THE NEW NATURALIST

A SURVEY OF BRITISH NATURAL HISTORY

INSECT NATURAL HISTORY

The aim of this series is to interest the general reader in the wild life of Britain by recapturing the inquiring spirit of the old naturalists. The Editors believe that the natural pride of the British public in the native fauna and flora, to which must be added concern for their conservation, is best fostered by maintaining a high standard of accuracy combined with clarity of exposition in presenting the results of modern scientific research.

The text and line illustrations are here reproduced unaltered, but the process of manufacture used to achieve an economic price does not, unfortunately, do full justice to all the photographs; and those originally in colour appear in black and white.

THE NEW NATURALIST

INSECT
NATURAL HISTORY

by

A. D. IMMS
M.A. D.Sc. F.R.S.

LATE HONORARY FELLOW OF DOWNING COLLEGE AND READER
IN ENTOMOLOGY, CAMBRIDGE UNIVERSITY

Bloomsbury Books
London

First Edition 1947
Second Edition 1956
Third Edition 1971
Reprinted 1973

This edition published 1990 by
Bloomsbury Books an imprint of
Godfrey Cave Associates Limited
42 Bloomsbury Street, London WC1B 3QJ
under license from William Collins Son's & Co. Ltd.

ISBN 1 870630 39 4

TO

MARJORIE FLORENCE

ON HER RECOVERY

CONTENTS

COLOUR PLATES *(continued)*

It should be noted that throughout this book Plate numbers in arabic figures refer to Colour Plates, while roman numerals are used for Black-and-White Plates.

ix

PLATES IN BLACK AND WHITE

ILLUSTRATIONS IN THE TEXT

DISTRIBUTION MAPS

NOTE TO THIRD EDITION

Dr. A. D. Imms died on 3 April, 1949, and the text of this book was revised for the Second (1956) Edition by Dr. G. C. Varley, Hope Professor of Entomology at the University of Oxford, and by his colleague Dr. B. M. Hobby.

For this Third (1971) Edition Mr. Michael Tweedie has kindly re-written Chapter 3 'On Wings and Flight' and has supplied a new Fig. 18 in that chapter.

EDITORS' PREFACE

THE natural history of British insects will never be written. This subject, too vast to be treated as a whole, must be treated in part ; and there are several ways of doing this, both special and general. At one end of the scale is the history of a group—an example is Dr. E. B. Ford's *Butterflies* in this series. Only 68 species have been recorded wild in the British Isles at one time or another ; and every one of them was dealt with and illustrated in that book.

The number of species of British beetles, however, is 3,690, and of two-winged flies over 5,200. Groups like these clearly demand a different treatment. So at the other end of the scale comes the integrative work, the essay on and the discussion of British insects as a whole—their place in nature, and the principles which govern their lives.

Dr. A. D. Imms' *Insects* is of this kind. No attempt has been made to deal with the 20,000 known British species of insects individually. The main emphasis is on the characteristics of insects in general, and on the ways in which they have adapted themselves to the environment provided by the British Isles. Some of these adaptations are beautiful, others extraordinary. Some are quite bizarre.

The late Dr. Imms was pre-eminently qualified to write such a book. In his years as Reader in Entomology at Cambridge he dispensed an immense store of knowledge on the habits, the physiology, the structure, and the classification, as well as the economic importance, of insects.

At least five-sixths of all the species of animals in the world are insects (in spite of their virtual absence from the sea, which is the major part of the area inhabited by life). Insects show the successes and failures of a section of life which has evolved along lines entirely different from those followed by our own ancestors. Further, insects are of immense importance economically and medically to man, and provide the chief food of many higher vertebrates.

All these are matters which Dr. Imms has considered and illustrated from among the insect inhabitants of our country. In our opinion he has achieved a signal success in his treatment of this complex and difficult group.

THE EDITORS

AUTHOR'S PREFACE

THE aim in writing this book is to induce those who happen to read it to become better acquainted with the natural history of our native insects. Many people are interested in these creatures and are anxious to know something about them. But apart from Butterflies and Moths, difficulty is experienced in finding out how they live, to what kinds so many of them belong, whether they are harmful or not, and so on. An acquaintance with our commoner insects adds to the pleasure of the country-dweller and of those who take walks or holidays beyond the bounds of bricks and mortar. It will be understood, therefore, that this book is intended for general readers, while teachers of nature study or of elementary biology may also find it an aid to their work.

It would have been a more satisfactory task had it been possible to continue the subject into a second volume. As it is I cannot pretend to have done more than skirt the fringe of the subject in so limited a space, nor can I pretend that I have been impartial in my treatment of it. I realise how unpromising it would have been to divide the space impartially. Such well-proportioned treatment would savour of lifelessness and defeat the object in view. Consequently I have written at greater length about the feeding habits of insects, about aquatic insects and on social behaviour, for example, than about other things. The reason for this partiality is because so much that is remarkable or characteristic about insect life is betrayed in these particular manifestations. It will be noted that no mention is made of the great subject of inheritance or of the origin of the British insect fauna. Both these aspects are so well treated in Dr. Ford's book on Butterflies, in this same series, that it is undesirable to tread much the same ground again. Furthermore, these two subjects are better explained in Butterflies than in other insects where they have been much less fully explored.

Effort has been made to avoid the use of terms only familiar to students of zoology and to refrain from giving details of anatomy and of classification. Nor indeed are such details needed from the viewpoint of the general reader. A certain number of unfamiliar words such as the names of the major groups of insects and those of a few of the parts of the insect body are necessary. The plan that has been followed is to refer to each kind of insect under its popular name and only to quote its scientific name where mention of a particular insect is made for the first time in each chapter. This good intention cannot always be followed for the simple reason that so many insects have no individual proper names. A few technical names and terms may convey a superficial impression of difficulty but this is only so long as they remain mere sounds. When an acquaintance is gained with what they stand for they soon lose much of their unfamiliarity and their necessity will become realised. A few words are needed about the scientific names of the different insects that are mentioned. In a general book of this kind it is desirable to use those names that are in widest circulation in order to avoid confusing the reader when looking up other works on a particular subject. In a few cases, therefore, the latest names resulting from application of the rules of nomenclature have not been employed for this reason.

Some readers may feel encouraged to become acquainted with the ways and means of insect life beyond the scope of this book. For them the Documentary Appendix at the end provides a guide to books and papers that will widen their horizon and enlarge their acquaintance with many aspects of the subject.

It will be noted that comparatively little is said about the ever-popular order of the Butterflies and Moths. This omission is intentional for the reason that these insects are, or will be, dealt with in separate volumes in the present series.

As regards the plates that accompany this book the credit is due to Mr. S. Beaufoy, who took the original kodachromes for almost all the colour plates and the negatives for many of the black and white illustrations. With scarcely any exceptions they were taken from the living insects : in a few cases a mild anaesthetic had to be given in order to restrain the movements of the more active kinds. Care was taken not to kill them with an overdose, and consequently they display their natural colours and appearance. The colour-photographs of set specimens were taken by Mr. Z. Wegner. The specimens were arranged by myself and, after various technical difficulties had been overcome, were photographed by him. Several of the specimens were from the Cambridge University Museum of Zoology.

I am much indebted to Dr. Julian Huxley, F.R.S., for valued help by way of criticism while the book was in manuscript. Also I owe a debt of gratitude to those who kindly supplied me with necessary living material for photographic purposes and in particular to the Rev. C. E. Tottenham and to Messrs. S. Beaufoy and R. P. Bumstead.

Nearly all the text-figures illustrating this book are original. In the case of the few that are from borrowed sources acknowledgment is made where due in the appropriate legend.

I am indebted to my daughter, M. F. Imms, for carefully reading the proofs when in galley form.

A. D. I.

Note.—Since the original edition was published in 1947 various minor changes in this book are now desirable, but the book remains substantially as Dr. Imms wrote it. A number of small errors of fact have been corrected and some references to recent key works will be found in the documentary appendix.

G. C. Varley, B. M. Hobby, Hope Dept. of Entomology, University Museum, Oxford.

INTRODUCTION

THE name insect is very commonly given to any small creeping animal with a ringed or segmented body and several pairs of legs. Not many people, excepting entomologists and trained biologists, could give a proper definition of an insect that would distinguish it from its near relatives. In the first place it needs to be borne in mind that insects belong to the great group of invertebrate animals known as the Arthropoda. These creatures have the body divided into more or less separate rings or segments, of which a variable number bear jointed limbs. Their whole body and the limbs are covered with a specially hardened cuticle forming an external skeleton. Between the segments, and at the joints of the limbs, there is flexible connecting membrane which allows of freedom of movement. An arthropod, in fact, is encased in a tubular outer skeleton, in striking contrast with a vertebrate animal whose skeleton lies within the body. The functions of the skeleton, whether it be an inner or an outer one, is to give attachment to the muscles and general support to the body. The word insect is derived from the Latin *insectum*, meaning " cut into," and refers to the way in which its body is made up of a series of ring-like pieces.

Fully 85 per cent, possibly more, of all the known kinds of animals are arthropods. It is only necessary to visualise such creatures as lobsters, crabs and shrimps ; also spiders, centipedes and their like, besides insects, to gain an idea of the almost infinite variety of forms that belong to the arthropods. This brings us to the definition of an insect. It is an animal whose body is divided into head, thorax and abdomen ; the head bears a pair of feelers or antennae and attached to the thorax are three pairs of legs and usually wings. It is useful to remember that while all winged invertebrate animals are insects not all insects are winged—a feature that will be referred to again on a later page. The definition just given may seem clear enough and in so far as it applies to *adult* insects it is a sound one. No general definition, however, will cover immature insects also, for many young insects show no separation into thorax and abdomen. Others seem to be without a head or antennae : some have legs on many of the segments while others bear no legs at all. The reader will gradually become acquainted with these forms and it will not be found difficult to identify them individually (see Chapter 2).

Spiders and scorpions, together with harvestmen, mites and ticks, are not insects. They form a separate class of arthropods called the Arachnida. Their special features are a head and thorax completely merged into a single region : the absence of antennae : and the possession of four pairs of legs. They are, therefore, easily separated from any member of the Insecta. The same applies to the millipedes and centipedes. They form the class Myriapoda, whose distinguishing features are a single pair of antennae (as in the Insecta) ; a trunk which shows no separation into thorax and abdomen ; and the possession of many pairs of legs. Shrimps, lobsters, crabs and woodlice are Crustacea. Unlike the members of the other classes mentioned they are almost entirely denizens of the sea or of fresh water : only a very few, such as the woodlice, have invaded the land. Crustacea usually have two pairs of antennae, the head and thorax are merged together into one region, and there are numerous pairs of limbs.

The distinctive features of the four main classes of arthropods may be epitomised in the following way :

   a. With three pairs of legs : antennae present and usually wings. INSECTA.
   b. With four pairs of legs : antennae absent. ARACHNIDA.
   c. With many pairs of legs : antennae present.
      c^1. Head distinct : one pair of antennae : terrestrial in habit. MYRIAPODA.
      c^2. Head merged with the thorax : two pairs of antennae : almost always aquatic in habit. CRUSTACEA.

It is scarcely possible to go out of doors, in town or country, except in winter, without meeting, often by actual contact, at least one insect. Notwithstanding their abundance, man has been too absorbed in himself to take much notice of such small creatures until comparatively recent times. The great Swedish naturalist Linnaeus (1707–78), for instance, only knew of 1,929 different kinds of insects. To-day the picture is very different. The number of known species is not far short of one million and several thousand new ones are discovered, named,

PLATE I

S. BEAUFOY

a. Common Cockroach, *Blatta orientalis*, male (right), female (left), and egg-purse or ootheca (middle). (Slightly less than actual size) [etherised]

S. BEAUFOY

b. Great Green Gasshopper, *Tettigonia viridissima*, female (× ½)

COCKROACHES AND GRASSHOPPER

PLATE 2

S. BEAUFOY
a. Alder-fly, *Sialis lutaria*, and egg-batch

S. BEAUFOY
b. Common Earwig, *Forficula auricularia*, male (right), female (left), [etherised]

S. BEAUFOY
c. Long-horned Grasshopper, *Meconema thalassina*, male
(All are slightly enlarged)
ALDER-FLY, EARWIGS AND GRASSHOPPER

and described in every normal year. The question which naturally arises is what has caused so many different kinds of creatures, all showing the same general plan of organisation, to come into existence ? The answer to this enigma can be conveyed in four words—flight, adaptability, skeleton and size.

1. *Capacity for Flight.*—The majority of insects are not by any means wholly confined to the ground and vegetation. Having developed wings, they are able to use the air to their own great advantage. Being able to fly gives them exceptional means for spreading themselves far and wide over the world. It likewise gives great advantages in finding their mates ; in searching for food and in making good their escape from enemies. Such a combination of advantages is not enjoyed by any other invertebrate animals for the simple reason that they cannot fly.

2. *Adaptability.*—No other animals have so persistently thrust themselves throughout the world. Insects are found from arctic regions to the equator. Snow or ice are not impassable barriers to their enterprise, neither are hot springs, salt lakes or deserts, which all have their quota of insect life. Every kind of flowering plant is used as food by one or more kinds, while decomposing organic matter attracts and supports many thousands of species. A very large number live as parasites on or within the bodies of other insects and of very different animals including vertebrates.

The soil and fresh water have their own great populations of insect life. The sea is the only medium that has proved a barrier to all but a few forms of insect life.* The most unpromising substances, left severely alone by other animals, are by no means despised by insects. One or more kinds are known to feed for instance on peppermint, ginger, licorice, musk, hides, corks of wine-bottles, paint brushes, carpets, stuffed natural history specimens, mummies, etc. Even more enterprising insects have lived on such eccentric diets as argol (potassium bitartrate), lump opium, aconite, Cayenne pepper, cigarettes and sal ammoniac, which shows how hard-bitten they can become and what they can tolerate. The palm for enterprise, however, must go to a small fly, called *Psilopa petrolei*, which spends its immature stages in the pools of petroleum around the oil-wells of South California and is not known to live anywhere else.

* Wherever this sign is used it indicates that reference should be made to the Documentary Appendix under the chapter and page concerned.

3. *The Skeleton.*—The external skeleton has been of immense help in contributing to the success of the insect plan of structure. Since it is in the form of a cylinder surrounding the body it is the strongest type of construction that is possible with a given amount of material. Furthermore it is virtually unbreakable and much lighter than bone. This kind of skeleton has enabled insects to solve one of the great difficulties that face all animals which live on land, viz. the need to guard against water-loss. General protection against drying is afforded by the impregnation of the skeleton with a substance that makes it impervious to water. Without such protection insects would have to live entirely in moist places, like earthworms, or in water.

The horny substance that forms the insect skeleton lends itself in a most remarkable way to almost infinite modifications of bodily structure for different uses. Especially to be noted are the ways in which it has become moulded to provide the range of form and size of the jaws ; in the growth of horns, spines and other projections from the body ; in the clothing of bristles, hairs and scales ; in membranous wings and horny or leathery wing-cases ; in the different kinds of legs adapted for different uses ; in needle-like egg-laying organs, stings and so forth.

4. *Size.*—The small size of insects gives them many advantages in the struggle for existence. The quantity of food needed to nourish them individually is in itself very small. Many are, therefore, able to live on such insignificant amounts of food material that they would be of no use to larger animals. Their small size also enables them to occupy niches in their surroundings that afford security from a whole range of enemies and often provide them with food at the same time. Thus, one or more leaf-mining insects can feed and grow in the tissue between the upper and lower surfaces of one small leaf ; a weevil will undergo its complete growth within a single small seed ; and a very moderate-sized fungus will support large populations of small beetles and flies.

An insect has to face certain disadvantages should it be either very minute or relatively gigantic in size. Such extreme forms are by no means common, most insects being of small or moderately small size. Among the smallest of all insects are certain minute beetles which live among fungi and measure no more than 0·2 mm. (0·007 in.) long ; also some of the Fairy Flies are only a little longer. These mere specks are helpless if they become wetted. The reason is because the smaller an animal becomes the greater in proportion is its surface area. If then it has the misfortune to be wetted by rain or dew the weight of the encompassing water speedily exhausts the creature's efforts to free itself. With larger insects and a relatively smaller surface area this complication has less vital consequences. Most insects, therefore, manage to avoid being too small and they also escape the other pitfall of growing too big. It is not just chance that so few have bodies more than $\frac{1}{2}$ in. to $\frac{3}{4}$ in. in thickness. Something prevents them becoming as large as lobsters or crabs and the key to the matter is in their particular way of breathing. As is explained on p. 15, insects breathe by means of internal air-tubes which end in extremely fine capillaries. Although these capillaries can only be seen under high powers of the microscope they are the final conveyers of oxygen to the tissues. The only way this gas can travel along vessels of such minute calibre is by diffusion. Now diffusion is effective over very short distances but should an insect tend to become too large it would experience oxygen-want and become too lethargic to survive. This is because diffusion is rapidly slowed down when the capillaries lengthen and their distance from the outside air oversteps a certain limit.

It is consequently interesting to note that the largest insects are mostly creatures with very long bodies or relatively big wing-expanse. Thus, there are attenuated Stick Insects in the tropics that are not far below a foot in length, and small-bodied moths that measure 11 inches across the wings. In the Coal Measure period there were fossil Dragon-flies with a wing expanse exceeding two feet, but they have long been extinct and nature has not repeated the experiment. It is very rarely that an insect has the massive proportions of the African Goliath Beetle with a length of 4 inches and a breadth of 2 inches.

Among British insects our largest and bulkiest species is the Silver Water-beetle (*Hydrophilus piceus*), which reaches a length of $1\frac{7}{8}$ in. with a breadth of $\frac{7}{8}$ in. The Death's Head Hawk-moth (*Acherontia atropos*) has the largest wing-span—$5\frac{1}{4}$ in.—while our longest-bodied insect is the Emperor Dragon-fly (*Anax imperator*), which attains 3 in. in length (Map 1 and Pl. 6, p. 15).

The more insects are studied the more unique they are found to be and the less they have in common with so many other animals. They are among the most permanent and persistent kinds of animals nature has evolved. Even in that remote geological period, perhaps 500 million years ago, when mighty forests flourished that are now coal we suddenly come upon remains of " a wild riot of teeming insect life." By the time man was evolving from his simian ancestors every major group of insects had already come into existence. In this vast interval of geological time the insect type had become fitted to every sort and condition of life. Bearing these remarks in mind we need to consider briefly what the structure of these remarkable animals is like, how their organs work, and what happens during their transformations.

" A magnificent temple is a laudable monument of national taste and religion, and the enthusiast who entered the dome of St. Sophia might be tempted to suppose that it was the residence, or even the workmanship of the Deity. Yet how dull is the artifice, how insignificant is the labour, if it be compared with the formation of the vilest insect that crawls upon the surface of the temple ! "—GIBBON, *Decline and Fall of the Roman Empire*, chap. XL.

INSECT STRUCTURE AND TRANSFORMATIONS

IT WILL help in understanding the structure of an insect if it be remembered that it is an almost complete inversion of what prevails in a vertebrate animal. Its skeleton for instance is, as already noted, an outer shell or case: the heart lies above the gut or alimentary canal, and the nervous system mostly lies on the underside of the body. The senses operate in a very different way from those of a vertebrate and seem to us to be lodged in fantastic positions. Thus, insects smell by means of long feelers and some have ears placed close to the knees or on the abdomen. Although they have no larynx, many can produce very creditable sounds simply by rubbing one part of the body against another. Moreover, an organ in an insect may become altered in its use in a most disconcerting way. Thus, the usual salivary glands produce silk in the caterpillar and other glands function in secreting the saliva. Jaws used for biting the food in a cockroach become transformed into sharp needle-like lancets in a mosquito. The hind-wings in flies have become changed into balancing organs, and the egg-laying organ of grasshoppers has become changed into a sting in bees and wasps. Insects are indeed strange animals: the more one comes to know about them the more incredible they seem to be.

The skeleton or cuticle of an insect is made up of non-living material that is secreted by the epidermis or outermost cells of its body. Chemically the skeleton is a complex mixture of different substances, and its most notable property is its power of resisting decay or corrosion. It is this property that enables insects to be kept for several centuries in a life-like state in collections. Its main constituent is chitin, which is chemically a nitrogenous polysaccharide with an empirical formula $(C_8H_{13}O_5N)_x$. It is horn-like and extremely resistant to concentrated alkalies and dilute acids. If a whole insect be boiled in caustic potash all its soft parts are dissolved and only its skeleton remains. The hardness of the insect skeleton is due to the chitin being impregnated with another substance, called sclerotin or cuticulin; but not much is known about it chemically. It dissolves in caustic alkali,

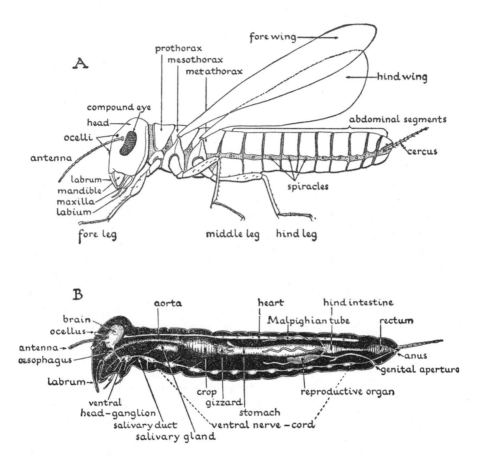

FIG. IA-B.—General structure of an Insect (Diagrammatic).
A, external features. B, internal organs (side wall of the insect removed).

but unlike chitin it is insoluble in concentrated mineral acids. In the maggots of Flies and the grubs of Bees and Wasps the cuticle is soft and thin as compared with that of a Beetle. It is interesting to know that the cuticle covers every external part, even the eyes and body-hairs. A very thin layer of it also lines the throat and the hind-gut and also the breathing tubes.

EXTERNAL STRUCTURE (TEXT-FIG. 1A)

In order to gain an insight into insect anatomy it is desirable to use a relatively large example such as a cricket, cockroach or wasp. The division of the body into head, thorax and abdomen will be easily recognised (Text-Fig. 1).

THE HEAD :—The head of an insect (Text-Fig. 2) is its feeding and sensory centre. It bears the antennae, eyes and mouth-parts. The antennae, or feelers, show great variety of form and are sometimes very different in the two sexes. They are chiefly concerned with the senses of smell and touch. The eyes are of two kinds, i.e. compound eyes and ocelli. Compound eyes (or faceted eyes) are situated one on each side of the head and are formed of a number of individual lenses or facets closely arranged in a honeycomb-like manner. Each lens is commonly hexagonal in form and is associated with a separate under-lying visual element. There are, for example, about 4,000 lenses to each compound eye in the House-fly. The ocelli (or simple eyes) are usually three in number, arranged in a triangle above or between the origins of the antennae. Each consists of a strongly biconvex lens overlying a number of visual elements. Whereas compound eyes are

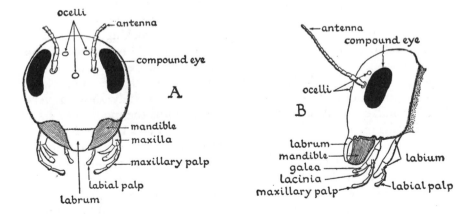

FIG. 2A-B.—Head of an Insect with ordinary biting mouth-parts. A, front view. B, side view.

rarely absent, ocelli are often wanting, as happens for instance in Mosquitoes and most Beetles.

The mouth-parts (Text-Fig. 2) comprise three separate pairs of jaws which are placed one behind the other. They are subject to great variation in form and function according to the nature of the food. A knowledge of the general type of mouth-parts found in different groups of insects is of much help in understanding their habits and also in classification. Typically the mouth-parts are organs for biting and chewing and work in the horizontal or transverse plane. Such biting mouth-parts consist (1) of a pair of strong, toothed principal jaws or mandibles. Behind them is (2) a pair of accessory jaws or maxillae : each maxilla bears an outer and an inner lobe, termed the galea and lacinia respectively ; at the base of the galea there is a sensory append-age or maxillary palp. Finally, there is (3) a second pair of maxillae, which are united to form a lower lip or labium ; its free margin may bear as many as four lobes, together with a pair of labial palpi that are sensory in function. Overlying the mandibles, and projecting in front of the head as a kind of flap, is the labrum or upper lip. Such, in brief, are the chief features of biting mouth-parts. Organs of this kind prevail in all insects which feed upon solid food, e.g. Cockroaches, Crickets, Grasshoppers, Earwigs, Dragon-flies and Beetles.

There are, on the other hand, many forms of insect life that subsist entirely upon a fluid diet and have the mouth-parts specially modified accordingly. The mechanisms of these mouth-parts are less easy to understand than those of the biting type. It will help a good deal if it be remembered that the individual organs of sucking mouth-parts have developed by modification from corresponding organs of the biting type. Both sorts of mouth-parts begin their development in the same way and it is only later that those destined to become sucking organs grow along lines of their own and ultimately show a very different make-up. Among Butterflies and Moths the mouth-parts are used for sucking only : the same happens in most flies but the suctional mechanism is brought about in a different way. In Mosquitoes, Horse-flies, Fleas, etc.—creatures that feed upon blood—the mouth-parts are veritable lancets used for piercing the skin so as to allow of free suction of the blood. Again all Plant-bugs, Greenfly and the like, also have piercing and sucking mouth-parts which enable them to penetrate the tissues of plants and imbibe the sap. The whole subject is full of interest and for this reason it is further dealt with in Chapter 6.

PLATE 3

a. May-fly, *Ephemera danica*, subimago (× 1¾) and b. Adult (× 1)

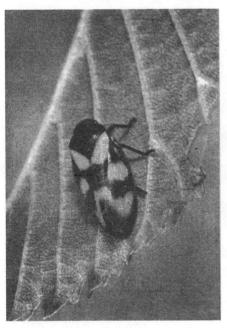

c. Frog-hopper, *Cercopsis vulnerata* (× 3)　　d. Green Lace-wing and eggs (attached to leaf above the insect) (× 1½)

MAY-FLY, FROG-HOPPER AND LACE-WING

Photographs a, b, c, by S. BEAUFOY: d, by E. J. HUDSON

PLATE 4

a. Demoiselle, *Agrion splendens*, male

b. Demoiselle, *Agrion splendens*, female

c. Damsel-fly, *Coenagrion puella*, female

d. Damsel-fly, *Coenagrion puella*, male

DRAGON-FLIES (ZYGOPTERA) (× 1)

Photographs by S. BEAUFOY

THE THORAX :—The thorax (Text-Fig. 1) is the locomotory centre of an insect. It comprises three segments, each bearing a pair of legs. These segments are called the prothorax, mesothorax and metathorax respectively. Among most insects the second and third of these segments have each a pair of wings. The number of legs is so constant (i.e. six) that any segmented creature which has six legs will, almost certainly, be an insect. Among immature insects, caterpillars have a number of false unjointed legs in addition to true or jointed legs, while wasp and bee grubs and fly maggots have no legs at all.

The parts of a leg are easily made out (Text-Fig. 3). First, a basal piece or coxa which is hinged to the underside of the segment. The coxa is joined to the femur or thigh by a small intermediate part called the trochanter. The femur is followed by a more slender tibia or shank, which carries the tarsus or foot. The tarsus is usually subdivided by several joints and bears a pair of claws at its free end. Between the claws there is a pad or sometimes a pair of such pads, which aid in climbing. If a surface is sufficiently rough an insect can climb by holding on by means of its claws. Where a surface is too slippery for the claws to obtain a foothold the pad or pads referred to come into use. Their underside is clothed with numerous fine hollow hairs with expanded tips that are moistened by a secretion. How they actually operate is controversial, and the subject has not so far been fully explored. Some authors claim that the secretion is a sticky fluid and that it is its cohesion which holds the insect to the surface. In many cases it seems likely that the hairs are applied so closely to the surface that the fluid film between each and the surface breaks and seizure or adhesion takes place ! In other words the insect is held by what the physicist terms molecular forces.

Insects use their legs in manifold ways, for they are exceptionally adaptable organs. It does not require a very profound acquaintance with these animals to be able to deduce something about their modes of life from an examination of their legs (Text-Fig. 3). Those which are active runners, such as Earwigs, Beetles, Cockroaches and Plant-bugs, have a large free prothorax, with the three pairs of legs alike and rather slender. In the act of walking or running an insect does not move the legs of the two sides together in pairs as might be imagined. Instead, they are used so that the fore and hind-legs of one side and the middle leg of the opposite side are raised and advanced almost synchronously. In this way the body is momentarily supported

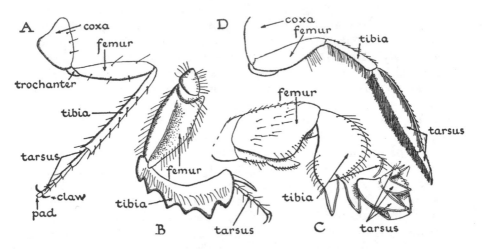

FIG. 3A-D.—Fore-legs of different Insects.
A, Cockroach (*Blatta*). B, Dor-beetle (*Geotrupes*). C, Mole-cricket (*Gryllotalpa*).
D, Water-boatman (*Notonecta*).

on a tripod formed by the remaining three legs. It is worth noting that a tripod involves the smallest number of supports that gives a stable equilibrium whether the insect be moving or stationary (Text-Fig. 4).

Water insects very commonly have their hind-legs, and sometimes the middle pair also, flattened and oarlike. A closely set fringe of hairs, which adds to the surface area, helps them to function as oars in swimming. In the Crane-flies, Bee-flies and also Mosquitoes (Pls. 22 [p. 111], 28 [p. 159] Fig. 19, and Text-Fig. 28) the long and exceedingly slender legs are used for alighting and scarcely for walking or running. Among Grasshoppers, Crickets and the Flea-beetles the femora of the hind legs are very characteristically enlarged in order to accommodate the powerful extensor muscles that are used in leaping. Digging insects, such as the Mole-cricket and the Dung-beetles, can be recognised by the form of the front legs, which are short, very broad and thickened scoop-like organs. In the Mole-cricket the fore-legs are perfect digging organs. Also, the first two divisions of the tarsus are armed with large tooth-like outgrowths that work in conjunction with very similar tibial teeth. The combined organs operate like a pair of shears and are used for cutting through the roots of plants, well below the surface of the soil.

Wings are membranous outgrowths of the thoracic wall : their possession is one of the most obvious features in the majority of insects. Some insects, however, have never acquired wings—this is the case with the lowly Silver-fish of kitchens and bakehouses and the fragile white *Campodea* of the soil. Their wingless state is, therefore, a primary condition, whereas in worker ants and the females of certain moths,

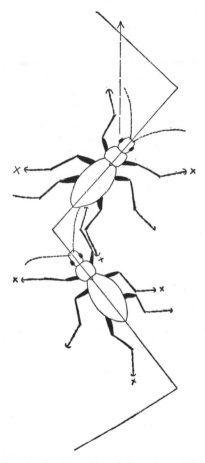

FIG. 4.—A Beetle walking in the direction of the arrow. The continuous line shows the track the insect follows : the crosses show which of the legs rest on the ground in the two phases represented. (Adapted from v. Lengerken.)

for example, it is a secondary feature because they have lost the wings which their ancestors possessed. A typical wing is supported by a tubular framework of ribs or veins, often strengthened by connecting ribs or cross-veins. The arrangement of these structures in the wing is known as the venation and is of paramount importance in the classification of insects. Wings undergo many modifications, and these are dealt with in the groups wherein they occur. There are many interesting features concerning these organs, and for this reason Chapter 3 is devoted to the subject.

THE ABDOMEN :—The abdomen (Text-Fig. 1) is the centre where digestion and excretion take place together with those functions associated with sex. This region of the body is made up of a number of clearly indicated segments, eleven being the most found in any insect. At the apex of the abdomen is situated the anus and on either side of this opening there is, in many insects, a pair of cerci or tail-feelers. Very long and thread-like in May-flies, short in Grasshoppers and Crickets, they are reduced to tubercles in some other insects. The long tail-feelers act as posterior antennae and are sensitive to touch and also to sound vibrations. In many insects the 9th abdominal segment in the male carries a pair of claspers or pairing appendages used for holding the female during mating. In the female there is very commonly an ovipositor, or egg-laying instrument, which is made up of three pairs of outgrowths beneath the 8th and 9th segments. This organ is broad and knife-like in Long-horned Grasshoppers and needle-like in Crickets and Ichneumon-flies. In other cases it is invisible except when functioning. Among Bees and Wasps it has lost its egg-laying function and has become converted into the sting—which explains its absence in the male or drone.

INTERNAL STRUCTURE (TEXT-FIG. 1B)

The general make-up of the internal anatomy of an insect will be better appreciated by referring to Text-Fig. 1B than from a lengthy description. It must first be pointed out that the digestive canal and all the other organs which lie in the body-cavity are immersed in blood. This is because the body-cavity in an insect is an expanded part of the blood-system and there are very few true blood-vessels. In the

PLATE 5

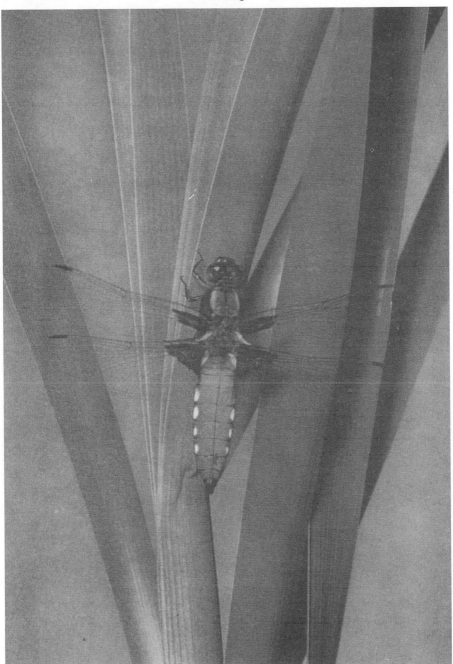

S. BEAUFOY

Libellula depressa, male (× 1)
THE BROAD-BODIED *LIBELLULA* DRAGON-FLY

PLATE 6

S. BEAUFOY

Anax imperator, female, newly emerged. It has not yet acquired its full colour ($\times \frac{5}{6}$)

EMPEROR DRAGON-FLY

vertebrate animal the body-cavity is devoid of blood, the latter being confined to an elaborate system of blood-vessels. In this respect insects seem at first sight to have a great advantage over vertebrates because the digested food percolates through the walls of the stomach directly into the blood and thus speedily reaches the different organs of the body. In the vertebrate it has to traverse the lymphatic vessels and pass into the arteries, arterioles and capillaries before it can be distributed to the different parts.

When an insect such as a Cockroach masticates its food, it is mixed with saliva, whose enzyme or ferment acts upon the starch and other carbohydrates present. The stomach produces numerous enzymes which complete the digestion of starch and sugars and also deal with proteins and fats. These enzymes are passed forward into the crop where the actual digestion occurs. The gizzard, apart from grinding up the food, acts as a strainer which allows only fluid matter to enter the stomach. Insects have no organ comparable with the liver ; and also no enzyme of the pepsin kind (together with hydrochloric acid) is secreted. The enzyme present in the stomach is more comparable with the trypsin of the vertebrate pancreas. Absorption of the digested food takes place in the stomach and the faecal matter passes *via* the hind intestine to the exterior. Where the stomach joins the hind intestine a group of Malpighian tubes take their origin. They function as the kidneys of the insect, and derive their name from that of the Italian anatomist Marcello Malpighi (1628–94), who was their discoverer. The Malpighian tubes separate waste substances from the blood and discharge them into the hind intestine. In most insects the chief nitrogenous waste product is uric acid. Among the maggots of some of the Blow-flies (*Calliphora, Lucilia*) ammonia is excreted instead —a very economic procedure, since no loss of unused carbon occurs !

Insects have no lungs and breathe by means of an elaborate system of air-tubes or *tracheae*, which branch in an intricate manner among the organs of the body. The larger and more active insects exhale and inhale, not through the mouth and nostrils but through breathing pores or *spiracles* placed on each side of many of the body-segments (Text-Fig. 1A). The ultimate branches of the air-tubes are microscopic capillaries less than 1 μ ($\frac{1}{25,000}$ in.) across, and it is in these minute vessels that the interchange of gases takes place. In many insects oxygen diffuses through the spiracles into the whole respiratory system and there is no mechanical ventilation. It will be gathered therefore

C

that the blood of insects does not act as the oxygen-carrier as in vertebrates. It is commonly pale yellow or green in colour ; it contains no red corpuscles and has very little to do with respiration.

Circulation is effected by the pulsations of a long tubular heart which runs along the middle line of the back. This results in the blood being drawn from the body-cavity into the heart, through minute valves in the heart-wall, and it is thence propelled forwards through the aorta or main blood-vessel. It is then returned to the body-cavity to circulate among the different organs. The chief function of the blood is to carry the necessary nutriment, derived from the food, to all parts of the body. As already mentioned, the whole process of circulation is much simpler than what happens for example in a mammal.

The central nervous system, excepting the brain, lies beneath the digestive canal and other organs. On referring to Text-Fig. 1B the brain is seen to be located in the head over the oesophagus. It is joined to a creamy-white ventral nerve-cord which runs down the length of the body. At intervals along its course the ventral cord shows swellings that constitute the ganglia or nerve-centres.* The brain is the receiving centre for whatever is perceived through the senses. It is also the co-ordinating centre which governs the movements of the whole animal in accordance with the sensations experienced. The ventral head-ganglion (or suboesophageal ganglion) is the feeding centre which controls the mouth-parts ; the ganglia in the thorax control walking and flying ; and those in the abdomen act to a considerable extent as independent centres for their respective segments. It will be evident, therefore, that the nervous functions of an insect are localised in the brain to a much lesser degree than in a vertebrate. Removal of the brain does not kill an insect ; it makes it inert and unable to start any act of its own accord. Thus a brainless insect can eat, fly or lay its eggs but, since the centre for initiating these acts has been removed, none of them can be performed unless the insect be suitably stimulated. It is unable to seek its food : the food must be placed in contact with the mouth-parts before it can feed. Raising a brainless insect from the surface on which it is resting provides the stimulus that sets the flight mechanism working ; while stimulating the abdomen induces egg-laying.

Among other striking things in the make-up of insects is their great strength. Thus, they are able to raise weights much greater than that of their own bodies and they can leap astonishingly long distances. Performances of this kind have given rise to the popular idea that their muscles must be immensely powerful. The physiologist tells us, however, that the power of a muscle varies as the square of the area of its cross-section while the volume of the body of an animal varies as the cube of its linear dimension. A simple calculation will show that the relative power of a muscle increases as the body of an animal becomes smaller—hence the apparent great strength of a small animal like an insect. The *absolute* power of a muscle is the load it can raise for each centimetre of its area in cross-section. When looked at in this way the absolute power of human muscle is rather greater than that of an insect. Insect muscle, however, is unique in its power of endurance, as witnessed by the high frequency of the wing vibrations. These may amount to about 15,000 beats per minute in the Hive-bee ! Such rapidity of muscle action is linked up with the direct air-supply and the speedy conversion of food materials into muscular energy.

The reproductive organs comprise the testes or ovaries, as the case may be, and their ducts, together with certain accessory glands, etc. The ovaries of insects are unique in that they are formed of separate egg-tubes. The eggs develop in these tubes in successive series ; the youngest eggs lie nearest the apex of a tube and the most mature nearest to the passage which conveys them to the exterior. The striking features of reproduction among different insects are much more varied than in other animals and form the subject of a later chapter.

The so-called fat-body is in the form of irregular masses of cells that occupy much of the space around the internal organs. It is a particular feature in an insect's economy and serves for the storage of reserve food-substances (not merely fat, but also protein, glycogen, etc.), which tide the creature over during critical periods. These reserves are drawn upon, for instance, during metamorphosis (see p. 21) ; they are extensively used during hibernation, besides providing nutriment for the developing eggs in the body of the female.

GROWTH AND TRANSFORMATION

When ready to emerge from the egg the young insect has, in some manner or other, to force its way through the egg-shell in order to reach the outer world. In some cases the egg-shell is fitted with a neat cap or lid which is merely pushed open to allow the insect to escape. In others the young insects have special temporary devices, called egg-bursters or hatching spines, for tearing open the egg-shell. Caterpillars have no such appliances and merely gnaw their way out. Very commonly insects swallow air and fluid while still in the egg, which makes them more turgid and able to exert more pressure until the shell bursts.

Growth in an insect is not gradual and continuous as that of an infant, for instance. It takes place in cycles which are interrupted by periods of moulting.

The amount of growth that takes place can be found out in various ways. One of the most reliable is by measuring the increase of weight that takes place during the time spent as a nymph or a larva, as the case may be. This is shown for several insects in the table below :

Name of Insect	*Period*	*Increase of Weight*	*Name of Investigator*
Larva or grub of Hive-bee (*Apis*)	$4\frac{1}{2}$ to 5 days	About 1,500 times	J. A. Nelson, *et al.*, 1924
Caterpillar of Goat-moth (*Cossus*)	3 years	72,000 times	P. Lyonnet, 1762
Larva or maggot of Flesh-fly (*Sarcophaga*)	71 hours	451 times	W. B. Herms, 1907
Larva or grub of Great Water-beetle (*Dytiscus*)	51 days	52 times	H. Blunck, 1923

It will be seen from this table how variable is the rate and amount of growth among different insects. The rapidity of the process in the

Plate I

THREE-PRONGED BRISTLE-TAILS

S. BEAUFOY

S. BEAUFOY

a Silver-fish, *Lepisma saccharina* (× 4)   *b* Fire-brat, *Thermobia domestica* (× 3½)

These very active creatures had to be etherised to allow of the photographs being taken

Plate II

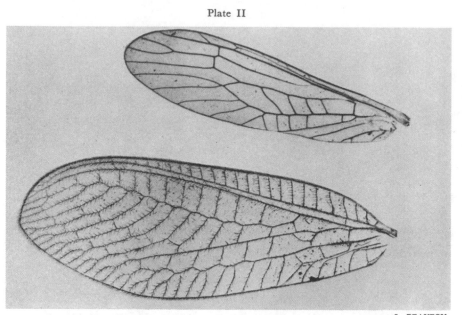

S. BEAUFOY

a Stone-fly (× 5)   Lace-wing (× 6) [from specimens mounted in euparal]

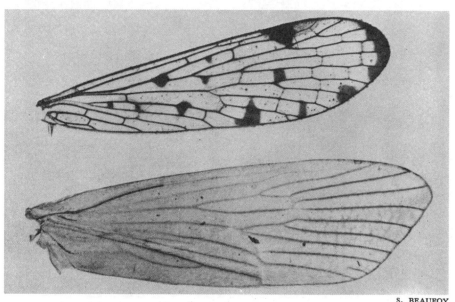

S. BEAUFOY

b Scorpion-fly (× 6)   Caddis-fly (× 6½) [from specimens mounted in euparal]

FORE-WINGS SHOWING VENATION IN DIFFERENT INSECTS

Hive-bee and Flesh-fly is no doubt connected with the very nutritious nature of the food and the fact that the young insect is literally surrounded by a superabundance of it. The Goat-moth caterpillar, on the other hand, lives in the wood of trees, which has a low nutrient value.

Rate of growth, as in all cold-blooded animals, is also very much affected by temperature. Let us take the case of the maggot or larva of the House-fly (*Musca domestica*). This insect requires only about $5\frac{1}{2}$ days after leaving the egg until it transforms into a pupa, provided the temperature be kept at 86° F. (30° C.) ; at 68° F. (20° C.) it takes $9\frac{1}{2}$ days, and at 50° F. (10° C.) it requires as long as 34 days. At the same temperatures the times for the caterpillar of the Small Garden White butterfly (*Pieris rapae*) after emerging from the egg until it changes into a chrysalis are $8\frac{1}{2}$, $15\frac{1}{2}$ and 55 days respectively.

Because the cuticle of an insect is hard and inelastic it does not allow for growth in size or for change of form. This difficulty is overcome simply by getting rid of the old cuticle and growing a new one. The latter, being at first soft and pliable, is able to adapt itself to any increase in size and change of shape, etc. that the creature may have acquired.

Moulting is rather like changing a suit of worn-out clothes in a growing boy and getting him a new one which is a size larger. The process in itself is not quite so simple as this, and in order to understand how it happens the reader will note (Text-Fig. 5) that the skin of an insect consists of a layer of cells, or epidermis, which produces the hard covering or cuticle. The nature of the cuticle has been previously referred to, and it may be added that the outer layer is impregnated with sclerotin whereas the inner layer is not. Just before moulting the insect ceases to feed, and certain glands in the skin—termed moulting glands—become active and discharge a secretion which dissolves the inner cuticle, but leaves the outer cuticle unaffected. The epidermal cells soon begin to form a new cuticle, which is thus separated by a space from the outer layer of the old cuticle. The insect then proceeds to get rid of the latter by exerting pressure from within ; this causes the skin to rupture down the back of the thorax. It then works its way out through the split thus formed (Pl. XXVI, Fig. b). The whole business is often helped by gravity, because many insects hang downwards during moulting. As it escapes from the old skin its limbs are drawn out of the coverings and the creature emerges in a brand-

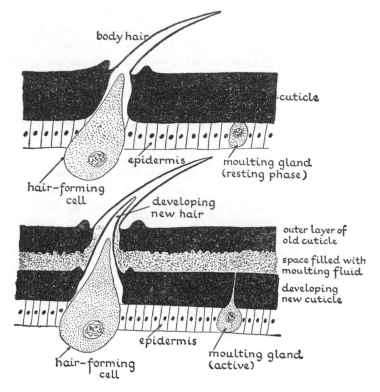

FIG. 5—*Above* : Structure of the integument. *Below* : The process of moulting. (Diagrammatic)

new suit of clothes. This soon darkens and hardens, and the insect then resumes its staple occupation of feeding.

The number of times moulting happens varies a good deal in winged insects. Grasshoppers, for instance, often moult 5 times before reaching the winged state, while the Cockroach (*Blatta orientalis*) moults 7 times. Fly maggots during their short lives only cast their skins twice. At the other extreme we have May-flies and Stone-flies, which hold the record. Species of both these kinds of insects spend two or more years in the water before becoming winged and in this period they may moult between 30 and 40 times. The caterpillars of butterflies and moths moult from about 5 to 9 times, the number being often, but not always, constant for each species.

Recent discoveries in the physiology of insects have removed some of the mysteries connected with moulting.* Certain ductless glands have been discovered in the head which produce a hormone when the time for moulting approaches. This substance is discharged into the blood and acts as a sort of messenger which causes the moulting glands to become active and the epidermis to produce a new cuticle. We know that such a substance is in the blood at such times because it is possible to transfuse blood from an insect near the time for moulting into another individual in a normal condition, with the result that a premature moult follows. It is interesting to note that this insect hormone is produced by ductless glands which are innervated by the sympathetic nervous system, just as with the thyroid and pituitary glands of man. In both insects and man the hormone is discharged into the blood and acts in a very definite way on growth or other functions of the body.

It is characteristic of most insects that they emerge from the egg in a very different form from the adult. The growth-changes that take place are termed metamorphosis ; metamorphosis in fact means change of form during growth. Some insects, like the Silver-fish (*Lepisma saccharina*), change their form so little during growth that they cannot be said to pass through any metamorphosis. Most of the lower groups of insects, however, pass through a direct or incomplete metamorphosis. They hatch out from the eggs in a form closely resembling the parent except in size and in the absence of wings and the external organs of reproduction. Their lives and mode of feeding are usually very similar to those of the adults. The possession of compound eyes is a further point of resemblance between them. Young insects of this kind are known as nymphs. Their growth into the adult or imago shows, therefore, no marked changes of form ; in fact they simply just grow bigger. The most noticeable thing is the growth of the wings, which start as two pairs of buds or outgrowths from the side-walls of the meso- and metathorax. After each moult the insect comes out a size larger, and the wing-buds normally grow at a faster rate than the rest of the body. The metamorphosis of a Grasshopper is shown in Text-Fig. 6 ; that of Cockroaches, Earwigs and Aphids is of a similar kind.

In May-flies and Dragon-flies the nymphs are sombre-coloured creatures that lurk about the bottoms of ponds and streams. It is an astonishing thing that they transform into winged adults that are aerial things of great beauty. Their nymphs have gills and other organs that enable them to live an aquatic life and for this reason they differ from the adults more noticeably than is the rule among other insects with incomplete metamorphosis.

FIG. 6.—Three stages in the metamorphosis of a Short-horned Grasshopper.

The higher groups of insects, such as Butterflies and Moths, Beetles, Flies, etc., pass through an indirect or complete metamorphosis. They hatch from the eggs at an earlier stage of development than nymphs and in a form very different from the adults. The differences are so great that it seems at first almost incredible that the one grows into the other. The young insects are termed larvae ; familiar examples are caterpillars, the maggots of Flies and the grubs of Wasps and Bees. In larvae the wing-buds lie inside the body and remain invisible externally. Their methods of feeding and ways of life are generally very different from those of the adults. Also the visual organs of larvae are not compound eyes but temporary or provisional organs of a more rudimentary kind. The differences between the two kinds of metamorphosis are great. Where there is incomplete metamorphosis the process is one of gradual transformation from the young to the adult and feeding goes on throughout. With complete metamorphosis, the life of the insect is drastically interrupted and a resting pupal stage is entered upon when no feeding is done. The larval period is given over to growth and feeding, only broken at certain brief intervals by moulting. Ultimately the larva completes its growth and no longer feeds : it then lapses into a state of immobility and, having passed through its last change of skin, becomes a pupa. While the pupa shows every sign of outward quiescence, it is in reality the seat of intense biological activity within. It is at this time that the wings become evident externally and reconstruction and transformation of the larval organs and tissues into those of the adult insect take place. The complexity of these changes is, even to-day, only imperfectly understood, notwithstanding the efforts of some of the most famous biologists to unravel them. Not much imagination is called for to realise the

profundity of the task nature has set herself to accomplish in transforming the sluggish leaf-eating caterpillar into the immensely active
nectar-sucking Butterfly ; or the conversion of the degenerate, eyeless,
limbless grub so that it finally appears as a highly endowed Wasp or
Bee.   The gist of the process may be epitomised as follows.   Those
organs of the larva which are no longer required undergo dissolution
and their remains provide the material and energy for building up the
adult organs.   The latter arise, for the most part, from nests of cells
known as imaginal buds, which resist the disruptive process and grow
into new organs or parts.   The buds of the future wings have already
been referred to : those of the legs and antennae are at first rather
similar, but the germs or forerunners of the different parts of the
digestive canal, of the muscles and so forth are more obscure and
difficult to detect.   When the transformation is less drastic, certain of
the larval organs pass over with but little alteration to become those
of the adult.   When the changes are profound, as in the Blow-fly
(*Calliphora*), the whole larval system is broken down, and it seems
that wandering blood-cells or phagocytes play the major part in the
dissolution process.

Many theories have been advanced to explain what causes a
caterpillar to transform into a chrysalis.   Recent discovery indicates
that, just as with moulting, the change is induced by the action of a
hormone.   The latter is produced either in the immediate vicinity of
the brain or by gland-cells located in that organ.   Removal of the
brain from a caterpillar before a certain critical period (before the
hormone is active) prevents the creature from turning into a chrysalis.
If the experiment be done after the critical period (when apparently
the hormone has been discharged into the blood) the transformation
takes place in the usual way.   Interesting results have also been
obtained by ligaturing Blow-fly larvae just behind the brain so as to
prevent free communication with the blood in the part posterior to
the ligature.   If the ligaturing be done before the hormone is discharged
into the blood, only the part in front of the ligature shows characters
of the pupa, the hind part being unchanged.   If the operation be done
after the hormone has been discharged into the blood, change to the
pupa takes place both in front and behind the ligature.

The commonest type of pupa is shown in Text-Fig. 7.   It will be
noted that the legs, wings, antennae and mouth-parts are encased in
sheaths which lie free.   An exception is met with in the familiar

chrysalis of Butterflies and Moths. In this kind of pupa the above-mentioned sheaths are closely soldered to the body so that the pupa as a whole presents a relatively smooth contour. The term chrysalis, it may be added, refers in particular to the metallic-coloured pupae of certain Butterflies. Among many kinds of Flies the pupa is protected by the last larval skin, which is not cast off. Instead, it remains and becomes barrel-shaped, hardened in texture and brown in colour. This pupal covering is called a puparium (Pl. XIV, p. 115, Fig. b).

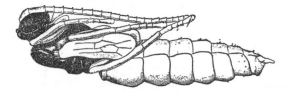

FIG. 7.—A typical pupa. (Enlarged.)

It will be evident to the reader that the pupa is a singularly helpless and vulnerable stage in the life of an insect. Salvation, in such a phase, usually lies in concealment from all and sundry enemies. Adverse weather conditions, shocks and other mechanical disturbances have also to be guarded against. Provision against such influences has to be made by the larva in its last stage. It selects the driest and best concealed site that is available. The earth itself is the most favoured situation; very many larvae bind together soil particles to form cells deep in the ground wherein to pupate. Perhaps the largest number of insects construct cocoons (Pl. XII, p. 107) either of silk or of extraneous material bound together by threads of that substance. In this way many wood-boring larvae utilise wood particles: some hairy caterpillars mix their body-hairs with the silken framework of their cocoons, while that of the Puss-moth (*Cerura vinula*) makes an exceedingly hard and most skilfully camouflaged cocoon of gnawed fragments of bark that merges perfectly with its surroundings (Fig. f). The dense cocoons of pure silk formed by the caterpillars of many moths afford very efficient protection from enemies as well as insulating their occupants from the effects of excessive wet, cold, or other adverse influences. The caterpillars of Saw-flies make cocoons of parchment-like or horny consistency and in some cases an outer cocoon encloses an inner one of more delicate texture (Fig. c). Among Butterflies the pupae are often unprotected and are situated nakedly on leaves, etc., or on fences (Fig. d). In such cases the absence of a cocoon is compensated for by the very close colour and other resemblance such chrysalides bear to their immediate surroundings. Among Flies a cocoon is absent, the pupae being protected by the puparium (p. 24) or in other ways. Among Wasps and Bees the change to the pupae takes place in the cells wherein the larvae developed. Ants, on the other hand, often construct dense cocoons ; their pupae, thus enclosed, are frequently collected and sold as fish food under the name of " ants' eggs."

On the arrival of the time for an insect to emerge from the pupa, it undergoes its last moult, which consists in shedding the pupal covering. If the insect finds itself within a cocoon, this has to be negotiated before it can reach the outer world. Many just gnaw their way out by means of their mandibles : in others temporary mandibles or special " cocoon-cutters " are borne by the pupa and are used for rupturing the protective case and for no other purpose.

On issuing from the pupa the main problem facing an insect is to ensure that the full expansion and hardening of its organs and parts is accomplished. When freshly emerged the creature is soft and helpless : it climbs up a stem or other support with its unexpanded wings hanging down in a flaccid condition (Pl. 9, p. 34, Fig. a). Blood-pressure, aided by muscular contraction, causes them to straighten out and expand to their full extent. Fraenkel has shown that the newly emerged Blow-fly increases its volume 128 per cent by swallowing air : by this means, it is enabled to exert considerable pressure during the process of wing-expansion. If a wing be punctured at this time blood oozes through the perforation and expansion ceases. On the other hand, if the Fly is only allowed to take in very little air and is then placed in a vessel of pure carbon dioxide gas, which diffuses very rapidly into the gut, greatly distending the fly, the result is that the wings expand in a few seconds, instead of the usual period of 20 to 30 minutes.

When in the adult state, or imago, an insect no longer grows or moults* : small Flies, for example, do not grow into larger Flies—they are separate kinds or species. The only change that takes place in this phase of existence is the maturing of the organs of sex. Being solely for the maintenance and dispersal of its kind, an adult insect rarely lives more than a few weeks. In some of the May-flies it is only a matter of a few hours. At the other extreme are many Butterflies and

Moths which appear in autumn but do not lay their eggs and die until the following spring. Such species spend a large proportion of their adult life in a comatose state, since they hibernate throughout the cold months of the year. The queens or functional females of the social insects live longest of all. In the security of their nests they devote themselves to egg-laying and are constantly fed by the workers. A Queen Bee will live six or seven years if allowed to do so by the beekeeper, and a queen ant will live much longer and go on laying eggs. Donisthorpe kept one for 15 years and he considered, from the size of the nest when he found her, that she must have been eighteen when she died.

" Wherefore we ought not childishly to neglect the study even of the most despised animals, for in all natural objects there lies something marvellous."—ARISTOTLE, *De Partibus Animalium*, I, 5.

Plate III

S. BEAUFOY

K. C. WILLIAMSON

a Nymph of Damsel-fly, *Coenagrion puella*   *b* Larva of Alder-fly, *Sialis lutaria* (× 2)
(× 2)

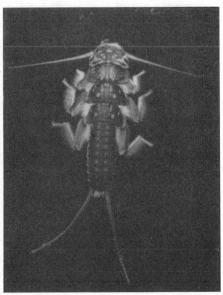

S. BEAUFOY

K. C. WILLIAMSON

c Nymph of May-fly, *Cloeon dipterum* (× 2)   *d* Nymph of Stone-fly, *Perla bipunctata* (× 1½)

AQUATIC INSECTS I

Plate IV

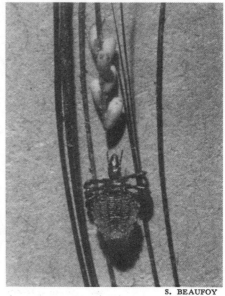

S. BEAUFOY

a Bed-bug, *Cimex lectularius* (× 6)
[etherised]

S. BEAUFOY

b Hog-louse, *Haematopinus suis* and eggs on
hairs of pig (× 6½) [etherised]

W. S. RICHARDS

c **Book-louse**, *Liposcelis bostrychopilus* (× 50)

S. BEAUFOY

d Nymph of a Bug, *Nabis lativentris* (× 6)
which bears a close resemblance to an
ant [from a set specimen]

BUGS AND LICE

CHAPTER 2

HOW INSECTS ARE CLASSIFIED
AND NAMED

THE object of classifying any large assemblage of animals is to arrange its members in some kind of logical order. The system in general use is one based as closely as possible upon what are believed to be natural relationships.

Each kind or species of animal is given a name for convenience of reference ; the system of naming in current use is international and has the advantage of applying to all groups of animals.

> " What's the use of their having names," the Gnat said, " if they won't answer to them ? "
>
> " No use to *them*," said Alice, " but it's useful to the people that name them, I suppose."
>
> LEWIS CARROLL : *Alice Through the Looking-Glass.*

As was pointed out in the Introduction, insects are one of the four great classes of animals that collectively form the invertebrate phylum known as the Arthropoda (Gr. *arthron*, a joint and *pous*, gen. *podos*, a foot).

Let us take some individual insect and try to classify and name it. A large sturdy Dung- or Dor-beetle will serve the purpose admirably. We have no doubt about its being an insect because its body is divided into head, thorax and abdomen : the head bears one pair of antennae and the thorax carries three pairs of legs. Furthermore, since it has two pairs of wings it is obviously a member of the subclass Pterygota, all of whose members are winged or, if wingless, they were derived from winged ancestors (Pls. 18 [p. 79] Fig. 16, and XI [p. 106] Fig. c).

Insects themselves are divided into 22 different major groups called *orders*, so we must now settle to which of these orders our specimen belongs. With the aid of a simple pocket lens it is easy to see that its mouth-parts are clearly of the biting kind. Also, the fore-wings are represented by horny sheaths or elytra that cover the membranous hind-wings folded away beneath them. Also, we notice that the elytra do not overlap but meet in a straight line down the middle of the back, when closed. This combination of features shows that our insect belongs to the order Coleoptera (Gr. *coleos*, a shield, and *pteron*, a wing). The next step is to sort out the specimen from among the Coleoptera. The latter are divided into two *suborders*. The Dor-beetle is a member of that suborder termed the Polyphaga (Gr. *poly*, neut. singular of *polys*, many, and *phago*, to eat). All members of this suborder have no oblong closed cell in the hind-wings and the cavities into which the coxae of the hind legs fit do not divide the 1st ventral plate of the hind body into two pieces.

In the descending scale the next step is to note that a suborder is divided into groups of *families* known as *superfamilies*. The Polyphaga contain six of these groupings. Two features in the Dor-beetle give a useful clue as to which one it belongs, i.e. :—(1) the antennae end in a sort of club made up of separate plates ; and (2) the legs are very stout and spiny and are formed for digging. Now the only super-family that displays these characters is the Lamellicornia (L. *lamella*, a thin plate, and *cornu*, a horn, from the characters of its antennae). The British Lamellicornia are composed of two families only. One is the Lucanidae or Stag-beetles and the other is the Scarabaeidae (L. *scarabaeus*, a scarab). It is easy to settle where the Dor-beetle belongs because it has the plates of its antennary club very thin and closely compacted as in the Scarabaeidae, whereas in the Lucanidae the plates of the club are much thicker and are spaced apart.

If the reader has followed the argument this far the task can be completed by using a pocket lens more freely than before as some of the characters to be relied upon are not so easily seen. With its help we trace our specimen down to the *subfamily* Geotrupinae. Reasons for this are because the hind-body is made up of 6 segments and the breathing pores along its sides are covered by the elytra. Also the scutellum (Text-Fig. 15, p. 56) is very distinct and there are 11 segments to the antennae.

The next step is to find out to which *genus* the beetle belongs. There are only two genera to be concerned with, viz. :—*Ceratophyus* and *Geotrupes*. Now an examination of the thorax shows that since it is smooth and without a trace of projecting horns our creature is a *Geotrupes* (Gr. *geios*, of the earth and *trupa*, a hole). All that remains now is to find out to which kind, or *species*, of *Geotrupes* the insect belongs. There are six species of *Geotrupes* in Britain. In separating them we note that the groove-like lines or striae down the elytra are strongly marked, that each wing-cover bears 7 of them (between the middle line and the shoulder), and that there are few or no cross-lines between them. Also, the hind-body underneath is clothed all over with fine hairs and has a dotted or pitted cuticle. This combination of small characters proclaims the insect to be *Geotrupes stercorarius* L. (Latin *stercorarius*, having to do with dung: Pl. 18, p. 79, Fig. 16).

It will be convenient to summarise these conclusions in tabular form, thus :—

PHYLUM : Arthropoda (insects, centipedes, crustaceans, spiders, mites and the like).
   CLASS : Insecta (insects).
     SUBCLASS : Pterygota (winged insects).
       ORDER : Coleoptera (Beetles).
         SUBORDER : Polyphaga (all Coleoptera excepting Ground-beetles and their allies).
           SUPERFAMILY : Lamellicornia (Stag-beetles, Dung-beetles, Chafers and the like).
             FAMILY : Scarabaeidae (Dung-beetles and Chafers).
               SUBFAMILY : Geotrupinae (Dung-beetles).
                 GENUS : *Geotrupes* (Dor-beetles).
                   SPECIES : *stercorarius* Linn. (the common Dor-beetle).

The system of naming animals that is in universal use is *binomial*, i.e., each kind of animal is referred to by two names, one is that of the species or kind to which it belongs and the other refers to the genus. This system dates from the 10th edition of the *Systema Naturae*, written by the great Swedish naturalist Linnaeus (often shortened to Linné) and published in 1758. In this work binomial naming was first used for zoology and has persisted ever since. No one has been able to devise a better plan. Since Linnaeus' day the subject of nomenclature has become very complex and a series of " Rules of Nomenclature " has been adopted by international sanction and agreement. These rules lay down that the scientific names of animals must be of Latin or Latinised form, or considered and treated as such when not of classical origin. The name of a family is formed by adding the suffix *-idae* to the stem of the name of the type genus of that family, e.g. :— *Scarabaeus*, Scarabaeidae. Similarly the name of a subfamily is formed by adding *inae* to the stem of the name of its type genus, as *Geotrupes*, Geotrupinae.

A genus is essentially a group of closely related species that show certain characters in common. Its name is a substantive in the nominative singular. The name of a species must be either an adjective agreeing grammatically with the name of the genus, e.g. :—*Musca domestica* ; or a substantive in the genitive case, e.g. :—*Vanessa urticae* ; or a substantive in apposition with the generic name, e.g. :—*Stratiomys chamaeleon*. The name of the author (abbreviated) who first described and named a given species is quoted after the specific name without a mark of punctuation, e.g. :—*Geotrupes stercorarius* Linn.

It is not easy to define what is meant by the term species.* For general purposes, however, a species may be regarded as an assemblage of individuals showing a common distinctive likeness of structure and having a common area of geographical distribution. Further, these individuals freely interbreed, or are presumed to do so, and do not usually cross with those of other communities. For many years the infallible criterion of a species used to be its infertility when crossed with individuals of another species ; or if the cross be fertile the hybrids it yielded were infertile. While this definition still holds good in the vast majority of cases it needs to be borne in mind that crosses between species do happen, in both plants and animals (though much more frequently in the former), and may yield fertile offspring.

With increased knowledge more and more cases are being discovered where species are divisible into groups of individuals showing distinguishing characters of a lower grade than those which separate one species from another. For example some species can be subdivided into groups of individuals distinguishable from one another in certain characteristics and occupying different geographical areas. These are known as *subspecies*. Each subspecies is given an additional name so that the binomial system of Linnaeus becomes a trinomial one. The three names indicate the genus, species and subspecies respectively. The particular subspecies to which the species name was originally given takes that same name also, while different names are given to each of the other subspecies. As an example the Rove Beetle, *Philonthus varius*, may be mentioned. In its typical form (*Philonthus varius varius*), found in most parts of Britain, the elytra are black with a greenish metallic sheen. In Orkney and Shetland it is replaced by the subspecies *shetlandicus*, which has the elytra entirely red. The full name for this subspecies is consequently *Philonthus varius shetlandicus*.

Again, individuals of a species may show differences of coloration or other features, insufficient in themselves to be of specific value. Such

PLATE 7

S. BEAUFOY

a. *Libellula depressa*, female (× 1)

S. BEAUFOY

b, *Aeshna grandis*, male (× ½)

THE BROAD-BODIED *LIBELLULA* AND BROWN *AESHNA* DRAGON-FLIES

PLATE 8

Aeshna cyanea, young male.　The eyes and spots on the hind body become blue when fully mature ($\times \frac{7}{8}$)

A COMMON DRAGON-FLY, THE SOUTHERN *AESHNA*

individuals inhabit the same area as do typical members of their species (with which they freely interbreed) and are regarded as belonging to a separate *form* or *variety*. The latter word, however, has been used to convey several different meanings and for this reason should no longer be used. The common two-spot Ladybird (*Adalia bipunctata*) has typically red elytra each with a black spot. Along with it there are often found individuals with red spots on a black ground. The forms freely interbreed and have the same range of distribution. One form, with two red spots on each wing-cover, is *Adalia bipunctata* form *quadrimaculata* and another which has three red spots on each wing cover is the form *sexpustulata* (see Plate 16, p. 75, Figs. c, d and e).

In a third category are those cases where a species is divisible into groups of individuals differing from one another in their habits with little or no difference of colour or structure. The differences are, therefore, mainly biological and groups of individuals of this kind are often described as *biological races*. The differences of habits in such cases may be quite as distinct as those between different species. A good instance is afforded by the Plant-bug *Plesiocoris rugicollis* which has become a serious pest of the apple. It is practically certain that it was not an apple pest in England before 1900, and since that time a biological race appears to have developed which has adopted this tree as its host in preference to willows which are its usual food-plants. The change seems to have involved some readjustment in the life of the insect, since on willow it usually occurs from June to August : whereas on apple the adults are found from about the first week in June until the end of July. Its whole life-cycle, therefore, seems to have been advanced by about one month. These two biological races appear to be sufficiently distinct to deserve trinomial recognition by having special names.

Another instance of a species divided into biological races is afforded by the Human Louse (*Pediculus humanus*). This insect exists as two separate races known respectively as the Head Louse (*Pediculus humanus capitis*) and the Body Louse (*P. humanus corporis*). Apart from differences of habit the two races show slight differences in form and colour. They interbreed freely under experimental conditions and the hybrids are usually fertile (see also p. 43).

Very often species or genera are described and named in ignorance of the fact that they had already been designated perhaps many years previously. The rules of nomenclature lay down that the valid name of a species or genus is that under which it was first properly described. Unless these rules are adhered to endless confusion may result. Efforts to regularise nomenclature are very evident when the scientific names of insects as given in older works are compared with those quoted in the most modern writings.

Insects may be conveniently divided into two main subclasses that are based upon the presence or absence of wings and the nature of the transformation which they undergo during growth. Comprised in these two groups are some 22 orders or smaller divisions that are represented in the British Isles.*

Subclass I. APTERYGOTA. Small or minute wingless insects in which the wingless condition is primitive or original. They undergo no true metamorphosis and the young closely resemble the adults except that they are smaller and not sexually mature.

Order	1.	Diplura.	Two-pronged Bristle-tails (p. 33).
Order	2.	Thysanura.	Three-pronged Bristle-tails (p. 34).
Order	3.	Collembola.	Spring-tails (p. 34).
Order	4.	Protura.	Proturans (p. 35).

Subclass II. PTERYGOTA. Normally winged insects or if wingless they are derived from winged ancestors. Metamorphosis, either slight or pronounced, present. The young are very varied in form and, in many orders, are very unlike the adults.

Orders 5 to 13 are known as Exopterygota because the wings develop outside the body. Metamorphosis is incomplete, there being no pupal stage. The young are nymphs that are generally similar in form to the adults but are smaller and have the wings only partly grown. In orders 6, 8 and 9 the nymphs are aquatic and differ from the adults more noticeably than in the other orders.

Order	5.	Orthoptera.	Cockroaches, Grasshoppers, Crickets (p. 35).
Order	6.	Plecoptera.	Stone-flies (p. 37).
Order	7.	Dermaptera.	Earwigs (p. 38).
Order	8.	Ephemeroptera.	May-flies (p. 39).
Order	9.	Odonata.	Dragon-flies (p. 40).
Order	10.	Psocoptera.	Book-lice (p. 42).
Order	11.	Anoplura.	Bird-lice and Sucking Lice (p. 42).
Order	12.	Thysanoptera.	Thrips (p. 43).
Order	13.	Hemiptera.	Plant-bugs, Aphids or Green-fly, White-flies, Scale-insects, etc. (p. 43).

Orders 14 to 22 are known as Endopterygota because the wings develop inside the body. Metamorphosis is complete, a pupal stage always being present. The young are larvae that bear little or no resemblance to the adults.

Order 14.	Neuroptera.	Alder-flies, Snake-flies, Lace-wings (p. 47).
Order 15.	Mecoptera.	Scorpion-flies (p. 49).
Order 16.	Trichoptera.	Caddis-flies (p. 50).
Order 17.	Lepidoptera.	Butterflies and Moths (p. 52).
Order 18.	Coleoptera.	Beetles and Weevils (p. 55).
Order 19.	Strepsiptera.	Stylops (p. 60).
Order 20.	Hymenoptera.	Ants, Bees, Wasps, Ichneumon-flies (p. 60).
Order 21.	Diptera.	True Flies (p. 61).
Order 22.	Aphaniptera.	Fleas (p. 64).

Only two orders, viz. the Isoptera or Termites and the Embioptera or Web-spinners, are unrepresented in Britain. All the others have a more or less world-wide range, becoming scarcer and scarcer towards the two poles and attaining their greatest abundance in the tropics.

At this stage it will be convenient to give a short account of the different orders noting how their British representatives are to be recognised. At the end of the title heading of each order the number of British species of that order is shown in brackets, thus (Brit. spp. about 10).* Altogether there are about 20,000 different kinds of insects to be found in the British Isles.

Order 1. DIPLURA (*diplos*, double ; *oura*, a tail)
TWO-PRONGED BRISTLE-TAILS (Brit. spp. about 10) †

Insects with long antennae and two very long tail filaments or cerci. The only British members belong to the genus *Campodea* with several species, but little is known as to their distribution and relative abundance. They are white creatures, about ¼ in. long and eyeless. They are found beneath the soil, among rubbish or under stones or logs, often in gardens and always where conditions are sufficiently moist. Special interest is associated with the Diplura because they are the nearest living descendants of the ancestral insects from which all others are believed to have been evolved.

Order 2. THYSANURA (*thusanos*, a fringe ; *oura*, a tail)

THREE-PRONGED BRISTLE-TAILS (Brit. spp. about 12) †

Insects with long antennae and three very long tail filaments. The British members are ⅓ to ¾ in. long when fully grown. They bear compound eyes and the whole body is clothed with scales. The commonest and most familiar species is the Silver-fish (*Lepisma saccharina*) found in kitchens, pantries, etc., and in bakehouses, where it runs about the floors and shelves attracted by sugary or starchy foods. Its name is given on account of its glistening silvery white appearance (Plate I). Other kinds of Bristle-tails occur among leaves in woods, on hill-sides, under stones on the sea coast, etc., but very little is known about them.*

Order 3. COLLEMBOLA (*kolla*, glue ; *embolon*, a peg)

SPRING-TAILS (Brit. spp. 260)

The Spring-tails are all very small insects, seldom more than 5 mm. (about ⅕ in.) long. The antennae have only four segments and the abdomen differs from that of all other insects in having only six segments. The first of these bears a sucker-like ventral tube and on the fourth segment there is usually a forked springing organ. Spring-tails are seldom noticed except by entomologists: when disturbed they can leap a distance of several inches. They are often exceedingly abundant in number of individuals and live on or beneath the soil, among herbage, in decaying organic matter, under bark, etc. An acre of meadow land has been found by John Ford to support nearly 230,000,000 of these insects, from the surface down to a depth of 9 in. in the soil. They are found almost all over the world and are one of the few orders that seem to be as well represented in temperate as in tropical lands. While most Collembola are linear, some are more or less globular in form. Among the latter, the green *Smynthurus viridis* is abundant in clover fields and has become a pest in South Australia. The blue-black *Anurida maritima* is common along our coasts, both on the sand and on the surface of rock pools. It is one of the few marine insects and is daily submerged by the tides. It has no springing organ and consequently is unable to leap. The name Collembola has reference to the ventral tube which was believed by some authorities to act as an adhesive organ, but is now known to absorb water from moist surfaces.

PLATE 9

DRAGON-FLIES

S. BEAUFOY

a. Emperor Dragon-fly just emerged from its nymphal case and holding on to it. The white threads are the cast-off linings of the breathing tubes of the nymph ($\times \frac{1}{2}$)

S. BEAUFOY

b. Large Red Damsel-fly, *Pyrrhosoma nymphula*, male (left), and female (right) ($\times 1$)

PLATE 10

S. BEAUFOY

a.   Dragon-fly nymph, *Libellula depressa* (× 1)

P. L. EMERY

b.   Side-view of *Aeshna* nymph showing mask folded away beneath the head and
between the fore-legs (× 6)

DRAGON-FLY NYMPHS

Order 4. PROTURA (*protos*, first ; *oura*, a tail)

(Brit. spp. 17)

These very minute white creatures are seldom more than $\frac{1}{20}$ in. in length : as may be imagined, considerable skill is needed in order to find them. They live beneath tree bark, under stones, in turf and in light but moist soil. Being without antennae, the functions of these appendages are performed by the fore-legs, which are held forward. The name Protura refers to the primitive nature of the abdomen.

Order 5. ORTHOPTERA (*orthos*, straight ; *pteron*, a wing)

COCKROACHES, GRASSHOPPERS, CRICKETS, ETC. (Brit. spp. 38) †

These insects have long, narrow, leathery fore-wings called tegmina and much broader membranous hind-wings with a net-like venation. Some kinds have lost their wings, others have them much reduced and non-functional. The antennae are long and most often thread-like ; cerci, sometimes difficult to see, are present, and the mouth-parts are of the ordinary biting type.

Cockroaches or Blattidae (Pl. 1, p. 2, Fig. a) are easily separated from our other Orthoptera in being flattened, with the legs about equal in size and formed for swift running. They always lay their eggs in purse-like cases which are sometimes seen protruding from the hind-body of the females. Several species have become spread over the world through commerce and shipping : these cosmopolitan immigrants are the only kinds usually encountered in Britain.

The remaining Orthoptera, which are known collectively as the Saltatoria, or jumping forms, are more attractive creatures than the Cockroaches. They have the power of leaping by means of the hind legs, which have enlarged femora. Almost all our Saltatoria hatch from the eggs about May and are found as adults from mid-July until some time in September. The winter, it will be noted, is passed as eggs. Relatively little is known about their life-histories or even of their distribution in this country. All the species will repay rearing and observing from the egg onwards. Being a small group, whose members are easy to identify, they are one in which the amateur entomologist can do really useful observation. There is scope for much more collecting which will enable us to have a fuller acquaintance with the range of the different species and the localities they frequent (Maps 4 and 5). The chirping or stridulation of Grasshoppers and Crickets is familiar to every one but it is not generally known that it is only the males that have this power. On the other hand, the individuals of both sexes have tympanal organs or ears. It does not take very long to recognise our few British species by their individual songs.

The Acrididae or Short-horned Grasshoppers have rather stout and short antennae about as long as the head and thorax combined. They stridulate in full sunshine and the hotter the day the noisier their

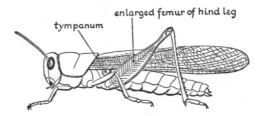

FIG. 8.—A Short-horned Grasshopper.

chirping becomes. The sound is made by rubbing the inner surface of the hind femur, which bears a row of fine points, against a projecting vein on the outside of the tegmen. Their ears are membranous drums or tympana, on either side at the base of the abdomen (Text-Fig. 8).

The Tettigoniidae are the Bush Crickets or Long-horned Grasshoppers (Pls. 1 and 2). Their thread-like antennae are longer than the head and thorax combined ; and the females, unlike those of the Acrididae, have a broad sword-like ovipositor. This instrument is used for laying the eggs deep in the soil or for cutting slits in stems or twigs for their reception. The family is, in every way, more nearly related to the Crickets than to the Grasshoppers. Its members stridulate by rubbing the right tegmen against the left one : the former bears a hardened area or scraper and the latter has a prominent vein with a surface like a file. The ears are borne on the tibiae of the fore-legs just in front of the knee-joint.

The Crickets or Gryllidae are easily distinguished by their long cerci and filamentous antennae: the tegmina lie flat on the back and are sharply bent down over the sides of the body. They stridulate by rubbing the two tegmina together backwards and forwards. Unlike the Bush

Crickets, both tegmina bear a file and scraper : the ears are placed on the front tibiae. Of the four British species the Mole-cricket (*Gryllotalpa gryllotalpa*) is over 2 in. long and is nocturnal and sub-terranean but occasionally flies when above ground. It is perfectly modified for an underground life, with the front legs formed for digging, rather like those of the mole (Text-Fig. 3, p. 12). Although this very remarkable insect is seldom seen it is probably not rare in parts of Southern England especially in the New Forest area (Map 2). The yellowish-grey House-cricket (*Acheta domesticus*) is the celebrated " Cricket on the Hearth " whose familiar chirping is often heard in kitchens and bakeries. It is sometimes found out of doors in warm weather in old rubbish dumps.

Before passing to the next order reference needs to be made to Locusts. These noxious creatures are, in fact, large Grasshoppers that have developed habits of swarming and migrating at certain periods. Occasionally stragglers reach the British Isles but they are unable to survive the climate and breed here.

Order 6. PLECOPTERA (*plekein*, to fold ; *pteron*, a wing)

STONE-FLIES (Brit. spp. 32) †

Stone-flies are rarely found far from the water in which their nymphal life is spent. They need searching for under stones, on tree trunks, etc., and the green forms lurk among foliage. When disturbed they mostly run, unless it is sunny, when many take to the wing, but their flight is very weak. Stone-flies vary much in size: the common *Dinocras cephalotes* has a wing-span of about 1½ to 2⅜ in. but most species measure about ¾ in. or less. In colour they are some shade of brown or grey or, in some cases, pale green. The antennae are long and thread-like and cerci are always present, being long and filamentous in the large species but very reduced and inconspicuous in the smaller kinds. The two pairs of wings are long, narrow and membranous, the hind pair being the broader (Plate II, p. 19, Fig. a).

These insects might be confused with some of the Neuroptera (p. 47) but those species with long tail filaments are easily separated from Neuroptera which never bear cerci of any sort. Other differences are as follows. In Plecoptera the wings are closed flat over the back whereas in Neuroptera they are sloped roof-wise along the sides : the hind-wings are broader than the fore pair but in Neuroptera they are of equal size : and the tarsi are 3-segmented while in Neuroptera they have always 5 segments.

Stone-fly nymphs (Pl. III, p. 26, Fig. d) occur in streams, rivers and lakes, where they live beneath stones and debris : the largest number of kinds are to be found in hilly or mountainous country. They are slenderly built and have long antennae and tail-filaments very much as in *Campodea* (p. 33). They breathe often by means of tufts of thread-like gills situated on the thorax or near the cerci : when gills are absent they respire through the skin. Most kinds feed upon plant material but the larger species also consume other small aquatic creatures.

Order 7. DERMAPTERA (*derma*, skin ; *pteron*, a wing)

EARWIGS (Brit. spp. 5) †

The Common Earwig (*Forficula auricularia*) is familiar to everyone. The fore-wings are small leathery flaps and the large, elegant hind-wings are folded in two directions so as to be stowed away beneath them. Although the hind-wings are so well developed this insect has only very rarely been seen to fly. The two sexes are easily recognised, the male having arched forceps or callipers, whereas those of the female are nearly straight as shown in Pl. 2, p. 3, Fig. b. The adults hibernate during winter and egg-laying takes place between late January and the end of March. The female excavates a cavity in the soil wherein she deposits her eggs in a group. She watches over them, and after they have hatched also shows parental care until the very young nymphs shift for themselves. The Common Earwig is nocturnal in habit and feeds both on animal and vegetable food : its partiality for the latter is a sore point with gardeners when they grow Zinnias and Dahlias. During day-time it hides away in narrow crevices, beneath bark, in hollow dead stems or canes ; in fact in almost any dry situation where there are narrow upright crevices. The ordinary name of the insect in most European languages refers to a widely spread belief that it creeps into the ears of sleeping persons. Rare chance entries into the ears of people sleeping on the ground have probably been responsible for the name. Excepting the very small Tawny Earwig *Labia minor*, which often flies on hot days, the other British species are confined to the south and south-east of England.

Order 8. EPHEMEROPTERA (*ephemeros*, living a day ; *pteron*, a wing)*

MAY-FLIES (Brit. spp. 47) †

May-flies are probably better known to fly-fishermen than to many other people, for most of their " duns," " spinners " and several of the " drakes " are made up to represent different kinds of these insects and are used at times when they are on the wing. The association of their scientific name with the Ephemerides of Grecian mythology expresses the brief aerial life of May-flies, which in some species lasts only a few hours. Others may live for one or two days and some a little longer. Since the mouth-parts are aborted May-flies take no food during their aerial life. This brief adult existence is compensated for by the length of life of the nymphs which may require a year or more in order to complete their growth. The nymphs are water-dwellers, and the winged adults into which they transform often emerge towards sundown in great numbers on the borders of rivers and lakes. May-flies have broad transparent fore-wings and a much smaller hind pair. When at rest the wings are held vertically over the back, closely apposed, like those of a Butterfly. The compound eyes are very large, especially in the males but, on the other hand, the antennae are so small as to seem like mere bristles. The legs are only for grasping, being quite ineffective for walking or running. The body ends in three, or sometimes only two, long tail-filaments, together with a pair of prominent claspers in the male.

The nymphs (Pl. III, p. 26, Fig. c), like the corresponding adults, have either two or three tail-filaments : their antennae are better developed and along the sides of the abdomen are pairs of gills, of varied character in different species. They inhabit slow and fast streams, rivers large and small, ponds and lakes. Their staple food is vegetable matter. When fully grown the nymph crawls from the water and then undergoes an astonishing and unique transformation. It changes into a fully winged insect known as the subimago—the " dun " of the fly-fisher. The wings are dull and opaque with hair fringes, while the legs and cerci are as yet not fully grown. After a short period of rest the subimago goes through a moult during which it sheds a delicate pellicle from its whole body, including the wings, and issues as the imago or " spinner " (Pl. 3, p. 10). These cast skins retain their form as replicas of May-flies and are common objects on the borders of the waters from which their owners originally came.

The adult May-fly is shiny and pigmented with transparent wings. At certain times of the day these insects congregate in swarms, in which males predominate, and perform their famous dances above the water. Mating occurs during these aerial evolutions, which consist of a vertical up-and-down motion—a fluttering and rather quick ascent is followed by a more leisurely descent, many times repeated. The eggs are laid in the water and in some species the adult insect descends beneath the surface for the purpose.

Notwithstanding their name, May-flies occur, on and off, during the whole summer, first appearing as a rule during the month of May. Those most commonly noticed are two mottled brownish species of *Ephemera*. They are among our largest May-flies having a wing-spread of about 1½ in. Most other May-flies are much smaller, some only ¼ in. from tip to tip of the wings.

Order 9. ODONATA (*odous*, gen. *odontos*, a tooth)*

DRAGON-FLIES, DAMSEL-FLIES (Brit. spp. 43) †

A Dragon-fly scarcely needs description ; with its four gauzy net-veined wings, its huge head and eyes and long slender body it is known to almost everyone. The great development of the compound eyes in Dragon-flies is in contrast to their insignificant bristle-like antennae which are poor in sense organs and of less importance than with most other insects. Dragon-flies consequently rely much more upon their keen vision than upon antennal perception. The four wings are of nearly equal size and each bears a small oblong darkly coloured mark or stigma towards the apex. The legs are attached to the body just behind the mouth—an arrangement well suited for seizing and holding the prey while it is being devoured. All Dragon-flies, it may be added, are carnivores, hawking and catching other insects while on the wing. The position of the legs makes walking hardly possible but grasping is, on the other hand, very efficient.

The mating process in Dragon-flies is quite unique among insects. The male seizes the female with his tail claspers, either by the head or neck. Thus firmly gripped, the female then curves her body round so that her genital opening comes into contact with a peculiar special apparatus under the 2nd abdominal segment of the male. Prior to mating the male apparently curves the abdomen forward so as to charge the apparatus just alluded to with spermatozoa. The mating process often takes place in the air, when the two individuals fly in unison. Afterwards the female is either released or, as in some species, she remains held by the male during egg-laying and when this happens the two individuals are in tandem during flight.

Many Dragon-flies are notable for the beauty and brilliancy of their coloration; the females, however, are often of more sombre hues than the males. In our common *Pyrrhosoma nymphula* (Pl. 9, p. 34) red is the predominant colour while *Coenagrion puella* (Pl. 4, p. 11, Figs. c and d) is cerulean-blue. Our most brilliantly coloured Dragon-flies belong to the genus *Agrion* (Pl. 4, Figs. a and b): thus, in the Demoiselle, *A. splendens*, the male is metallic ultramarine-blue with smoky brown clouded wings showing beautiful deep blue and purple reflections, while the female is metallic emerald with pale yellow-green wings. In some other Dragon-flies the male is covered with a powder-blue exudation or " bloom", very easily rubbed off (Plate 5, p. 14).

The larger and more stoutly built Dragon-flies belong to the sub-order Anisoptera (Pls. 5 [p. 14], 6 [p. 15] and 7 [p. 30]). They are easily recognised by their powerful darting flight. Their wings have broad bases and, when at rest, are held stiffly outspread at right angles with the body. The remaining Dragon-flies, or Damsel-flies and Demoiselles, form the suborder Zygoptera. They are smaller insects with very slender bodies, often little thicker than a stout darning needle. It was these creatures that Dante Gabriel Rossetti must have had in mind when he wrote the lines :

> Deep in the sun-searched growths the dragon fly
> Hangs like a blue thread loosened from the sky.

Their flight is generally very weak : the wings have narrow bases and when at rest are held vertically apposed over the back (Pl. 4, Figs. a, b).

Dragon-fly nymphs (Pls. III [p. 26], XXV [p. 226]) are always aquatic. Those of the Anisoptera are large and stout-bodied with very short tail appendages. In the Zygoptera the nymphs are slender-bodied with three long tail-lamellae. All the nymphs possess a unique structure called the "mask" (Pl. 10, p. 35, Fig. b). It is the highly modified labium, whose palpi are converted into organs for seizing insects or other small denizens of the water upon which the nymphs feed. When not in use the mask is folded up beneath the head and between the fore-legs. While capturing the prey the whole apparatus is shot forward with great rapidity by means of powerful muscles and the unwary creature becomes impaled by the labial palpi (Plate XXV, Fig. f).

Search for Dragon-fly nymphs is best made among water-plants in ponds or dykes, marshes, canals and streams. They are mostly denizens of still or slowly moving waters : those of the Demoiselles (genus *Agrion*) are rather exceptional in that they also frequent swift streams.

Dragon-flies* are still regarded with awe in some country districts owing to the belief that they sting—the local names of " horse-stingers " and " devil's darning needles " exist in folk-lore. It scarcely need be added that these insects are incapable of stinging : they are, in fact, to be regarded as beneficial in view of the number of noxious insects which they consume as food.

Order 10. PSOCOPTERA (genus *Psocus* ; *pteron*, a wing)

PSOCIDS, BOOK-LICE (Brit. spp. 68)

These are minute or very small soft-bodied insects with long thread-like antennae and no cerci (Pl. IV, p. 27, Fig. c). Many kinds are winged, others, such as the Book-lice and their allies, are not. The last-named are the only kinds of these insignificant creatures likely to be noticed by the ordinary observer, because they occur in houses. They frequent accumulations of books and papers and feed on the paste of the bindings and on dried cereal products. The majority of Psocids are found on palings, tree trunks, under bark, among chaff, etc. The young are mottled objects, often found sheltering under a thin silken canopy. The Common Book-lice are species of *Liposcelis*.

Order 11. ANOPLURA (*anoplos*, unarmed ; *oura*, a tail)

SUCKING LICE AND BITING LICE (Brit. spp. 286)

Sucking Lice (Plate IV, Fig. b) are only found on the bodies of mammals whereas Biting Lice live mostly on birds with only a few species on mammals. Their eggs are attached to the hair or feathers as the case may be. Lice very soon die if removed from their host. Being tough-skinned, and flattened in contour, with stout legs and big clinging claws, they take a lot of biting, pecking, or scratching to crush or dislodge them. Always wingless, with short antennae and no cerci, they are dark brown or yellowish in colour and, on an average, about ⅛ in. long. Almost every mammal has its own species of Sucking Louse living upon it as a blood-sucking parasite. Man is no exception, neither

PLATE II

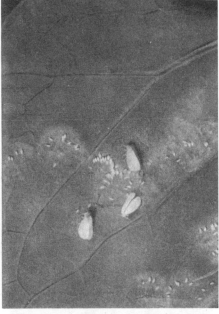

a. Shield-bug, *Elasmucha grisea* and progeny   b. Cabbage White-flies, *Aleyrodes broletella*, and eggs

c. Shield-bug, *Sehirus bicolor*   d. Mealy-bugs, *Pseudococcus* sp.

PLANT-BUGS AND THEIR ALLIES (× *circa* 2)

Photographs by S. BEAUFOY

PLATE 12

a. Crane-fly, *Nephrotoma maculata*, female

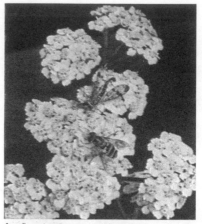

b. Scorpion-fly, *Panorpa communis*, male, and Hover-fly, *Syrphus nitidicollis*

c. Scorpion-fly, *Panorpa germanica*, male

d. Bibionid-fly, *Bibio hortulanus*, male (right) and female (left)

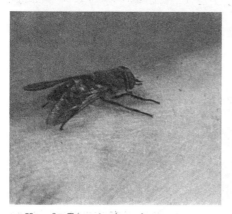

e. Horse-fly, *Tabanus bromius*, on human arm

f. Drone-fly, *Eristalis tenax*, male

(a, b, natural size; c to f, slightly magnified.   a, e, etherised; b, c, d, f, temperature controlled)

FLIES (DIPTERA) AND SCORPION-FLIES (MECOPTERA)

Photographs by S. BEAUFOY

are elephants nor seals ! The Human Louse (*Pediculus humanus*) exists in two races—the Head-louse (*capitis*) and the Body-louse (*corporis*). The Body-louse is a great pest during wars, causing much discomfort among front-line troops. It is also liable to be a very dangerous enemy, especially in Eastern Europe, since it conveys the micro-organism causing epidemic typhus from man to man. Even in England to-day the Head-louse is frequent where people live under unhygienic conditions. Recent surveys have shown that it is much commoner on children than adults and more girls than boys become infested.

Whereas the Sucking Lice form the suborder Siphunculata the Biting Lice are known as Mallophaga. They have biting jaws and do not suck blood : they feed on epidermal products such as flakes of skin and fragments of hairs or feathers. In this way, and by the scraping action of their claws, they cause birds much irritation, often leaving bare patches of skin through loss of feathers.

Order 12. Thysanoptera (*thusanos*, a fringe ; *pteron*, a wing)

Thrips (Brit. spp. about 180)

Thrips seldom come into the ken of anyone other than an entomologist unless really searched for. They escape observation because they are so small (usually ⅛ in. or less in length) not because they are rare. Thrips are very common in flowers, especially those of the daisy or Composite order where they will generally be found among the florets. They are mostly black or yellowish in colour and usually have two pairs of very narrow, strap-like wings margined with elegant fringes of long hairs. The majority of the species obtain their nutriment from the tissues of plants, which they pierce with their peculiarly formed mouth-parts, and imbibe the sap. In this way certain kinds are injurious, especially such species as the Pea Thrips and the Onion Thrips. Some are predatory.

Order 13. Hemiptera (*hemi*, half ; *pteron*, a wing)

Plant-bugs, Water-bugs, Leaf-hoppers, Aphids, Scale-insects, etc.
(Brit. spp. about 1,410)

Included in this order is a whole collection of often unfamiliar and apparently dissimilar insects. They are classified into two suborders. Normally they have four wings but the ordinal name refers to the anterior pair in the suborder Heteroptera only, whose members have the base of the wing leathery and the tip membranous (Text-Fig. 9). In the other suborder—the Homoptera—the fore-wings are of the same texture throughout, being either leathery like the tegmina of Orthoptera, or wholly membranous ; many species however bear no wings at all (Plates 37 [p. 238] Fig. a, and 38 [p. 239] Fig. a).

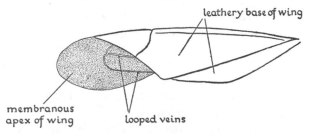

FIG. 9.—Left fore-wing of a Plant-bug of the family *Capsidae*. (Magnified.)

The mouth-parts offer the most constant criterion for recognising members of this order and a good pocket lens is desirable in order to make them out. These organs are of the same type irrespective of the stage the insect may be in. They consist of four very fine bristles (the greatly modified mandibles and maxillae) which lie when at rest in a sort of beak or proboscis formed by the labium (Text-Figs. 10 and 11) : there are no palpi. Mouth-parts of this type fit together so as to form an instrument for piercing and sucking. The great majority of Hemiptera feed on the sap of plants, some species causing great losses to agricultural crops. A small number of kinds have taken to sucking blood.

The two suborders may now be looked into a little further. The Heteroptera are easy to recognise by the wing-characters already mentioned. Another feature to notice is that the wings are closed flat over the back, whereas in the Homoptera they slope roof-like over the sides of the body (Pl. 37, Fig. a). The Heteroptera (Plant-bugs, Water-bugs) are generally larger than Homoptera but by no means so abundant. Those most likely to be found are the Capsid-bugs (family Capsidae) of which there are nearly 190 British species. They are generally green or brownish insects from $\frac{1}{4}$ to $\frac{1}{2}$ in. long, of slender build and with the membranous area of the fore wings supported by two looped veins as shown in Text-Fig. 9.[1] Special mention may be made

[1] More rarely with a single looped vein.

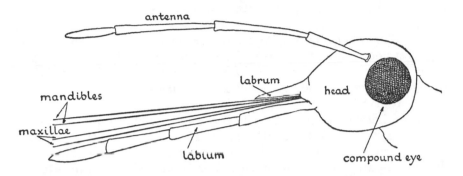

FIG. 10.—Mouth-parts of an Hemipterous Insect, side view. (Diagrammatic.)

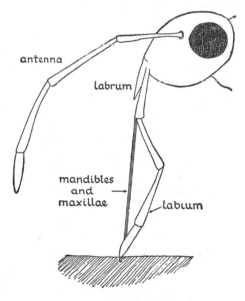

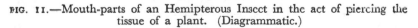

FIG. 11.—Mouth-parts of an Hemipterous Insect in the act of piercing the tissue of a plant. (Diagrammatic.)

of the Apple Capsid (*Plesiocoris rugicollis*), which is also abundant on willows and sallows (see p. 31). Another species is shown on Pl. 39, p. 254.

The Shield-bugs (family Pentatomidae) include some of the largest and most stoutly built members of the suborder (Pls. 11 [p. 42] Fig. a and 15 [p. 74] Fig. a). They have 5-segmented antennae and a very large triangular dorsal shield, or scutellum. Shield-bugs are much less common than Capsids ; some kinds occur on bushes or low trees, others on herbaceous plants. The Bed-bug (*Cimex lectularius*) belongs to the family Cimicidae (Pl. IV, p. 27, Fig. a). Since its fore-wings are reduced to mere pads, and it has no hind-wings, the structure of the mouth-parts provides the main evidence that this creature belongs to the Hemiptera. It frequents unhygienic dwellings and feeds upon the blood of man. Although liable to cause much irritation when present in numbers it is not known to be implicated in the spread of any disease. A number of Heteroptera are aquatic in habits and are dealt with in Chapter 11. These include the Pond-skaters, the Water-boatmen, the Water-scorpions and their allies.

The second suborder, or Homoptera, includes a great variety of often very dissimilar-looking insects. Notwithstanding their small size they are of enormous economic importance on account of the injurious propensities of many species. A very characteristic feature of their economy is the almost continuous discharge through the vent of a sugary waste product or " honey-dew ", especially notable in Aphids.

The Cercopidae or Frog-hoppers derive their popular name from their somewhat frog-like appearance due to their broad heads, coupled with their propensity for leaping. The few British species, although unprotected as adults, live as nymphs within a frothy exudation popularly called Cuckoo-spit (see also p. 206). The commonest of them is *Philaenus leucophthalmus*, about ¼ in. long, which lives on a great variety of wild and cultivated plants (Plates 37 [p. 238] and 38 [p. 239]).

The family Cicadellidae is abundantly represented by very small, rather elongated insects called Leaf-hoppers. They leap and fly with agility and various kinds are readily obtained off nettles, rose-bushes, apple trees, beech, etc. They are separated from Frog-hoppers by their slender hind tibiae which bear longitudinal rows of bristles: in the Frog-hoppers the hind tibiae are stouter and end in a cluster of spines with two others along their outer edge.

Most people are familiar with Aphids or Plant-lice (Aphididae)

Plate V

S. BEAUFOY

a Pear-midge, *Contarinia pyrivora* (× *circa* 10) [from a specimen mounted in euparal]

S. BEAUFOY

b Mymarid or Fairy-fly (× 22) [from a specimen mounted in euparal]

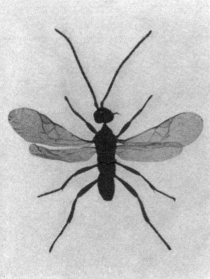

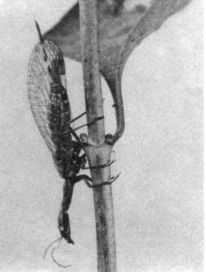

S. BEAUFOY

c Ichneumon-fly (Braconidae), *Apanteles glomeratus* (× 8) [from a set specimen]

A. D. IMMS

d Snake-fly, *Raphidia maculicollis*, female (× 2) [from a living example]

SOME DIVERSE TYPES OF INSECTS

Plate VI

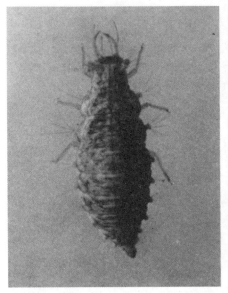

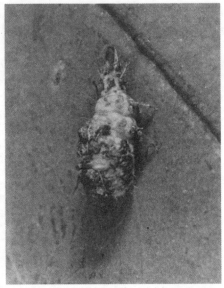

A. D. IMMS

c Green Lace-wing larval (*Chrysopa*) after removal of debris

S. BEAUFOY

b Green Lace-wing larva (*Chrysopa*) carrying debris [subjected to low temperature]

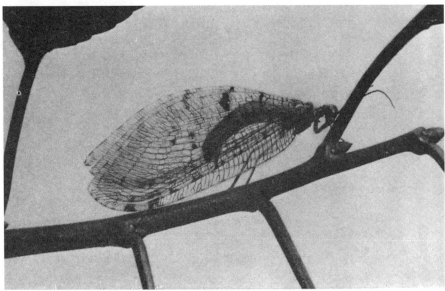

S. BEAUFOY

c Giant Lace-wing, *Osmylus fulvicephalus* (× 3)

STUDIES OF LACE-WINGS

which live in colonies on the leaves and shoots of so many plants (see also pp. 113 and 220). They are very small, soft-skinned insects with long antennae and usually a pair of processes or cornicles on the upper side of the 5th abdominal segment. Both winged and wingless adults occur and are about equally abundant. Both pairs of wings are delicate membranes with few veins, the hind pair being much the smaller. While many Aphids are predominantly green in colour, the Broad-bean Aphid is black and others are yellowish or brown. The Woolly Aphis or American Blight of the apple is covered with a coating of waxy threads. Several kinds of Aphids are shown in Pls. 17, 29 and 38.

The White-flies or Aleurodidae (Pl. 11, p. 42, Fig. b) are minute creatures liable to be mistaken for very small moths. Their opaque white appearance is due to the body and wings being coated with a fine powdery wax. Among the British species the Cabbage White-fly (*Aleyrodes proletella*) and the Greenhouse White-fly (*Trialeurodes vaporariorum*) rank as pests.

The family Coccidae includes the Mealy-bugs and Scale-insects (Plates 11 and XXI). In spite of being very small and inconspicuous they are remarkable owing to the extraordinary disparity of form between individuals of the two sexes. It was many years before the females of some of the species were recognised as being living animals at all. It is said that one kind was only eventually decided to be an insect, and not a seed, as the result of a lawsuit, many years ago. The Mealy-bugs (Pl. 11, Fig. d) derive their name from the mealy or waxy exudation which covers them. The females, like those of all Coccidae, are devoid of any wings, but retain the nymphal capacity for free movement. In the true Scale-insects, which are in the majority, the body of the female is covered with a " scale " formed by the persistent skins of previous stages glued together by a variable amount of dermal secretion. In many cases the legs and antennae are much reduced or lost and the animals remain fixed for life on the food-plant. Male Coccidae are very minute and fragile, devoid of mouth-parts and with only a single pair of wings.

Order 14. NEUROPTERA (*neuron*, a nerve ; *pteron*, a wing)

ALDER-FLIES, SNAKE-FLIES, LACE-WINGS, etc. (Brit. spp. 60) * †

The Neuroptera are mostly slenderly built, soft-bodied insects that are very weak fliers. They bear two pairs of gauzy, net-veined wings

E

which are closed roof-like over the body when at rest ; the wings of a
side are closely alike in size and shape (Pl. VI, p. 47, Fig. c). The
antennae are rather long and thread-like and there are no cerci.
Perhaps they are most easily recognised by the close meshwork of
wing-veins and by the ladder-like series of veinlets along the front
margin of each wing (Pl. II, p. 19, Fig. a). It is true that Dragon-flies
show these same features but their much larger and more robust build,
minute bristle-like antennae and 3-segmented tarsi (5-segmented in
Neuroptera) serve to distinguish them.

The Alder-flies (*Sialis*) have smoky wings and the two British
species are found resting on vegetation bordering streams and canals,
flitting away weakly if aroused. The greyish eggs are laid in cake-like
masses of about 500 to 700 in May–June on Grasses, Sedges, etc. (Pl. 2,
p. 3, Fig. a). They hatch into aquatic larvae of the kind shown in
Pl. III, p. 26, Fig. b. When fully grown they leave the water, burrow
in the earth nearby and pupate, becoming adult insects a few weeks
later.

The Snake flies (*Raphidia*) include three British species (Pl. V, p. 46,
Fig. d): they are distinguished by the elongated neck-like prothorax
and the long needle-like ovipositor. They are not really common
insects but are to be found in wooded country among rank herbage,
on tree-trunks, or among May-blossom and other flowers.

The Green Lace-wings (*Chrysopa*), which are familiar objects in gardens in summer, are delicately built creatures, often with iridescent pale
green bodies and wing-veins, and eyes of gleaming gold (Pl. 3, p. 10).
Other species are yellowish green and two are brown. The rather
common *Chrysopa carnea* often enters houses, barns, etc., to hibernate,
and during this time it undergoes a striking colour change. It alters
from green to reddish but, on the advent of spring, it regains its original
colour. It is stated that the colour change is caused by an increase of
red colouring matter in autumn and to its absorption in spring. The
eggs of Green Lace-wings are attached to the summits of tall stalks (see
p. 212 and Pl. VII, p. 62) and are found on the vegetation frequented
by the larvae. The latter are true friends of the horticulturist since they
are wholesale devourers of Aphids and other small insects. The larvae
(Pl. VI, p. 47) have long caliper-like jaws projecting in front of the
head ; well-developed eyes, antennae and legs ; and bristly tubercles
are present on the body in many species. Some of them hide themselves
under a coating of debris carried on their backs. When fully grown

the larvae spin tough oval or globular cocoons of white silk on leaves, bark, fences, etc., the silk being produced by transformed Malpighian tubes and delivered through an anal spinneret (Pl. XII, p. 107, Fig. e).

The Brown Lace-wings constitute the family *Hemerobiidae* (28 British spp.) ; they resemble Green Lace-wings but are smaller and of a sombre brown or greyish colour. They and their larvae similarly feed upon Aphids and other small insects, mites, etc. The eggs are elongate oval in shape and are not supported on stalks. The larvae are easily mistaken for those of Green Lace-wings but the jaws are shorter, thicker and less curved : also, they lack bristly tubercles and do not carry debris. Allied to the Brown Lace-wings are the species of *Sisyra*. They are dull-coloured insects, measuring not more than $\frac{1}{2}$ in. across the wings, and inhabit the banks of canals, rivers and lakes. The larvae are parasitic on fresh-water sponges and are stated to probe the sponge tissues for nutriment, using their very long bristle-like jaws. The largest British member of the Neuroptera is *Osmylus fulvicephalus*—a beautiful insect with blotched wings attaining an expanse of 2 in. (Pl. VI, p. 47). It occurs along the banks of woodland streams where there is dense overhanging vegetation. It is very local but not rare and occurs in various counties, especially in the southern part of England. The larva lives in wet moss or under stones bordering streams (Map 3).

Order 15. MECOPTERA (*mekos*, length ; *pteron*, a wing)

SCORPION-FLIES (Brit. spp. 4) *†

This very small order is separable from the Neuroptera by the absence of the ladder-like arrangement of veinlets along the front margins of the wings (Pl. II, p. 19, Fig. b) and by the head being pro-longed downwards into a strong beak. The four wings are transparent but spotted with brown and are of equal size with narrow bases (Pl. II). The antennae are long and thread-like. The name Scorpion-fly is due to the habit of the male of holding the end of the body upturned over the back rather like the way a scorpion carries its tail. Both larvae and adults are carnivorous. The common Scorpion-Fly (*Panorpa communis*) occurs along hedgerows and the borders of woods (Pl. 12, p. 43, Figs. b and c). Its larva is subterranean but not often found : it is to be looked for in and around crumbling damp tree-stumps and resembles a small greyish brown caterpillar.

Order 16. TRICHOPTERA (*thrix*, gen. *trichos*, a hair ; *pteron*, a wing)

CADDIS-FLIES (Brit. spp. 188)

Caddis-flies are small to moderate-sized sombre-coloured insects whose bodies and wings are densely clothed with hair. Generally of some shade of light brown, buff or black, they are exceedingly moth-like in appearance and are likewise mostly nocturnal in habits. The two kinds of insects are, in fact, so similar that there can be little doubt that both groups were evolved from a common ancestral type. If Caddis-flies bore scales instead of hairs on their wings and bodies they would be hard to separate from sombre coloured moths. The real distinction between the two, however, is in the mouth-parts. These in the great majority of moths form a coiled sucking proboscis whereas such an organ is never found among Caddis-flies. Caddis-flies are incapable of taking food requiring mastication, since they have no functional mandibles. Their mouth-parts serve to lap or lick up fluid matter and some kinds will visit and feed on the moth-collector's sugar mixture when applied to tree-trunks, etc. Herbage and bushes at the edge of lakes, rivers and streams yield many Caddis-flies, which fly out when disturbed. A number of different kinds rest during daylight, like moths, in the crevices of the bark of tree-trunks, on fences, etc. After dark a bright light attracts them on a warm night, when they often enter houses. The flight of many, but not all, Caddis-flies is weak and, when resting, the wings are closed roofwise along the sides of the body (Pl. 13, p. 66, Fig. d). The fore-wings are rather narrow and often bear an obscure pattern, whereas the broader hind-wings are of a uniform smoky tint (Plate II, p. 19, Fig. b).

Notwithstanding the close resemblance between these insects and moths they show great differences both in structure and habits in their immature stage. The eggs are laid in water or on aquatic plants or on overhanging trees or bushes. They are deposited in masses, often enveloped in a kind of mucilage which rapidly swells when wetted. The larvae or caddis-worms are aquatic throughout their life and many kinds make shelters or caddis-cases within which they live. The caddis-cases are composed of a lining of silk to which various foreign materials are added. The silk, it may be added, is emitted from glands that discharge into a spinneret on the floor of the mouth. The cases are commonly tubular with an opening at either end. The front opening is large and allows of the head and thorax of the larva being protruded. The larva (Text-Fig. 12) is somewhat fleshy with a hard head, and

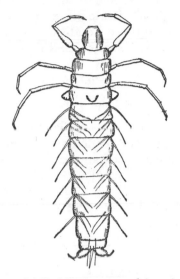

FIG. 12.—Larva of a Caddis-fly removed from its case. (×2.)

antennae so small as to appear to be wanting. The thorax has the upper or tergal plates hard and shiny and the legs strong and well formed. At the end of the body is a pair of grappling hooks: it is by means of these devices that it holds on to the end of its case and thereby drags it along as it crawls about. The abdomen also bears a series of gills which look like fine whitish threads. The variety of cases made by these insects is very great, most kinds of material found in the water being used for the purpose by one or other species. Leaves, pieces of leaves or stalks, straws, bits of stick are often used while other species select sand, particles of gravel or even the empty shells of small water snails (Pl. XXX, p. 259). A current of water is kept flowing through the case by means of periodic undulatory movements of the body.

Before turning into a pupa a caddis-worm fixes its habitation to some object in the water. A silken grating is formed across either end which allows for the ingress and egress of the water but keeps out intruders. The pupa has powerful mandibles to bite its way through the case. After emergence it makes an upward passage through the water either by swimming or by crawling ; in the former method the middle legs are used as oars and are fringed with rows of long hairs. In some species the pupae become so active that they are able to swim about until they can find a suitable place to leave the water. In those kinds living in swift streams the Caddis-fly breaks out of the pupa as soon as the latter reaches the surface, and flies away immediately.

Order 17. LEPIDOPTERA (*lepis*, gen. *lepidos*, a scale ; *pteron*, a wing)

BUTTERFLIES and MOTHS (Brit. spp. 2,187) *

The Lepidoptera are an order familiar to everyone. It is common knowledge that these insects have four wings covered with flat scales that adhere to the fingers like powder if the wings be handled or touched (Pl. VIII, p. 63). The mouth-parts consist of a sucking proboscis or trunk that is formed into a tube by the combined galeae of the two maxillae, these parts being greatly drawn out and modified for the purpose. With rare exceptions mandibles are wanting or reduced to mere nodules. Various Moths belonging to very different groups have no functional mouth-parts and consequently do not feed as adults. In this category are the Eggars and Lappet-moths ; the Emperor (*Saturnia pavonia*) ; the Goat-moth (*Cossus cossus*) ; and the Swift-moths (*Hepialus*).

There is usually not much difficulty in separating a Butterfly from a Moth. In the former the antennae end in a club or knob whereas in Moths there are many types of antennae but they are always without a knob at the extremity. In the Skipper Butterflies (*Hesperiidae*) the antennal club is more tapering and drawn out at its tip into a point

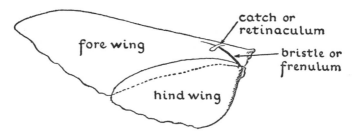

FIG. 13.—Underside of right wings of a Hawk-moth showing how they are linked together in the male. (Enlarged.)

or minute hook. This same feature is seen in some of the Hawk-moths, Clearwings, and Burnets and, in cases of this kind, the presence or absence of an interlocking mechanism, coupling the two wings of a side together, gives the clue ; among Butterflies there is no such device, whereas in the majority of Moths the base of the hind-wing bears a very long projecting bristle, or group of bristles, which become engaged in a hook-like catch on the under side of the fore-wing (Text-Fig. 13). All Moths likely to be mistaken for a Butterfly bear this mechanism.

In many cases the sexes are so very different that the males and females may be separated at a glance. This feature is well displayed in the examples shown on Pl. 14, p. 67, where the individuals of the two sexes are so different as to suggest separate species. Among some of the larger Moths, e.g. the Wood Leopard (*Zeuzera pyrina*), the Drinker (*Philudoria potatoria*) and the Emperor (*Saturnia pavonia*), the male is decidedly smaller than the female and has the antennae branched or comb-like (Plate 14). In the two last-named the males are also more brightly and deeply coloured. The most striking differences in the sexes are met with among these Moths with flightless females, their wings being either absent or aborted to mere vestiges, whereas the males are fully winged. About a dozen kinds of British Moths of the family Geometridae display this peculiarity, the spider-like females of the Winter Moth (*Operophtera brumata*) and of the Mottled Umber Moth (*Erannis defoliaria*) being familiar examples. The same thing happens in the Vapourers (*Orgyia*) and in the curious Psychids whose females live in the caddis-like cases made by the caterpillars. Since quite a number of the Moths whose females have lost their wings are very common insects it is clear that this feature is not in any way a handicap to them. It is, however, by no means confined to Moths and for this reason its implications are further commented upon in Chapter 3.

Although most people know a caterpillar by sight they can rarely say correctly how many legs it possesses. The usual number is 8 pairs— 3 pairs of thoracic legs and 5 pairs of abdominal feet. The abdominal feet are separated by a gap from the thoracic legs and are borne on segments 3 to 6 and 10 of the hind body. These feet have fleshy soles that are used for grasping the object they are resting upon. Their grip is helped by numerous small hooks or crochets which are grouped in circles or in crescents or bands. The whole business in life of a cater- pillar is eating and consequently the head is hard and firm so as to

give a rigid base for the strong muscles that move the jaws. The
antennae are very small and peg-like and just behind them on either
side is a group of six very small simple eyes. Projecting from the middle
of the labium is a minute spinneret through which silk is discharged.
In the family Geometridae the caterpillars only possess abdominal feet
on segments 8 and 10. They move in consequence by a looping action
and are often known for this reason as " loopers " or " Geometers "
(" earth measurers "). They progress by holding on by the thoracic
legs and then drawing up the hind body so that the abdominal feet

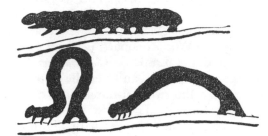

FIG. 14.—*Above :* a typical Caterpillar. *Below :* two phases in the locomotion
of a Geometer Caterpillar.

come close up to the thorax, thus bending the abdomen into a pronounced loop (Text-Fig. 14). The abdominal feet then grip the
support and the whole body is extended forwards. The looping action
is then repeated.

Various kinds of caterpillars are familiar to dwellers in the country.
Many others need diligently searching for, being hidden away or
camouflaged to match their surroundings. Some idea of their diversity
of form and coloration is conveyed in Plates 34, p. 207, and 35, p. 222,
while the significance of these features in the economy of nature is
discussed in Chapter 9.

Whereas the caterpillars of many kinds of Moths spin dense silken
cocoons, those of other species make cocoons of particles of wood, soil
or other extraneous material bound together with silk (Pl. XII, p. 107).
Among Butterflies a cocoon is wanting and in the Peacock (*Vanessa io*)
and the Tortoiseshell (*Vanessa urticae*) the larva merely weaves a pad
of silk and the chrysalis hangs head downwards with the tail-end,
which bears minute hooklets, attached to it. In the Swallow-tail
(*Papilio machaon*) and the Pierid or White Butterflies the chrysalides

are suspended in an upright position by means of a silken girdle, the tail-end being likewise attached to a pad of silk (Pl. XII, Fig. d).

Order 18. COLEOPTERA (*coleos*, a sheath ; *pteron*, a wing)

BEETLES (Brit. spp. 3,690) *

Beetles outnumber in species every other order of animals ; it is estimated that about 250,000 different kinds have already been described and given names but many hundreds of new species are being discovered even in a single year. Beetles are ubiquitous, being found almost everywhere from the seashore to the tops of mountains ; ponds, streams, marshes, woods, moors, lanes, cliff-sides and fields all provide their quota of different kinds. Their habits are extremely varied, but large numbers are inhabitants of the ground, either living in the soil itself or frequenting the various decaying animal or vegetable substances present. Dung, carrion, refuse of all kinds, rotting wood and fungi all support large associations of Beetles. The members of five families are truly aquatic (see p. 230). The often brilliantly coloured Leaf-beetles, and numerous kinds of Weevils, are only found associated with living plants. A considerable number of different Beetles occur in close relation with man, being found in wood, fur, hides, furniture, seeds, museum specimens and in dried stored foods and drugs.

Before proceeding further it is necessary to state what features qualify an insect for inclusion within the Coleoptera. In the first place the fore-wings are in the form of dense, usually horny sheaths called elytra which are devoid of any visible veins and meet in a straight line down the back (Text-Fig. 15). As a rule the elytra cover, or almost cover, the hind body but in the Rove-beetles (Pl. X, p. 99, Fig. c) and the Oil-beetles (Pl. XI, p. 106, Fig. d) the abdomen is freely exposed. The hind-wings are the functional organs of flight. The elytra play no active part in propulsion and when a Beetle is in the air are held at an acute angle with the body. When not in use the hind-wings are folded up in a complicated way and stowed away beneath the closed elytra. Whereas many Beetles have fully developed membranous hind-wings (Pl. IX, p. 98, Fig. a) a considerable number are unable to fly, owing to these organs being reduced to mere flaps or lost altogether.

The mouth-parts are of the biting or chewing kind with strong toothed mandibles, well-developed maxillae and a somewhat reduced labium. The antennae are so variable in character that no one type

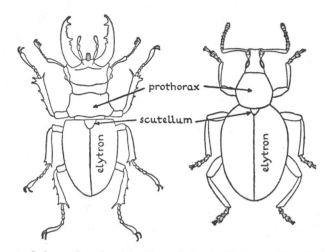

FIG. 15.—*Left :* a Stag-beetle. (Actual size.) *Right :* a Weevil. (×3.)

is characteristic of the order as a whole. The prothorax is large and very evident and the only other part of the thorax visible when the elytra are closed, is a little dorsal shield or scutellum (Text-Fig. 15) belonging to the mesothorax. The legs are just about as variable as the antennae and the tarsal segments often differ in number in the different groups.

The reader may often be puzzled in finding out which creatures are beetle larvae and which are not, so great is their diversity of form and habits. Those that are active, and seek out and catch other insects that constitute their prey, have well-formed legs and antennae. Their eyes and other sense-organs are well-developed and likewise the tail-feelers or cerci. The larvae of Ground-beetles (Pl. X, p. 99, Fig. a) and of carnivorous Water-beetles (Pl. XXVII, p. 234, Fig. a) are examples of this kind. Many other beetle larvae live near their food and consequently have not far to go for it. In such cases they have short but obvious legs and their other appendages are likewise reduced. Wire-worms and Ladybird larvae come under this category. There are again Beetle larvae that live immersed in their food. Creatures so placed no longer need legs, eyes or other sense-organs to enable them to discover it. Weevil larvae are good examples, also those larvae that live in decaying wood, dung, etc.

Beetle pupae (Pl. XII, p. 107) are most often located in cavities or cells in the ground: others occur within the larval food-plants; but cocoons are not so frequently found as in Lepidoptera and silk does not so often participate in their formation.

Among the different groups of Beetles most likely to be met with, the Ground-beetles, which are discussed on p. 127, occur almost everywhere in the soil. The Rove-beetles or Staphylinidae have very short elytra which usually only cover a small part of the hind-body. They are very common insects about the soil, especially among decaying vegetation, dung, etc. The vast majority of the 700 odd species of this family are very small creatures and perhaps only one species—the Devil's Coach-horse (*Staphylinus olens*)—is known to the casual observer (Pl. X, p. 99). Dull black, as if in mourning, and over 1 in. long, it is often seen on pathways and in gardens (see also p. 188). Out in the country one is sometimes afflicted by a minute black insect entering the eye and causing much irritation. The culprit, according to N. H. Joy, is probably a very small Rove-beetle of the genus *Oxytelus*. The larvae of Rove-beetles (Pl. X, Fig. b) are very like those of Ground-beetles, but the claws of their feet are single whereas in the last-named creatures they are paired.

Most readers are probably aware of the economic value of the Ladybirds or Coccinellidae and their larvae as destroyers of Aphids (see also p. 128). Their small yellow eggs are laid in groups, often on the undersides of leaves infested with Aphids. The slate-blue larvae, which are tuberculated and spotted, taper posteriorly and have well-developed legs (Pl. 16, p. 75). Each larva lives about three weeks and in that time devours several hundred aphids. When fully grown it attaches itself beneath a leaf or other support and passes into the pupal stage (Plate 16). The pupa, it will be noted, is not concealed and has the cast-off larval skin associated with it. From among about 50 British Coccinellidae one of the most familiar is the Two-spot Ladybird (*Adalia bipunctata*), which most often has red elytra and two black spots (see also p. 31). It is, however, very variable in colour and is frequently black with 4 or 6 red spots (Plate 16). The Seven-spot Ladybird (*Coccinella septempunctata*) is about equally familiar and differs in being very constant in its colour-markings (Pl. 15, p. 74, Fig. c). *Adalia decempunctata* is another common and extremely variable species. As an occasional visitor in gardens the small lemon-coloured *Thea vigintiduopunctata* (Plate 16) is sure to attract notice. Other kinds, which likewise generally derive their names from the number of spots on the elytra, are to be met with in different types of country.

The Click-beetles or Skipjacks (family Elateridae) are mostly elongated insects of sombre hues but a few are red or have metallic colours. The " Fireflies " of the tropics are members of the same family. Most Elateridae have a curious faculty of being able to jerk themselves upwards into the air when lying on their backs, hence their name of Skipjacks. They are also called Click-beetles because this feat is often achieved with a clicking sound. An account of the habit and its significance is given on p. 188. The larvae of the genera *Agriotes* and *Athous* are the notorious Wireworms of the agriculturist. They live up to five years at the roots of grass and when the latter is ploughed in they attack the supervening cereal or other crop (see p. 122). A Wireworm (Pl. 17, p. 78, Fig. a) is a slender hard-skinned yellowish-brown creature with very short legs and a pointed hind extremity. It pupates deep in the soil. Larvae of other kinds live in dead, decaying trees, etc.

The Chrysomelidae or Leaf-beetles include nearly 250 British species. They are an attractive group of shining or brightly coloured insects of small or moderate size (Pl. 18, p. 79). The larger number feed as larvae on the foliage of various plants and, for this reason, some, such as the Colorado Potato Beetle (*Leptinotarsa decemlineata*), the Flea-beetles (*Phyllotreta*) and the Asparagus Beetle (*Crioceris asparagi*) (Pl. 19, p. 94, Fig. a) are very destructive to specific vegetables. The first-named was accidentally introduced into France about 1922 and, despite measures of eradication, has now become firmly established in Western Europe. An outbreak in the Tilbury-Gravesend district of England in 1933 was successfully dealt with, but sporadic occurrences of the same type are liable to recur with the spread of this insect on the Continent. The larvae of Leaf-beetles are soft and fleshy, often brightly coloured and with short stumpy legs. They are very sluggish and when fully fed pupate in the soil. Many species of *Chrysomela*, *Cryptocephalus* and other genera are brilliant metallic beetles, often found in grassy, flowery localities where the larval food-plants occur (Pl. 15, p. 74, Fig. f). Browning must have had some of these creatures in mind when he wrote:

> Where one small orange cup amassed
> Five beetles—blind and green they grope
> Among the honey-meal.

The Weevils or Curculionidae are the largest family group of any kind of animals. With a world total of over 40,000 species our British fauna with about 450 kinds seems very meagre. Weevils show a pronounced family likeness owing to the front region of the head being drawn out into a beak or rostrum of varying length and thickness. This projection bears the mouth-parts and also the very definitely elbowed antennae (Text-Fig. 15). Weevils, both as larvae and adults, are plant-feeders and some are very destructive to grain, seeds, fruit, etc. Their larvae are crescentic, whitish, blind grubs devoid of limbs, their degeneration being associated with the fact that they live amidst an abundance of food which they have not to seek for themselves. Among the most familiar kinds are the golden-green members of the genera *Phyllobius* and *Polydrusus* (Pl. 19, p. 94, Figs. d, e) that occur in early summer on nettles and other wayside plants and on young oaks. Anyone who has never seen these resplendent but small Weevils should tap any of the plants named into an open umbrella or butterfly-net when some will usually oblige by revealing themselves. Other kinds of Weevils are discussed on pp. 115 and 120. Closely related to the Weevils are the Bark-beetles or Scolytidae that are among the most serious enemies the forester has to contend with (see p. 113).

The important family of the Cerambycidae is associated with wooded areas, their larvae boring into the trunks and branches of the trees, often causing damage to valuable timber. An account of these beetles is given on p. 116. Among other wood-boring Beetles the Furniture-beetles, including the famous Death-watch, the Powder-post Beetles and the Pinhole-borers are dealt with on pp. 118 *et seq.*

Other interesting and familiar beetles belong to the superfamily Lamellicornia, so called because the end segments of the antennae are flattened into plates or lamellae (Pl. VIII, p. 63, Fig. a). Most of them are Scarabaeidae—beetles whose habits the French naturalist Fabre has so interestingly described. The bulky Dor-beetles (*Geotrupes*) come in for mention on p. 154, while Chafers are discussed on p. 123. Among the largest of all our beetles is the Stag-beetle (*Lucanus cervus*), also mentioned on p. 189. It is not uncommon in parts of southern England (Pl. IX, p. 98, Figs. c, d), where its larva feeds on the wood of the roots and trunks of dead trees. The *Dorcus* (Pl. XI, p. 106, Fig. a) is a much commoner insect.

Order 19. STREPSIPTERA (*strepsis*, a twisting ; *pteron*, a wing)

STYLOPS (Brit. spp. 16)

These minute insects are related to the Coleoptera ; they are, however, seldom found, even by many entomologists. The males have branched antennae ; the fore-wings are altered into club-like organs and the hind-wings are very large. Strepsiptera pass their larval stages as internal parasites of certain bees, wasps, plant bugs, etc. This habit is retained throughout life by the females, which are greatly modified in structure as the result.

Order 20. HYMENOPTERA (*hymen*, a membrane ; *pteron*, a wing)

SAW-FLIES, ANTS, BEES, WASPS, ICHNEUMON-FLIES, etc. (Brit. spp. over 6,100) *

Hymenoptera possess two pairs of more or less transparent, membranous wings, which are usually rather narrow with few veins, the hind pair being smaller (Pls. 20 [p. 95] and 21 [p. 110]). The wings of a side are linked together by minute hooklets in the manner shown in Pl. XIII, p. 114. Their mouth-parts are formed for chewing and licking. A large proportion of them have a narrow waist and this will always serve to identify wingless members of the order. An ovipositor is always present though sometimes converted into a sting.

There are two main divisions of the order. The first division (or Symphyta) includes the Saw-flies and their allies (Pl. 21, p. 110, Figs. 15-16). They have no constriction or waist and the ovipositor is modified to form a saw. With this instrument the female literally saws slits or pockets, in which to place her eggs, in the leaves or stems of those plants upon which the larvae will feed. The larvae, it may be added, are caterpillars very closely resembling those of the Lepidoptera. The easiest way to separate them is to use a pocket lens and note the single eye on each side of the head instead of a group of these organs as in the caterpillars of Lepidoptera. Also, the abdominal feet in the saw-fly caterpillar often number 6 or more pairs whereas in the Lepidopterous larva the usual number is 5 pairs. When fully-fed the saw-fly caterpillar makes a cocoon, sometimes on its food-plant but more often beneath the soil. Everyone who grows a little fruit must have come across the yellowish spotted caterpillars of the Gooseberry Saw-fly (*Pteronidea ribesii*) (Pl. 34, p. 207, Fig b), which also devours the leaves of

Currants. The orange and black caterpillars of the Poplar Saw-fly (*Priophorus viminalis*) feed in companies on the leaves of the poplar, while another kind (*Phymatocera aterrima*) often plays havoc with the leaves of the Solomon's Seal (Pl. 25, p. 142, Fig. c). The finest members of the Saw-fly group are the Wood-wasps. The female Giant Wood-wasp (*Urocerus gigas*) measures nearly 1½ in. long without reckoning the stout ovipositor (Pl. 20, p. 95, Fig. 12). This instrument is used for boring (rather than sawing) through the bark into the wood of conifers, a single egg being laid in each hole thus formed. The white sluggish larvae burrow into the heart-wood, often causing much damage.

The members of the second main division (or Apocrita) have a constriction or waist between the fore- and hind-body : in some kinds it is prolonged to form a stalk or petiole. Many of them have lost their wings : this feature prevails in all the ants (excepting the functional males and females), besides happening here and there among the so-called Parasitica. The larvae are legless grubs, often crescentic in form. The Apocrita are divided into two groups, viz. the Parasitica and the Aculeata. The Parasitica are so called because their larvae live as parasites of other insects (see p. 144). The Ichneumon-flies and Chalcid Wasps are well-known examples. They use their ovipositor for laying their eggs on or within the bodies of insects that are destined to serve as their hosts. The Aculeata are stinging insects. In them the ovipositor is modified into a sting or defensive organ and is no longer used for egg-laying. The eggs are discharged from the body of the female through an opening at the base of the ovipositor. In this category are included the Bees (p. 260), Wasps (p. 275) and Ants (p. 283). A special characteristic is the attention and care which so many of them give to their young. In the case of some of the bees and wasps, together with all the ants, this habit has become developed into an elaborate form of social life (see p. 258).

Order 21. DIPTERA (*di*, two ; *pteron*, a wing)

TRUE FLIES, MOSQUITOES, MIDGES and the like (Brit. spp. over 5,200) *

The Diptera are one of the largest orders of insects and have a world total of more than 80,000 described species. They seem to us to be the most cosmopolitan of all insects. There is hardly anywhere on earth where man can live that Flies, and especially the House-fly (see p. 103), have not followed on his tracks and established themselves.

Most kinds of flies are very easily recognised but some, owing to their special form and coloration, are liable to be mistaken for bees or wasps unless examined more closely. The presence of only a single pair of wings is their special distinguishing feature (Pl. 23, p. 126). Two very small organs—the halteres—take the places of hind-wings. Each haltere consists of a slender stalk surmounted by a minute knob: such organs are very readily seen in Crane-flies. They illustrate a remarkable case of change of form and function of organs, being in reality the greatly modified hind-wings. Their function is sensory; without halteres Diptera lose control when trying to fly and fall downwards (see p. 97).

The mouth-parts of Flies are formed for sucking (Text-Fig. 22) or for sucking and piercing combined (Text-Fig. 26). No fly can masticate solid food—it can only imbibe it in liquid or minutely particulate form. The so-called biting Flies (see p. 133) feed mostly upon blood and usually retain their mandibles in order to use them in conjunction with the lobe of the maxillae as piercing organs. Examples of this kind are Mosquitoes, Punkies or Blood-sucking Midges and Horse-flies. Other kinds of flies, notably the Robber-flies (p. 132) are predators that have strong mouth-parts capable of piercing other insects and sucking their blood. The majority of Flies, however, do not suck the blood of man or of any other animal but feed on many kinds of fluid matter including the nectar of flowers.

The antennae of Flies are extraordinarily variable in form. They are often thread-like with many segments—as in Crane-flies and Midges—but many species have only three segments. In the House-fly, the Blow-fly and their numerous allies the very short antennae hang down in front of the head, instead of projecting outwards as in those flies in which these organs are many-segmented (Text-Fig. 22).

The larvae of flies are legless. Those of Mosquitoes, Midges and their relatives have distinct heads and ultimately transform into pupae of the ordinary kind. Many of these larvae (and pupae) are aquatic and for this reason they are discussed at length in Chapter 11.

The largest number of species of Flies have larvae of the kind so often known as maggots, which are creatures that wriggle and squirm in their movements. In form they taper towards the front end where the head is reduced to a mere papilla; at their broader or tail end there is a pair of enlarged darkly-coloured breathing pores that can be seen through a pocket lens. The most familiar maggots are those

Plate VII

C. L. WITHYCOMBE

a Chrysopa flava (× 4): stalks of eggs merged together

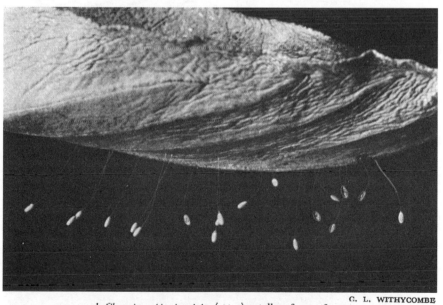

C. L. WITHYCOMBE

b Chrysopa septempunctata (× 3): stalks of eggs free

EGGS OF GREEN LACE-WINGS

Plate VIII

E. A. PHOENIX

a Extremity of antenna of male Cockchafer,
Melolontha melolontha (× 10)

H. E. ELTRINGHAM
b Portrait of the late Sir Edward
Poulton, F.R.S. [from a photograph taken through the eye of
a glow-worm. By the courtesy of
the Royal Entomological Society
of London]

S. BEAUFOY
c Scales from the wing of a Butterfly

S. BEAUFOY
d Wing of a Mosquito, *Theobaldia annulata*

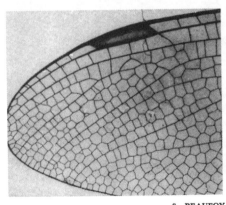

S. BEAUFOY
e Tip of wing of a Dragonfly (*Aeshna*)

S. BEAUFOY
f Antenna of Emperor Moth, *Saturnia
pavonia*, male

WINGS, ANTENNAE, ETC.

belonging to the House-fly (*Musca domestica*), the Blow-flies (*Calliphora*), Flesh-flies (*Sarcophaga*), Dung-flies (*Scatophaga*) and their like. All the foregoing kinds feed upon various sorts of dead or decaying organic matter and are dealt with later on in this book. Others such as those of the Frit-fly (*Oscinella frit*) and the Celery-fly (*Philophylla heraclei*) live within and injure economic plants. The larvae of the Warble-flies (*Hypoderma*) injure the hides of cattle, and those of numerous other flies are noxious in various ways. As an offset to these injurious propensities the maggots of a great many Flies are beneficial to man, especially those of the Hover-flies (p. 132) and the Tachinid flies (p. 151). When the time comes for a maggot to pupate it has a method all its own. Instead of casting off the last larval skin, as almost all insects do, this coat remains and hardens into a darkly coloured barrel-shaped capsule or puparium (Pl. XIV, p. 115, Fig. b). Within this covering and protected by it the maggot changes into an ordinary kind of pupa.

At the time of emergence the fly has somehow to break through the hard wall of the puparium before it can reach the outer world. Most of them achieve this by means of a frontal sac, which is protruded through a special slit-like opening on the front of the head where it expands into a minute bladder. The whole business is brought about by muscular contraction of the hind-body which forces blood into the frontal sac so as to make it turgid. The pressure exerted by this quite unique device enables the fly to rupture the hard wall of the enclosing capsule and crawl out (Plate XIV, Fig. c). The actual break takes place along certain pre-determined lines of weakness that result in a more or less circular piece becoming detached. Having achieved its function the frontal sac is then withdrawn permanently into the cavity of the head. But if a Blow-fly or House-fly be put into a killing bottle and when dead squeezed in the region of the thorax with fine forceps, blood will be forced into the head and the frontal sac become everted ; as soon as the pressure is released it slips back again into the head.

Finally it may be added that the order Diptera is one of immense economic importance. The injurious propensities of some of their larvae have been briefly mentioned, while those adult Flies that have acquired blood-sucking habits are of great significance in regard to medicine. The pathogenic organisms of some of the most virulent diseases, such as malaria, yellow fever, elephantiasis, and sleeping sickness, are transmitted to man through the intermediary of blood-sucking Diptera. The occasional incidence of malaria in England, and its insect carrier, are discussed on p. 138.

Order 22. APHANIPTERA (or SIPHONAPTERA) (*aphanes*, not apparent ; *pteron*, a wing)

FLEAS (Brit. spp. 47) *

Fleas are hard-skinned, laterally flattened, wingless insects whose adults live on the bodies of warm-blooded animals (see also p. 143). Their food is blood and their mouth-parts are modified into organs for piercing the skin of the hosts. Their larvae are very like those of Diptera : they have biting mouth-parts and feed upon organic matter in the host's lair or, in the case of the human flea, upon such material among the dust and dirt of floors. The maximum vertical leap of the Human Flea (*Pulex irritans*) is said to be 7¾ in.

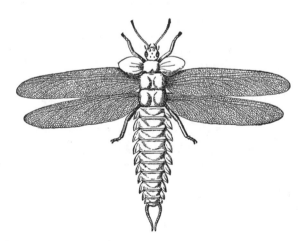

FIG. 16.—Restoration of a fossil Insect of the extinct order Palaeodictyoptera, showing wing-like expansions on the prothorax. (After Handlirsch, × ½.)

ON WINGS AND FLIGHT

INSECTS learned to fly in the evolutionary sense long before any other group of animals. The earliest fossil of a winged insect dates from the Upper Devonian period. It was a creature rather like a cockroach, and it inhabited the region that now lies west of the Ural Mountains over 350 million years ago; it has been given the name *Eopterum* or "Dawn-wing". In the Upper Carboniferous period, about 300 to 270 million years ago, a variety of winged insects already existed, including true cockroaches and primitive Dragon-flies and May-flies, some of the Dragon-flies being gigantic, with wings spanning well over two feet. Some orders also existed at that time which have become extinct; one of the most important of these was the Palaeodictyoptera, a word meaning, by derivation from the Greek, "ancient-net-wing". A member of this order is illustrated at Fig. 16.

Unlike those of birds, bats and pterodactyls, the wings of insects are not limbs, developed primarily for running and modified to function as organs of flight. The most probable explanation of their origin is that they arose from lateral expansions of the thoracic segments called *paranota*. In the very primitive Palaeodictyoptera the second and third thoracic segments bore wings, as in modern insects, and on the first segment there was a pair of paranota. Although there is no direct fossil evidence, it seems likely that the ancestors of these ancient winged insects bore paranota on all three thoracic segments and that some of them took to jumping, like modern Grasshoppers and Crickets. In these the paranota became sufficiently enlarged to form gliding planes, and later those of the hinder two thoracic segments acquired basal articulations and muscles and evolved into wings. Support for the paranotal theory is afforded by the fact that the Silver-fish, a very primitive modern insect, has paranota containing tracheae recalling those of the pads that represent the wings during the early stages of a winged insect's life history.

The wing of an insect is composed of two very thin and often transparent layers of chitin. When it is fully formed these are closely adherent and appear as a single sheet, just as a flattened paper bag does, but the layers can readily be separated in an insect that has just emerged from the pupa. The wing is strengthened by a framework of hollow rods of sclerotin usually called the *veins*, and their arrangement in the wing is termed the *venation*. Although their primary function is to afford support to the wing, the term "vein" is not wholly inappropriate to them as they do play the part of blood-vessels during the development of the wing, and in some insects a circulation of blood is maintained in them after the wings become functional.

The arrangement of veins in the wing is far from being a haphazard network. On the contrary it is virtually constant for each species, and the different orders (and smaller taxonomic groups as well) usually show characteristic features in the venation which are of great importance in classification; four examples are shown on Plate II.

One interesting reason why the wing venation is such a valuable feature in classification is that the wings of insects are more often found in a good state of preservation as fossils than any other parts of them. In very fine-grained sediments imprints of wings, flattened between the bedding planes, may give a picture of the venation almost as complete and clear as the wing of a modern insect mounted on a microscope slide. For this reason the evolution of insect wing venation can be studied in detail, not only by reference to living types, but through a great part of the geological record as well.

Studies of this kind have led to the establishment of a hypothetical primitive wing-type in which the longitudinal veins and their branches are given names. To a large degree the venation in all the orders of winged insects can be related to this primitive model, and the same names used for veins which appear to be homologous, just as the same system of nomenclature can be applied to the bones in the fore limb of a man, a horse and a bat. The uniformity of structure of vertebrates implies that all land vertebrates are descendants of one ancestral group of amphibians. Similarly it is inferrred that wings have been developed by insects only once in their evolutionary history, though they appear to have divided very early into two separate branches. One of these, the Palaeoptera, is represented today only by the May-flies and Dragon-flies, all other living winged insects being included in the Neoptera.

It must not be supposed that determination of homologies in the veins of insects' wings is a simple matter. On the contrary it is a complex and difficult branch of entomology, and in many cases, especially among the Hymenoptera, the relationships of the veins are still uncertain.

In the earliest winged insects the main longitudinal veins were joined by a close network of cross-veins, and this primitive condition is seen today in Dragon-flies and May-flies. The tendency in evolution has been towards reduction in the number of veins, especially in the cross-veins, and towards thickening and strengthening of those which remain. In particular the veins at and near the front margin become thickened and also tend to lie closer together than those in the middle and hinder part of the wing. The result is to stiffen and strengthen the front or leading edge of the wing, which is the part which bears the greatest stress in flight.

Flies and Beetles have only one pair of wings, most other kinds of winged insects have two pairs. They may work independently, but the Hymenoptera

PLATE 13

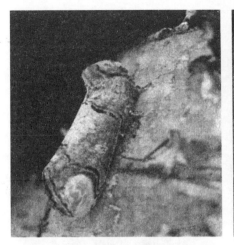

E. J. HUDSON

E. J. HUDSON

a. Buff-tip Moth, *Phalera bucephala*

b. Caterpillar of Buff-tip Moth, *Phalera bucephala*

E. J. HUDSON

S. BEAUFOY

c. Chrysalis of Large White Butterfly, *Pieris brassicae*

d. Caddis-fly, *Limnophilus*

(All larger than actual size)

LEPIDOPTERA AND TRICHOPTERA

PLATE 14

PLATE 14   67
SEXUAL DIFFERENCES IN BUTTERFLIES AND MOTHS

1
CHALK HILL BLUE
Lysandra coridon
MALE

6
CHALK HILL BLUE
Lysandra coridon
FEMALE

2
DRINKER
Philudoria potatoria
MALE

7
DRINKER
Philudoria potatoria
FEMALE

3
ORANGE TIP
Euchloë cardamines
MALE

8
ORANGE TIP
Euchloë cardamines
FEMALE

4
GHOST SWIFT
Hepialus humuli
MALE

9
GHOST SWIFT
Hepialus humuli
FEMALE

5
PALE BRINDLED BEAUTY
Phigalia pilosaria
MALE

10
PALE BRINDLED BEAUTY
Phigalia pilosaria
FEMALE

(Wasps, Bees and Ants) and most of the Lepidoptera (Butterflies and Moths) have the fore- and hind-wings of each side coupled together so that they work in unison. In the Hymenoptera this is effected by a row of minute hooks along the leading edge of the hind-wing, which engage in a fold on the rear edge of the fore-wing (Plate XIII, b). In most moths the wing-coupling apparatus is, most curiously, different in the two sexes. The male has a bristle, the *frenulum*, near the base of the hind-wing, which is held by a hook-like *retinaculum* on the lower surface of the fore-wing (Fig. 13, p. 52). In females the frenulum consists of several bristles and the retinaculum is differently formed and situated. The wings of Butterflies, and of some Moths, merely overlap to such an extent (fore-wings over hind-wings) that the down-stroke, powered mainly by the fore-wing, is applied to both simultaneously.

In most insects both lift and propulsion are produced by the actual movement of the wings rather than by the air flow resulting from the insect's forward motion, and the analogy of a helicopter is closer than that of a conventional aeroplane. This is particularly true of the more advanced types of flying insects, such as Flies, Bees and Moths, which can hover or even fly backwards. The main difference is, of course, that the wings of an insect oscillate, with an up-and-down motion, instead of rotating, but in both insect and helicopter propulsion lift and control are obtained by changes in the angle of attack of the wing in different parts of its stroke.

In simple terms an insect's wings work by flapping up and down, at the same time twisting at the base in such a way that the costa or leading edge is below the hinder edge on the downstroke and above it on the upstroke. The effect of this action is to fan a stream of air downwards and backwards, so that a region of low pressure is created just in front of and above the insect, and one of increased pressure behind and below it. As a result the insect is drawn forward into the region of low pressure and at the same time supported against the pull of gravity.

The way in which power and control are applied to the wings is interesting and extremely complicated.* In each of the two thoracic segments that bear wings, the mesothorax and metathorax, nine or ten functionally distinct pairs of muscles may be involved in flight. They are classified in three groups: the direct wind muscles, which are inserted on the base of the wings, the indirect muscles, running right across the segment internally, and the accessory indirect muscles, which also join one part of the thorax internally to another. The direct wing muscles are important in the Dragon-flies, Grasshoppers and Cockroaches and in the Beetles, but in all the more advanced flying insects the indirect wing muscles are the largest in the body, supplying the power for flight by deformation of the walls of the thorax, not by directly moving the bases of the wings.

Text Fig. 17 gives a much simplified picture of how the indirect muscles work. In the type illustrated there are two pairs of these indirect muscles, a vertical and a longitudinal pair. When the vertical muscles contract they cause the roof of the thorax to become depressed. This results in the wings being forced upwards, owing to the peculiar way in which they are hinged to the thorax. When the longitudinal muscles contract the roof of the thorax bulges upwards, which causes the wings to make a downward stroke. The direct muscles may assist in powering the downward stroke, but they are more usually concerned with producing the accurately synchronised twisting of the wings already described, and with the variations in the degree of twisting by which the insect steers and controls its flight. The accessory indirect muscles have the function of bracing the walls of the thorax against the forces imposed on them by the other muscles, and so of adjusting their elastic properties to the action of certain other flight mechanisms.

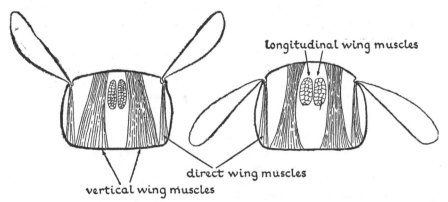

FIG. 17.—Diagrammatic cross-section through the thorax of an Insect showing the wing-muscles. *Left:* vertical muscles contracted forcing the wings upwards. *Right:* longitudinal muscles contracted forcing the wings downwards. (Adapted from R. E. Snodgrass.)

The most important of these is the so-called "click-mechanism", which was first demonstrated in Flies but has since been discovered in other groups of insects. By a complicated modification of the hinge of the wing the indirect muscles do not merely push the wing up and down as they contract and relax. The wings are held in their up and down positions by minute locks or catches, which are not released until deformation of the walls of the thorax by the muscles reaches a certain degree of tension. This build-up and sudden release of tension causes the wings to move with a snapping motion which gives increased speed and efficiency to their strokes.

The principle is the same as when an archer uses muscular power to draw his bow; the power is stored in the flexed bow (equivalent to the elastic walls of the thorax) and is suddenly released to shoot the arrow with much greater velocity than that of a thrown spear.

Independent movement of the two pairs of wings is seen in Locusts and other Orthoptera and reaches its greatest development in the Dragon-flies. In such insects the flight muscles are developed in both the mesothoracic and metathoracic segments, but in the other main orders the action of the wings is synchronised, or one pair ceases to function as wings, and the muscles are developed mainly in one segment or the other. In those insects in which fore- and hind-wings are coupled together, Bees, Wasps, Moths and Butterflies, power is applied mainly to the fore-wings. The Flies have carried this subordination of the hind-wings further and dispensed with them altogether. In their place is seen a pair of little knobbed stalks, called the *halteres*, which control equilibrium in flight. They vibrate with the same frequency as the wings and are believed to function as gyroscopic organs.

The fact that the halteres are indeed modified hind-wings is convincingly shown by one of the many mutations observed in the Fruit-fly (*Drosophila*) in the course of genetical studies. In this mutation the halteres are replaced by a pair of functionless but quite recognisable hind-wings.

Beetles, by contrast, have the hind-wings developed as the sole organs of flight; the fore-wings have the form of horny sheaths called elytra under which the membranous hind-wings lie folded and protected. Here, of course, the flight muscles are confined to the metathorax.

There is no doubt that the greatest efficiency in insect flight is achieved by development of the fore-wings at the expense of the hind-wings. The large Hawk-moths probably have the most powerful flight of all insects, and control surely reaches its acme in the Flies. A Hover-fly appears to be poised motionless over a bush in a woodland glade, but it is really flying in a complex of currents and eddies of air. It probably maintains its position by visually "locking" itself to selected landmarks and making instantaneous adjustments in flight to eliminate any movement of itself relative to them. However it achieves it this is a truly remarkable performance, far more accurate and refined than that of any helicopter.

The wings of many insects possessing the click mechanism beat at very high frequencies; more than 1,000 beats per second has been recorded for one of the small biting midges called *Forcipomyia*. Wing-beats at this rate could not possibly be controlled by a separate motor nerve-impulse for each beat. It has been found that the flight muscles of such insects are of a special type called fibrillar muscle, which has the property of contracting as a direct and immediate response to being stretched. The vertical and longitudinal indirect muscles are arranged in antagonistic sets, that is to say the one set will be stretched when the other relaxes. As the immediate response of the stretched muscle is to contract, and then to relax at the finish of the wing-stoke it has actuated, repeated cycles of contraction and relaxation are set up. These cycles are entirely automatic and independent of nerve-impulses, and can operate at fantastic speed. The twisting of the wings that accompanies flight is no longer under muscular control, but is brought about by further elaboration of the articulation at their bases. Other figures for rate of wing-beats per second are: Butterflies, 8 to 12; Locusts, 18 to 20; large Moths, 50 to 70; Bees, 190; House-fly, 200; Mosquitoes, up to 600. The figures are for the complete up-and-down stroke.

The speed at which insects fly is difficult to estimate and has often been exaggerated. Some years ago a claim was made that a kind of Bot-fly could fly at 800 m.p.h. This is still occasionally quoted as a fact, but it is known to have been based on an unsound observation. The truth is that insects cannot fly very fast. Bees and Butterflies travel at from 6 to 10 m.p.h. Horse-flies follow vehicles (taking them presumably for large mammals) at speeds up to 25 to 30 m.p.h. and a maximum speed of 36 m.p.h. has been calculated for a large Australian Dragon-fly. The big Hawk-moths, such as the Convolvulus Hawk, probably have the most powerful flight muscles of any insects, and their fore- and hind-wings are coupled together, an arrangement which is believed to promote efficiency in flight. It is possible that some of these Moths may be swifter fliers even than the big Dragon-flies, but they are only active at night and observations of their flight are very difficult to make.

Soaring flight, with the wings extended and motionless, is rarely encountered among insects. Alpine Butterflies, notably the Apollo Butterfly, have been observed flying in this way in the rising air on sunlit hillsides and covering long distances without moving their wings. Winged Aphids, taking advantage of rising currents in their dispersal flights, are also known to "ride the air" with motionless extended wings.

Although the flight of insects is extremely efficient it consumes a great deal of energy. Insects such as the Blow-fly, which "burn" carbohydrate as fuel to motivate their wings, consume 27 to 35 per cent of their weight in an hour's flying. Those which store their energy in the form of fat do rather better; a Locust consumes 0·8 of its body weight in an hour. All insects which undertake long migratory flights must have recourse to the more efficient type of fuel. Butterflies and Moths (many of which are migrants) take their food in the form of carbohydrate, "honeydew" and the nectar of flowers, but convert it to fat before using it as a source of energy.

Insects often fly great distances, involving hundreds or even thousands of miles; such flights are of two types. Firstly, many kinds of very small insects get carried by upward thermal currents into the regions of the atmosphere where strong, steady winds are blowing, and so are dispersed over great distances. Insects that travel in this way are almost all day fliers, because the thermal currents are caused by the sun warming the air in contact with the ground. Their journeys may start with a deliberate upward flight, but otherwise depend entirely on the wind, and these insect voyagers are often called collectively the aerial plankton, by analogy with the small marine animals that are carried about by ocean currents. On a warm day the air from 1,000 to 5,000 feet contains vast numbers of insects among which aphids and small flies predominate, and some birds, the swallows, martins and swifts, depend entirely upon this aerial plankton for their subsistence. Insects have been caught at all heights in the air up to 16,000 feet and also over the oceans at great distances from the land.

Methods of collecting the aerial plankton for study involve the use of large nets which are allowed to blow out from the masts of ships, from kites and from points at different heights along the mooring cables of barrage balloons, the captive balloons used in the Second World War to form a barrage against raiding aircraft. For sampling at greater heights nets are towed behind aeroplanes. The study is of importance as some of the Aphids that are agricultural pests are dispersed in this way. The Black-fly or Bean Aphid (*Aphis fabae*) arrives in southern England in the early summer from Continental Europe in great numbers, carried on the prevailing south-westerly winds, and another very harmful Aphid, *Myzus persicae*, which carries the virus of potato leaf-roll, is dispersed in the same way. Winged Aphids begin their dispersal flights by a deliberate upward movement, apparently attracted by the ultra-violet light of the sky. If they then encounter an ascending air current they may set off on a long journey, but if not they descend and continue to feed on the plants in the region of their origin.

The second type of long-distance flying is that in which the insects orientate themselves and direct their flight independently of the wind. This is more akin to the true migration of birds, and Butterflies, Moths and Dragon-flies afford well known examples of it. In the Northern Hemisphere it usually consists of a northern flight, often in the form of conspicuous swarms, in the spring or early summer, and a far less conspicuous southward return of the descendants of the spring migrants in the autumn.

One of our most notable migrant species is the Painted Lady Butterfly. Accounts have been published of the hatching and departure of huge swarms of this Butterfly from localities in the northern African deserts. The earliest observation was made in 1869 in the Sudan. An explorer noticed that a great area of grass was being shaken, although there was no wind. On dismounting from his camel he found that myriads of Painted Lady pupae were hatching, and he stayed to watch the butterflies dry their wings and fly off in a swarm eastwards towards the Red Sea. A similar mass hatching was reported in 1948 from an area of sand dunes on the coast of Algeria; in this case the butterflies flew northward over the Mediterranean. Members of such swarms may reach Britain in the spring in large numbers, and in some years they press on to the north and are recorded in Finland and Iceland, 2,000 miles from their point of departure.

In their southern habitat these Butterflies breed continuously all the year round, but in the colder latitudes they are able to breed only during the summer and normally complete only one generation: our summer and autumn Painted Ladies are the offspring of migrants that arrived in the spring. This Butterfly cannot live through the British winter in any stage of its life history, and its occurrence in this country depends entirely on the yearly arrival of migrants. The same is true of two other familiar insects, the Red Admiral Butterfly and the Silver Y Moth, and of a number of less common species, including several of the larger Hawk-moths. The urge to dispersal by migratory flights in the Painted Lady is so strong that it has led to the Butterfly having a virtually world-wide distribution without any well-marked local races or subspecies.

It is usually impossible to be sure that a particular insect has migrated from the main breeding grounds of its species, as an intermediate generation may have occurred at some point on its route as the warmth of the spring season advances northward. Some years ago, however, evidence was obtained in a quite dramatic way of a 1,500-mile flight made by a small Pyralid Moth, the Rush Veneer (*Nomophila noctuella*), well known to be a migrant. In February 1960 the French Government made tests of nuclear explosives in the Sahara, and in March Dr. H. B. D. Kettlewell captured near Oxford a specimen of this moth containing a radioactive particle of a type which could be identified with the explosion. This furnished proof that the moth had actually performed the journey from northern Africa to Britain.

Evidence for a return flight of northward migrating insects has long been established for the Monarch Butterfly (*Danaus plexippus*) in North America; specimens marked in late summer in the northern regions have been recaptured later, far to the south. Evidence of this kind has not been obtained in Europe, but migratory insects, including the Red Admiral, Painted Lady and Silver Y (which flies both by night and day), have been observed flying southwards in the autumn. The most likely object of such a flight would seem to be a return to the Mediterranean region where breeding is continuous, but we know nothing of what proportion of the migrants attain this destination.

The direction of flight of these larger insects, Butterflies, Moths, Dragon-flies and (in more southern latitudes) Locusts, is not dependent on wind direction.   They usually fly at no great height and swarms have been observed going against and across the wind just as frequently as with it.

The northward migration of insects in Europe occurs on a far greater scale in some years than others, and at long intervals real "bumper" years are experienced. The most recent of these was 1947; in that year not only were many of the migrant butterflies and moths unusually abundant, but thirty-two specimens of the Migratory Locust (*Locusta migratoria*) were taken in southern England.

Every species of winged insect holds its wings in some characteristic position when at rest. This position may also be characteristic of the whole order, as in May-flies, which all rest with the wings held vertically over the back, or it may vary within the order; Butterflies and Moths hold their wings in a variety of positions (Plate 24). The earliest flying insects are believed to have held them extended on each side, like those of "set" specimens in a collection. This primitive condition is seen today in the larger Dragon-flies (Anisoptera), which are primitive insects and have probably held their wings in this way throughout their evolutionary history (Plates 5, 7, 8). Their close relatives the smaller Dragon-flies or Damsel-flies (Zygoptera) usually carry their wings as May-flies do, vertically over the back (Plate 4). This involves little adaptation of the wing articulation beyond an upward extension though ninety degrees of the movement used in flying. It is thus also a primitive condition, only one step removed from that shown by the big Dragon-flies.

Most of the more advanced flying insects close the wings so that they lie back, covering the abdomen. They may lie flat, one pair covering the other as in Bees and Flies, or side-by-side. In this case the wings usually meet in the middle line and slope down on each side, forming a roof-like cover to the body; Caddis-flies and Lacewing-flies show this condition. The wings themselves are often folded. In the Social Wasps both pairs are folded longitudinally and lie back parallel with each other when the insect is at rest. The hind-wings of Grasshoppers fold right up like a fan and lie under the narrow leathery fore-wings, and those of Beetles and Earwigs are folded under the modified fore-wings in quite an elaborate manner. Among Butterflies and Moths almost every resting position that has been mentioned is found in one group or another. The two primitive positions have been adopted secondarily; the Pug Moths (genus *Eupithecia*) and various other groups among the Geometroidea or "loopers" rest with the wings extended sideways, and most butterflies and a few Moths hold them vertically as May-flies and Damsel-flies do. The majority of Moths fold the wings back in the normal "advanced insect" manner, in which case they may overlap or meet in the middle line. In these Moths the hind-wings are folded fan-wise, and in some groups, such as the Plume Moths (Pterophoroidea), both

PLATE 15

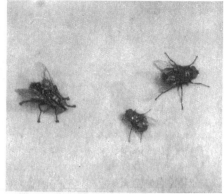

a. Shield-bug, *Troilus luridus*

b. Flesh-fly *Sarcophaga* (left), Green-bottle *Lucilia* (centre), Blow-fly, *Calliphora*

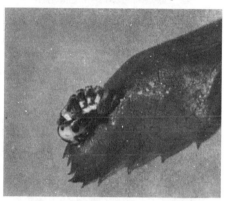

c. Seven-spot Ladybird, *Coccinella septempunctata*, and larva

d. Pupa of Seven-spot Ladybird, *Coccinella septempunctata*

e. Weevils, *Apoderus coryli* [temperature controlled]

f. Leaf-beetle, *Cryptocephalus aureolus*

(b, natural size; remainder slightly enlarged. b, etherised)

A SHIELD-BUG, SOME COMMON FLIES AND BEETLES

Photographs by S. BEAUFOY

PLATE 16

a. Larva of Two-spot Ladybird

b. Pupa and eggs of Two-spot Ladybird

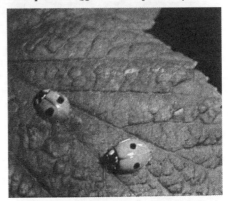

c. Two-spot, typical form mating with form *quadrimaculata;*

d. Two-spot, typical form

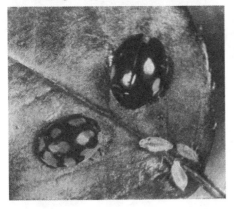

e. Two-spot, form *quadrimaculata,* and Ten-spot, *Adalia decempunctata*

f. Twenty-two-spot, *Thea vigintiduopunctata* [etherised]

(All larger than actual size)

LADYBIRDS AND THEIR METAMORPHOSIS

Photographs a, b, c, f, by S. BEAUFOY; d, by P. L. EMERY; e, by E. J. HUDSON fore- and hind-wings are folded or rolled in a way quite peculiar to themselves. There is a good reason for this diversity of wing-posture among the Lepidoptera, which will appear when we discuss the subject of wing coloration in insects.

The elytra or modified fore-wings of Beetles are very variously coloured, but will not be further discussed here as they are not wings in any functional sense. The majority of insects have the wings colourless and more or less transparent, though in Scorpion-flies, in some flies and Dragon-flies and here and there in other orders there are dark pigmented spots or bands in the wings, or they may be pigmented all over. Brightly coloured wing membranes are rare, but are found in certain Grasshoppers (*Oedipoda*) in which the hind-wings are bright blue or red. One of these, a species with blue hind-wings, is common in France and is said to have occurred in the Scilly Islands. These insects afford a good example of "flash coloration" (p. 205), the brilliant blue being concealed when they are at rest and startlingly revealed when they fly.

Only one group of insects has, in the course of its evolution, hit on a means by which wings can be marked with diverse and intricate patterns having an unlimited range of colour. This is, of course, the Lepidoptera; in the Butterflies and Moths the colour and pattern on the wings is determined in the same way as tesserae determine the features of a mosaic. The wings are covered with minute overlapping scales (Plate VIII, c), each one self-coloured but varying among themselves to an almost infinite degree. The scales may be pigmented or they may display structural coloration due to interference, effects similar to those seen when water is covered by a film of oil. The yellow and orange colours of Pierid Butterflies like the Brimstone and the Orange-tip are due to pigments called "pterines"; the brilliant metallic colours of the Blue and Hairstreak Butterflies are structural.

The versatility of this mode of wing coloration has led to its featuring in a wide variety of adaptations apart from those concerned with flight. Cryptic colours and patterns or "camouflage" are often seen on the wings of moths that sit on the bark of trees or among foliage. The bright colours of butterflies' wings serve the purpose of enabling members of the same species to recognise each other. An accurately painted paper cut-out of a Fritillary Butterfly has been used to lure down to it males of the species represented, showing that they are attracted by visual recognition of a particular pattern. Warning coloration (p. 194) is often displayed on the wings of Butterflies and Moths: the brilliant and sluggish Burnet Moths, red-spotted on a metallic blue or green ground, are both nauseous and poisonous, and gain protection from the fact that a bird which has once tried to eat a Burnet can hardly fail to recognise one when it sees it again. More than one type of colour adaptation can be developed in the same insect. With the wings spread as it feeds on a flower a Comma Butterfly is conspicuous and easily recognised by others of its species, but it is alert and wary too; when it settles down to the deep sleep of hibernation the Comma closes its wings, exposing only the dark brown mottled under-surface. Now the colour and irregular outline of the wings perfectly simu-lates a withered leaf, and the hungry, questing birds pass the insect by. Many Moths, such as the Red- and Crimson-underwings (*Catocala*) have the fore-wings cryptically coloured for protection at rest and the hind-wings brightly coloured to achieve the flash coloration effect when the insect flies.

Now it becomes clear why the Lepidoptera afford examples of so many types of resting wing posture. The great range of adaptive wing coloration that their scales enable them to achieve can only be exploited to the full by a corresponding diversity in the way in which the wings are held when the insect is not flying. The day-flying Butterflies must hold their wings in the primitive "May-fly" fashion in order to conceal their bright recognition colours when they are resting. A Pug Moth must spread its wings out to flatten itself against a piece of bark; a resting Red-underwing must keep its hind-wings concealed. The most perfect correlation of wing pattern and wing posture is seen when both fore- and hind-wings are exposed to display a coincident pattern (Fig. 18).

FIG. 18.—The Blood-vein Moth (*Calothysanis amata*) at rest on a leaf. The dark bands on the fore- and hind-wings are aligned to form a "coincident pattern", giving the effect of a continuous band from wing-tip to wing-tip.

No dissertation on insect wings can be complete without some account of the lack of them. Only the most primitive insects such as the Silver-fish and the Springtails are regarded as primarily wingless, that is without winged ancestors. The rest are believed, for various reasons, to have been descended from ancestors having the power of flight. Almost every order of insects whose members normally possess wings has at least some flightless species, and these do not have primitive characters suggesting that they represent the wingless ancestors of the rest. In two orders, the Anoplura or Lice and the Siphonaptera or Fleas, all the members are wingless, but these are orders specialised for a parasitic existence in which wings would be an embarrassment, and they can well be supposed to have lost them in the evolutionary course of becoming parasites. The larvae and pupae of Fleas suggest that they have a common ancestry with Flies.

Loss of wings in normally winged orders may also be associated with parasitism, as in the Fly known as the Sheep-ked (*Melophagus*) and other peculiar wingless Flies that live on bats, but it is most commonly found in insects that live among debris or underground. Most of the very numerous wingless beetles are of this type.

In many species of insects there are both winged and wingless forms. In Ants the males are winged and the queens, or reproductive females, have wings when they emerge from the pupa. After the marriage flight the males die and the queens descend to the ground, where they deliberately break off their wings before seeking a situation in which to found a new nest. The sterile female ants or "workers" never possess wings. Ants therefore have the best of both worlds: they secure dispersion of their species by flight, the most efficient means of all, and are at the same time adapted for their usual underground existence by lacking wings. In the parasitic Deer-fly (*Lipoptena*) both sexes are winged and fly in search of deer, among whose hair they live. As soon as they find a host these flies cast off their wings, just as queen ants do.

A more usual state of affairs is seen in insects in which the male is always winged and the female always wingless, or at any rate flightless. The female Glow-worm is wingless, but her partner is fully winged and is believed to be guided to her by the light she emits. In a number of moths the females are wingless or have tiny aborted wings. It is difficult to see what advantage they gain from this, but it is interesting to note that Moths with flightless females belong most often to species in which the adults are abroad in the cold months of the year. When they hatch the females crawl up the trunks of the trees and bushes on which they fed as larvae and await the arrival of the winged males. It is possible that if they possessed functional wings themselves they would be in danger of being blown away by storms, when torpid with cold, before they had any opportunity to lay their eggs. The males retain their wings to enable them to seek out the females. Of course they encounter the risk of being blown away, but their lives are less essential to the survival of the species than those of the females, as each male is usually capable of mating several times. This argument fails, however, to account for the wingless female of the Vapourer Moth, in which the adults are out in the summer.

The main problem these moths with wingless females must encounter is that of dispersal of the species, as freely flying males cannot achieve this alone. It seems likely that the newly-hatched caterpillars may be dispersed by the wind, especially if they have long hairs, as those of the Vapourer Moth have. In the allied Gipsy Moth, of which the female rarely if ever flies (though she is fully winged), the small larvae are known to be wind-borne.

Winged and wingless individuals often occur in the same species among the Bugs (Hemiptera). This is clearly seen in the Aphids, in which these occur at definite stages in the annual reproductive cycle in such a way that rapid growth and proliferation on plants is combined with efficient and well-timed air-borne dispersal (p. 219). In Bugs of the suborder Heteroptera macropterous (large-winged) and micropterous (small-winged and flightless) individuals of the same species often occur in a manner that seems to bear no definite relation to their life-cycle or to any other aspect of their biology, though in general small-winged forms are characteristic of cold regions and high altitudes. Sometimes a species may be normally macropterous or micropterous, the alternative form occurring only as a rarity, and one gets the impression that one form is replacing the other, which will eventually disappear. Such phenomena as this are reminders that the process of evolution is not simply a thing of the past that has led up to the present state of affairs: it is going on all the time.

PLATE 17

a. Wireworm (× 3)

b. Ground-beetle, *Carabus violaceus* (× 1¼)

c. Gall on root of young Cabbage caused by the Weevil, *Ceuthorrhynchus pleurostigma* (× ⅓)

d. Woolly Aphid, *Eriosoma lanigerum*, on apple (× ½)

INJURIOUS AND USEFUL INSECTS

Photographs b, c, d, by S. BEAUFOY; a, by E. J. HUDSON

PLATE 18

PLATE 18

79

COLEOPTERA OR BEETLES (× 1)

1	9		22	29
TIGER-BEETLE	WEEVIL	18	DEATH-WATCH	GROUND-BEETLE
Cicindela campestris	*Cionus*	SPANISH FLY	*Xestobium rufovillosum*	*Pseudophonus rufipes*
		Lytta vesicatoria		

23
LEAF-BEETLE
Cryptocephalus aureolus

2
WATER-BEETLE
Acilius sulcatus
MALE

19
THE TIMBERMAN
Acanthocinus aedilis

30
SUMMER CHAFER
Amphimallon solstitialis

10
FLEA-BEETLE
Phyllotreta nemorum

24
COLORADO BEETLE
Leptinotarsa decemlineata

11
GORSE WEEVIL
Apion ulicis

3
WATER-BEETLE
Acilius sulcatus
FEMALE

31
ROSE CHAFER
Cetonia aurata

12
POWDER-POST BEETLE
Lyctus linearis

13
LEAF-BEETLE
Lema melanopa

4
LEAF-BEETLE
Sermylassa halensis

14
WHIRLIGIG-BEETLE
Gyrinus natator

32
GARDEN CHAFER
Phyllopertha horticola

25
LEAF-BEETLE
Chrysolina polita

5
LEAF-BEETLE
Chrysomela populi

15
GLOW-WORM
Lampyris noctiluca
MALE

33
LONGICORN
Leiopus nebulosus

26
WEEVIL
Cryptorhynchidius lapathi

6
LEAF-BEETLE
Chrysolina graminis

16
DOR-BEETLE
Geotrupes stercorarius

20
LONGICORN
Rhagium bifasciatum

34
POPLAR LONGICORN
Saperda populnea

7
CLICK-BEETLE
Athous haemorrhoidalis

27
BOMBARDIER-BEETLE
Brachinus crepitans

8
MINOTAUR
Typhaeus typhoeus
MALE

17
MINOTAUR
Typhaeus typhoeus
FEMALE

21
LONGICORN
Strangalia maculata

28
LONGICORN
Tetropium gabrieli

35
LONGICORN
Saperda carcharias

THE SENSES
AND OTHER ATTRIBUTES

IT IS by means of its senses that an insect, like any other animal, becomes aware of the outside world. Insects are able to react to very much the same stimuli which impart definite impressions in man. Thus they react to light, touch or contact, smell, taste and sound. We are not, however, in a position to assert that they see, feel, smell, taste, or hear in the same way as we ourselves do. In fact it is very improbable that they do so because the organs by which they react to such stimuli are of a very different nature to those used for the same purpose in man. But on these points more will be said later.

The sense-organs of insects lie in the integument. They are for the most part microscopic in size but are often present in very large numbers, especially on the antennae. Each sense-organ is covered by a specially modified part of the cuticle that is able to transmit a particular kind of impulse. At the base of a sense-organ there is a sense-cell that is continuous with a fibre of a sensory nerve. Impulses received on the sense-organs are sent along the sensory nerves to the brain where a particular kind of sensation is experienced and acted upon. The behaviour of insects is influenced profoundly by the stimuli received *via* the sense-organs. But it is only by closely observing behaviour that we learn about the uses of their sense-organs. The two subjects are inseparable but in order to understand why insects behave as they do their sense-organs must be considered first.

The simplest kind of sense-organ is an innervated hair. Many other kinds are derived from this type by modification of the shaft of the hair in different ways. Thus, it may be shortened into a rod-like structure, or may be modified still more to form a peg-like projection, while, in other cases, all that is left of the original shaft is a mere dome-like area, or just a flattened plate lying flush with the general surface of the cuticle. In each case the nervous mechanism is of the same general kind as that associated with a simple hair, except that there may be groups of sense-cells, instead of a single element, at the base of a particular kind of sense-organ.

Innervated hairs are concerned with the most universal of senses, touch. They are abundant on the antennae, besides having a scattered distribution over the body; they are also found on the legs, mouth-parts, cerci and even on the wings. The whole insect is, therefore, more or less sensitive to touch but the sense is most highly developed on the antennae.

On referring to Text-Fig. 19 it will be seen that each sensory hair is attached at the base by a fine membrane to the wall of its socket. Any pressure on the hair would cause the hair to move in its socket

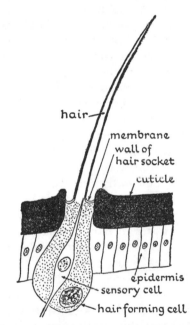

FIG. 19.—Diagram of the integument of an Insect showing a sensory hair. (Much enlarged.)

and set up an impulse that is transmitted to the central nervous system. It is by means of these tactile or touch hairs that insects explore the nature of surfaces upon which they are crawling. In this way they experience different sensations according to the degree of roughness or smoothness or other texture such surfaces may present. This can be observed by watching a Cockroach, Silver-fish, Earwig or other insect, as it moves along, with its antennae in rapid palpation, eagerly exploring the nature of the different surfaces with which it comes into contact.

Some insects when they come to rest show a marked contact-response to surrounding objects. The sense-organs concerned are the tactile hairs over the general surface of the body. An Earwig penetrates dark narrow crevices so that when it comes to rest its body is pressed against the available surfaces. Many Beetles and other insects that hide away beneath loose bark on trunks and branches of trees display this same trait. If an Earwig be placed in a glass vessel or a shallow box it will tend to press one side of its body as closely as possible against the wall of the receptacle and, in the case of a circular vessel, the insect will even curve the side of its body so as to conform with the contour of the vessel. This marked contact-reaction to surfaces provides a ready means of trapping Earwigs in the garden, where they are so often destructive. Hollow upright stems or canes, bark-covered posts, inverted plant-pots filled with tightly wedged paper or straw and placed upon the top of upright sticks, all provide the necessary conditions that enable Earwigs to satisfy their need to orient themselves in this particular way. Dark situations are normally resorted to because these insects are nocturnal in habit and, given free choice, they will select those crevices that are sufficiently narrow to enable them to make contact with their surrounding walls. Many insects only display this contact-reflex when about to change from the larva to the pupa. At such a time they seek fissures in bark or dark crevices or bury themselves beneath the soil. Previously they lived openly on foliage and showed quite different behaviour. In the case of the caterpillar of the Codling-moth (*Enarmonia pomonella*), if a dark cavity or crevice be not available it will spin its cocoon and turn to a pupa in a well-lighted cranny. Here it is evident that the contact-reflex is the overmastering one. Also, many moths rest during the day in fissures and crannies in the bark of trees where they often harmonise closely with their immediate surroundings. In these cases it seems that the determining influence, causing them to select these situations, is the contact reflex.

The body-hairs of some caterpillars not only respond to touch but also to sound-waves. In these cases sensitivity to sound is little more than a highly refined sense of touch. Caterpillars respond to sound-waves so long as their body-hairs are intact and free. Singeing, dusting with flour, spraying with water through an atomiser, smearing with vaseline, etc., tend to destroy this response. In responding to sounds caterpillars throw the front part, and sometimes the hind part also, upward or sideways; even a headless body will display this same reflex. Among caterpillars that are known to behave in this way are those of the large Cabbage White Butterfly (*Pieris brassicae*), but the responses have been more fully explored in America in regard to larvae of the Mourning Cloak Butterfly (*Nymphalis antiopa*).[1] In this insect responses were obtained from vibrations ranging from 32 to 1,024 per second. Caterpillars are also sensitive to air currents and, if these are prolonged, response to sound waves becomes interfered with. It is possible that the responses of sensory hairs on the bodies of caterpillars are not a feature of any real significance in the lives of these creatures. It is well-known that a cord of a one-stringed instrument responds to another instrument set in vibration in a particular key and that a bowl will ring in "sympathy" to a particular note!

In Grasshoppers, Crickets, Cicadas and many Moths there are elaborate structures called tympanal organs for perceiving sound. These organs may with some justice be regarded as ears. They are present in individuals of both sexes and, with the exception of Moths, their possessors also have a well-developed capacity for sound-production. This latter is a property of the males only: the strident notes made by one or other of these insects are among the familiar sounds of the countryside. "Ears," on the other hand, are present in both sexes.

Each tympanal organ consists of a ring of cuticle over which is stretched a drum-like membrane. This latter is exposed on one side to the outer air and is set into vibration when sound-waves impinge upon it. Associated, or directly connected, with the inner side of this membrane is a group of sensory structures of a particular kind which are stimulated when the drum is caused to vibrate and the resultant impulses are sent by an auditory nerve to the central nervous system.

In the Short-horned Grasshoppers the tympanal organs are placed one on each side of the base of the hind-body close to where it joins the thorax (Text-Fig. 8, p. 36). In the Long-horned Grasshoppers and Crickets a very complex tympanal organ is present on either side near the base of the tibia of each fore-leg (Text-Fig. 20, p. 84). In the House-cricket the tympanal membranes are freely exposed and easy to see but in the Mole-cricket and the Great Green Grasshopper, for example, each tympanum lies in a cavity which has a slit-like opening com-

[1] A rare immigrant in Britain, where it is known as the Camberwell Beauty.

municating with the outside air. By moving themselves and their fore-legs in appropriate directions it would seem that these insects are able to ascertain the precise location from whence sound is emitted. This is especially the case where the tympanum is placed in a cavity,

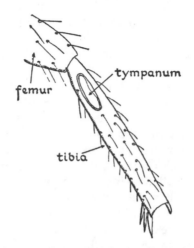

FIG. 20.—Tibia and base of femur of right fore-leg (outer side) of a Cricket. (Magnified.)

for the legs can be oriented in such a way that the slit-like openings come into a direct line with the sound-vibrations. L. J. Baier in 1930 carried out experiments with Field-crickets and Long-horned Grass-hoppers relative to the functions of their tympanal organs. Individuals of different sexes were kept apart, accustomed to life in cages, and then placed in different rooms sufficiently distant to be out of range of hearing the sounds produced by their mates. A microphone, placed in the cage containing the males, was connected by telephone with a receiver in the cage containing females of the same species. The females responded to the stridulation of the males by orienting them-selves when they perceived the sound: this they did by approaching the receiver with actively moving antennae and by performing move-ments indicative of search for the summoning partners. When the current was temporarily interrupted, the females might move away from the receiver, and in any case no longer betrayed their former signs of attention. On restoring the circuit the females at once approached the receiver again. The cages, it may be added, were insulated so as to guard against solid vibrational stimulation conveyed through the ground. Females whose tympana were excised showed none of these responses, and a local anaesthetic (ethyl chloride) applied to these organs had the same effect but only so long as its influence lasted, normal responses being ultimately restored. The use of gramophone records of the males' stridulatory notes had an effect similar to that exercised by the living insects themselves.

Close to the junction of the hind-body with the thorax there is, in many Moths, a rather conspicuous opening on either side. It leads into a cavity whose inner wall is formed by a delicate glistening membrane of tympanum. Closely associated with this membrane is a group of sensory structures that form the endings of the fibres of a special tympanal nerve. The openings of these tympanal organs are easily seen in many Moths if the scales be first removed with a fine brush from the region concerned. The Large Yellow Underwing (*Triphaena pronuba*) or the Brimstone (*Opisthograptis luteolata*) are suitable Moths for this purpose and easily obtained. It is curious that tympanal organs are wanting in Butterflies, Hawk-moths, Clothes-moths and their allies, and others. It is easy to show that those that possess them respond to high-pitched sounds such as the squeak caused by turning the glass stopper in the neck of a bottle, or the supersonic vibrations from a Galton whistle. Resting moths respond by active vibration of the wings, by running, or by flying. The function of these complex organs remained a puzzle until it was discovered that the insect-eating bats navigate in the dark, avoid obstacles and locate their prey by echo sounding. The rapidly repeated supersonic cries of the bat are at just the frequency to which the moths' hearing organs are particularly sensitive. Artificially produced supersonic vibrations of the right frequency beamed onto a flying moth have a dramatic effect. The moth instantly changes the direction of its flight, dashes wildly about and may even dive into the cover of low vegetation. The complex hearing organs of these night-flying moths enable them to detect the presence of a hunting bat at sufficient distance for them to take avoiding action.

No insect has a true voice. One of the commonest ways of making sounds is by stridulation, that is by the rubbing of one hard part of the body against another. This is the prevailing method among the Orthoptera: a short account of it is given on p. 36. The sounds made by both Grasshoppers and Crickets are undoubtedly an important means of bringing together the members of the two sexes in a species. Temperature has considerable influence on the rate of chirping in Crickets for instance, which becomes accelerated as the temperature rises. It has been said that if the number of chirps made by a Cricket in fourteen seconds be counted and 40 be added to it the answer, in nine cases out of ten, will be the correct temperature within a couple of degrees (Fahrenheit).[1] This rough computation seems to be borne out by a formula given by an American, A. E. Dolbear, who claims that the temperature $= 50 + \dfrac{N - 40}{4}$, where N is the rate of chirping per minute. Below 50° F. a Field-cricket is said to chirp 40 times per minute and above it there is an increase of 4 to 4·7 chirps for each degree rise of temperature.

The notes emitted by different species are very distinctive and some are definitely more pleasing than others to human ears. Thus W. H. Hudson in his attractive book *Hampshire Days* remarks on " the intrinsic beauty of the sounds " of the Field-cricket and contrasts them with the coarser and " more creaky " notes of the House-cricket. Gilbert White in the *Natural History of Selborne* (1789) stated that a Field-cricket, " when confined in a paper cage and set in the sun, and supplied with plants moistened with water, will feed and thrive, and become so merry and loud as to be irksome in the same room where a person is sitting." Much has been written about the penetrating " song " of the Great Green Grasshopper. W. H. Hudson admired its music and thought that the males express rivalry in their singing, which he regarded as a sort of contest rather than a means of attracting the female. In the south of Europe, where it is known to French children as " la cigale," its notes are very familiar in the trees of gardens and boulevards. R. Laddimann in 1879 wrote about this insect that " The males commence their stridulations just before sundown, which extend far into the night, and the performance of several of these insects in close proximity is almost deafening. . . . The male takes up his position on the topmost twig in the hedgerow—often on an ear of corn—which position he will maintain during the whole of the evening, and will there ' rasp ' away unceasingly for hours, if not disturbed ; he will often be found performing on or near the same twig the next evening. Three years ago I turned out a male of this insect in my garden, who perched himself on the topmost branch of a tall larch tree, where he

[1] *The Weather.* By G. Kimble and R. Bush. Penguin Books, 1943.

carried on his harsh evensong for more than a week, when I missed him and never heard him afterwards. These insects seem to be gifted with a species of ventriloquism, for it is often extremely difficult to mark the spot whence the ' singing ' appears to proceed."

The notes of the Mole-cricket are very different. Gilbert White remarked that " just at the close of day they begin to solace themselves with a low, dull, jarring note, continued for a long time without interruption, and not unlike the chattering of the fern-owl, or goat-sucker."

The musical powers of stridulating insects are appreciated by certain peoples, especially the Japanese, whose country is rich in numbers of kinds of these creatures. Lafcadio Hearn,[1] in particular, stresses this fact and mentions that, long before it became the fashion to keep " singing-insects " in cages, their music had been celebrated by poets as one of the aesthetic pleasures of the autumn. Later, when the breeding and sale of these creatures became a lucrative industry, the custom of going out into the country to hear them gradually declined. Visitors to Japan, he exhorts, should go to at least one temple-festival—*en-nichi*—preferably at night. Among the " dazzling lanes of booths," he writes, " full of toys indescribable—dainty puerilities, fragile astonishments, laughter-making oddities—ultimately the visitor will pause to look at a booth illuminated like a magic-lantern, and stocked with tiny wooden cages out of which an incomparable shrilling proceeds. The booth is the booth of a vendor of singing-insects ; and the storm of noise is made by the insects." The insects in all cases are various kinds of Grasshoppers and Crickets—Cicadas are never caged, Lafcadio Hearn tells us ; they are relegated to the vulgar place of chatterers.

One need not go as far as Japan in order to experience caged musical insects. In parts of Italy Field-crickets are kept for the sake of their song. The same happens in Portugal where, according to A. E. Eaton, Crickets of this species are sold in miniature cages in Lisbon and Oporto because the inhabitants like to have them in their rooms and make pets of them.

It is not generally known that many kinds of Beetles also stridulate. In these insects usually one part of each stridulating organ is a file-like area and the other is a scraper which is rasped across it. Thus, the Musk-beetle often stridulates audibly, making a squeaking note, when

[1] *Exotics and Retrospectives*, 1898, pp. 38–80.

held between the fingers. This it does by rubbing the hind edge of the prothorax against an area on the mesothorax, just in front of the scutellum. The Death-watch (p. 118), on the other hand, makes its characteristic tapping sound by striking the underneath of the front of its head against the surface upon which it is resting.

A surprising thing is that the subterranean larvae of Dung- or Dor-beetles (*Geotrupes*) also stridulate. This they do by rubbing the much reduced hind-leg, which bears a kind of strigil composed of minute points, against a finely ridged area on the base of the 2nd leg. The larva of the Stag-beetle, which lives deep in decaying wood, does the same. It has been suggested that, when during tunnelling through the same stump the burrows of two larvae approach one another, stridulation serves to warn them of their close proximity so that they can change their direction. However no one has found any organs for sound-perception in these grubs, which makes the reason for their stridulation still more enigmatical. Perhaps some of the sensory hairs on their bodies react to sounds very much as in caterpillars !

Cockchafers, Dor- or Dung-beetles and Bumble-bees make a familiar humming or buzzing sound when flying, owing to the vibration of the wings. A high-pitched singing note is emitted by various Flies, particularly Hover-flies, and can be heard when these insects are on the wing and while they are nesting. The cause of this sound has led to speculation but no one seems to have gone into the matter very thoroughly. Some authorities think that it is caused by the vibration of a fine membrane situated just internal to the thoracic breathing pores. Another authority says that, in the Blow-fly, blocking up these openings with gum or wax causes the sound to cease. Removal of the wings, it may be added, does not influence the sound. It is a nice little problem for some enthusiast to try to elucidate.

Insects have a highly developed chemical sensitivity that seems to correspond in a general way to our own senses of smell and taste. It has long been known that insects are highly sensitive to volatile substances and that the antennae are the chief seat of odour perception. Elongated freely movable appendages like antennae that project outwards from the head seem to be specially well suited to carry the organs of smell. They give an insect better means of exploring the air in its vicinity than if odoriferous particles had to be drawn into a nasal chamber as in man and other terrestrial vertebrates.

As the antennae are also highly sensitive tactile organs, they may provide the insect with means of perception different from any available to man. Such perception may be a combination of smell with shape, just as our eyes plus our fingers give us a solid picture which is a combination of sight with shape.

The sense of smell is chiefly located in the antennae.* If these appendages be coated with vaseline, paraffin wax or other impervious material, or be amputated, an insect will become largely or wholly insensitive to odours. In some insects, however, the labial and maxillary palpi are also capable of perceiving odours but they have a lesser range of sensitivity than the antennae. Strong or irritant odours, especially those which do not enter into the normal experience of an insect, may produce merely irritant sensations capable of affecting almost any kind of sense-organ—after the analogy of pungent vapours which may affect the eyes, nose and throat in human beings. This general sensitivity seems to have given rise to the wrong belief that the organs of smell are widely distributed over the insect body.

If the antennae of a Hive-bee be examined under a microscope the last eight segments will be seen to bear large numbers of minute plate-like sense-organs that are wanting from the remaining segments. K. von Frisch noticed this about 25 years ago, and he also found that if these eight segments be removed from both antennae a Bee becomes insensitive to odours. He pointed out that Bees trained to respond to a particular colour will still seek that colour, and no other, after amputation of their antennae. He concluded, therefore, that the loss of response to scents is not due to the shock of amputation but to depriving them of their organs of smell.

Smell plays a vital part in the lives of many insects. Let us take the mating process as an example because it is by means of smell that the male detects the presence of the female. The males of some Moths enjoy the very remarkable faculty (known as " assembling ") of discovering their mates from considerable distances away, possibly up to three miles. This habit is characteristic of the Emperor Moths and their allies, the Eggar* and Vapourer Moths, of certain Hawk-moths, the Peppered Moth and others. In general they possess branched or "feathered " antennae (Pl. VIII, p. 63, Fig. f), and this increase of antennal surface allows for the accommodation of a much larger number of sensory organs than is borne on the simpler and more thread-like antennae of the corresponding females. The latter bear scent-producing organs near the tip of the hind body and the odour which they diffuse is the stimulus that lures the males from a distance. Sometimes as many as 40 or 50 eager males may cluster around a single female. It is noteworthy that only unmated females exercise this attraction. Even an empty box recently inhabited by one of these virgins will prove as attractive as the insect herself. All the evidence points to the odour being carried over distances by air-currents. If the males are elsewhere than in the current of air blowing directly over the females, few or none respond to the attraction. If a female be confined in a box, the covering must be of muslin or gauze and not of wood or other impervious material, otherwise the odour becomes imprisoned instead of diffusing into the air. If the antennae be coated with glue, shellac or paste the male is rendered incapable of finding the female. Blinding by coating their eyes with impervious material does not affect the reactions of the males.

The distances over which the males are attracted are probably often exaggerated. In many cases it is not known how far the males travel before they pick up the scent. Thus a marked male may be liberated 3 miles distant from a female but he may perform erratic flights until he happens to encounter an odour trail, perhaps only 500 yards away. Where, however, as P. and N. L. Rau have recorded, Moths have been liberated a mile distant and have reached their mates in 10 to 12 minutes there seems little doubt that they have been directly attracted from that distance. Finally, it needs to be stressed that each species of Moth has a rhythmic periodicity in its time of flight and that it is only at a definite period in each 24 hours that they are on the wing and mating occurs. This habit needs to be borne in mind by anyone who plans to carry out tests regarding the "assembling" capacity among British Moths. Properly planned experiments, it may be added, are much needed. It is, indeed, remarkable, considering the numbers of collectors and others who are interested in these insects, that so little is known regarding their mating behaviour.

The sense of smell also plays a predominant part in the discovery of their food by many insects. Females when egg-laying are largely guided by this sense to the appropriate plants. Many Flies and Beetles lay their eggs in dung or carrion and discover such substances by their sense of smell. Ichneumon-flies are known to find their respective hosts by this same sense. The Chalcid-wasp (*Trichogramma*), which is an egg-parasite (see p. 149), can even detect the odour imparted to eggs when another female has walked over them and consequently avoids them.

The gregarious caterpillars of the Large Cabbage White Butterfly emit a specific odour of their own and keep together in groups by following trails of this odour.

The transition from smell to taste is a gradual one and it is very probable that, in many cases, insects do not experience smell and taste as separate and distinct sensations. The sense-organs present on the underside of the labrum are apparently only adapted to receive chemical stimuli by actual contact. It may, therefore, be inferred that they function as taste-organs. Various other sense-organs occur on the mouth-parts but we do not know to what extent they perceive stimuli by actual contact (taste) or at a distance (smell) or whether they are sensitive in a general way to both kinds of stimuli. There is consequently much to be said for using the words taste and smell in regard to insects with reservation. Since these sensations result from chemical stimuli many biologists no longer refer to organs of smell and taste and use instead the general term of *chemoreceptors*.

Various insects, notably Blow-flies (*Calliphora*) and their allies and certain Butterflies, betray a remarkable sensitivity to even very dilute chemical stimuli by means of the tarsi. The Red Admiral (*Vanessa atalanta*) and the Camberwell Beauty (*Nymphalis antiopa*) were among the species used for experimentation. Experiments were carried out with starved individuals and the response was judged by the coiling and uncoiling of the insects' proboscides. The maximum duration of each individual trial was one minute and if no visible uncoiling of the proboscis took place during that interval " no response " was recorded. During the experiments the insects were held by the wings in a kind of clamp so that their tarsi were in contact with a pad that was moistened with the particular solution to be tested. Red Admiral Butterflies gave 100 per cent response to apple-juice when their feet were in contact with the moistened pad but when their feet were prevented from making contact, by means of an intervening screen, the responses were only 29 per cent. This same species shows an extraordinarily high tarsal sensitivity since its members are able to discriminate between distilled water and solutions of sucrose as low as $M/12,800$. This means that their feet are more than 200 times as sensitive to sugar as the human tongue. More recently it has been claimed that Blow-flies are able to distinguish between chemically pure saccharose solution and distilled water even when the tarsi are 3 mm. distant from these liquids. Here it would seem that we have an excellent instance of response by organs that are best termed chemo-receptors because they appear to be concerned with both " smell " and " taste " in the anthropomorphic sense with which those words are charged.

As has been previously mentioned the eyes of insects are of two quite different kinds, viz. the compound or faceted eyes and the ocelli or simple eyes.   Neither kind has any means of focusing and both are constructed on a plan totally unlike our own eyes.   Each compound eye is made up of a number of minute light-concentrating lenses or facets.   Beneath each facet is a visual unit.   Each visual unit consists of an elongated body called a cone which, together with the overlying facet, transmits the light to an elaborate system of rods, retinal cells and pigment cells and so to the nerve-centres in the brain. Space will not allow of a full description of the complicated structure of the compound eye.   It will suffice to add that because of their convex grouping each facet looks out in a slightly different direction from the others : thus, collectively, the visual units form a kind of mosaic picture of the whole field of vision.   This picture is not built up of as many separate complete images as there are facets to the eyes as was once popularly believed. It is, in fact, made up of a great number of separate partial images, each formed of the tiny part of the field of vision transmitted by the corresponding facet.   In other words a mosaic picture results owing to the combination of a large number of fractional images ; and these latter collectively make up a general image on the same principle that a half-tone picture in a newspaper, for example, is made up of a vast number of light and dark dots of varying intensity. Proof that images are formed in this way was first obtained by S. Exner in 1891. He used the eye of a Glow-worm for this purpose and, after removing the retinal and other elements, was able by means of an ingenious arrangement under the microscope to look through the facets and cones.   In this way he was able to see the kind of image that the insect itself would perceive.   What he saw and photographed was a simple, unmistakable, but rather indistinct erect image (see Pl. VIII).

Notwithstanding its elaborate structure the compound eye is not so efficient as the vertebrate eye. Since it has no focusing mechanism its capability for image-formation can only be effective in producing a clear impression within a very limited focal distance. The number and size of the visual units involved determines the sharpness of the picture because a large number of small visual units (represented by the number of eye facets) will produce a more detailed impression than if the same visual area be occupied by a smaller number of larger visual units. To return to the analogy of a half-tone illustration, the finer and more numerous the dots the sharper will be the picture. If each dot be supposed to represent the fraction of the image transmitted by a single visual unit then the more numerous the latter become the sharper will be the whole image that the insect sees.

The number of facets in a compound eye varies enormously among different kinds of insects. Thus, in the House-fly there are 4,000 facets to each eye : in the Water-beetle (*Dytiscus*) there are 9,000, and in the Glow-worm 2,500 in the male and only 300 in the wingless female. Among Ants the workers, that mostly lead subterranean lives, have the smallest number of facets, and the males, which pursue the females during their aerial flights, have the largest number. Thus, in *Formica pratensis* the worker has 600, the female 830 and the male 1,200 facets to each compound eye. In another British Ant, viz. *Solenopsis fugax*, the corresponding numbers are 6 to 9, 200 and 400 respectively. Among Dragon-flies the number ranges from about 10,000 to near 30,000 and in Butterflies from about 2,000 to 17,000.

Near objects are seen tolerably distinctly by insects but the picture rapidly becomes blurred as the distance increases. Their eyes on the other hand are specially adapted for perceiving movement. The movement of even a small object in the field of vision would be immediately registered on the mosaic picture received on the brain, which would become suddenly altered in consequence, and the insect would respond accordingly. It is often possible to approach an insect so gradually that the change of position is unnoticed by the creature. An object as large as a human being affects a large number of visual units equally and simultaneously and, if it is moving very slowly, the change in position only causes slight changes in the image as a whole. A sudden movement of any part of the body causes the insect's immediate departure owing to the fact that such a movement affects abruptly a number of visual units in succession.

The size of the facets (and consequently of the visual units) is not always uniform over the whole eye. In Horse-flies (*Tabanus*), for example, the facets are often larger in the males over the front and upper parts of the eye than elsewhere. In the males of the St. Mark's Fly (*Bibio marci*) and the Whirligig Beetles (*Gyrinus*) the two areas of differently sized facets are very distinctly separated. In the May-fly

Chloëon the two parts of the eye are likewise distinctly separated, the anterior division being raised above the other. The upper or anterior parts of these divided eyes are composed of larger facets than the lower parts and probably come into use to perceive variations in light-intensity, moving enemies, etc., when there is no occasion to perceive definite form. The lower area is clearly adapted for more acute vision and to receive the more detailed impressions produced by the immediate surroundings over which the insect may be walking or flying.

The eyes of many insects are able to adapt themselves for day or night vision by means of a device which regulates the amount of light entering each visual unit. Its effect is very much the same as the expansion and contraction of the pupil in the mammalian eye. Adjustment in the insect eye is effected by changes in the distribution of the black pigment which acts like a dark sleeve surrounding each visual unit. The pigment becomes diffused or localised in accordance with the amount of light available. Many night-flying Moths have eyes that shine in the dark like minute glistening globes of ruby or emerald. In such cases the pigment cells surrounding the visual units contain a special colouring substance. Between these cells there are longitudinal bundles of fine air-tubes that reflect back the light entering the eye, thus causing the pigment to glisten in the way just mentioned by reflecting whatever light there may be available. The same effect is produced in a different way when the eyes of night-roaming animals reflect the glow from the head-lights of a motor vehicle.

There seems to be no doubt that insects perceive differences in differently coloured but otherwise similar objects, but this perception does not extend over the whole range of the spectrum visible to man. They are, on the other hand, particularly sensitive to the shorter wave-lengths including the ultra-violet rays, beyond human visible range. The Hive-bee can be trained or conditioned to associate certain colours with food. By using a number of pieces of paper of diverse colour, but of similar shape and size and arranging them in chequer-board fashion, K. von Frisch carried out some interesting experiments with this insect. A watch-glass containing an inodorous sugar solution was placed over one of the colours while empty watch-glasses were placed on the other squares. After repeating this a number of times (*until the Bees had learned to go to this particular square*) von Frisch then omitted the food-solution ; but the bees still went straight to that colour over which he had previously placed the filled watch-glass. By means

PLATE 19

a. Asparagus-beetles and larvae

b. Cardinal-beetle, *Pyrochroa serraticornis*

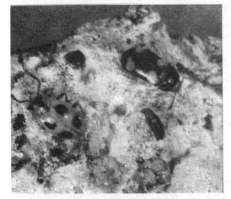

c. Fungus feeders: see p. 125

d. Green Weevils, *Phyllobius pomaceus*

e. Green Weevils, *Phyllobius argentatus*

f. Ant-beetle, *Thanasimus formicarius*

(All are somewhat enlarged. a, c, etherised; d to f, temperature controlled)

COLEOPTERA OR BEETLES

Photographs by S. BEAUFOY

PLATE 20

PLATE 20

95

BEES, WASPS AND THEIR ALLIES

1
ICHNEUMON-FLY
Ichneumon suspiciosus
MALE

12
GREAT WOOD-WASP
Urocerus gigas
FEMALE

18
SAND WASP
Ammophila sabulosa

2
SOLITARY WASP
Cerceris arenaria

19
HIVE BEE
Apis mellifera
DRONE

3
SPIDER-HUNTER WASP
Anoplius nigerrimus

20
HIVE BEE
Apis mellifera
WORKER

4
SPIDER-HUNTER WASP
Anoplius fuscus

13
ICHNEUMON-FLY
Rhyssa persuasoria
FEMALE

21
HIVE BEE
Apis mellifera
QUEEN

5
SOLITARY TRUE WASP
Ancistrocerus parietinus

22
SOLITARY BEE
Andrena fulva
FEMALE

6
SOLITARY TRUE WASP
Eumenes coarctata

23
SOLITARY BEE
Andrena fulva
MALE

7
SOLITARY WASP
Clytochrysus cavifrons

10
SOLITARY BEE
Anthophora acervorum
MALE

16
SOLITARY BEE
Andrena albicans

24
SOLITARY BEE
Andrena cineraria

8
SOLITARY BEE
Osmia rufa
MALE

14
CARDER BEE
Anthidium manicatum
MALE

11
SOLITARY BEE
Anthophora retusa
FEMALE

17
COMMON WASP
Vespula vulgaris
MALE

9
SOLITARY BEE
Osmia rufa
FEMALE

15
COMMON WASP
Vespula germanica
QUEEN

25
LEAF-CUTTING BEE
Megachile centuncularis
FEMALE

of these and other experiments von Frisch showed that bees are unable to distinguish between red, black and dark grey : they are, in fact, red-blind. He also found that they fail to discriminate between yellow-orange or yellow-green or between blue and violet, their colour sense being much less developed than in man. The possibility that bees have no real colour-sense and were distinguishing colours by their relative brightness and not by differences of quality was not over-looked by von Frisch. He exposed the colour to which bees had been trained on a chequer-board made of a complete range of shades of grey. They were able in all cases to separate blue or yellow from the greys but could not be trained so that they came to an individual shade of grey. It was in this way that doubts on the subject were removed. Another possibility also presented itself : namely that the Bees were distinguishing the different coloured papers because these were reflecting different amounts of ultra-violet rays. Ever since Lubbock showed, many years ago, that Ants are very sensitive to ultra-violet rays, various other insects have been found to react similarly. In order to answer criticism of this sort von Frisch covered the chequer-board of coloured papers with a sheet of glass and still found that the Bees reacted in a similar manner. This innovation is not conclusive for the reason that a certain amount of ultra-violet is often transmitted by ordinary glass. Later investigators by using other methods have, however, substantiated the conclusions of von Frisch. The available evidence, therefore, points to the conclusion that the Hive-bee is able to distinguish differences in colour within the limits indicated.

The sensitiveness of many insects to ultra-violet is very remarkable. Moths, for example, will flock to a glass screen transmitting ultra-violet rays though to man it appears opaque to all light. Bees are able to distinguish between two very similar white surfaces when one reflects

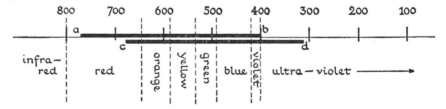

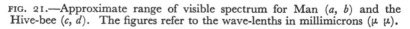

FIG. 21.—Approximate range of visible spectrum for Man (*a*, *b*) and the Hive-bee (*c*, *d*). The figures refer to the wave-lenths in millimicrons (μ μ).

ultra-violet and the other does not. Although Bees are normally red-blind they can distinguish some red flowers from others if such flowers reflect ultra-violet rays. In the accompanying diagram (Text-Fig. 21) the approximate limits of the visible spectrum for man and the bee are shown. Most insects, it may be added, are insensitive to red except in its paler shades near to the orange band of the spectrum, but can appreciate rays far into the ultra-violet end (to 257 $\mu\mu$).

Ocelli or simple eyes occur on the upper side of the head in nymphs and adult insects. Their functions are very enigmatical, especially for the reason that while they are found in many insects they are absent in numerous others. They are hardly ever present in Beetles, for instance, while in Flies they occur in many families and not in others. Among Moths they are much hidden by scales and in bees by the hairs. Some authorities consider that they are for seeing very near objects, others think that they serve to detect small changes in the light-intensity. It is significant that if the compound eyes be coated with an opaque varnish and *not* the ocelli, Bees and Flies behave as though they were blind. On the other hand, if the ocelli only be blackened these same insects respond more tardily to light received through the compound eyes. Some modern authorities believe, in consequence, that the ocelli are stimulatory organs that serve to maintain general visual sensitivity.

The lateral ocelli of larvae are provisional visual organs that function in the absence of compound eyes. While they serve much the same uses as the latter their visual capacity is much inferior. Each ocellus, it may be added, has a single biconvex lens overlying a small number of visual units.

The organs which enable insects to exercise a general sense of balance or orientation are unknown. Peculiar microscopic structures called chordotonal organs occur in symmetrical pairs or groups in different parts of the body. In an American species of Grasshopper at least 76 pairs of these organs have been detected by E. H. Slifer and there is no reason to believe that our English kinds are very different in this respect. It seems very possible that these organs detect strains or stresses caused by muscular action and thereby lead to their being redressed so as to be equally adjusted on the two sides of the body. Possibly it is by means of such sense-organs that most insects are able, when in flight, to maintain themselves on " an even keel."

The halteres of Flies (see p. 62) are often termed balancers. Many of these insects show complete loss of equilibrium in the air after removal of the halteres. Hence it would appear that these organs exercise a kind of balancing function. Readers interested in problems of physics will appreciate the fact that when a Fly is in normal flight the halteres are thrown into vibration in the vertical plane. Equal and symmetrical impulses are conveyed to sense-organs at the bases of the halteres and no shearing strains are set up. It is believed that the haltere with its end-knob behaves as an alternating gyroscope. If from any cause the insect, and consequently its halteres, deviates from the plane of vibration of the latter shearing forces will be set up. These forces act as messages that are perceived by the sense-organs and thereby enable the insect to restore its balance.

The foregoing remarks on the senses of insects will serve as a pre-amble to understanding the simpler ways in which they behave. It is noteworthy that while many of their actions are automatic and inborn, some are modifiable or plastic, in the sense that they can be altered in accordance with circumstances.

A striking example of automatic behaviour is instanced in the case of a male Moth that is lured from a distance by a virgin female. As previously noted, he smells his way until he meets the partner emitting the guiding scent. His behaviour is so absurdly automatic and different from our own emotional manifestations that it is difficult for us to conceive. The Moth has no idea of his partner as an individual ; he merely possesses the mating instinct. This reaction is released by the stimulus of the scent emitted by the female. The empty box in which she was imprisoned will serve equally well. Even the excised scent-glands from the apex of her hind-body will release the full instinctive urge. The male will attempt to mate with them, and not with the female herself, even when she is nearby in the same cage.

As an example of plastic behaviour the visits of Hive-bees to Buck-wheat may be quoted. According to the apiarist H. von Buttel-Reepen, Bees are very active among this crop from early morning up to about 10 a.m. Much of the rest of the day they are resting but restart their activities at the same time each following day. The Buckwheat, it may be mentioned, only secretes nectar during the earlier part of the morning and the bees very soon learn this fact and avoid embarking on useless midday visits.* Notwithstanding the field being in full flower and giving off a pervading perfume this author says that he noticed very few Bees in the field once the secretion of nectar lapsed. In this

Plate IX

a Burying-beetle, *Necrophorus humator* with wings extended

b Silver Water-beetle, *Hydrophilus piceus*

c Stag-beetle, *Lucanus cervus*, male

d Stag-beetle, *Lucanus cervus*, female

COLEOPTERA OR BEETLES I (× 1)

BEETLE LARVAE

Plate X

a Larva of Ground-beetle, *Pterostichus* (× 2½) [subjected to low temperature]

S. BEAUFOY

b Larva of Devil's Coach Horse, *Staphylinus olens* (× 2½) [subjected to low temperature]

S. BEAUFOY

c Devil's Coach Horse, *Staphylinus olens* (× 2½) [subjected to low temperature]

S. BEAUFOY

d Larva of Cardinal-beetle, *Pyrochroa* (× 3)

S. BEAUFOY

behaviour both adaptability to meet circumstances and a capacity for memory are involved.

Another example is afforded by the behaviour of Cockroaches (*Periplaneta*) in regard to light. Normally they avoid the light and seek dark places, only coming out of hiding at night. By devising a container with light and dark ends, and giving the insects slight electric shocks each time they settle at the dark end, they can be taught to remain in the light region. Individuals vary very much in the length of time they can retain what they learn from this association of sensory experience, and also as regards the number of shocks necessary before they acquire this change of behaviour. Different individuals required from 18 to 118 shocks before they behaved in the way indicated, and memory of the experience lasted from about 5 minutes to one hour.

Turning now to more complex kinds of behaviour, the route-finding instincts of Ants and Bees will serve our purpose admirably. The methods used by these insects involve the co-ordination of multiple impressions, including those derived through a contact-odour sense, by visual recognition of landmarks, and by light-compass orientation. A contact-odour sense is believed to be involved when Ants, for example, follow trails laid down by themselves and other members of their colony. They appear constantly to be exploring, by means of their antennae, the sides and surfaces of a given track. In this way they appear to receive both tactile and olfactory stimuli, which probably merge into a common sensation. This the Swiss master of myrmecology, A. Forel, called the contact-odour sense. He further suggested that Ants also possess a sense of odour-shape so that smells along their tracks may have triangular, circular, pointed or other pattern of distribution which may be further combined with roughness or smoothness, according to the nature of the surfaces from which they emanate.

Among Ants of the genus *Formica* the contact-odour sense plays very little part in connection with their route-finding instinct. They rely much more upon visual impressions. If their eyes be obscured by an opaque varnish they are no longer able to find their way. The very opposite prevails in another Ant (*Lasius fuliginosus*), which with varnished eyes finds its way as it did before. Bees have remarkable powers of finding their way. They learn to do this by taking, at first, very short exploration flights so as to learn the lie of the land in the immediate vicinity of the hive or nest. The flights become longer and longer until a radius of perhaps two or more miles is learned. If a Bee be taken beyond the radius of familiar territory it will either make a tardy return or become lost altogether. Colours aid Bees in finding their way and something can be done to help them by making use of discoveries in their colour-vision already referred to. If you put a yellow hive next to one painted blue it will aid their recognising their own home, but if a red hive be next to a dark grey one no help at all is given because these two colours look alike to them. Von Frisch mentions how the monks of the monastery of St. Ottilien in Bavaria conducted a large apiary along modern scientific lines. They painted their hives in accordance with recent discoveries and whereas in two previous years 16 out of 21 young queens apparently lost their way and failed to return, in the next five years after their hives had been suitably painted, out of 42 queens only 3 failed to return.

Ants, Bees and many other insects have the power of guiding themselves to and from their nest by the direction of the sun. This behaviour has been followed more closely in Ants than among Bees. If an Ant be taken up when on its way to its nest, and then put down again in another place, it starts off in the original direction but along a path parallel to the old one, whether it leads to the nest or not. Ants keep in a straight line by moving at a definite angle to the sun's rays. If, for instance, they are held captive for an hour or so when on one of their excursions, and then liberated, they will be seen to follow a route that makes an angle with the original route equal to the angle that the sun has moved through in the meantime. This kind of behaviour is termed " light-compass " orientation.*

It has only been possible, in the space available, to deal very inadequately with the subject of insect behaviour. In his book *Mechanistic Biology and Animal Behaviour*, T. Savory wrote—" If it is difficult for a practised novelist to describe life through the eyes of a railway porter or a house-parlourmaid, how much harder is it for the biologist to understand the activities of a snail or a starfish." This remark of course is equally applicable to the activities of insects, which are much more complex than those of either of the two kinds of animals just quoted. The experimentalist who isolates an animal in a laboratory is too prone to interpret its behaviour exclusively on the basis of reflexes and instincts. The naturalist who only observes the same creature in its native surroundings is liable to credit it with higher psychological implications than are warranted. While the behaviour of insects predominates in complex instinctive acts these do not provide the whole key to the subject. The ability of insects to adapt themselves to new circumstances, without the guidance of hereditary experience of similar adjustments, has often been designated "intelligence." Plastic behaviour, however, is a preferable expression. It is possible that in it is betrayed the first manifestation of a rudimentary intelligence. The relatively small size of insects, however, has severely limited their brain-size and consequently they have only a small number of brain-cells. This latter feature has made it impossible for them to develop the numerous alternative brain-pathways and tracts that are apparently needed for the development of the higher mental processes.

CHAPTER 5

CONCERNING
FEEDING HABITS

ALMOST every kind of substance of plant or animal origin serves to nourish some insect or other. It would be tiresome to enumerate all the different things insects use as food. It will suffice to say that they range from fluids such as blood and plant-sap to the heartwood of trees, bones and other seemingly indigestible substances. Even dried drugs, hair, feathers, fungi and decaying materials of almost every sort are resorted to. There are in addition numerous insects, or their larvae, that must have animal food in order to live ; most of them are hunters that seek out living prey and utilise them in their own particular ways.

It is, therefore, not surprising that with so diversified a menu the food-getting mechanisms of insects display an extraordinary range of devices. The largest number of insects have ordinary mouth-parts of the biting or chewing kind as shown in Text-Fig. 2, p. 9. Others require a siphoning apparatus in order to feed, many have devices for lapping up their food, and a large number have piercing instruments with which they gain access to their food and a special sucking apparatus for its extraction.

There is no reason to suppose that the food-requirements of insects are any simpler than those of vertebrates. We know that they all need water, salts and organic substances. There is rapidly growing evidence that accessory substances or vitamins are also necessary.

Food is required for two main purposes, i.e. (1) for growth and reproduction and (2) for energy-production. Cockroaches, for example, can maintain themselves for a long period on a carbohydrate diet, but in order to grow and reproduce they must have organic nitrogen in some form or other.

In a general way insects may be grouped into four categories as regards feeding habits. Firstly, those that are eaters of almost anything that has food value at all : these are the *omnivores*. Secondly, the eaters of living vegetable matter—the *vegetarians*. Thirdly, the devourers of animal substances—the *carnivores*. Fourthly, those that eat dead or decaying animal or plant materials—the *scavengers*. Let us take them separately.

OMNIVORES

True omnivores are not very widely represented in the insect world. Good examples are to be found in the Common Cockroach (*Blatta orientalis*) and others of its kind (Pl. 1, p. 2). These creatures are truly catholic in their tastes. Very few substances, ranging from new bread to old boots, seem to come amiss to them. This is one of the reasons why they are difficult to eradicate once they have established themselves in a human habitation. After all, since they are known to eat such unpromising materials as ink, boot-blacking, films on photographic plates, bones, book-bindings, whitewash, emery-paper, not omitting the dead bodies and cast skins of their friends, it will be realised that they cannot be easily starved out. It is, however, some comfort to know that cucumber, putty and a few other things are stated to disagree with them.

Most of us human beings very definitely loathe domestic Cockroaches and legitimately seek to destroy them. Their habits are such that they foul and contaminate even more substances than those they actually eat. The reader may be glad to know that a mixture of half powdered borax and half sodium fluoride sprinkled liberally over their haunts, and left there for a week, will usually do away with them. The insecticide known as D.D.T. is said to be even more effective.

Only two things can be said in favour of Cockroaches. One is that their size and simple structure make them very suitable subjects for teaching beginners the elements of insect anatomy. Every zoological laboratory and medical school consequently places much reliance on the Cockroach fraternity. The other thing seems only to have been proclaimed by A. E. Shipley (later Sir Arthur Shipley) who tells us that Cockroaches are said to form the basis of the flavouring of a well-known sauce (he did not divulge the name of that particular sauce) !

The Common House-fly (*Musca domestica*) is another omnivorous feeder that is particularly associated with the haunts of man. It has followed man all over the world wherever he lives and has become a menace to his health. The true significance of this insect is not generally appreciated even to-day, and what can be written about it does not make pleasant reading. If a House-fly (Pl. 23, p. 126, Fig. 1) could keep a diary of its doings it would be a most sordid document.

John Ruskin wrote about the House-fly " feasting at his will with rich variety of feast from the heaped sweets in the grocer's window to those of the butcher's backyard, and from the galled place on your horse's neck to the brown spot on the road from which, as the hoof disturbs him, he rises with angry republican buzz."

Human faeces have a great attraction for House-flies, which feed greedily on such material. In the process their feet and mouth-parts become contaminated with the living germs of many diseases that it so often contains. Sooner or later they fly to human foods—sugar, jam, milk, bread, cheese, syrups, fruits, meats, etc. are all powerfully attractive to them. While feeding they frequently void excrement, which very often contains unaltered disease germs. In summer such germs multiply rapidly, especially in fluids such as milk, and the contaminated foods are consumed by human beings. In this way the micro-organisms causing such diseases as cholera, typhoid, dysentery, summer diarrhoea, etc. become diffused. In Britain the House-fly is believed to be responsible for the spread of summer diarrhoea among infants, resulting from drinking fly-contaminated milk.

So much then for the feeding habits of the House-fly : but where does it breed ? Accumulations of fresh horse-manure form the preferred breeding places but almost any kind of fermenting dung or other organic matter may be utilised, including household refuse. The length of time development takes depends very much upon temperature and also on the nature of the food. In Britain during a hot summer only about three weeks may be required from when the eggs hatch until the Flies they give rise to are laying eggs on their own account.

We still do not know exactly how the House-fly spends the winter. It is found sometimes in houses until quite late on in the cold weather, but there is no proof that such individuals live until the next spring and then reproduce their kind. Possibly enough survive as pupae in manure and refuse-heaps to carry on until the next season.

Various kinds of Flies are found on window panes and are often mistaken for House-flies. It is still necessary to tell people that the smaller kinds are not youthful growing House-flies—no insect grows after reaching the fully winged state—they are of different species. Also, the House-fly does not change its habits in late summer and start biting people ; it is a separate kind of fly—known as the Stable-fly—with quite different mouth-parts that causes this annoyance.

Unlike the Cockroach the House-fly cannot bite solid food. Its mouth-parts are so much altered and modified that it takes an entomologist to explain what has happened. The labium is the principal organ for feeding : there are no mandibles, and all that is left of the

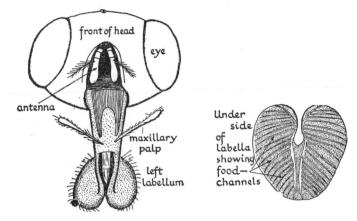

FIG 22.—Head of House-fly, seen from the front, and under side of labella or " tongue." (Highly magnified.)

maxillae are their palpi (Text-Fig. 22). The labium forms a trunk or proboscis which is expanded at its lower end into a pair of soft pads or labella. When in use the whole organ is made turgid through blood being forced into it from the head. When feeding is no longer going on this pressure is relaxed and the flaccid organ is drawn up and stowed away under the head. The labella are closely applied to any substance that is being used for feeding and the food is sucked up through minute openings that lead into a series of food-channels. There are about 30 of these channels in each labellum and they conduct the food into a main collecting channel from whence it is drawn into the gut. Since the openings into the food-channels are so minute that particles larger than 0·003 mm. cannot be eaten it will be readily appreciated that the Fly can only feed normally upon liquids.* The same applies to hosts of other Flies, including the Blow-fly, the Flesh-fly, the Greenbottle-fly, etc., whose feeding organs are constructed upon the same plan as those of the House-fly.

Three things, among others, have greatly reduced the prevalence of House-flies under modern conditions of living. These are motor vehicles, efficient sanitation and dust-bins. The internal combustion engine has wellnigh supplanted the horse as a motive power. Consequently stables and mews have largely disappeared, together with the manure-heap which is the favourite breeding ground for the House-fly.

Wherever the " midden privy " system has been replaced by modern sanitation another resort of the House-fly has become abolished. The same is true of the open " ash-pit " as the dumping place for garbage and all kinds of organic refuse. This contraption was only cleaned at long irregular intervals and provided the House-fly with another rendezvous for purposes of breeding. The adoption of closed dust-bins instead marked a simple but very definite advance in hygiene. We may take comfort in the thought that the weekly removal of their contents by municipal authorities prevents our dwellings from being invaded by hordes of newly-developed Flies.

Notwithstanding what has just been said the House-fly still finds plenty of opportunity for evil. It is abundant in the poorer quarters of our towns, about farms and in country dwellings. It is still unrivalled among insects in this country in importance from the standpoint of public hygiene. Useful practical information about this creature is available in a pamphlet entitled *The House-Fly* published by the British Museum (Natural History), price 6d. It can be had at the Museum or through a bookseller.

Brief mention may be made of two other insects that possess omnivorous habits although in a more restricted way—the House-cricket and the Common Wasp. The first-named insect eats any scraps available on the floors of kitchens and bakeries. Small insects and decaying vegetable matter are also devoured, while in greenhouses it sometimes chews parts of living plants. The Common Wasp feeds on liquid substances ; its narrow mouth, being guarded within by a comb-like arrangement of closely-set bristles, only allows of the passage of microscopic solid particles. Its tongue-like labium also is adapted for licking up materials in liquid form. Those of high sugar-content are most favoured, being energy-yielding substances. In this category are nectar, ripe and over-ripe fruits, manufactured sweets, molasses, etc. At times animal substances are resorted to, especially the juices of insects and of dead vertebrates. It is, however, not always easy to ascertain whether a Wasp is feeding on an animal substance itself or merely collecting such food for its brood which are carnivorous.

Plate XI

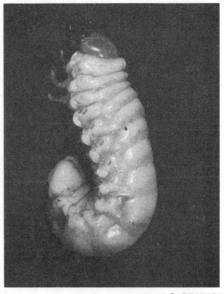

S. BEAUFOY

a Lamellicorn, *Dorcus parallelipipedus*—an ally of the Stag-beetle [subjected to low temperature]

S. BEAUFOY

b Larva of Lamellicorn, *Dorcus parallelipipedus* [subjected to low temperature]

S. BEAUFOY

c Dor-beetle, *Geotrupes* [subjected to low temperature]

A. D. IMMS

d Oil-beetle, *Meloe proscarabaeus*

COLEOPTERA OR BEETLES II (× 2)

Plate XII

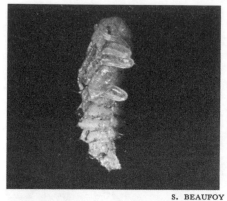

S. BEAUFOY

a Pupa of Cardinal-beetle, *Pyrochroa, serraticornis* (× 2½)

H. MAIN

b Pupa of Stag-beetle, *Lucanus cervus,* male (× 1)

S. BEAUFOY

c Cocoon of Saw-fly, *Trichiosoma lucorum,* on Hawthorn (× 2)

A. D. IMMS

d Pupae of Swallow-tail Butterfly, *Papilio machaon* (× 1)

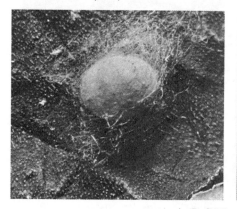

A. D. IMMS

e Cocoon of Lace-wing, *Chrysopa flava* (× 6)

S. BEAUFOY

f Cocoon of Puss-moth, *Cerura vinula* (× ½)

PUPAE AND COCOONS

VEGETARIANS

" Thus are my blossoms blasted in the bud
And caterpillars eat my leaves away."

Any and every part of plants is used as food by some insect or other. Many insects are simply leaf-feeders, roaming at will over the branches and devouring the leaves as they encounter them. Others live more protected lives and consequently burrow into their food-plants. Many of these are leaf-miners, others bore into the wood or feed at the roots. To these must be added leaf-rollers, case-builders and the great host of creatures that feed by sucking the sap. Nor must it be forgotten that large numbers of insects feed upon flour, meal, and other dried plant-products.

Almost all the caterpillars likely to be found by the ordinary observer are leaf-feeders. They obtain their nourishment from the contents of the cells. The cell walls and skeletal parts pass through the gut apparently unchanged chemically, for caterpillars have no ferment capable of breaking down and making use of the cellulose.

Sometimes caterpillars are so numerous that they strip a plant of its leaves; the kinds that do this are aptly termed defoliators. Among Moth caterpillars those of the Cinnabar (*Callimorpha jacobaeae*) often denude the Ragwort down to its bare main stems. The Pea-green Moth or Green Oak-roller (*Tortrix viridana*) is our best known defoliator of trees. Its caterpillars make shelters, spinning leaves together with silken threads. Periodically it becomes so abundant in the older Oak woods in the southern half of England as to leave the trees bare over considerable areas of country. Of our two native kinds of oak the Pedunculate Oak is usually much more heavily attacked than the closely related Sessile Oak which is often left unharmed.

Among Saw-fly caterpillars the two most familiar defoliators in gardens are those of the Gooseberry Saw-fly (*Pteronidea ribesii*) (Pl. 34, p. 207, Fig. 15) and of the Solomon's Seal Saw-fly (*Phymatocera aterrima*). Both these species often entirely defoliate the plants with which they are associated. Those of the Solomon's Seal Saw-fly (Pl. 25, 142) begin feeding on the undersides of the leaves, then they eat out large tracts of tissue between the veins, and finally entirely strip the plants of their leaves. Conifers suffer at times from the attacks of the two close y related Pine Saw-flies (*Diprion pini* and *Neodiprion sertifer*) whose larvae eat up the young needles. In this way they may partially or wholly defoliate pine plantations, as happened in East Anglia during the years 1926-29.

Defoliators are serious enemies of the forester, but under British conditions it is rare for them to kill the trees. However, they usually check the production of annual rings of wood or interfere with growth in other ways and in this manner reduce the commercial value of the timber.

Leaf-miners find board and lodging between the upper and lower epidermis of leaves. In this microcosm they spend their time mostly devouring the green tissue between these two membranes by mining or burrowing into it. In this way they leave behind them tracks of various shapes. Generally speaking these mines are of two main types, either narrow winding galleries that increase in calibre as the miner grows: or broad irregular blotch-like patches (Pl. XV, p. 122). But there are many varieties of each type and some mines start as narrow galleries and alter later into the blotch type. Others are in the form of most attractive scrolls that almost suggest an artistic temperament on the part of the miner concerned. Wherever there is plenty of green vegetation, be it herbage, trees or bushes, these leaf-miners are to be found. Gardens, lanes and meadows will yield plenty of different sorts to anyone who takes the trouble to search for them. No adult insect seems to have adopted the mining habit, all being larvae; they mostly belong to the orders Diptera and Lepidoptera.

Lepidopterous leaf-miners are almost all of them the caterpillars of some of our very smallest Moths.* Notwithstanding the minute size of so many of them they are often exceptionally beautiful creatures and it is a pity that more people are not attracted to studying them and their life-histories. The very common Lilac Leaf-miner (*Gracillaria syringella*) is to be found in many gardens all over Britain. Each mine (Pl. XV, Fig. d) is the work of several of its caterpillars operating in company. At first they make a conspicuous blotch mine in a Lilac leaf or in one of Privet and Ash. The affected part shrivels and turns brown. After a while these caterpillars tend to outgrow their confined quarters so they vacate the mine and feed outside the leaf. When this change happens they roll the leaf so as to form a funnel-like shelter wherein they continue feeding.

A large number of other minute Moths belong to the genus *Lithocolletis*, of which we have about 50 kinds in Britain. They form small blotch mines on various herbs, shrubs and trees. They do not leave their mines like the *Gracillarias* and, when fully grown, they pupate in these quarters. One surface of the mine is lined with silk which

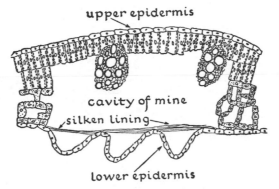

FIG. 23.—Transverse section of a Leaf, taken across a mine made by the Caterpillar of a small Moth (*Lithocolletis oxyacanthae*). (Adapted from Hering.)

causes it to shrink so as to leave a small hollow wherein the caterpillar lives (Text-Fig. 23). They are very particular and exact as to the sites of their mines. Some species, for instance, mine beneath the upper surface of a leaf and others affect the lower tissue—no species mines both surfaces indifferently. As a result, the contracted surface referred to is either on the upper or lower side of a leaf according to the species that makes the mine. Thus, the common *Lithocolletis coryli* forms whitish blotch mines in the upper tissues of Hazel leaves (Pl. XV, Fig. b). On Hawthorn there are two different species: one of them, *Lithocolletis oxyacanthae*, mines the lower side of the leaves, while the other, *L. corylifoliella*, excavates in the upper layers. All three kinds are to be found in July and again in the autumn.

Nepticula includes the smallest of all Moths—some of them measure no more than 3 mm. (0·117 in.) from tip to tip of their outstretched wings. Their caterpillars mostly form serpentine tunnels, sometimes very little thicker than threads. They are constructed usually just below the upper surface of leaves, chiefly those of trees and shrubs. Among the commonest kinds *Nepticula aurella* mines the leaves of the

PLATE 21

ANTS, BEES, WASPS AND SAW-FLIES ($\times$ 2)

1
SOLITARY BEE
Prosopis hyalinata

7
YELLOW ANT
Acanthomyops flavus
QUEEN

12
YELLOW ANT
WORKER

2
SOLITARY BEE
Prosopis pectoralis

8
PARASITIC BEE
Sphecodes monilicornis

13
PARASITIC BEE
Nomada goodeniana

3
CHALCID WASP
Habrocytus bedeguaris

4
CHALCID WASP
Torymus sp.

9
CHRYSID OR RUBY-TAIL WASP
Omalus ignita

14
GOOSEBERRY SAW-FLY
Pteronidea ribesii

5
WOOD ANT
Formica rufa
DEALATED QUEEN

10
CHRYSID WASP
Ellampus aeneus

15
SAW-FLY
Tenthredo perkinsi

6
WOOD ANT
Formica rufa
WORKER

11
QUEEN ANT
Acanthomyops fuliginosus

16
SAW-FLY
Zaraea fasciata

PLATE 21

PLATE 22

S. BEAUFOY

a. Heather beetle (*Lochmaea suturalis*)

S. BEAUFOY

b. Ladybird (*Coccinella hieroglyphica*)

S. BEAUFOY

c. Heather weevil (*Strophosomus lateralis*)

Blackberry (Pl. XV, Fig. a) and *N. anomalella* affects both wild and cultivated Roses. Considering how minute these Moths and their larvae are, and how difficult they are to handle without injury, it is surprising that as many as 67 species have been bred and identified in our British fauna. The best way to become acquainted with these mere specks of insect life is to collect mined leaves and breed out the Moths. Since the latter require to be mounted before they can be identified their manipulation needs deft fingers.

A Dipterous leaf-miner can be distinguished from a caterpillar of similar habit because it is less flattened and more cylindrical. Also, it is devoid of legs and has no apparent head. At the mouth end of the body it carries a pair of minute black hooklets whose backward and forward scraping action excavates the mine. It is true that some mining caterpillars have no traces of legs but they can be separated from Fly larvae by the other characters mentioned.

Among the common blotch mines caused by larvae of Diptera one of the best known is the work of the Celery-fly (*Philophylla heraclei*)—a small Fly with brown mottled wings and bright green eyes. When present in numbers, its mines affect a large area of leaves and consequently check the growth of the plants. It also mines weeds of the same natural order (Umbelliferae) and it is from these wild hosts that it has come to invade both Celery and Parsnip under cultivation. Several larvae occur in a mine: they are short and barrel-shaped, and when fully-grown they pupate in the soil.

In some years the Holly Leaf-miner (*Phytomyza ilicis*) is so abundant that most of the leaves of its food-plant seem to bear one or more of its blotch-like mines. The larvae pupate within the mine. The insect seems to be confined to its single food-plant—the Holly. This is in contrast to the Chrysanthemum Leaf-miner (*Phytomyza atricornis*), which has over one hundred different plant hosts. These include many wild and cultivated Compositae besides members of many other plant orders. Its serpentine tunnels are often in evidence in the leaves of garden Chrysanthemums, Michaelmas Daisies, etc. and of such weeds as Sow-thistle, etc.

There is a very numerous company of insects that feed by piercing and sucking the tissues of plants. The majority belong to the Hemiptera or Plant-bug order. Their mouth-parts differ completely from the simple biting type and are represented by a set of instruments beautifully adapted for this particular way of feeding. The mandibles and maxillae are not recognisable as such, for they have become completely changed into two pairs of needle-like stylets, but of infinitely finer calibre than any man-made needle. When not in use they are neatly stowed away in a groove in the lower lip. In this position they are hidden and the lower lip is usually the only part of the mouth-organs that can be seen without a pocket lens (Text-Fig. 10, p. 45). When a Plant-bug, or an Aphid begins to feed, the lower lip is shortened by becoming bent or looped so as to expose the stylets, as shown in Text-Fig. 11, p. 45. The mandibles are used to puncture the plant and the combined maxillae form the organ for sucking up the sap.

This particular way of feeding by extracting the sap causes severe injury to many plants. When the insects are abundant the leaves flag, curl up, often becoming brown, and then fall off. In severe infestations the plant may become stunted and dwarfed if not actually killed. The insect inserts its stylets into the plant until they reach the vascular bundles and, in particular, the phloem, which is then tapped for the nourishment its cells contain. Before feeding actually begins, saliva is injected so as to mix with the sap around the puncture and predigest it before being imbibed by the insect. In most cases the saliva seems to be responsible for changes in colour or growth that are set up in the plant by the feeding activities of these insects. Thus the punctures made by the Apple Capsid cause blister-like patches on the skin of the fruit, which render it largely unsaleable. Dr. Kenneth Smith tried dissecting out the salivary glands from this particular Capsid-bug and then inserting them, with the aid of a fine needle, beneath the skin of some Apples. The same blisters resulted, just as if the insect had been feeding on the fruit, thus providing a neat proof that the saliva is the cause of the change. It needs scarcely to be added that merely piercing the skin of the Apple with a bare needle does not have this effect.

The feeding activities of Aphids cause all sorts of changes in the plants they infest. In some cases the leaves become rolled or blotched, or galls of various sorts may develop (Plate 31, p. 190).

Sap-sucking insects are also of great economic importance in another connection. In recent years they have been proved to be the culprits causing the spread of virus diseases from one plant to another. Whether the viruses themselves are ultra-microscopic living organisms or not is disputed, but what is not disputed is that they cause a large number of serious diseases. The chief offenders are Aphids, which carry the viruses of diseases of the Potato, Sugar-cane, Sugar-beet and other plants. In Britain, for example, the Potato suffers severely from virus diseases mostly spread by Aphids. Leaf-hoppers come next in importance. What happens in all these cases is that the insect sucks up the virus that is in the sap of an infected plant. If it then flies to a healthy plant and feeds on it that plant becomes contaminated and develops the particular disease.

Another thing connected with sap-sucking insects is the production of a sweetish substance known as honey-dew. Its origin has given rise in the past to much speculation. Thus Gilbert White (1720–93) wrote about it in his *Natural History of Selborne* as follows—" that this clammy sweet substance is of the vegetable kind we may learn from the bees to whom it is very grateful : and we may be assured that it falls in the night because it is always seen on warm still mornings." This rather mystical conception of honey-dew was not shared by Kirby and Spence (1815), who remarked " You doubtless observed what is called the *honey-dew* upon the maple and other trees, concerning which the learned Roman naturalist Pliny gravely hesitates whether he shall call it the sweat of the heavens, the saliva of the stars, or a liquid provided by the purgation of the air ! Perhaps you may not be aware that it is a secretion of *Aphides*, whose excrement has the privilege of emulating sugar and honey in sweetness and purity."

Various Hemiptera exude honey-dew, but more especially Aphids and Scale-insects. It is a clear fluid that is discharged through the vent on to the ground or the surrounding vegetation. Insects such as Aphids seem to feed continuously and have to take in large amounts of cell-sap in order to obtain sufficient nutriment from it. In the process they imbibe far more sugar and other constituents than they can make use of, and these unwanted products pass directly through the digestive system and out by the anus. This discharge, then, is honey-dew and it is much sought after as a delicacy by Ants, Bees, certain Flies, etc. The passion Ants have for Aphids is entirely connected with the provision of honey-dew by the latter. Ants only fraternise with certain kinds of Aphids whose honey-dew appeals to their taste—other kinds they ignore and have no use for.

Among the numerous other kinds of insects with vegetarian habits, bark-feeders, wood-borers,* seed-feeders, root-feeders and fungus-feeders all betray special features of interest. We will take bark-feeders first.

Bark-feeders are mostly Beetles belonging to the family Scolytidae.

They are very closely related to the Weevils but lack the usual prominent snout of the latter. The Scolytidae are commonly referred to as Bark-beetles or Engraver-beetles. They tunnel between the bark and the wood of trees and shrubs, making very characteristically patterned galleries in the process. The tunnels, or gallery systems, assume diverse patterns in different members of the family. Some of them rather suggest ancient hieroglyphics engraved in the tree. They often afford a far easier and readier means of identifying the various Bark-beetles than the examination of these small insects themselves. A vast amount of damage to valuable timber trees results from their activities and consequently Bark-beetle control forms a major programme in forest protection.

If pieces of loose bark be stripped off the trunk of a dead elm, or from logs of that same kind of tree, galleries of the pattern shown in Pl. XVI, p. 123, very commonly reveal themselves. These elaborate patterns are the work of the Large Elm Bark-beetle (*Scolytus scolytus*). Like other members of its family it feeds on the starches, sugars and other substances encountered during its tunnelling activities. The female Beetle first cuts a short entrance tunnel in the bark, which leads into a main gallery or egg gallery. At its commencement this gallery is widened so as to form a pairing chamber where mating takes place. While she excavates the main gallery she gnaws niches at intervals along its walls and deposits an egg in each. When the larvae emerge they gnaw side galleries for themselves : these extend outwards and more or less at right angles to the main passage. The latter, it will be noted, runs in a vertical direction and the separate larval galleries are very evenly spaced. Furthermore as the larvae grow in size their galleries show a corresponding increase in calibre until they finally end in pupal cells. The newly-developed Beetles then gnaw the shortest tunnel that enables them to reach the outside of the tree.

In the branches of Conifers, and especially Pine and Spruce, there are often star-shaped gallery systems, each arranged around a central pairing chamber. The patterns (Pl. XVII, p. 162) are mostly gnawed out of the surface of the wood and are the work of the Two-toothed Bark-beetle (*Pityogenes bidentatus*). The second (or specific) Latin name of this insect has allusion to the two hook-like teeth at the end of its wing-covers. This insect is polygamous, whereas the *Scolytus* is strictly monogamous. What happens in the case of the *Pityogenes* is that the male mates with several females in the pairing chamber. Each fertilised

Plate XIII

a Frame with comb and workers of Hive Bee (× ¼). A number of the cells are capped (or closed over)

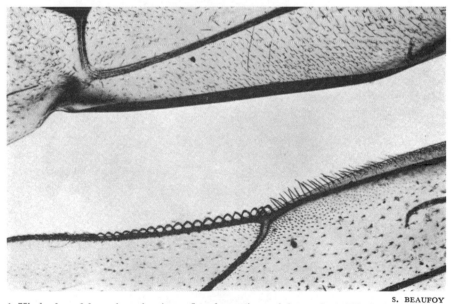

b Hind edge of fore-wing, showing reflexed margin, and front edge of hind-wing, showing row of hooklets, of a Bumble Bee (× 32)

CONCERNING BEES

Plate XIV

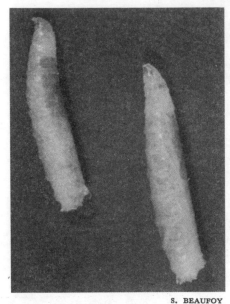

a Larvae [etherised]

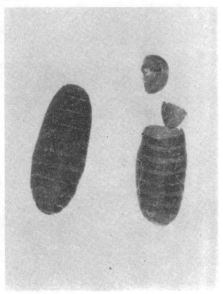

omplete and a ruptured puparium

c Fly newly-emerged from puparium. Note half-developed wings and the frontal sac seen as a white area at the extreme front of the head [from a preserved specimen]

d The same at a slightly later stage with the frontal sac withdrawn into the head: the insect has become deeper pigmented but the wings are still only half-developed [from a preserved specimen]

BLOW-FLY (*CALLIPHORA ERYTHROCEPHALA*) (× 3)

female makes her own main gallery leading from the pairing chamber, which accounts for the star-like pattern of the tunnel system. In the Elm Bark-beetle, on the other hand, since there is only one female on the scene there is but a single main gallery. The outcome is that a very different pattern becomes evolved.

In the Ash Bark-beetle (*Hylesinus fraxini*), which is common all over England, the main gallery is two-armed and horizontal with the larval galleries short and spaced very closely together (Plate XVII, Fig. d). Where the two arms of the main gallery join there is a pairing chamber and the usual entrance hole leading from outside the tree.

Among other bark-feeders are certain Weevils. The most destructive of these is the Pine Weevil (*Hylobius abietis*), which measures from $\frac{1}{3}$ to $\frac{1}{2}$ in. in maximum length. The Scots Pine is its favourite tree but all conifers are liable to attack. It eats into the bark of the younger branches in order to reach the more succulent tissues beneath and, in this way, it interferes with the flow of the sap. Young conifer plantations provide this Weevil with a feast that it fully appreciates to the detriment of the trees. Its larva curiously is not directly injurious since it lives mainly in the stumps of felled trees. When considerable woods of Pine are cut down, these provide the breeding grounds for future mass-populations of the Weevil to arise.

Wood-borers eat into the wood of trees for two purposes ; firstly they do it in order to obtain their food, and secondly they excavate borings or tunnels as habitations wherein they may live. A great many borers seem to get nothing of food value from the woody substance itself and live on the starch and sugar contained in its cells. Others secrete enzymes or ferments which act chemically on the wood so that it becomes converted into substances upon which they can feed. In some cases this chemical process is done for them by cellulose-digesting bacteria that live in their digestive canal.

Wood-borers are mostly larvae and many of them transform into large and handsome adult insects as shown in Pls. 18 (p. 79), 26 (p. 143). Their way of living renders some of them harmful to our meagre timber supplies since the tunnellings that they make are liable to render the wood useless for constructional purposes. In many cases, however, they only attack trees that are past their prime or are unhealthy.

Many wood-borers show surprising variation in the length of the lives and in the size of the adult insects they grow into. Both these features are traceable to differences in the nutritive properties of the wood in which they happen to feed and in the amount of moisture it contains. Generally borers take much longer to grow in dry old wood and produce much smaller adults than those which develop in newly killed or fresher timber. The time difference may be a matter of several years: in exceptional cases a larval life of over 20 years has been recorded with borers living in furniture.

The great Wood-wasps confine their attention to conifers and leave broad-leaved trees severely alone. The two commonest kinds are the Hornet-like *Urocerus gigas* (Pl. 20, p. 95, 12) and the resplendent blue *Sirex cyaneus*. The females of these insects use their stout saw-toothed ovipositor to drill holes into the solid wood where their eggs are laid. The larvae tunnel deeper into the wood and since they live from $2\frac{1}{2}$ to 3 years it is not surprising that their burrows may be a foot long. When the time comes to pupate they work their way to within about $\frac{1}{2}$ in. of the surface so that the mature Wood-wasps have only to gnaw a short exit to reach the outer world. Many people seem to be scared stiff when they encounter a Wood-wasp but the creature does not sting and cannot harm them in any way.

The caterpillars of the Goat-moth (*Cossus cossus*), on the other hand, are found only in broad-leaved trees such as Elm, Ash and Poplar. They make great burrows, often big enough to admit a finger, and have to ingest a vast amount of wood in order to get enough nourishment out of it to live. A person of an enquiring turn of mind gave some of these caterpillars beetroot to bore into instead of wood. The surprising thing was that they liked it and found it so nutritious that they became fully grown in one year instead of the more usual three years.

The most numerous of the wood-borers are the larvae of Longicorn Beetles, of which there are about 60 kinds in Britain. They form an important item in the diet of woodpeckers, which only peck into affected trees where there are juicy morsels in the form of Longicorn grubs or other insects to be extracted from the wood.

Some adult Longicorns are portrayed on Plates 18 and 26. They are attractive and often handsome insects but are not usually noticed by the layman. As a rule they are found near the trees wherein they lived as larvae. If they are not to be met with on or beneath the bark of the trees they are addicted to, they are very likely to turn up on neighbouring wild flowers where they sun themselves and feed upon pollen. These beetles mostly belong to the family Cerambycidae (p. 59).

Among broad-leaved trees, Oaks, Willows and Poplars are most frequently attacked by the larvae. The large yellow-green *Saperda carcharias* bores into the solid wood of Willows and Poplars, making conspicuous tunnels like those shown in Pl. XVII, p. 162, Fig. c. If fortunate we may find among Willows the resplendent Musk-beetle (*Aromia moschata*) which measures over 1 in. long (Pl. 26, p. 143, Fig. c). Very often it can be smelt before it is actually seen on the tree, for it diffuses a pleasant odour. Placed in a handkerchief for a few minutes, one of these Beetles will impart a scent that will last for some time. It is a harmless enough insect to handle and if any prejudice against holding it for a few moments be overcome it will often make a squeaking noise by rubbing the head and thorax together. The Wasp-beetle (*Clytus arietis*) is usually commoner and more generally distributed than the Musk-beetle and lives as a larva in the wood of posts and palings. Something further about this Beetle and its unusual livery will be found on p. 201, and its portrait appears on Pl. 36, p. 223, Fig. a.

Conifers provide board and lodging for a number of other kinds of Longicorn larvae. Those most likely to be found in Pines belong to the species *Rhagium bifasciatum*, while the usual kind found in Larch is *Tetropium gabrieli* (Pl. 18, p. 79, Fig. 28). In Perthshire and neighbouring areas of Scotland the Timberman (*Acanthocinus aedilis*) is sometimes found in forest glades (Fig. 19). The male flies in sunshine with its antennae, four times as long as its body, streaming behind. When these insects settle on the felled trunks of pines their antennae are extended like a pair of callipers, a trait that has caused them to become known as the " Timberman " in several European countries.

Several kinds of Longicorn beetles have almost certainly been introduced into Britain in shipments of foreign timber. Later they have become permanent residents in our woodlands. The Timberman is probably one of them and also the species of *Tetropium*. With increased imports of foreign woods this immigration is likely to go on, with the result that further species will become added to our fauna. A good deal of doubt exists as to whether any of the handsome Wood-wasps are truly native to Britain and have not entered in the same way. Some of them are certainly aliens. In recent years Wood-wasps have become established in New Zealand where they now provide the forester with an additional problem.

Longicorn Beetles are by no means the only kinds whose larvae are wood-borers. The Furniture Beetles (family Anobiidae)*bore into the

timber of ancient buildings and into furniture. They are mostly small
insects and their larvae tunnel into the wood but make no very definitely
patterned galleries (Pl. 18, Fig. 22). The notorious " Death-watch "
(*Xestobium rufovillosum*) is the largest of them, measuring up to $\frac{1}{3}$ in.
long. It lives in decaying Oaks, Willows, Hawthorns and other hard-
wood trees. Also, it invades the structural timbers of ancient buildings,
including cathedrals, churches, city and college halls and houses. At
one time it caused extensive damage to the roof of Westminster Hall.
In the course of their activities the larvae play havoc with woodwork,
rendering the affected parts unsafe, so as often to necessitate replace-
ment (Pl. XVII, p. 162, Fig. a). The presence of borings or dust ejected
from the burrows of this insect is much surer evidence of its existence
than that afforded by damaged timbers : the Beetle may have left
perhaps 100 years ago and no longer be a source of trouble !

The name " Death-watch " refers to an old superstition that the
sound made by these beetles, which resembles the ticking of a watch,
heralds an approaching death in the house where it is heard. The
ticking sound, it may be added, is made by the Beetles tapping the
front of their heads against the wood on which they are standing. It
is a mating call that is most often heard in April and May. Dean
Swift erroneously attributed the sound to the larva in the following
lines :—

> With teeth or with claws it will bite or will scratch,
> And chambermaids christen this worm the death-watch,
> Because like a watch it always cries click ;
> And woe be to those in the house who are sick !
> For, sure as a gun, they will give up the ghost,
> If the maggot cries click, when it scratches the post.

The most usual wood-borer in the household is the Furniture
Beetle (*Anobium punctatum*) and not the Death-watch. It does not
exceed $\frac{1}{5}$ in. long but the activities of its larva may reduce pieces of
woodwork to mere powder. The Beetles lay their eggs in cracks or
crevices of the furniture and do not themselves burrow. A smooth
uncracked surface is stated to be immune. The Beetles that develop
from the larvae bore their way to the surface and escape by making
circular exit-holes about $\frac{1}{16}$ in. across. The presence of these " worm-
holes " is often supposed to be a guarantee of the antiquity of a given
piece of furniture as they only affect the well-seasoned older heartwood.

It is said that they are occasionally to be found in cleverly disguised modern " antique " furniture. A sound of firing, as from a shotgun, is stated to have emanated on more than one occasion from a certain factory addicted to producing faked antiques. There may be, therefore, a sort of Gilbertian drama sometimes enacted when " worm-holes " are being provided by means other than by Beetles.

Of other wood-borers brief reference must be made to the Pinhole Borers and the Powder-post Beetles. The Pinhole Borers are closely related to the Bark-beetles. The female Beetles eat narrow cylindrical burrows deep into unseasoned timber ; the name " pinhole " refers to the holes, which scarcely exceed the diameter of a thick pin. These burrows are black or dark brown owing to the development of a mould on their walls. This mould was first termed " ambrosia " and these insects are often referred to as Ambrosia Beetles. The mould, it may be added, is brought into the burrows by the female Beetles, who cultivate it as food for themselves and their larvae. Each Beetle makes a carefully prepared layer of borings and excreta upon which the fungus develops. Once established it spreads to the neighbouring galleries, staining them in the way previously mentioned owing to its action on the wood itself. We have not much information as to how the fungus spreads from tree to tree. In the Beetle *Xyleborus*, of which we have two species in Britain, it is stated that the conidia, or reproductive bodies of the fungus, are either voided in the excreta or carried in the crops of the female Beetles and regurgitated when a fungus-bed is being prepared. In other cases the conidia adhere to groups of hairs on the heads of the Beetles and get rubbed off once the insects are established in their burrows. Ambrosia Beetles are abundant in the tropics where one species (*Xyleborus perforans*) has become known by the name of " tippling Tommy " because it has the habit of boring into the staves of wine, rum and beer casks, thus causing leakage of the contents. My friend the late Prof. William Morton Wheeler, of Harvard University, suggested that this insect might be adopted by prohibitionists as their totem-animal.

The Powder-post Beetles (family Lyctidae) comprise several species of *Lyctus* (Pl. 18, p. 79, Fig. 12) that have become introduced into Britain. They have entered during the last 15 years or so in American, Japanese and other foreign timbers. They are chiefly found in timber yards and furniture workshops. Their name refers to the fine powdery products of their borings. They deposit their eggs chiefly in those woods that have large pores or vessels of sufficient bore to allow of the Beetles inserting the ends of their egg-laying tubes.   The consequence of this is that Powder-post Beetles mainly affect Oak ; Ash, Walnut, Hickory and a few other trees are also attacked.   Their burrows are confined to the sapwood.   Damage by the larvae may continue when the wood is manufactured into furniture, etc.   The exit-holes made by the Beetles resemble those made by Furniture Beetles but the activities of the latter can be recognised by the products of their borings being granular rather than like fine dust.

Among seed-feeders the long-snouted Weevil shown in Plate 36 is worthy of attention.   It is known as a Nut Weevil, from its habit of tunnelling into nuts, and there are several kinds in Britain.   The snout is longest in the female who uses it as a tool ; by means of the small but hard pair of jaws at its extremity she gnaws a tubular passage into the centre of a young Hazel-nut or acorn.   Having accomplished this feat she then turns the opposite end of her body to the hole thus made and lays an egg in the soft tissue within.   Our most plentiful species, *Curculio nucum*, utilises Hazel-nuts for this purpose, selecting those that are green and young.   By the time the egg has hatched and the larva has begun to feed the entrance hole has healed up.   Eventually the nut falls to the ground, by which time most of the kernel has been consumed.   The larva gnaws its way out by making a small round exit-hole in the shell and turns to a pupa in the soil.   Other members of the genus attack acorns in the same way.

The doings of this Weevil have been recounted in verse and it is a temptation to quote the lines in question.

> So sleeps in silence the Curculio, shut
> In the dark chamber of the cavern'd nut ;
> Erodes with ivory beak the vaulted shell
> And quits on fairy wings its narrow cell.

It is, however, to be regretted that this graceful poetic reference is marred by wholly wrong suppositions, for the " Curculio " does not, as we have just seen, inhabit the nut in Beetle form or use its beak upon the shell in order to escape.

The Gorse Weevil (*Apion ulicis*) is another example of a seed-feeder. Like all members of the large genus *Apion* it is a small creature (Pl. 18, p. 79, Fig. 11), only $\frac{1}{8}$ in. long, but nevertheless an interesting one and easy to find. It is pitchy black but most of the body is densely coated with white scales that give it a grey colour. In May, or a little earlier in the south of England, the female Weevil begins the business of egg-laying. She bores a hole with her snout into the young pod of the Gorse plant. This often takes her several hours to accomplish ; when it is finished to her satisfaction she turns round so as to use the other end of her body and lays about half a dozen eggs in a batch within the pod. There may be several groups of eggs in a single pod when more than one Weevil has been at work. The larvae feed on the seeds and although there are rarely more than six seeds per pod more than a dozen Weevils may be produced in the one pod. The larvae turn to pupae within and the Beetles normally emerge only when the pods dehisce on dry days. The crackling sound of Gorse-pods splitting open in the sunshine is a familiar sound wherever there is gorse. This dehiscence or bursting open of the pods results in the seeds being scattered through the air. The same thing happens when the seeds are eaten up by the Weevils ; the only difference is that when bursting takes place it is the Beetles themselves that are hurled through the air. It is a curious thing that, although this Weevil has a pair of good mandibles, it does not gnaw its way out. In a wet season the splitting-open of the pods is often much delayed and the Beetles remain imprisoned therein, but they are able to remain alive for several months. The Gorse Weevil abounds in Britain wherever there are areas of Gorse, from Caithness to Cornwall. It destroys a large amount of the seed of this plant—sometimes as much as 90 per cent.

Root-feeders are mostly larvae of Beetles and Flies. The farmer comes in contact with many of them in his daily routine and anyone who regularly digs a garden usually notices a few kinds without probably knowing what they are. The creatures named Wireworms (Pl. 17, p. 78, Fig. a) are the most notorious and widely spread of all root-feeders. They are the larvae of Click-beetles (Plate 18, Fig. 7), of which something more is said on p. 188. Being worm-like in form, they are well adapted to travel beneath the soil ; their colour is brown or yellowish with a shining polished skin and there are three pairs of short legs just behind the head.

The breaking up of permanent grass and its conversion into arable land was of vital importance in both the World Wars of the present century. It was imperative in those critical times that this country should greatly increase its production of cereals and other food-crops.

The greatest enemy of this scheme was the Wireworm,* whose normal diet consists of the roots of grasses and of many roadside weeds. When grassland is ploughed in and the sod broken up and buried, the Wireworms turn their attention to the crop that is growing on the land thus prepared. Cereals suffer the heaviest destruction, especially Oats and Wheat. Flax, Linseed, Peas and Beans are least attacked. Potatoes and root crops occupy a more or less intermediate position. Since 1940 a method of sampling has been adopted which enables an estimate to be made of the approximate number of Wireworms present per acre in grassland before it is ploughed up. Thus forewarned the farmer is forearmed. If Wireworms number only about 300,000 per acre, or less, it is safe to grow almost any farm crop provided other conditions are satisfactory : an infestation of from 300,000 to 600,000 per acre is not heavy enough for cereals to suffer to any serious extent but such a population increases the risk for Potato growing. Over 600,000 per acre are a menace to most crops on light land but on heavy soils barley is likely to succeed, and also pulse. Populations of over 1,000,000 per acre are definitely dangerous ; and the least susceptible crops stand the best chances of success. Wireworms are sometimes found in the soil of weedy gardens but the adult Beetles prefer grassy places. They are often common on roadside flowers, especially those of the Umbelliferae. The adult Click-beetles (see p. 58), it may be added, do not cause appreciable injury to crops and not one farmer in a hundred connects them in any way with Wireworms !

Along with Wireworms there are often found large numbers of Leather-jackets—greyish or brownish legless larvae with a tough leathery skin and 1–1½ in. long. They turn into Crane-flies or " Daddy-long-legs " (family Tipulidae). The most abundant kinds are the greyish Common Crane-fly (*Tipula oleracea*) (Pl. 22, p. 111), the reddish Marsh Crane-fly (*T. paludosa*) and the black and yellow striped species of *Nephrotoma* (Pl. 12, p. 43, Fig. a). Leather-jackets injure a great many crops, particularly Potatoes, Mangolds, and young Oats, besides a variety of garden plants. The larvae of several kinds of *Tipula* and other Crane-flies are aquatic and their respiratory system is modified accordingly (see also p. 238). Their breathing pores lie on a disc-like plate at the tail end of the body and are surrounded by a rosette of short lobes. This apparatus is kept at the surface of the water so that air can enter the tracheae or breathing tubes. Now Leather-jackets have just the same device notwithstanding they live

Plate XV

F. C. BROWN

a Serpentine mine in Blackberry leaf made by the caterpillar of the Moth, *Nepticula aurella*

F. C. BROWN

b Blotch mine in Hazel leaf made by caterpillars of the Moth, *Lithocolletis coryli*

S. BEAUFOY

c Leaves of Lilac showing work of the Leaf-cutting Bee, *Megachile centuncularis*

F. C. BROWN

d Leaves of Lilac showing blotch mines made by caterpillars of the Moth, *Gracillaria syringella*

LEAF-MINES AND LEAF-CUTTINGS (less than actual size)

Plate XVI

S. BEAUFOY

Two vertical main galleries or egg-galleries are shown and at the upper end of each is a small pairing chamber appearing in shadow as a dark spot. From the main galleries numerous larval galleries extend outwards on either side, their calibre increasing as the larvae grow. At their extremities they become expanded to form pupal cells

GALLERIES OF THE BARK-BEETLE, *SCOLYTUS SCOLYTUS* BENEATH
BARK OF ELM

on land, and there seems no doubt that they were derived from aquatic antecedents. It is, therefore, not surprising that they thrive best in damp or wet soils and readily succumb to drought conditions.

Various sorts of Chafer are root-feeders during their larval stages. Four kinds will be mentioned here. Portraits of the Beetles are shown on Pls. 18, p. 79, Figs. 30-32, and 27, p. 158, Fig. a. The Cockchafer (*Melolontha melolontha*) is the largest and has a black head and thorax with the wing-cases reddish-brown. The Summer Chafer (*Amphimallon solstitialis*) is rather smaller and entirely reddish- or yellowish-brown with a very hairy covering. The Garden Chafer or June-bug (*Phyllopertha horticola*) is the smallest of the four kinds and has a metallic bluish-green thorax and reddish-brown wing-cases. The Rose-chafer (*Cetonia aurata*)* is of a beautiful golden metallic green speckled with whitish flecks; it is much less often found than the three other kinds.

Chafers often occur in swarms, flying around the tops of trees and shrubs with a loud humming sound. The two first-named kinds fly towards dusk in May and June, whereas the other two species are mostly diurnal in habits. They feed on the leaves of various trees and bushes, excepting the Rose-chafer which is prone to eat the petals and other parts of flowers, especially those of the Rose. Chafer larvae are mostly long-lived creatures : in the case of the Cockchafer the life-span is 2 to 3 years. It is one of our longest-lived insects, if Wireworms, which live up to about 5 years, be excluded. Chafer larvae appear very much alike and they usually attract attention, on account of their large size and C-shaped form, when dug up in the soil. They are whitish objects with brown heads and rather long legs situated very far forwards. They feed especially on the roots of grasses but are also often very destructive to young trees in forest nurseries.

One does not associate caterpillars with a subterranean life but there are a few kinds that are root-feeders. Those of the Swift Moths all have this habit and feed on the roots of grasses and many wild and cultivated plants. The larva of the Ghost Swift (*Hepialus humuli*) is commonest in weedy grassland while that of the Garden Swift (*H. lupulinus*) is frequent in herbaceous borders where it often pays too much attention to our Delphiniums, Lupins and Peonies, etc. We have five species of these Moths and their larvae are all pale whitish caterpillars with a reddish-brown head and scattered hairs over the body (Pl. XVIII, p. 163, Fig. a). The pupae show considerable activity and work their way to the soil surface to allow of the exit of the Moths.

Where these insects are common the empty pupal coverings are frequently to be found lying about on the soil.

The last group of vegetarian feeders we shall discuss are the fungus-feeders. Many of them are of special interest in particular ways and much still remains to be discovered regarding their economy. It has already been noted that the egg-laying females of Ambrosia Beetles infect their burrows with moulds that grow on the dead wood and serve as food for the larvae. The female Wood-wasp apparently does something of the same kind. At the base of her ovipositor there is a pair of glands that contain conidia or fruiting bodies of a particular kind of fungus. These conidia pass with the eggs into the borings made by the insect in the wood, and these later develop a crop of the mould on their walls. It remains to be determined how the Wood-wasp herself becomes infected in the first place and, secondly, what part the mould plays in the nutrition of the larvae. We are beginning to discover that some borers cannot digest any constituent of the wood and have to rely upon moulds as food. In other cases the fungi appear to break down the wood into substances that the insects are able to digest. There are, however, various borers, such as the larva of the Death-watch, that produce a ferment in their alimentary system which converts the cellulose of the wood into digestible glucose so that they are independent of other agencies.

Apart from some wood-borers of the kinds just mentioned there are large numbers of other insects that have simpler relations with fungi. They literally inhabit the fungus where they find it since it affords them both board and lodging. In early summer, for instance, certain common grasses, such as Cock's-foot, are often seen to be girdled with a belt formed by a white fungus for about an inch of their length (Pl. XIX, p. 170, Fig. b). The fungus in question is of the mould type and is known as *Epichloë typhina* ; it behaves as a parasite on the grass and checks its growth. If the reader will take a pocket lens and examine these patches when they are quite fresh many of them will be seen to bear a creamy glistening and rather longish insect egg, deposited near its centre. The egg has been laid by a small Fly* (*Egle radicum*) which has the general look of a House-fly but is of smaller size. So far as is known this Fly lays its egg nowhere else. Its larva makes excursions through the fungus patch in a radiating manner; it eats its way through this luxurious pasture, leaving wide sinuous tracks in its wake. How far it acts as a natural check on the fungus is uncertain and its whole life-cycle would repay more careful scrutiny than has so far been devoted to it.

Beds of the edible mushroom are often infested with the larvae of small Flies called Fungus-gnats (family Mycetophilidae). These larvae are very like whitish worms with dark brown or black heads. They feed primarily on the decaying parts of mushrooms but they may stray afield from there and ultimately ruin a whole crop. Spring-tails (Collembola) are also very prone to feed on mushrooms and are sometimes present in the beds in immense numbers. They are very liable to reduce the value of the crop or even render it unsaleable where mushrooms are cultivated under glass. But Fungus-gnats and Spring-tails are found in many different sorts of fungi. The bracket and other types growing on trees also support a number of kinds of small Beetles and their larvae. The largest populations are met with in autumn and in fungi that are just beginning to decay. Such inhabitants are virtually scavengers but since they feed on the living parts also we have classed them among vegetarians. Besides many small Rove-beetles, other fungus-feeding Coleoptera include the brilliant-scarlet *Endomychus coccineus*,[1] which bears a superficial likeness to a Ladybird. A more abundant kind is the brown spotted *Mycetophagus quadripustulatus*,[2] and there are hosts of others. Since there does not seem to be anything special regarding their economy individual mention of other kinds is unnecessary.

Here these remarks on plant-feeders must be brought to a close. So far nothing has been said regarding carnivores and scavengers. Since both these ways of living are abundantly represented among insects they form the subject for the next chapter.

[1, 2] On Pl. 19, p. 94, Fig. c, these two fungus-feeders are shown: on the left, *Endomychus coccineus;* on the right, *Mycetophagus quadripustulatus.*

PLATE 23
DIPTERA OR TRUE FLIES

1
HOUSE-FLY
Musca domestica

2
CLUSTER-FLY
Pollenia rudis

3
Hilara maura
MALE

4
YELLOW DUNG-FLY
Scatophaga stercoraria
MALE

5
REED GALL FLY
Lipara lucens

6
Protocalliphora azurea

7
ROBBER-FLY
Laphria marginata

8
DRONE-FLY
Eristalis tenax
FEMALE

9
DRONE-FLY
Eristalis tenax
MALE

10
HOVER-FLY
Volucella pellucens

11
DUNG-FLY
Mesembrina meridiana

12
PARASITIC FLY
Echinomyia fera

13
PARASITIC FLY
Echinomyia grossa

14
ROBBER-FLY
Philonicus albiceps
MALE

15
ROBBER-FLY
Philonicus albiceps
FEMALE

16
ST. MARK'S FLY
Bibio marci
MALE

17
CLEG
Haematopota pluvialis

18
HORSE-FLY
Tabanus bromius

19
CRANE-FLY
Ptychoptera paludosa

20
HORSE-FLY
Tabanus sudeticus

21
Thyridaanthrax fenestralis

22
CRANE-FLY
Ctenophora ornata
MALE

PLATE 23

PLATE 24

E. J. HUDSON
a. Silver-Y Moth, *Plusia gamma*

E. J. HUDSON
b. Small Copper Butterfly, *Lycaena phlaeas*

ERIC HOSKING
c. Red Admiral Butterfly, *Vanessa atalanta*
RESTING ATTITUDES IN LEPIDOPTERA

CHAPTER 6

CONCERNING FEEDING HABITS
(*continued*)

CARNIVORES

" It is a wise dispensation of Providence to keep every animal in check by some other that is either more powerful or more sagacious than itself."

THE word carnivore is used here to include not only the flesh-eaters but also blood-suckers and parasites. In the broad sense they all feed upon living animal tissues of one kind or another.

1. PREDATORS.—The true carnivores are the predators, i.e. those creatures that go forth and seek their prey where they can find it. They include the lions and tigers of the insect world. For the most part they prey upon other insects and, on this account, they play an important part in the economy of nature by acting as a check or restraint upon the inordinate abundance of insect life.

As a general rule predators are well endowed with organs of special sense and are particularly agile in their movements. Only a few of them are more or less sedentary and catch their prey by snares or by deception. A Ground-beetle (family Carabidae) provides an excellent example of a general predator. Its long slender legs, those of the three pairs being of about equal size, betoken agility in running (Pl. 17, p. 78, Fig. b). It rarely seems to fly and many kinds have the hind-wings rudimentary. The elongated sensitive antennae, large protuberant eyes and mobile palps to the maxillae and labium provide a very complete outfit of special sense-organs. Such an equipment, of course, is essential in creatures that mainly live by the aid of their wits. The larvae betray the same general characteristics and often have in addition well-formed tail-feelers or cerci (Pl. X, p. 99, Fig. a). Both larval and adult Carabidae are soil insects and their victims are small insects and other creatures that inhabit the same medium. During feeding the prey is seized with the mandibles and torn to pieces with the aid of the other mouth-parts. The mandibles, it will be noted, project well forwards, especially in the larva. They and the maxillae are sharply pointed and prominently toothed—once the prey is seized it has little chance of escape.

I.N.H.   K

We have more than 700 species of Ground-beetles in Britain. They include such relatively large insects as the common *Carabus violaceus* (Pl. 17, p. 78, Fig. b), and its near relatives, to the small burnished species of *Notiophilus* and *Bembidiom*. Every garden contains at least a few kinds, including generally one or more of the larger Carabi that lurk by day under stones and logs. Most members of the family display grace of form and some have bright metallic colours, especially the rare and beautiful *Carabus nitens*. A few of these Beetles show unusual habits. Thus *Calosoma inquisitor* frequents Oak woods, where it climbs the trees in search of its prey (Map 6). It is most frequent in the New Forest and the Forest of Dean, where it feeds upon defoliating caterpillars, especially those of the Pea-green Moth and the Winter Moth. The very common *Pseudophonus rufipes* shows vegetarian tendencies and has been found damaging strawberries (Pl. 18, p. 79, Fig. 29).

The Cicindelidae or Tiger-beetles are another family of hunters and are closely allied to the Ground Beetles. They are largely tropical insects and consequently only five species extend their range into the British Isles. The beautiful and elegantly shaped *Cicindela campestris* (Plate 18, Fig. 1) is the kind most usually met with and is mostly found on sandy heaths and moorlands, where it runs and flies in sunshine with a speed that makes its erratic movements hard to follow. It has all the attributes of a hunter and slayer intensified ; with long, very slender legs, ample wings and protuberant eyes, it is well fitted for the chase. Prominent and formidably toothed mandibles give it a fearsome hold on its prey once it is captured.

The Tiger-beetle larva on the other hand is a sluggish animal that lives in a vertical tubular burrow extending into the ground to a depth of about a foot. It lies in wait for its prey with head and prothorax occupying the entrance to the burrow while its curiously bent body, aided by its legs and a pair of hooks on its back, enables it to keep its position and maintain a firm grip on to the walls of its abode. When an unsuspecting insect wanders too near the entrance to this death-trap the larva makes a rapid jerking movement and seizes it with its long sharp mandibles. It then hauls the prey down to the bottom of the dark passage and devours it. Text-Fig. 24 conveys an idea how the Tiger-beetle larva awaits its prey to come along.

Among other beetles Ladybirds (family Coccinellidae) and their larvae are predominantly carnivorous in habit [(Pls. 15 p. 74], 16 [p. 75]). They do not, however, so openly display their traits in their bodily make-up as we have seen is the rule in the two families just discussed. The main reason for this lies in the nature of their prey. This consists of Aphids and related small insects which are all helpless sedentary and thin-skinned creatures that almost seem to invite the attention of any predator that comes along. Lady-birds and their larvae have become so addicted to a diet of Aphids that they will seldom trouble to look for anything else. The spirit of the chase does not enter into their lives for they are too much pampered by their mothers. What the parent Beetle does is to lay her eggs in small groups in the vicinity of a pro-mising colony of Green-fly. The young larvae on hatching find their

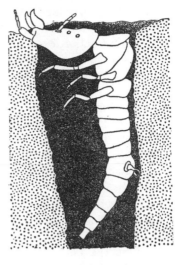
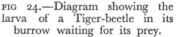

FIG 24.—Diagram showing the larva of a Tiger-beetle in its burrow waiting for its prey.

living meals already provided and near at hand. Hence it will be clear that neither wits nor agility are any special asset to these creatures. At least they have not to chase their prey, consequently no particular development of their sense-organs is called for and their mouth-parts need no special adaptations in order to cope with such soft and help-less victims. Another large group of carnivores includes the Great Water-beetles (family Dytiscidae). Their lives are discussed in Chapter 11, and for this reason only passing mention is needed here.

The family Cantharidae (Pl. 39, p. 254, Fig. 3-5, 11) includes many carnivorous Beetles and their larvae. The Glow-worm is their most noted member (Pl. 18, p. 79, Fig. 15) : it feeds upon snails and slugs when in the larval stage. The Beetles themselves seem to take very little food of any kind. The larval Glow-worm has sharp sickle-like mandibles each traversed by a fine canal. The prey is seized by means of these appendages and a dark-coloured fluid is injected down the canals just mentioned into its body. The fluid evidently has the property of breaking down and partly digesting the tissues of the victim. It will be observed that digestion occurs partly outside the insect and it is only after this preliminary treatment that the larva proceeds to eat

its meal.   Since the food has by now become liquefied no mastication
is needed and what it does is to suck it in through the mouth by means
of a pumping action exercised by the pharynx.   This kind of feeding,
which is known as external digestion, is probably widespread among
carnivorous insects and especially in Beetles in which salivary glands
are absent.   In the place of salivary secretion the stomach juices are
regurgitated and predigest the food.

Anyone who has much to do with Pine woods sooner or later comes
across the rather strikingly marked Ant-beetle (*Thanasimus formicarius*)
shown in Pl. 19, p. 94, Fig. f.   It roams over the tree trunks, seizing
and devouring any Bark-beetle it meets.   The larva is rose-red with a
dark head and two hooks at the tail end.   It inhabits the galleries in
the bark, feeding upon the eggs, larvae and pupae of Bark-beetles.
This Beetle and its larva are, therefore, true friends of the forester and
should never be destroyed.

Leaving the Beetles we are now in a position to note what other
kinds of predators there are among insects.   The Dragon-flies and
their nymphs are among the most thoroughgoing of all such hunters,
but since they are dealt with in Chapters 3 and 10 they only call for
passing mention here.   The Lace-wings (order Neuroptera) are slow-
flying, creatures of such delicacy of build that few people associate
them with predatory behaviour.   Yet there seems no doubt that Aphids
form a large part of their diet.   According to F. J. Killington three
examples of the Brown Lace-wing (*Megalomus hirtus*) kept in captivity
for nine weeks consumed an average of 315 Aphids.   This same
authority comments upon the fact that small Moths also figure among
the diet of Lace-wings and he believes that these are caught either while
resting and stationary, or when injured or dead.   It is, however, quite
evident that not much is known about their feeding habits.   Their
larvae, on the other hand, have been well explored.   Their staple food
consists of Aphids, Leaf-hoppers and other small soft-bodied insects.
They have also been noted to attack Mites, small Spiders, insect eggs,
etc.   But Aphids are undoubtedly their favourite diet and the larva
of a Green Lace-wing will consume at least 100 average-sized Aphids
during its life.   They seize their prey with their long mandibles and
suck out their juices in much the same way as a Glow-worm does to
a snail.   In captivity I have often noticed that they do not seem at
all particular as to the kind of Aphid provided.

The larvae of Green Lace-wings are of two types, viz. those which carry debris on their backs and those which do not. The debris-carriers are broader and shorter than the other type of larva and bear projecting tubercles capped with bristles. They also bear rows of small hooked bristles across most of the body segments. The debris is chiefly composed of such gruesome objects as the empty skins of their victims, besides fragments of dry plant remains, etc. (Text-Fig. 25). In covering itself with debris a larva seizes the materials with its mandibles and bending its neck so that its head points backwards it places them in

FIG. 25.—Larva of a Green Lace-wing showing covering of debris (*Chrysopa*).

the required position. Each piece is finally settled into place by wriggling movements of the hind-body and is held in position by the hooked bristles and the tubercles previously alluded to. The function of the debris seems to be that of a protective covering that shields them against the attacks of enemies. The process of making the covering can be observed by stripping one of these larvae of its debris and placing the remains, along with the insect, in a small glass vessel. The larva evidently feels its nakedness and has the urge, if uninjured, to restore its covering very soon after having lost it. Those Lace-wing larvae not addicted to covering themselves with debris are more slender and longer-bodied ; they have no side tubercles and their skins are smoother (Plate VI, p. 47). None of the Brown Lace-wings is a debris-carrier.

The Asilidae or Robber-flies are another family of predators. In contrast to Lace-wings they are vigorous, robust creatures addicted to catching their prey on the wing. Rather more than 20 species inhabit Britain and several are very large powerful Flies. An inspection of Pl. 23, p. 126, Figs. 14, 15 will give a general impression as to what they are like. If one of these Flies be looked straight in the face the horny downwardly-directed proboscis attracts notice and a characteristic tuft of hairs known as the "mouth-beard" is a conspicuous feature. Large bulging eyes and long spiny legs ending in a stout bristle between the claws of each foot are other items in their outfit. Robber-flies, like

Dragon-flies, capture their prey while on the wing, seizing and holding them with their strong legs. Once the victim is within its clutches the insect pierces it with its proboscis. When this happens the prey collapses and becomes motionless. The effect is so sudden and remarkable that something more than merely inserting the proboscis appears to have occurred. It strongly suggests that a toxic or narcotic substance is injected at the same time, but no one seems to have performed any experiments to test the truth of such a supposition. Robber-flies seem to be endowed with plenty of courage for they never appear to hesitate to attack prey often larger and more formidably armed than themselves. Their favourite victims are other Flies, but the larger kinds tackle Grasshoppers as big as themselves, besides Spiders, Beetles and even Bees and Wasps.

Our largest Robber-fly, *Asilus crabroniformis*, is a most striking creature (Pl. 28, p. 159, Fig. 9). It inhabits sandy localities in southern England. I have seen it settle on cliff-paths near Shaldon (Devon) darting away on short flights when approached and then settling again. Among its prey, as recorded by E. B. Poulton, Sarel Whitfield and others, are Blow-flies (Pl. 15, p. 74, Fig. b), Drone-flies (Pl. 12, p. 43, Fig. f), the wasp-like fly *Sericomyia borealis* (Pl. 28, p. 159, Fig. 4), and also *Volucella pellucens* (Pl. 23, p. 126, Fig. 10) and *Mesembrina meridiana* (Pl. 23, Fig. 11). These are all large robust Flies, well adapted to look after themselves one would think, but, nevertheless, they fall victims. To these must be added several kinds of Grasshoppers, the Beetles *Sermylassa halensis* (Pl. 18, p. 79, Fig. 4), *Aphodius rufipes* and others. It is, however, among the Hymenoptera that more formidable insects feature as its victims. Thus the Hive-bee, the Solitary Bee *Andrena fulva* and the German Wasp (*Vespula germanica*), including the queens, are recorded victims. Such powerful and well-armed opponents would, as Sarel Whitfield observes, most certainly have killed their captors unless immediately deprived of their power of doing so. Another large Asilid Fly the bee-like *Laphria flava* (Pl. 28, p. 159, Fig. 8) has been less fully observed but is known to prey upon Ladybirds, Chafers, Ants and other insects.

Finally, we must not overlook the Hover-flies (family Syrphidae) since many of them are predators in their larval stages. The Hover-flies themselves feed on nectar, etc. and are quite unable to negotiate prey of any kind. Among those that have predacious larvae the commonest include many species of *Syrphus*, the much larger *Scaeva pyrastri*, and various others that are also abundant on Composite flowers in gardens (Pl. 28, Figs. 11, 16). They lay their eggs near colonies of Aphids and it is among these insects that the soft-bodied, rather slug-like Syrphid larvae are to be found. Such larvae are flattened beneath and as they move over the leaves they moisten the surface with a lubricant which seems to be saliva. They are pale-coloured, marked with green or brown, and measure when fully grown from about ⅛ to ⅝ in. long, according to the species (Pl. 29, p. 174, Fig. b). Ordinarily they only feed upon Aphids. They seize these creatures with their mouth-hooks and suck out the entire soft interior leaving only shrivelled skins behind.

It may have occurred to the reader how frequently Aphids become the victims of predators for we have already recorded that they are the staple food of Ladybird Beetles and their larvae, of Lace-wing larvae and finally of Hover-fly larvae. When the enormous capacity for multiplication possessed by Aphids is taken into account it is scarcely possible to overrate the value and importance of such predators as natural controlling agents. The fact that a single Syrphid larva kept in captivity has been found to devour 800 to 900 Aphids will serve to emphasise the foregoing statement.

Hover-flies are plentiful, they are not difficult to rear or to identify. For these reasons an amateur naturalist, needing a subject to explore, might well consider taking up these Flies whose economy provides much that is unusual and interesting and a field that has been very little investigated.

Before leaving the subject of predators the reader may be reminded that the Long-horned Grasshoppers also come under this category and so do most of the Water-bugs : these and their like are, however, dealt with in other pages of this book.

2. BLOOD-SUCKERS.—The numerous blood-sucking Flies* that torment man and his domestic animals are predators of sorts. The difference is of course that they take a meal here and there at the expense of their vertebrate hosts, instead of devouring the latter wholesale after the manner of true predators. A short digression will, therefore, be in order if we discuss the private lives of Mosquitoes, Midges and a few other creatures. They are commonly referred to as " biting flies " but in reality they do not and cannot bite. They have no jaws for the purpose and, instead, their mandibles are transformed into needle-like piercing stylets and their use involves a different action

from biting in the accepted sense of that word. It is more correct to call them " piercing flies " because when they want a blood meal they do actually pierce the skin of the animal concerned.

There are in Britain 29 different kinds of Mosquitoes but surprisingly little is known about the range and distribution of many of them in our land. The commonest of them is *Culex pipiens* (Pl. XXVIII, p. 235, Fig. a), and if this Mosquito be examined under a good pocket lens the typical features distinctive of these creatures will be seen. They are :— a slender body and very slender legs : an elongate proboscis projecting from the head : narrow wings clothed with scales and the presence of 9 longitudinal veins that end on the wing-margin (Pl. VIII, p. 63, Fig. d). The male is easily recognised by its bushy plume-like antennae whereas those of the female are simpler and not endowed in this manner. The mouth-parts are only fully developed in the female and it is only the female that has blood-sucking habits. Rudyard Kipling's dictum " The female of the species is more deadly than the

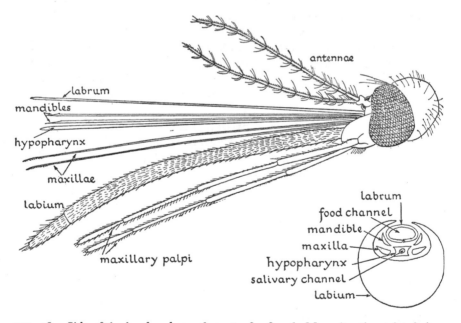

FIG. 26.—Side of the head and mouth-parts of a female Mosquito, the stylets being separated from the groove of the labium. On the right is a transverse section showing the position of the stylets in the groove of the labium. (Diagrammatic.)

male " is, therefore, particularly appropriate to Mosquitoes since it is the female alone who has developed the blood-sucking habit.

The proboscis in the female Mosquito is made up of the lower lip which is deeply grooved so as to receive a set of six minutely fine lancets. There are two pairs which are the transformed mandibles and maxillae together with an upper lip that is deeply furrowed beneath, and arising from the floor of the mouth is another stylet, called the hypopharynx, which (Text-Fig. 26) bears the salivary channel. When a mosquito is about to partake of a blood meal the first warning of her approach is usually a high pitched " piping " sound caused by her vibrating wings. It reminds us of the lines by John Keats :—

> Then in a wailful choir the small gnats mourn
> Among the river sallows, borne aloft
> Or sinking as the light wind lives or dies.

Anyway, she soon settles down on the skin with a lightness that is unperceived. She then brings her set of tools into practice. The mandibles and maxillae make the puncture while the upper lip and hypopharynx soon follow.

Before making the actual puncture a Mosquito feels over the skin of the victim with the tips of its maxillary palpi in order to find a nice soft spot. The mouth-stylets are then brought into operation. At first they are protruded between the two lobes at the end of the lower lip which act as a kind of guide. As the stylets are forced deeper into the skin the lower lip becomes drawn further and further back, or looped as it were, so as to be out of the way (Text-Fig. 27). Saliva then soon begins to flow down the excessively minute channel that traverses the length of the hypopharynx. This fluid is stated to cause the irritation and swelling that so often results from the Mosquito punctures but there is still difference of opinion on this matter. The actual blood-meal is sucked up in the groove along the underside of the upper lip, and in this way reaches the gut. In addition to blood the female Mosquito feeds on nectar and fruit juices. In the male the paired mouth-stylets are always insufficiently developed for piercing and he is a compulsory vegetarian in consequence, imbibing fluids, wherever he finds them.

In Britain the female *Culex pipiens* very rarely sucks human blood, but mainly resorts to birds. Until recently it was believed that a blood-meal was essential for the growth of fertile eggs of all Mosquitoes,

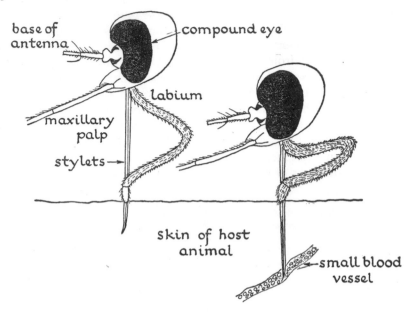

base of
antenna

compound eye

labium

maxillary
palp

stylets→

skin of host
animal

small blood
vessel

FIG. 27.—Diagram showing two stages of a Mosquito piercing the skin of its host. N.B. Only the head of the Mosquito is shown.

but we now know that it is not an invariable rule. *Culex molestus*, for example, which is an inveterate blood-sucker of man, can lay at any rate one batch of fertile eggs without ever having tasted blood, but she requires a blood meal in order to lay any more.

In Britain we have five species of domestic Mosquitoes, i.e. those that pass the winter in cellars, outhouses, attics, lofts and farm buildings. Only three of them are common. *Culex pipiens* is the one most usually found and sometimes occurs in hundreds settled on the walls of a dark room or shed. *Theobaldia annulata* is our largest Mosquito : it is about half as large again as *C. pipiens* and is a most ornamental fellow with many white rings on the legs and hind-body. It is often roused during mild spells in winter and it then takes a blood-meal off any two- or four-legged animal it meets. Its punctures are exceptionally severe to some human beings and in order to avoid the results of this intensified susceptibility or allergy it is as well to " swat " this Mosquito whenever met with. Our third common domestic Mosquito is *Anopheles maculipennis*. There are four species of *Anopheles* in Britain, all of which are capable of transmitting malaria among human beings ; but *A. maculipennis* is the only kind that regularly enters buildings. When settled on a wall or other surface a Mosquito of the genus *Anopheles* can be distinguished from any other kind by the attitude it assumes. As seen in Text-Fig. 28, it rests with the long axis of the body inclined at an angle with the supporting surface, whereas all other Mosquitoes rest with the hind-body more or less parallel to that surface. The larvae of *Anopheles* are astonishingly different from those of other Mosquitoes but since all such larvae are aquatic in habits they are dealt with in Chapter 11.

When an *Anopheles* feeds on a human being affected with malaria the organisms which cause this disease enter the insect along with the blood. Eventually they find their way into the salivary glands of the Mosquito. When this happens the insect is capable of infecting another human being with malaria. Actual infection is brought about by the disease organisms being conveyed in the saliva down the minute groove that traverses the hypopharynx and in this way they mix with the blood. As Shipley has aptly observed, the hypopharynx is much the most dangerous weapon in the whole armoury of *Anopheles* ; he goes on to remark :—" Down this minute, microscopic groove has flowed the fluid which has closed the continent of Africa for countless centuries to civilisation, and which has played a dominant part in destroying the civilisations of ancient Greece and of Rome." It was not until 1897 that Ronald Ross made his great discovery that Anopheline Mosquitoes carry the malaria organism from man to man. Armed with this knowledge we have the means to guard against malaria by destroying the Mosquito and its breeding places or by preventing the insect from having access to man. It is not generally known that a malaria-infected Mosquito develops relatively huge tumours on the walls of its stomach as the

FIG. 28 —*Above*, an Anopheline and *below* a Culicine Mosquito in their characteristic resting positions

result of the disease. These growths must cause the insect intense discomfort and worse suffering than man himself has to endure from malaria!

A very interesting story is connected with the former prevalence of malaria in England. As J. F. Marshall, then the authority on Mosquitoes, tells us (1938), up to about 60 years ago malaria—under the name of the ague—was very general in some parts of the country. It was apparently as popular a topic of conversation as influenza is to-day : the polite enquiry " Have you had ague this spring ? " being a sort of conversational opening. In the Fenland and low-lying coastal areas, from Suffolk to Kent, malaria once used to undermine the health of the people. Between about 1860 and 1870 it began to die out and finally almost completely disappeared. During the Great War of 1914–18 soldiers invalided home with malaria were often sent to eastern coastal districts in order to convalesce. They unwittingly became reservoirs for the transmission of the malaria organism to healthy persons with the result that a considerable amount of temporary malaria became prevalent.

This state of affairs led the powers that be to look into its causes and it has now become known that *Anopheles maculipennis* is represented in England by two separate species, which have hitherto been regarded as biological races, viz. *messeae* and *atroparvus*. *Anopheles maculipennis messeae*, to quote its full name, breeds in the non-saline waters of inland ponds and streams : it rarely attacks man and does not tend to frequent human habitations. *Atroparvus*, on the other hand, is chiefly a coastal species that breeds in saline waters and frequents warm dark ill-ventilated quarters, especially where there are human beings or domestic animals. These facts explain the peculiarly localised distribution of ague and the carrying Mosquito. Improvements in the living conditions of human beings have reduced the chances of the insect obtaining blood-meals off man, with the result that this Mosquito is no longer a reservoir of endemic malaria in England. It can, however, disseminate imported malaria when infected cases become introduced into its area of distribution. *

Probably most people who happen to read this chapter have been annoyed at one time or another by the attentions of minute blood-sucking Midges. These creatures measure only about $\frac{1}{10}$ to $\frac{1}{8}$ in. in length, but size is no criterion of the irritation they may cause to susceptible persons. On a hasty glance they look like mere black specks but more careful scrutiny will reveal that they have a dark clouding or spotting on their wings. Their piercing mouth-parts are formed on much the same plan as those of Mosquitoes. As with the last-named

FIG. 29.—A small blood-sucking Midge (*Culicoides*). (× 10).

insects the males are distinguishable on account of their densely bushy antennae and by the lack of all blood-sucking propensities (Text-Fig. 29).

These minute Flies are usually called " Punkies " in the United States, but for our purpose it is preferable to refer to them as Midges, especially as the name was given to them by Thos. Moufet as long ago as 1634. According to F. W. Edwards the first account of their life-history was published in 1713 by W. Dereham, Rector of Upminster (Essex), in a work entitled *Physico-Theology : or a demonstration of the being and attributes of God, from His Works of Creation.* This account says :—" These Gnats are greedy Blood-suckers, and very trouble-some where numerous, as they are in some places near the *Thames*, particularly in the Breach-waters that have lately befallen us, in the Parish of Dagenham ; where I found them so vexatious, that I was glad to get out of those Marshes."

There are about 150 different kinds of these Midges in Britain : they are usually classified nowadays as a separate family of their own, the Ceratopogonidae. Only one genus, *Culicoides*, is known to suck mammalian blood in Britain. Members of the remaining genera either feed upon nectar, or other plant-juices, or upon various insect hosts. Soft-skinned caterpillars are favoured by some species, while others have the peculiar habit of piercing the wing-veins of Moths, Lace-wings and Dragon-flies, holding on tenaciously when these insects are in flight.

When on a blood-hunt, the *Culicoides* settle on any exposed and on some unexposed parts of the human body. They are very prone, for instance, to nose their way through the texture of women's stockings, which afford but little protection in consequence. The effect of their punctures causes intense irritation to some people, making it a torment to sit out of doors on a summer's evening. The discomfort may last even for several days. If the affected parts be moistened and some finely powdered sodium carbonate be rubbed over them the irritation very often ceases. One kind of Midge, notably the species *Culicoides impunctatus*, is especially troublesome in the Western Highlands of Scotland. It is referred to in a well-known textbook of Zoology with the comment that " its presence in conjunction with that of the kilt is said to have given rise to the Highland Fling."

Not much is known about the breeding habits of *Culicoides* : most of the larvae are believed to be aquatic but for some of them only moist soil and shade seem to be necessary. The liquid draining from manure-heaps provides the right conditions for certain kinds and the margins of shallow pools where there are plenty of Confervae for others.

In the British Isles there are some 28 species of Horse-flies belonging to the family Tabanidae. They are very stoutly built insects with broad heads and include our largest blood-sucking Diptera (Pl. 23, p. 126, Figs. 17, 18 and 20). In contrast to the members of the family just considered, the female of *Tabanus sudeticus*, for instance, has a wing-spread of nearly 2 in. and a length of 1 in. There are also other kinds almost equally large. If a living Fly of this family be examined the prominent glistening eyes with golden-green or purple markings immediately attract notice. After death these colours fade away speedily and are represented by a dull brown. Horse-flies occur all through the summer in fields, open spaces in woods and along country roads. The approach of the larger kinds is heralded by a deep and rather soft hum, but the others often only betray their presence when a sharp prick is felt on the skin as their mouth-parts get to work. They are often rather persistent in their attacks even after being repeatedly driven away. The punctures made by the larger kinds may be severe when they attack in numbers and blood freely exudes from them, but they do not transmit any disease organisms. In all cases it is only the female that sucks blood.

Among the species of *Tabanus*, *T. bromius* is one of those most usually encountered (Pl. 12, p. 43, Fig. e). The Clegs are small mottled-winged Horse-flies belonging to the genus *Haematopota*. They are by far the most abundant members of the family and often settle in dozens on horses and cattle. Being very bloodthirsty and persistent in their attacks they are often a veritable plague to farm-labourers and their horses when working in hot sunshine. The species of *Chrysops* are rather larger than the Clegs. They have marbled wings and exceptionally brilliant golden-green eyes, as implied by the generic name. The most usual kind is *Chrysops caecutiens* which is found all over the country up to the north of Scotland. Comparatively little is known of the breeding habits of Horse-flies and only a single species has been properly investigated. Cattle ponds, roadside runnels, damp soil and rotting wet wood are situations where the larvae have been found. Moisture seems essential and all kinds appear to be carnivorous in their habits.

3. PARASITES.—We now come to those carnivores known as parasites.* Parasitic insects are believed to have evolved from predatory ancestors and in some cases there is not very much to distinguish a predator from a parasite. But predators, as we have seen, seek out and devour other animals that form their prey. Parasites live on or within the bodies of other animals known as their hosts. A predator normally devours a number of prey in the course of its life whereas a parasite lives on (or within) the body of a single host.

Parasites are often grouped under two categories. These are the *true parasites* and the *parasitoids*.

In the category of true parasites are Fleas, Lice, Bed-bugs and their like. They suck the blood or other tissues of their hosts but very rarely kill them. Their hosts in fact are almost always birds or mammals and are consequently very much larger than themselves. A single host, more often than not, supports a number of individual parasites that enter into a sort of life relationship with it and consequently it develops a tolerance to their presence.

The parasitoids are very different. They include the Ichneumon-flies, the Chalcid Wasps and the Tachinid-flies. Their hosts are other insects and not so very much larger than themselves. They only lead a parasitic life as larvae and in the adult condition they are free-living insects mostly found on flowers, about herbage, etc. Para-sitoids usually begin by feeding on the blood or other body fluids but eventually they devour the other tissues and bring about the death of their hosts. In their early stages they abstain from injuring any vital parts : it is only when they are nearing the end of their growth period that they set to and devour the viscera and other essential organs.

True parasites are a motley crowd of mostly rather unpleasant creatures, although many of them have highly interesting biographies. With few exceptions they are external parasites or, in other words, they live on the outside of the bodies of their hosts. Some of them such as the Lice reside more or less permanently on their hosts. Others such as Fleas and Bed-bugs live intermittently on their hosts, without passing their whole lives on them. They are thus intermediate between free-living blood-suckers and true parasites.

True parasites are for the most part tough-skinned customers. To have a thick tough cuticle is a very definite asset that proves its worth when the host scratches itself vigorously, or bites itself, or rubs against outside objects. After all it is only by such means that it can relieve the irritation caused by such disturbance of its tranquillity. Very well, a tough skin then saves the lives of many such parasites. Also, they are drastically flattened in body-form. Most of them take after the Bed-bug and are flattened from above as if they had been trodden upon. This enables them to cling closer to the body of their host. The Fleas, however, found it to their advantage to develop a side-to-side compression. This certainly allows them to make their way among the hairs or feathers covering their hosts' bodies.

All true parasites have developed strong claws for holding on with, and many of them, like the Sheep-ked (*Melophagus ovinus*) and the Fleas, have completely lost their wings. The Lice have done the same and the Bed-bug has only mere vestiges of its fore-wings left. After all wings are not of much use, and are liable to be an encumbrance to any insect that spends the whole or the greater part of its life among feathers or hair. For this same reason eyes are not important and are either reduced to small proportions or lost altogether.

These parasites illustrate the fallacy that evolution always implies progress. In order to fit themselves for their restricted lives on their hosts we have just seen that they have sacrificed their powers of flight and often of vision also. Perhaps the most curious of all these degenerates are the Bat-parasites that form the small family Nycteribiidae. They are spider-like blind wingless Flies with long legs, that spend their lives among the fur of Bats, whose blood they suck. There are only

PLATE 25

a. Queen Hornet, *Vespa crabro*

b. Queen Wasp, *Vespula germanica*

c. Caterpillars of Sawfly, *Phymatocera aterrima*, on Solomon's Seal

d. Spangle galls caused by *Neuroterus quercus baccarum* f. *lenticularis* on Oak

(a, b, temperature controlled)

WASPS AND THEIR ALLIES (× 1½)

Photographs by S. BEAUFOY

PLATE 26

a, Longicorns, *Stenocorus meridianus* (black form) (etherised)

b. Caterpillars of Large White Butterfly with cocoons of the parasitic Ichneumon-fly, *Apanteles* (Family *Braconidae*)

c. Musk-beetle, *Aromia moschata* (etherised)

d. Seed-capsules of Figwort and four cocoons of *Cionus* Weevils

(All slightly reduced in size)

PARASITES AND BEETLES

Photographs by S. BEAUFOY

two species in this country, each about $\frac{1}{8}$ in. long, tawny in colour and about as " unflylike " as one can imagine. Among other wingless parasitic Flies the Sheep-ked is very common and is often wrongly called " Sheep-tick " (Ticks are 8-legged creatures allied to Spiders). The Bee-louse (*Braula coeca*) is an anomalous creature that forms a family of its own and is quite different from any other Diptera. It lives on the bodies of Hive-bees, chiefly workers and queens. I once found 14 examples of *Braula* on a single queen. *Braula* does not suck blood : when it wants a meal it moves right on to the very front of the bee's head but whether it feeds on the saliva exuded by the bee or on the honey as it is being taken up, has not been properly ascertained. The larvae form mines or burrows on the inside of the wax capping that closes the honey-cells of the comb.

Fleas for some reason or other provoke amusement ; most folk are quite unaware of the devastation they continue to inflict upon humanity. The Indian Plague Commission made it quite clear that the Bacillus causing Bubonic Plague is transmitted from man to man by means of Fleas. The kind most usually responsible is the Rat-flea. Bubonic Plague is a fatal disease of rats. When the dead bodies of these animals start cooling the Fleas leave them, just as rats leave a sinking ship, and seek other hosts. In this way they often take up a temporary abode on man and transmit the disease to their new victim.

As in all true parasites among insects, both sexes of Fleas are bloodsuckers. Most kinds of mammals have their own private kinds of Fleas but while these insects keep generally to their particular hosts this habit is not always a rigid one. The Human Flea, for instance, is also common on goats and pigs and sometimes infests farmyards. Its original hosts may have been the fox and the badger, which still often harbour it. It has been suggested that cave-dwelling man acquired the Human Flea originally from those animals. This particular kind of Flea has considerable power of discrimination for it shows a definite but unflattering preference for particular persons.

The dog has its special Flea and so has the cat : the two kinds of Fleas are often found on both these animals. The domestic cat sometimes returns from its nocturnal marauding with Rabbit-fleas among its fur which provide testimony as to how it has spent its time. The hedgehog is endowed with a specially large Flea and I have never seen so many Fleas on any animals as on young hedgehogs. The domestic fowl, which came from the Orient, has acquired its species of Flea originally from Tits : this particular kind will suck human blood when hungry.

Many naturalists rear batches of caterpillars in order to obtain the resulting Butterflies or Moths. But as often as not they suffer disappointment when some of their treasures die prematurely before transforming. Instead there appear either some rather ordinary looking Flies or other unwanted creatures of very different mien. The first reaction is to wonder how on earth these intruders gained entry into a securely closed box or vessel. Eventually it transpires that they have gained entry because they were already present in their larval, or grub stages within the caterpillars at the time the latter were collected. They have gone on living amid the blood and fat-body of their hosts until they had the urge to gnaw their way out through the skin. When this happened they were fully grown and ultimately gave rise to the alien creatures just referred to. We have here good examples of parasitoids, as they are sometimes termed. They might well be called internal predators or fatal parasites for the reason that their feeding activities nearly always culminate in the destruction of their hosts (Pl. XX [p. 171], XVIII [p. 163] Fig. b, 26 [p. 143] Fig. b).

There are several thousand species of these parasitoids in Britain and their host-relationships provide some of the most interesting chapters in biology. They are members of two orders only—Hymenoptera and Diptera. Their hosts are other insects which they may parasitise in any stage of growth from the egg onwards. There are very few groups of insects whose species are not attacked, some more heavily than others, by one or more kinds of these parasites. The latter rank in fact as one of the most efficient natural checks upon the unrestricted multiplication of insect life. Among Hymenoptera the most characteristic parasites are the Ichneumons and the Chalcid Wasps along with their allies. Dipterous parasites belong in the main to a very large family of bristly Flies known as the Tachinidae. Ichneumon-flies, it may be added, attracted the notice of the early naturalists who believed them to be generated from the tissues of their hosts in some mysterious way. It is rather remarkable that this fallacy was corrected as long ago as 1671 by a Cambridge naturalist named Martin Lister (1638–1712) who showed by his own observations that Ichneumon-flies proceed from eggs laid in caterpillars or other hosts.

Ichneumon-flies comprise two distinct though related groups of Hymenoptera, the families Ichneumonidae and Braconidae. There

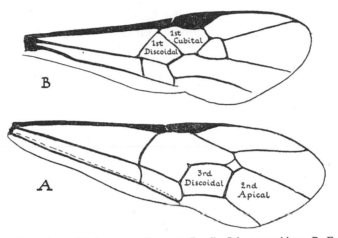

FIG. 30A-B.—Fore-wings of Ichneumon-flies: A, Family Ichneumonidae; B, Family Braconidae.

are many species of both found in Britain. On referring to Text-Fig. 30 it will be seen that differences in the venation of the fore-wings make it easy to discriminate between the two families.

One of the commonest members of the family Braconidae is *Apanteles glomeratus* (Pl. V, p. 46, Fig. c). It is an abundant parasite of the caterpillars of the Large Cabbage White Butterfly; it much less often attacks those of the Small Cabbage White. As the species is small in proportion to the size of the host a considerable number —over one hundred—can find sustenance in a single caterpillar. The female *Apanteles* pierces the skin of the caterpillar by means of her ovipositor and introduces her eggs in this way. The larvae on hatching feed upon the fat-body of their host and avoid the vital organs. When fully-grown they gnaw their way out throught the skin (Pl. XVIII, p. 163, Fig. b) and this happens just at the time the host caterpillar has spun its silken pad to which the pupa would normally become attached. But it never changes into a pupa: it dies instead, and the *Apanteles* grubs spin yellow cocoons surrounding its remains (Pl. 26, p. 143, Fig. b). A large number of the Cabbage White caterpillars will escape attack by *Apanteles* but they are liable to suffer heavy mortality from birds and disease. Those that survive all such adverse influences

are not, however, out of danger. There is a small dark-coloured
Chalcid Wasp known as *Pteromalus puparum* that specialises in laying
its eggs in pupae—it never seems to deposit them in caterpillars. As
the Frenchman F. Picard was the first to notice, the female *Pteromalus*
will settle down beside a caterpillar that is about to pupate, it may be
for several hours, and just wait until the event comes off. When the
transformation has taken place she mounts the pupa, stabs her

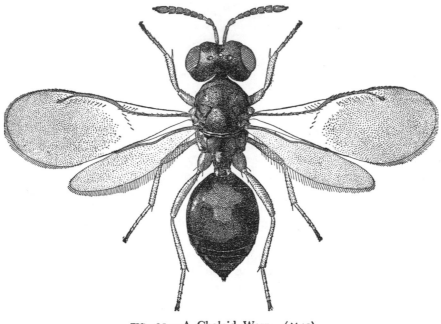

FIG. 31.—A Chalcid Wasp. (×40)

egg-laying tool into its vitals and deposits a number of eggs within.

At this point it must be mentioned that the Chalcid Wasps are very different in their appearance from Ichneumons. For one thing they are much smaller : further, they are of stouter build and often have brilliant metallic coloration not displayed by Ichneumons. The venation in Chalcid Wasps is very characteristic since it is reduced to a single vein along the front margin of each wing (Text-Fig. 31).

Having gone this far, we must complete the story of *Apanteles*. This insect has enemies of its own to contend with. Its larvae are by no means safe from attack because they are hidden away inside the bodies of unfortunate caterpillars. There are, in fact, other parasites that are real experts at detecting their presence. They have no scruples about driving an ovipositor through the skin and tissues of a caterpillar in order to reach the *Apanteles* larvae within. These enemies are literally parasites of parasites, or hyperparasites as they are termed. If a number of the sulphur yellow cocoons of *Apanteles glomeratus* be collected off garden fences and other situations some of them will most likely yield hyperparasites instead of their rightful owners. The small Ichneumon-fly *Hemiteles nanus* is the kind most likely to be present.

The reader needs to bear in mind that *Apanteles* is a direct or primary parasite of the caterpillar in question. The *Hemiteles* on the other hand is a secondary parasite of that same host : in other words, it does not parasitise it directly but through the primary parasite *Apanteles*. The same kind of caterpillar has also tertiary parasites associated with it. These are small Chalcid Wasps that are direct or primary parasites of the *Hemiteles*. Proof of this is obtained when a number of *Hemiteles* larvae are dissected and the Chalcid larvae are found inside them. We must therefore acknowledge the aptness of Jonathan Swift's hackneyed doggerel :—

> So, naturalists observe, a flea
> Hath smaller fleas that on him prey ;
> And these have smaller fleas to bite 'em,
> And so proceed *ad infinitum*.

We may review the situation as a whole in so far as the Large Cabbage White Butterfly is concerned. The best data available are those of J. E. Moss (1933),* who calculated that out of every 10,000 young caterpillars only about 32 Butterflies result, as shown in the table overleaf.

Cause of Mortality	Mortality	No. remaining
———	——	10,000
Disease of caterpillars	5,917=59·17%	4,083
Apanteles	3,438=84·21%	645
Disease of pupae	174=27·0 %	471
Pteromalus	14= 3·0 %	457
Birds	425=93·0 %	32

It is probable that the mortality due to *Pteromalus* is higher than given as the calculations were based only upon 86 pupae. On the other hand, that ascribed to disease is probably higher than what actually obtains. This, however, is offset by the fact that no account is taken of the destruction of the Butterflies' eggs or of destruction of the caterpillars by Tachinid Flies, both of which have an appreciable influence. Hence we may accept the final result as a more or less good approximation to what actually happens in the field. If it were not for these combined agencies of natural control the cultivation of vegetables of the cabbage tribe would not be worth while.

Aphids or Green-fly are often heavily attacked by parasites, especially by those belonging to the genus *Aphidius*, which, like *Apanteles*, belongs to the family Braconidae. Some species of *Aphidius* are often easy to find and to rear and are to be sought for among the leaves of Aphid-infested fruit-trees or other plants. The *Aphidius* lays its eggs singly, one in each suitable Aphid. When the larva is fully grown, and has consumed most of its host's tissues, it makes a slit in the skin of the Aphid's belly. It then weaves a warp of silk so as to fasten its dead victim down to the leaf and uses the empty skin as a cocoon within which it turns to a pupa. The straw-coloured skins of parasitised Aphids are often very common among colonies of the living insects : each harbours an *Aphidius* within. When the adult *Aphidius* is ready to emerge from its defunct host it makes a circular hole through which it issues into the world (Pl. XXI, p. 194, Fig. c). It is thus easy to ascertain whether a dead Aphid still harbours its slayer or whether the latter has emerged and flown away.

The genus *Praon* is closely allied to *Aphidius* and has much the same life-history up to the time when its members are ready to turn into pupae. Just before this crisis in its career occurs the *Praon* crawls out of its host and makes a curious tent-like cocoon for itself. And instead of fastening the dead Aphid host down to a leaf the *Praon* surmounts its cocoon with the dead skin of its victim.

The Chalcid Wasps (Text-Fig. 31) are another immense group of parasites. Many of them only attack the eggs of insects, others are exclusively larval parasites, or as we have already seen, pupal parasites. There are a few kinds that attack adult insects only, while many others are hyperparasites. Thus, they exhibit many different habits.

Among the Chalcid Wasps are the most minute of all insects—species in which each individual undergoes its whole metamorphosis within the egg of some other insect. The Mymaridae or Fairy-flies are the smallest of all (Pl. V, p. 46, Fig. b) ; some of them are mere specks of life less than $\frac{1}{50}$ in. long ; yet they manage to destroy an immense number of insect eggs. They seem especially fond of those of small Hemiptera like the Leaf-hoppers. One kind, *Caraphractus cinctus*, parasitises the eggs of Water-boatmen and is quite expert at swimming under water by means of its tiny hair-fringed wings.

The family Trichogrammidae are Chalcids that are likewise egg-parasites and are consequently also very minute creatures. The best known belong to the genus *Trichogramma* which parasitises almost all sorts of insect eggs, especially those of Moths. *Trichogramma evanescens* uses the eggs of more than 150 different kinds of insects, belonging to seven orders, as its hosts. G. Salt* has made a detailed enquiry into its habits, rearing it mostly from eggs of the Grain Moth (*Sitotroga*). When she discovers an insect egg to her liking the female walks over it and explores its surface preparatory to getting her ovipositor to work and laying an egg in its interior. This perambulation causes her to leave an odour trail behind on the host eggs which can be perceived by another female following on later. The picking up of this scent warns her that the egg is preoccupied and she therefore seeks another. If the odour be washed off the host egg the second female is unable to perceive that the egg has been already attacked but after merely pricking it with the ovipositor, she immediately becomes aware of its being already parasitised and leaves it without depositing her egg. If, however, she has very few hosts wherein to lay her eggs she will withhold them in her body for a time. Ultimately she can restrain herself no longer and is forced to lay her eggs in hosts already parasitised. If she has any choice at all she will select the largest eggs she can find for the purpose. All her progeny will perish if the host eggs be too small to provide the necessary food, or the individual progeny will emerge dwarfed or imperfect.

Salt also presented *Trichogramma* with the eggs of two different hosts simultaneously and found that the parasite always showed preference for the larger kind. Thus it preferred those of the Mediterranean Flour-moth (*Ephestia kühniella*) to the smaller eggs of the Grain-moth; but if the still larger eggs of the Large Yellow Underwing (*Triphaena pronuba*) were provided—they were preferred to those of the Flour-moth. In other trials he found that the eggs of the Bean-weevil (*Acanthoscelides obsoletus*) were preferred to those of the Grain-moth which are of smaller dimensions. The curious thing is that the Bean-weevil eggs are unsuitable for the growth of the parasites' progeny. But the instincts of *Trichogramma* seem to be by no means perfect. Salt was able to fool this parasite unmercifully by giving it false " hosts " such as sand-grains and Lobelia seeds. The creature could not even drive its ovipositor into these unpromising objects but did its best to do so. Apparently the sole reason for the preference showed by *Trichogramma* for these false hosts is because they were larger than the eggs of the Grain-moth. These eggs, it must be added, were available at the same time and in equal numbers to the false " hosts."

A number of years ago a Chalcid Wasp named *Blastothrix sericea* interested me very much. A good deal larger than *Trichogramma*, it is burnished with metallic blue-green. It uses for its host the Brown Scale *Eulecanium coryli*, that lives on the branches of hawthorn (Plate XXI, Figs. a and b) and other trees. What is peculiar about this parasite is the fact that its eggs have long stalks that project through the skin of the host into the open air. It took a little time to prove the reason for this but it eventually transpired that the young larva has but a single pair of breathing pores and these are placed at the tail end of its body. Now when it hatches the young larva remains with its tail end attached to the broken shell of the egg and uses the stalk as a kind of breathing tube. The stalk, it may be added, is specially modified in a way that suggests its being permeable to air.

This curious contrivance brings us to the general subject of respiration in parasites which yields some unexpected facts. Parasites that live on the outside of the bodies of their hosts respire in the usual way by means of breathing-pores along the sides of their bodies—their lives present no special difficulties. But parasites that live inside their hosts are sealed off from the free air and yet they have to breathe somehow. Whilst they are immersed in the blood of their hosts breathing-pores are of little use and are often absent. Instead, they breathe through the skin, after the manner of many aquatic insects, until the host is consumed. The host's blood contains a small amount of dissolved oxygen and this satisfies the meagre needs of such inert creatures as parasites. In the case of *Blastothrix*, however, free air seems to be needed the moment it issues from the eggs and this requirement is met by means of the device already described.

The larvae of the Tachinid Flies are common internal parasites of caterpillars. Their grubs or larvae all feel the need, sooner or later, for free air. This they obtain either by boring through the skin of their host or by breaking into one of its main tracheal tubes. In either case the Tachinid larva forces its tail end, which carries the breathing pores, into the lesion thus made.

It must not be concluded that all parasitoids live immersed in the rich stores of food provided by the tissues of their hosts. Some of them attach themselves to the outsides of their victims, holding on mainly by means of their mouth-parts which perforate the skin. In this situation they obtain all the nourishment they require simply by sucking in the host's blood. The large Ichneumon-fly, *Rhyssa*, mentioned in more detail on p. 214, provides an instance of this way of living. Various other parasitic Hymenoptera lead very similar lives but sooner or later their hosts become exhausted and succumb as the result of the insistent drain upon their vital energies caused by these tormentors.

Among Dipterous parasites the Tachinids are the most important. They are generally very ordinary looking Flies, the smaller kinds being not unlike the House-fly in appearance (Pl. 23, p. 126, Figs. 2, 12). Their life-histories on the other hand betray an extraordinary sequence of events. To begin with, their hosts comprise many groups of animals, including vertebrates. Their most frequent victims are other insects ; those most commonly selected are the caterpillars of Moths and of Saw-flies, but Beetles and Plant-bugs are also attacked. What determines their choice of certain kinds of hosts, when others apparently equally suitable are left untouched, has often puzzled entomologists. Thus, the common species *Compsilura concinnata* parasitises caterpillars belonging to no less than 18 families. As W. R. Thompson has observed, there appears to be no one distinctive character common to all its hosts—neither colour nor pattern : hairiness or absence of hairs ; herbage-feeders, bush-feeders or tree-feeders ; habit, whether gregarious or solitary, diurnal or nocturnal ; specific host food-plants, whether they be Gymnosperms, Monocotyledons, Dicotyledons or Lichens ; odour or absence of odour; presence or absence of urticating hairs, etc. All these features are represented among different hosts. From whatever standpoint this varied assemblage be considered the only feature its members have in common is that they are all hosts of the *Compsilura*. Many Tachinid Flies, however, have a very limited host-range. Thus one kind is only known to use the Common Earwig : others only select a few kinds of solitary Wasps or Bees : the larva of *Melinda* parasitises snails : that of *Pollenia rudis* (see also p. 252) lives in the body of a particular kind of earth-worm, and so on. A peculiar kind of Blow-fly, *Protocalliphora azurea* (Pl. 23, Fig. 6), clad in metallic blue, seeks out the nests of wild birds wherein to deposit her eggs. The larvae attack the nestlings and live by sucking their blood, particularly of sparrows, larks and swallows.

Among Tachinids in general at least five different chains of events may now happen. (1) The eggs, or sometimes the already hatched larvae, are deposited on the skin of the hosts. The larvae bore their way into the interior of their victims where they live by feeding at first on the blood and fat-body and later upon the more vital organs. This happens in the case of *Phryxe vulgaris* which is a common parasite of the caterpillars of the Large Garden White Butterfly and of many other Lepidoptera. Or (2) the female Fly is armed with a kind of piercer with which she perforates the skin of the host and lays an egg or a larva, as the case may be, in its interior. *Compsilura*, mentioned above, practises this innovation. Or (3) the female lays large numbers of very small eggs directly on the food of the future hosts. Some of them become swallowed by their victims, and the resulting larvae bore their way through the stomach wall to develop in some more suitable part of the body. Or (4) the eggs are laid in situations frequented by their hosts. The newly hatched larvae are very active and seek out their victims. Having discovered those to their liking, they bore their way into the interior of these hosts and complete their lives feeding upon the tissues. The two robust Flies shown in Figs. 12 and 13 develop from larvae that lead lives of this kind. Or (5) numerous eggs are laid under much the same conditions but the young larvae remain stationary. They stand upright on their hind extremity and when any moving object approaches they wave themselves about in a rotatory manner, ever striving to make contact with the kind of host within which they are enabled to grow and develop. Many come to a bad end either through never encountering a host of any kind or attaching themselves to one of the wrong sort. The parent Fly makes due allowances for such perils of life by laying so many eggs that wastage is well provided for.

It would be possible to devote a whole chapter to the lives of these sombre-looking Flies but pressure of space prevents this. We owe much to the Jesuit Father J. Pantel, of the University of Louvain, who devoted many years to unravelling the intricacies of the structure and biology of these insects. His published memoirs that adorn the pages of the Belgian journal *La Cellule* bear witness to his talents and industry.

SCAVENGERS

Scavengers are the members of nature's own sanitation department. Since they feed upon dead or decaying plant or animal substances they play a most important part in the economy of life. Their activities speed up the decomposition of such organic materials and promote their dissolution into substances that enrich the soil and finally become essential constituents of plant food.

As was pointed out in referring to fungus-feeders, it is not always possible to distinguish clearly between those insects that feed upon living substances and those that feed upon the same substances in a decaying condition, because there are some insects that feed upon both. Scavenging insects seem undoubtedly to have been derived from those that eat their food in the fresh living condition. They may be grouped into two series according to whether their food is of vegetable or animal origin.

Vegetarian scavengers are found almost everywhere. Every heap of rotting weeds or other plants has its quota. The leaf deposits carpeting woods and forests, rotting trees, and the humus of the soil are populated by many scavenging insects—mostly Beetles and their larvae and the larvae of Fungus Midges and of other Flies. This miscellaneous assortment can be passed by and we come to dung-feeders—in special those that find their wherewithal in the dung of our domestic and other herbivorous animals. Dung is mainly vegetable residues impregnated with secretions of the alimentary canal of the animals concerned. It provides the necessary diet for many insects that are found nowhere else. The most notable are the Scarabaeid beetles and their larvae. Among them the bulky Dor-beetles (*Geotrupes*) attract attention on warm summer evenings by their blundering flight and loud hum. *Geotrupes stercorarius* (Pl. 18, p. 79, Fig. 16) is often seen lying on its back with struggling legs, trying to right itself, with its amethystine violet underside revealed. This Beetle has been named the " Lousy Watchman" by country folk because it is so often infested beneath by a species of Mite. The latter inserts its mouth-parts between the Beetle's plates of mail so as to pierce the skin and obtain a blood-meal. The female Beetle burrows about 18 in. below a batch of cow- or horse-dung, and each burrow is filled at its blind end with a plug of dung which serves as food for the larva. The habits of *Geotrupes* recall lines by Arthur Waley which remind the present writer of this insect :

> Are you not he who, born
> Upon the dung-heap, coveted the sky,
> The clean and open air :

Another kind, the Minotaur Beetle, with its characteristically horned male (Plate 18, Fig. 8) is found in sandy places frequented by rabbits. It digs deep tunnels in the ground, provisioning them with the dung of these animals, in which it lays its eggs.

The Yellow Dung-fly (*Scatophaga stercoraria*) is another abundant scavenger, in fact it is one of the commonest of British insects. During the summer it frequents patches of fresh cattle-dung in large numbers. The yellowish hairy-bodied males are more likely to attract notice than the duller, greenish and non-hairy females (Plate 23, p. 126, Fig. 4). The eggs are laid in the dung, where the larvae feed and come to maturity. There is little doubt that these grubs help a great deal in bringing about the rapid disintegration of the unsavoury material wherein they live. Various other larvae of obscure-looking Flies also abound in dung. Not all are scavengers : some are predators that devour the real dung-feeders and in this way they tend to redress the balance, otherwise overcrowding would only too often result.

The large glistening black Fly, *Mesembrina meridiana*, that has conspicuous yellow-brown bases to its wings (Plate 23, Fig. 11) is of very general occurrence. It is essentially a sun-lover, the male resting on paths and fences while nearby the female is probably on the dung-patch. Her eggs are unusually large and according to D. Keilin she only lays about six in her whole life. The larva breaks out of the shell the moment the egg is deposited and comes to maturity in the course of a few days.

Among scavengers of animal carcasses the Burying Beetles (*Necrophorus*) are among the largest (Pl. 27, p. 158, Fig. d). They are strong fliers ; several kinds are adorned with orange bands, whereas others are uniformly black. These insects may be obtained in summer by setting baits in the form of dead rats, birds or rabbits out in the open where the soil is light ; the heads of poultry are also a good lure. When visited a few days later, if all goes well, the baits will be found partly sunk in the soil with the Beetles at work beneath them. Most of the digging is done with the legs, aided by the head which shovels the soil away. The object of burying the corpses is to provide a supply of food in a moist condition, in which the larvae may develop.

It is a matter of common knowledge that certain kinds of Flies are also attracted to dead flesh. Their scavenging propensities are most strongly evoked by any corpse when it begins to give off a gamey odour. The rôle of such Flies is to purge the land of death's impurities and in this good work they ably assist the Burying Beetles and the Carrion Beetles (*Silpha*). Sooner or later Rove-beetles and others join the community. The combined activities of such a population speedily reduce a carcass to skin and bone. They thus pave the way for the *Dermestes* Beetle and other late-comers that complete the task of disintegration.

Three kinds of Flies are particularly important as scavengers. They are the Bluebottles or Blow-flies (*Calliphora*), the Greenbottles (*Lucilia*) and the Flesh-flies (*Sarcophaga*). All three kinds are featured on Pl. 15, p. 74. Everybody knows the Bluebottle that scours the larder in search of meat and viands wherein to deposit her eggs, or settles on window panes. The glittering and magnificently metallic Greenbottles rarely forsake the sunshine for the interior of dwelling-houses and the Flesh-flies are much less prone to enter than Bluebottles. It would weary the patience of the reader to describe the detailed economy of these flies. It will suffice to say that their larvae are quite unable to chew the flesh that forms their staple food. They require it to be in the state of a broth or fluid before they can swallow it. What they do is to liquefy it beforehand : this they effect by means of enzymes or ferments that dissolve meat and other proteins before consumption. At one time it was thought that bacteria were responsible for this process but we now know that the larva of the Greenbottle-fly, for instance, is still able to prepare its meal in this way when reared under entirely aseptic conditions that exclude all micro-organisms.

Having got thus far it will be convenient to take stock of the contents of these two chapters on feeding habits. This can be done most advantageously by means of a tabular summary as given below.

1. **Omnivores.** General feeders upon both animal and plant materials.

2. **Vegetarians.** Feeders upon plants or on substances of a vegetable nature. They may be divided into :—

    a. Leaf- and shoot-feeders and defoliators.

    b. Leaf- and stem-miners.

    c. Suckers of plant sap.

    d. Fruit- and seed-feeders.

    e. Gall-formers.

    f. Bark-feeders.

    g. Wood-borers.

    h. Root-feeders.

    i. Fungus-feeders.

    j. Feeders on flour, grain and other dried plant-products.

3. **Carnivores.** Feeders on flesh and other animal tissues. They are divided into :—

    a. Predators or kinds that seek out and devour their prey, consuming many during their individual lives.

    b. Blood-suckers or kinds that take occasional meals of blood.

    c. Parasites or kinds that live on and at the expense of a single individual animal known as the host. Insect parasites are divisible into :—

        *c.*I. True or non-fatal parasites whose hosts are vertebrate animals much larger than themselves.

        *c.*II. Parasitoids or fatal parasites whose hosts are relatively small and are usually other insects.

4. **Scavengers.** Feeders upon dead and decaying organic substances. They are divisible into :—

    a. Feeders upon substances that are of vegetable origin.

    b. Feeders upon substances of animal origin.

INSECTS AND
BIOLOGICAL CONTROL

A PEST is an animal or plant that has become too abundant for man's comfort or convenience, or has even become a danger to his interests. Rats on a farm, for example, only too often satisfy this definition. The farmer who keeps terriers for the purpose of reducing the population of these rodents is practising biological control. The idea is to arrange for one kind of living organism to keep down the numbers of another and unwanted kind. But biological control is also practised by man in various other simple homely ways such as by keeping the domestic cat to kill off the mice ; by introducing snails in an aquarium to feed on the green algal growth that obscures the glass ; by keeping Golden Orfe or other fish in a garden pond to prey upon the larvae of Mosquitoes and Midges that would otherwise develop in unwanted numbers.

Under ordinary circumstances animals and plants are kept in a state of balance or numerical equilibrium by various natural influences. The most important of these controlling factors are food supply, disease, parasites and predators and weather conditions. The state of balance, of course, is not an actual stationary condition but is always fluctuating, usually on a small scale, about a common mean. Sometimes owing to scarcity of parasites or predators, or owing to unusually favourable weather the fluctuation is on a much larger scale and a particular kind of insect or other creature may multiply to such an extent as to become, temporarily, a pest. But sooner or later this state of affairs becomes redressed. Once an animal begins to increase in numbers more food becomes available for its parasites and predators. Yet the amount of food for the animal itself decreases and competition among its individuals for whatever is available becomes more intense. A general increase in natural enemies follows and ultimately they gain the ascendancy over the host species and bring down its numbers to more normal conditions.

Probably the most important of all agencies that upset the state of balance in nature is man himself. By his own activities he has again and again unwittingly converted an inoffensive animal or plant into a pest. The reason for this change is because man has provided suitable conditions for a particular species to multiply in a way it would never have been able to achieve if left to the undisturbed action of natural forces. Having thus brought about a state of affairs inimical to his own activities man has, therefore, to devise means of controlling the situation. Maybe he will try spraying with some chemical compound, or fumigation, or altering the usual method of cultivation, or some other method. Quite often these efforts prove unsuccessful or have been found impracticable or uneconomical to put into effect. It was under such circumstances that biological control first came to be tried out. According to W. A. Riley it was Erasmus Darwin, the grandfather of Charles Darwin, who was the first to point out the possibilities of applying biological control. In his *Phytologia, or the Philosophy of Agriculture and Gardening* (1800 ; p. 356) he suggested that Aphids might be counteracted by the propagation and distribution of their greatest enemies—the larvae of Hover-flies (see p. 132).

The special circumstances wherein biological control is most likely to be successful is when some particular kind of insect or plant has become accidentally introduced into a country it did not previously inhabit. Very often, in its new surroundings, an alien species finds itself in a sort of El Dorado, where controlling influences that held it under restraint in its original home are either ineffective or absent. Thus freed from natural controlling agents, the newcomer is liable to multiply to an extent that marks it out as a pest of the first order. The introduction of the Gypsy-moth, the Brown-tail Moth and the Japanese Beetle into North America ; of the Prickly Pear into Australia ; and of the Bramble into New Zealand, are examples of this kind.*

The aim of biological control is to redress the balance thus upset by introducing one or other of the missing biological factors, usually a parasite or a predator. It sounds all very simple and easy, but this is very far from the truth. While thrilling and most spectacular results have been achieved by means of biological control the method is not a universal panacea as the misinformed have been too prone to regard it.

Various attempts have been made to increase and distribute native parasites and predators, as suggested by Erasmus Darwin, but the results have been very disappointing. Such a procedure is not likely to be effective unless it be carried out by general agreement among

PLATE 27

a. Common Cockchafer, *Melolontha melolontha* (× 1)

b. Weevils, *Cionus scrophulariae*, on seed-capsules of Figwort (× 2)

c. Leaf-beetles, *Donacia semicuprea* (× 2) [etherised]

d. Burying-beetles: *Necrophorus vespillo* (above), *Necrophorus humator* (below) (× 1) [etherised]

COLEOPTERA OR BEETLES

PLATE 28

PLATE 28   159

INSECTS RESEMBLING BEES OR WASPS (× 1)

1
NARCISSUS-FLY
Merodon equestris

7
HOVER-FLY
Volucella bombylans

12
HOVER-FLY
Volucella bombylans

19
BEE-FLY
Bombylius major

13
DRONE-FLY
Eristalis intricarius

2
BEETLE
Trichius fasciatus

8
ROBBER-FLY
Laphria flava

20
HOVER-FLY
Criorhina floccosa

14
Conops flavipes

3
WASP-BEETLE
Clytus arietis

9
ROBBER-FLY
Asilus crabroniformis

21
HOVER-FLY
Helophilus pendulus

15
Conops quadrifasciata

4
HOVER-FLY
Sericomyia borealis

10
HOVER-FLY
Myiatropa florea

16
HOVER-FLY
Syrphus ribesii

22
OX WARBLE-FLY
Hypoderma bovis

5
HOVER-FLY
Arctophila fulva

11
HOVER-FLY
Scaeva pyrastri

17
HOVER-FLY
Chrysotoxum festivum

23
ICHNEUMON-FLY
Amblyteles palliatorius

18
BROAD-BORDERED BEE
HAWK-MOTH
Hemaris fuciformis

6
HORNET CLEARWING MOTH
Sesia apiformis

N.B. Figs. 7 and 12 are two different colour forms of the same species.

cultivators on a large scale and over a wide area. Individual efforts alone could only affect a fraction of the insect population and with no appreciable result to show for the expenditure of perhaps a great deal of labour. What seems easier, for instance, than to collect Ladybirds when they mass together prior to hibernation, or even to set up suitable quarters wherein they might congregate? When the due season arrives they might then be liberated in large numbers where they are most wanted. In practice it doesn't work because Ladybirds do not necessarily settle down in the districts where they are liberated. They are too prone to distribute themselves over wide areas and in this way nullify any preconceived plans.

In the uniform and confined surroundings of glasshouses biological control has worked very successfully in the case of the Greenhouse White-fly (*Trialeurodes vaporariorum*). This insect is destructive to Cucumbers, Tomatoes and various ornamental plants grown under glass. It has been known as a pest in England for about 40 years and has come to be regarded as a British insect. The probability is, however, that it is an immigrant from some warm country—Brazil has been suggested as being its real home. Anyway, it does not breed, except under the most favourable conditions, out of doors in England during the winter.

For a number of years past this insect has been controlled by fumigation, either with the dangerous hydrocyanic acid gas or by means of the more expensive tetrachlorethane. More recently the use of a minute Chalcid Wasp—*Encarsia formosa*—less than $\frac{1}{40}$ in. long has proved of greater advantage and much simpler for the grower to manipulate. Like its host, *Encarsia* is an alien and probably entered Britain along with nursery plants from abroad. A tropical origin seems to be indicated since it requires a heated glasshouse during winter to ensure its survival. It was first noticed in England in a small greenhouse at Elstree, Herts, in July 1926. E. R. Speyer, entomologist to the Experimental and Research Station, Cheshunt, was the first to rear this parasite and breed up a stock of it. By September of that year sufficient numbers became available for distribution among various houses at the Experimental Station and a considerable degree of control of the pest was achieved. In 1927 the White-fly was entirely wiped out by the *Encarsia* in certain Cucumber houses, and later a successful result was obtained in tomato nurseries. Since then consignments of the parasite have been sent all over

England : also to the Channel Islands, Canada and South Australia.

An interesting thing about this parasite is that it reproduces by parthenogenesis (p. 217), males being rare and probably functionless. It is the immature White-fly, or " scales " as they are often termed, that are attacked.   Sooner or later those that become parasitised show up very distinctly owing to the fact that they turn black (Plate XXI, p. 194, Fig. d).

In order to control an infestation of the White-fly, application should be made to the Cheshunt Experimental Station for a supply of the parasite.   What the grower will receive is a boxful of tomato leaves bearing parasitised " scales."   On their receipt the leaves are tied into convenient bunches and hung up at intervals in the glasshouses where the White-fly is prevalent.   Here they are left for about three weeks so as to ensure that all the parasites have emerged.   They freely distribute themselves by flight and in this way spread to other houses in the nursery.   The blackening of the immature White-flies is usually to be noticed about 14 to 21 days after the introduction of the parasite material.   A charge of 2s. 6d. is made for a consignment for a small greenhouse or a conservatory and 5s. for a box of material sufficient for a large glasshouse.   The demand for the parasite is usually greater than the available supply can meet.   Much can be done to further the good work if those who have already been able to clear their houses of the White-fly will distribute parasitised material among their neighbours.   Fellows of the Royal Horticultural Society are also able to obtain consignments, under the same conditions as at Cheshunt, by application to the Director, R.H.S. Gardens, Wisley, Ripley, Surrey.

It is important to note that the *Encarsia* needs a night temperature above 55° F. to maintain itself, and cannot do so unless the young stages of the White-fly are present, even if the adults are abundant. Very little breeding goes on between the months of October and April and consequently application for consignments of the parasite should be made between late April and early September.   It is desirable to establish the parasite as early as possible, so that it can multiply in sufficient time should the infestation it has to cope with be severe.

Another insect that is subject to biological control in many parts of the world is the Woolly Aphid or American Blight (*Eriosoma lanigerum*) of the Apple (Pl. 17, p. 78, Fig. d).   The name American Blight perpetuates an impression, never properly verified, that the insect originally came into Britain from the United States. Owing to its dense wool-like covering this insect is difficult to control by insecticides and the discovery in North America of the Chalcid parasite *Aphelinus mali* has greatly relieved the situation in some countries. This beneficial parasite has now been introduced into many lands where it has become established. In some cases, as in New Zealand, for example, where the pest was particularly severe, the *Aphelinus* has reduced its numbers enormously. In South America, parts of Australia and in Tasmania its introduction has also proved highly successful. On the continent of Europe it has not taken so readily to new conditions of life and in some countries little or no benefit has resulted from its introduction. In 1923 the Ministry of Agriculture attempted to establish the parasite in England. Colonies derived from stock originally of North American descent were obtained from France. These multiplied with great rapidity under artificial conditions and a considerable stock was thus built up. Liberations of the parasite were made in 1924 in a number of selected localities in southern England. Further attempts were made to establish it in 1928–31 and local control of the Woolly Aphid resulted in several localities for a limited period. Numerous failures, however, make it clear that the *Aphelinus* is difficult to establish under English conditions for it does not take kindly to our climate. If left to its own devices it seems likely to become effective only occasionally and under very favourable circumstances. In order to keep the Woolly Aphid permanently under restraint colonies of the parasites would probably have to be kept going under protected conditions throughout the winter, as is done with regard to *Encarsia*. This would enable the insect to be re-introduced periodically among infested orchards at favourable times.

England, however, is not the country to look for outstanding achievements in biological control. For these we must range further afield. We are fortunate, possibly owing to its humid and very change-able climate, in that so few alien pests of importance have been able to establish themselves in England. In regard to our indigenous insect pests a belief has grown up that the highest degree of biological control is already being exerted by native parasites and predators. Under such circumstances the introduction of other kinds would be ineffective. While this opinion may be justified it must be pointed out that it is not an ascertained fact but an unproven theory. In different parts of Europe there are different parasites of the same individual species of

Plate XVII

BEETLE-BORINGS IN WOOD AND BARK (× 1)

a Tunnellings of the Death-Watch Beetle, *Xestobium rufovill-osum*, in an Oak beam.

W. TAMS

b Galleries made by the Two-toothed Bark-beetle, *Pityogenes bidentatus*, in Pine. A central pairing chamber is seen with five main galleries radiating from it

W. TAMS

c Piece of Willow wood pierced by tunnels bored by the Longi-corn, *Saperda carcharias*

W. TAMS

d Galleries of Ash Bark-beetle, *Hylesinus fraxini*, showing two horizontal main galleries arising from a very small central pairing chamber (P). The larval galleries are very short and end as pupal cells which appear as small rounded holes

W. TAMS

Plate XVIII

S. BEAUFOY

a Larva of Garden Swift Moth, *Hepialus lupulinus*

S. BEAUFOY

b Larvae of the Ichneumon-fly, *Apanteles glomeratus* (Family Braconidae), spinning their cocoons after issuing from the body of a caterpillar of the Large White Butterfly, *Pieris brassicae* (See also Plate 26b.)

CATERPILLARS AND PARASITES (× 1½)

pest. In some cases it may be that geographical rather than climatic or other barriers have prevented their entry into Britain. It is possible, therefore, that good results might be obtained by the introduction of additional species of beneficial insects from other countries and thereby intensify the biological control of certain pests.

Many of our indigenous parasites have been shipped to other lands in attempts to repress introduced pests in such territories. In 1927 a special parasite-breeding laboratory was established at Farnham Royal in Buckinghamshire under the Imperial Institute of Entomology. During the first nine years of its existence this laboratory (popularly christened the Parasite Zoo) was able to send out, to various parts of the world, over 631 consignments including more than 11,000,000 individual beneficial insects. The latter were all enemies of noxious insects, many of them common in Britain, that had been accidentally introduced and become established in distant lands.

The Wood-wasps (*Sirex*) may be taken as an example. In Britain they are not very important pests and are subject to a considerable degree of biological control, notably by the large Ichneumon-fly *Rhyssa persuasoria*, discussed on p. 214. In New Zealand *Sirex noctilio* has become firmly established and its increase in numbers caused the government of that country anxiety over the welfare of the Dominion's pine woods. The Imperial Institute of Entomology was approached with the request for an investigation of the control of *Sirex* by biological means. As the result a start was made in 1928–29 by shipping about 1,300 *Rhyssa* larvae, collected in English woodlands, to New Zealand. The larvae were extracted out of infested tree-trunks, placed in gelatine capsules filled with sawdust, and transmitted successfully to their destination. When the adult Ichneumon-flies emerged they were liberated in infested areas. Reports indicate that the parasite is now well established in both islands of the dominion. Further consignments of *Rhyssa* larvae were sent out in 1931, and there is good reason to expect that adequate biological control will be the ultimate result of this work.

The accidental entry of the Small Cabbage White Butterfly (*Pieris rapae*) into New Zealand in 1929 presented a problem to vegetable-growers as the Butterfly spread very rapidly. By 1935–36 the invasion of that country was stated to be complete. The introduction of the Chalcid *Pteromalus puparum* (see p. 146), however, seems to have largely controlled this insect in a remarkably short space of time. In the summers of 1932-38 some 500 parasitised pupae of the White Butterfly were sent in cold storage to New Zealand from England. Over 12,000 parasites emerged and nearly 11,000 of these were liberated in the field. The next year further supplies of the Chalcid Wasp were received and liberated. Field surveys made that same year, by collecting pupae of the White Butterfly, showed that 89 per cent of them were parasitised. Since then the Butterfly has been well under control in most districts and affords a striking example of the repression of a pest by biological means. It is only in areas with high rainfall that the Butterfly seems better able to survive than its parasite. This seeming local failure of the *Pteromalus* might be offset by the introduction of some other larval parasites of the White Butterfly.

For a third example we will pass to British Columbia, where the Brown Scale (*Eulecanium coryli*) had become accidentally introduced in 1903. Most likely it came in on shade trees from England and had escaped notice at the time. In the absence of any natural enemy it increased enormously in its new environment. In the coastal region of British Columbia it became especially destructive. The city of Vancouver for instance repeatedly had to adopt oil spraying in order to check the premature leaf-fall of the maple and other shade trees attacked by the Scale-insect. In England this particular species is well controlled by parasites, among which the Chalcid *Blastothrix sericea* (see also p. 150) is the most important. The Scale-insect is not easy to find in England, where it seems to affect Hawthorn more consistently than other trees (Pl. XXI, p. 194, Fig. a). Recourse was made to introducing the *Blastothrix* into British Columbia in 1928. They were sent out in the adult stage and were transmitted in cold storage in glass tubes with split raisins as food. They were shipped to the Canadian Parasite Laboratory at Chatham, Ontario, and from there transhipped to Vancouver. The venture proved an outstandingly successful small-scale experiment in biological control. In the brief period of about four years this Scale-insect has been virtually exterminated from the infested territory.

The history of the many ventures that have been made in biological control, both the successes and the failures, makes an interesting story. But it is outside the scope of this book to pursue the matter further. Anyone who so desires will find references to sources of information in the Documentary Appendix.

One further excursus must, however, be made ; for it is hardly possible to overlook the biological control of noxious plants. It has already been mentioned that alien insects which have entered other countries unaccompanied by their natural enemies, may become firmly established in their new homes and entail great damage to cultivated crops, etc. This being so, surely there is no valid reason why the introduction of suitable kinds of plant-feeding insects, *free from their natural enemies*, should not likewise exercise a destructive effect upon weeds or other unwanted plants. This in fact is the principle that is involved. But it is not so simple as it appears on first impression. Extreme care, for example, must be exercised lest the wrong sort of insect be introduced, i.e. one that may turn its attention to cultivated plants, thus making the remedy perhaps worse than the disease. Exhaustive testing of the feeding propensities of any kind of insect it is contemplated to adopt for the control of pest plants is essential at the very beginning. Also it will be realised that, under the conditions demanded by noxious weed control, parasites and predators assume the opposite rôle to that which they perform in the control of noxious insects. In other words, parasites and predators require to be rigidly excluded in all cases of pest-plant control. Once they gained entry into the new environment they might easily prove impossible to eradicate and a whole campaign might be nullified as the result.

The outstanding example of pest-plant control hails from Australia in connection with those kinds of Cactus known as Prickly Pears. The history of this campaign makes a thrilling story of the application of technical skill in a scientific manner. On account of the ignorance of a well-meaning person (or persons) the Prickly Pear was introduced into Australia in 1787 in order to establish the cochineal industry. Prickly Pears, it may be mentioned, are the hosts upon which the Cochineal Insect grows and thrives. Commercial cochineal is the dried and ground-up remains of this particular kind of insect. Many other sorts of Prickly Pear have found their way into Australia but their origins cannot be traced. The two major pest species are *Opuntia inermis* and *O. stricta*. The rapidity with which these plants spread and increased is one of the botanical wonders of the world. The peak of the invasion was in 1925 when the area occupied by these plants in Queensland and New South Wales was computed to exceed 60,000,000 acres. The problems of control and clearance have been one of cost ; no feasible method is known that would be economically possible when applied to land worth less than £1 per acre. After a long period of inaction the governments concerned turned to men of science to help them out of the predicament. An expedition was sent to visit Mexico and other lands where the particular kinds of cactus live in their original homes. Some 150 different kinds of Cactus-feeding insects were discovered but of these only 12 sorts were ultimately allowed to be introduced into Australia. The scientists were really properly scared by their experience not only of Prickly Pear but of the rabbit and of other immigrants that have since run riot in Australia. They were not going to liberate any new creatures in that land until they had exhaustively tested them on every imaginable kind of plant, lest they might, in time, become unwanted enemies on their own account. What finally solved the Prickly Pear problem was the introduction of a small Moth—*Cactoblastis cactorum*—from the Argentine in 1925. The multiplication and spread of this insect has been little short of miraculous and completely outstripped other cactus-feeding insects that had been introduced. Only 2,750 eggs of *Cactoblastis* were obtained in all from overseas but between 1928 and 1930 about 3,000,000,000 eggs, laid by descendants from the original batch, were distributed in the Prickly Pear areas. The caterpillars feed in companies inside the Cactus tissues, disease organisms quickly follow in their wake and the combined effect results in the reduction of each plant to a rotting mass of pulp. The activities of *Cactoblastis* and other introduced insects have led to 22,000,000 acres of formerly dense Prickly Pear country in Queensland alone being selected for settlement. In New South Wales the greater part of the former Prickly Pear country has been brought into production. As a writer in *Blackwood's Magazine* has suggested, surely the *Cactoblastis cactorum* should be allotted a quartering on Australia's coat-of-arms !

The biological control of other pest plants seems to fade into insignificance in comparison with the great and highly successful Prickly Pear experiment. A few examples call for mention, however, because their control has been attempted by means of insects introduced from Britain. Among other harmful introduced weeds in Australia is the species of St. John's Wort, *Hypericum perforatum*. It entered the country in 1870 and has since become a widespread pest that eliminates pasture grasses and other low-growing vegetation, besides being poisonous to stock. The worst areas of infestation are in Victoria and New South Wales. Preliminary enquiries were made in 1917 with regard to the possibility of biological control by means of

English *Hypericum*-feeding insects. Eventually a number of kinds were introduced including three species of Leaf-beetles or Chrysomelidae and two kinds of Geometrid Moths, *Anaitis plagiata* and *A. efformata* whose caterpillars feed exclusively on St. John's Wort. Since these insects apparently failed to establish themselves under Australian conditions other enemies of *Hypericum* were subsequently introduced from southern France. Of these the root-boring Buprestid Beetle *Agrilus hyperici*, and the Leaf-beetle *Chrysolina gemellata*, have become established. The first-named has increased rapidly and it is hoped that an effect on the weed should be apparent in a few years' time. *Chrysolina hyperici*, one of the kinds introduced from England, has since been found to be established locally and is becoming increasingly abundant; retrogression of the weed is evident where this species is most numerous. The wide-spread area infested by St. John's Wort renders it evident that some years must elapse before any definite degree of biological control can be expected from the combined action of the insects mentioned.

New Zealand is troubled to a considerable extent with imported pest-plants, notably Blackberry (*Rubus fruticosus*), Gorse (*Ulex europaeus*) and Ragwort (*Senecio jacobaea*). With Blackberry the trouble at the outset lay in its close relationship with important economic plants such as Raspberry and Apple. The chances of introducing insect enemies that would confine their attentions to this plant are too remote to make biological control a safe proposition and the project has now been abandoned. With gorse, restriction of further spread of the plant was aimed at rather than its destruction. In this connection large numbers of the Seed-weevil *Apion ulicis* (see also p. 120) have been introduced from England. The Weevil is now well established and is infesting a high percentage of the pods in areas where it has been liberated. In the case of the Ragwort the Cinnabar Moth (*Callimorpha jacobaeae*) seemed to give promise of becoming a valuable enemy and large consignments were sent out from England. Where it became established in New Zealand its caterpillars produced a marked effect upon the weed concerned. The insect, however, has since steadily declined and is failing to hold its own. One of the causes is the extent to which its caterpillars are preyed upon by birds. According to D. Miller the bright colours of these larvae—which in England are a warning of nauseous properties to many would-be enemies—did not deter birds from gorging themselves until they could not take to the wing ! In order to offset the failure of the Cinnabar Moth a second kind of Ragwort-infesting insect was selected and imported into New Zealand from England.   This was the Ragwort Seed-fly (*Pegohylemyia jacobaeae*), whose larvae live in the developing florets and devour the young seeds. The insect is now well established and it is stated that of every floret it attacks practically all the seeds are destroyed. It may be said that good promise of success seems to be foreshadowed for the biological control of both Gorse and Ragwort in New Zealand.

In this chapter biological control has been interpreted as implying the repression of pests, whether they be animals or plants, by means of their natural enemies, particularly insects. It is, therefore, in direct contrast to artificial measures of control.   Some authorities take a much wider view and include under biological control all such factors as competition between different species, the destruction of alternative hosts, the breeding and adoption of resistant strains of races, crop-rotation, the effects of grazing and so on. While it is true that they are all of a biological nature and exercise a variable degree of con-trolling influence, the extension of the definition to include them becomes too wide and elastic to serve a useful purpose. Many of the methods just enumerated might be conveniently grouped under cultural control.

The advantages of biological control over physico-chemical methods are manifold. By using sprays, fumigants, poison baits and so on it is usually possible to reduce damage sufficiently to enable the farmer to grow a reasonable crop. Such methods, however, increase the cost of production and are at best only palliatives. Also, they have to be repeated year after year and their application often requires skilled knowledge. In some countries there is reason to believe that the repeated use of arsenical sprays may result in such compounds accumulating in the soil to the detriment of the vegetation. Also, it is noteworthy that certain noxious insects, especially Scale-insects, have become immune to the effects of some of the poisons used or now require a greatly increased dosage before they can be destroyed. Finally there are many pests that live concealed inside stems or fruits that cannot be reached by any known insecticide.

Biological control can never give immediate results like an insecti-cide, although in certain cases it has proved successful in a very short interval of time. The period between the colonisation of an enemy and the time when it is able to exercise sufficient control is often lengthy. This disadvantage is outweighed by the fact that in the successful cases a more or less permanent degree of control is obtained, usually at a very small and non-recurring cost. The planning of and provision for biological control has in practice to be undertaken by a central organisation of growers or by an agricultural department and consequently little or no financial responsibility for the work falls upon the individual grower. It is stated for instance that the cost of controlling the Levuana Moth, whose caterpillars wrought havoc among the coconut palms in Fiji, was only about £3,500, whereas the annual revenue lost owing to their ravages was computed at £1,000,000.

CHAPTER 8

ON GALLS

THE abnormal growths of plant tissues called galls* are caused by various kinds of living organisms. The largest number result from the activities of insects but by no means all galls are caused by them. There are in Britain, for instance, about 50 different kinds of galls that are produced by Mites, while others are caused by fungi and a few by Eelworms.

Galls display an immense variety of different forms and all parts of plants, from roots to the flowers, may be affected. The shape and position on the plant of each kind of gall is very characteristic. It is consequently usually far easier to identify a given gall than to name any particular causative insect without knowing the gall with which it is associated. The reader may be reminded that the gall-causer does not make the gall. Galls are vegetable growths entirely and are produced as the result of a particular stimulus imparted by the presence of the causer.

The greatest number of different kinds of galls caused by insects are found on Oaks; the next largest number are borne by Sallows and Willows. The Chestnut is one of the few trees that never seem to develop galls under English conditions and but rarely elsewhere.

The twiggy bunched growths, sometimes looking like birds' nests and known as "witches' brooms," are galls of a particular kind that are generally caused not by insects but by Mites. The most familiar of these galls occur on Birches and are especially conspicuous during the leafless season. The little tubular protuberances often so common on the leaves of the Lime tree, and called nail galls, are also caused by Mites. Big-bud in Black Currants also results from the activities of the same type of creature.

Galls are often so conspicuous, and sometimes such very attractive objects, that it is scarcely surprising that they have attracted the notice of observers from the earliest times; the Greek philosopher Theophrastus (378–286 B.C.), for instance, makes allusions to them. However, their true causes and origins remained quite unknown for many centuries. The prevailing ideas were that they were caused entirely

UNFAMILIAR STUDIES OF FLIES

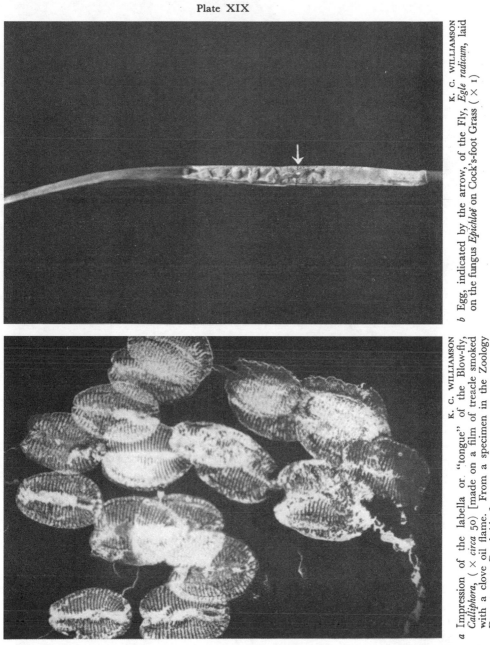

K. C. WILLIAMSON

a Impression of the labella or "tongue" of the Blow-fly, *Calliphora*, (× *circa* 50) [made on a film of treacle smoked with a clove oil flame. From a specimen in the Zoology Department, Cambridge]

b Egg, indicated by the arrow, of the Fly, *Egle radicum*, laid on the fungus *Epichloë* on Cock's-foot Grass (× 1)

Plate XX

S. BEAUFOY

a Mounting the host prior to egg-laying

S. BEAUFOY

b Inserting the egg-laying tool or ovipositor

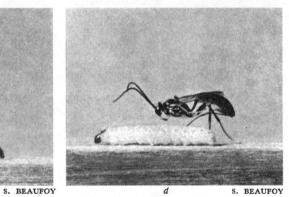

c   S. BEAUFOY

d   S. BEAUFOY

Positions assumed while driving in the egg-laying tool or ovipositor

S. BEAUFOY

e The organ inserted up to the hilt

S. BEAUFOY

f Having deposited her eggs the Ichneumon-fly walks away

STUDIES OF THE ICHNEUMON-FLY, *NEMERITIS CANESCENS*, EGG-LAYING
IN A CATERPILLAR OF THE MEDITERRANEAN FLOUR-MOTH (× 2½)

by the plants themselves and that the creatures found inside the galls came into existence as the result of spontaneous generation. The Italian anatomist Marcello Malpighi (1628–94), whose name has already been mentioned in another connection (p. 15), was not satisfied with this confession of faith and set himself the task of observing the growth and formation of galls. In this way he found out that they resulted where punctures were made in plants by certain kinds of insects. He believed that the insects injected a fluid into the plant that caused it to swell in a particular way ; in fact it appeared to be rather like the swelling that results after a person has been stung by a Bee or Wasp. How far such a contention is correct will become evident later in this chapter.

In addition to the original insects that cause the formation of galls a surprising variety of other inhabitants live in some of the larger kinds. They form a definite community of their own, all living within the confines of a single gall. Very often the relations of one species in this community to another are unknown or have been very little studied. I know of no case in which all the kinds of insects in any gall-inhabiting community have been adequately investigated. There is here, therefore, an extraordinarily interesting field of inquiry open to the amateur naturalist who cares to collect, observe and breed out the different inhabitants living in any of our galls, even the very commonest. Very often there are Chalcid Wasps whose larvae live as parasites that destroy the larvae or pupae of the original gall inhabitants. These parasites in turn are often attacked by other parasites, or hyper-parasites as they are termed (see p. 147). Then there may be predators that devour one insect after another. In addition to intruders of these kinds there are frequently uninvited guests or inquilines that feed upon the gall substance but do not directly attack the gall insects. The latter, however, may become starved out as the result of this kind of behaviour. Many of these inquilines are Cynipoid Wasps which are often mistaken for the true gall-causers ; others are the larvae of certain Flies, of Beetles and of several small Moths. The inquilines themselves, like the true gall-causing insects, are subject to attack by their own special parasites and hyperparasites. Thus we have a truly very mixed but highly interesting community.

The principal gall-causing insects belong to three different orders. They are (1) the Gall-wasps and some of the Saw-flies, belonging to the order Hymenoptera : (2) the Gall-midges and other true Flies of the order Diptera ; and (3) certain Aphids and their allies among the Hemiptera. Besides these a few galls are caused by certain Beetle larvae and others by the caterpillars of Moths.

(1) The Gall-wasps belong to the superfamily Cynipoidea*and are closely related to the Chalcid Wasps (see p. 147). The arrangement of the wing-veins, however, is somewhat different and their antennae are not elbowed as in the Chalcids (Text-Fig. 31, p. 146). Gall-wasps are all small or very small obscure looking creatures not likely to attract the attention of anyone other than an entomologist. It is a remarkable thing, as the American A. G. Kinsey has pointed out, that about 86 per cent of all the known kinds of Gall-wasps induce gall-formation on Oaks and on no other trees. About 7 per cent are found upon different species of Rose, while the remaining 7 per cent are found upon a wide variety of different flowering plants.

A great many Gall-wasps display what is known to biologists as alternation of generations. In each year there are two generations— one composed of females only and the other formed of individuals of both sexes. The bisexual generation is produced during the summer and gives rise to the unisexual one which passes through the winter. The extraordinary thing is that the females of the two generations are often so different that they were originally considered to be totally different species of Gall-wasps and received different names. The galls of the two successive generations are also often very different in appearance and may arise on different parts of the same plant.

There are other Gall-wasps in which males have never been seen at all although tens of thousands of females have been reared by naturalists in different countries. It is believed that in these cases a secondary simplification of the life-history has come about through the loss of the bisexual generation. Reproduction in such cases takes place entirely by virgin females that lay unfertilised eggs—a phenomenon called parthenogenesis, which is dealt with in Chapter 10.

The " oak-apple " is a good type of gall to start with especially for the reasons that it is plentiful and very easily seen where fully formed. It is caused by the Gall-wasp known as *Biorhiza pallida*. The name *Biorhiza* (from Gr. *bios*, life, and *rhiza*, a root) was given in allusion to the unisexual generation, which causes gall-formation on the roots of Oaks. The oak-apple (Pl. 30, p. 175, Fig. a) when mature has a rosy tint, and this hue together with its fruit-like appearance has suggested the popular name. If one of these galls be cut open it is seen to contain a number of cells or chambers in each of which there is normally a small larva or grub of the *Biorhiza*. The mature Gall-wasps eat their way through the gall to reach the outer world and their former presence is then revealed by their exit holes. The males are winged but the females are either wingless or have the wings reduced to vestiges making them quite useless for flight. After mating, which happens in July, the females crawl down the trunk of the tree and enter the soil. Here they make for the small roots, which they pierce with their ovipositors and lay their eggs within. The galls which result are rounded and berry-like about ½ in. in diameter. They occur singly or in groups up to a dozen or more (Pl. XXII, p. 195, Fig. c). The Gall-wasps that emerge are all wingless females which appear during the winter months and make their way to the soil surface. Having got thus far the real perils of life then begin ; they have to gain the tree-trunk, where they are exposed to the vicissitudes of the weather and to the perils of attack by hungry insectivorous birds. Those that reach the branches of the tree climb to the extremities of the shoots in order to lay their eggs in the terminal buds. Little or no change happens until early May, when the first swellings become evident. By the end of that month the " oak-apple " galls are mature and with the appearance of the bisexual generation of Wasps the life-cycle becomes completed.

Oak-leaves in or about July often bear circular lens-shaped growths, known as the " common spangle " galls, on their under surface. Often there are 80 or more on a single leaf. They are yellowish-green at first but this colour is concealed by a growth of reddish hairs. When mature in September they become detached from the leaves and fall to the ground. Each gall contains a single larva which continues to grow after its habitation has been separated from the parent tree. After passing the winter in the galls wingless female Gall-wasps belonging to the species *Neuroterus quercus baccarum* f. *lenticularis* appear in April. These females belong to the unisexual first generation and they lay their eggs deep down among the catkins or on the young leaves. The resulting galls occur in May and June and are berry-like in appearance, resembling red currants; their popular name of "currant galls" is therefore very appropriate (Pls. 31 [p. 190], XXII [p. 195]). The insects that emerge from these galls form the bisexual generation and were originally described as belonging not only to a different species but even to a different genus before their relationship with the spangle-galls became known.

The round, hard marble-galls caused by the Gall-wasp *Andricus kollari* are probably familiar to most readers. They are formed in the terminal or the lateral leaf-buds of the Oak. When fully grown they are pale to dark green according to whether they have developed in the shade or freely exposed to sunshine. In any case they change to brown in September (Pl. 30, p. 175, Fig. b) and in this dried state they may remain attached to the Oak many months after the gall-insects have emerged. Unlike the oak-apple gall, the marble-gall contains but a single original chamber which houses only one individual gall-insect. When other chambers are present, as is often the case, they are commonly made by inquilines. The Gall-wasps issue in September or October and each makes a circular exit-hole for the purpose. The smaller holes often seen in this species of gall are made by parasites and inquilines for the same purpose. Marble-galls are commonly about the size of large marbles but may be either smaller or larger. They occur either singly or in small groups on young Oaks and scrub Oaks found in hedgerows and coppices.

A curious thing is that *Andricus kollari* does not seem to be a native insect: it appears to have been introduced into Devonshire in imported galls about 1830 and from there it spread afield. By 1860 it was noted around Birmingham, and it now occurs in profusion even up into the north of Scotland. Why these galls were imported is uncertain but it has been suggested that it was in connection with the dyeing of cloth that was at that time extensively manufactured in the west of England. These galls, it may be added, are stated to contain about 17 per cent of tannic acid.

The Gall-wasps that issue from marble-galls are all females. Many years ago an official of the British Museum had one and a half bushels of these galls (which were collected in Devonshire) under observation and no male appeared among the 12,000-odd females that emerged. Every subsequent observer has had the same experience and it is uncertain whether the bisexual generation ever occurs—at any rate in Britain. It is suggested that the Gall-wasp called *Andricus circulans*, which causes very different and much smaller galls on the Turkey Oak (*Quercus cerris*), is the bisexual generation of the Marble Gall Wasp (*Andricus kollari*); but the subject is still in need of fuller investigation.

On many kinds of wild Rose there is found one of the most familiar of all galls, viz. the much admired "robin's pincushion," "bedeguar gall" or "moss-gall" as it is variously known (Pl. 32, p. 191, Fig. c).

PLATE 29

APHID STUDIES

s. BEAUFOY

a. Winged and wingless Aphids, *Macrosiphum rosae*, on Rose (× 2)

b. Hover-fly larva among a colony of Aphids (× 2)   s. BEAUFOY

PLATE 30

GALLS ON OAK

S. BEAUFOY

b. Marble galls ($\times \frac{3}{4}$)

S. BEAUFOY

a. Oak-apple galls ($\times \frac{1}{2}$)

The unusual word bedeguar is stated to be derived from the Persian *badawar*, meaning literally wind-borne. The gall is caused by an insignificant-looking little Gall-wasp—*Diplolepis rosae*, whose female lays her eggs in the young leaf-buds of the Rose in spring. The familiar reddish moss-like growths that envelop these galls do not seem to give the Gall-wasps protection against insect enemies for they are much persecuted by parasites, while numerous inquilines also find board and lodgings in the galls. Well-formed bedeguar galls measure an inch or more in diameter and present their best appearance by the end of July. The gall contains a number of cells, each harbouring a single *Diplolepis* larva.

If anyone is inspired to try and breed out the inhabitants of these galls,* the best time to collect them is at the end of winter when the majority of the insects within are fully-fed and ready to change into pupae. At this stage they are much less liable to be adversely affected by the severance of the galls from the living plant than at any other. A recent observer, E. McC. Callan, kept 1,015 of these galls, collected from a number of localities, on sand in glass jars covered with muslin and stored them in an open summer-house. Possibly these conditions were not completely satisfactory as only 815 of the galls produced insects. Anyway, the total number of insects that were bred out was 24,393. Of these some 6,007 were *Diplolepis rosae* and the rest either parasites or inquilines. A significant fact was that out of these 6,007 individual *Diplolepis* only 46, or 0·8 per cent, were males. The male in this case seems, therefore, to be on the way to becoming totally eliminated as in *Andricus kollari*.

In addition to the true gall-causer, *Diplolepis rosae*, a whole association of other creatures live within the gall. There is, for instance, another kind of Gall-wasp—*Periclistus brandtii*—which induces no gall-formation on its own account, but lives as a sort of Cuckoo-wasp or inquiline that lays its eggs only after the gall has been formed. Both the gall-causer and the inquiline are very subject to the attacks of insect parasites. Among these latter the resplendent metallic green and coppery Chalcid *Torymus bedeguaris* parasitises the *Diplolepis*. The female *Torymus* has a very long bristle-like ovipositor that she uses to pierce the matrix of the gall so as to reach the cells containing the larvae of its host. The *Diplolepis* larvae are also liable to be parasitised by the Ichneumon-fly *Orthopelma luteolator* which, in its turn, is attacked by the Chalcid *Habrocytus bedeguaris* (Pl. 21, p. 110, Fig. 3). But this by no means

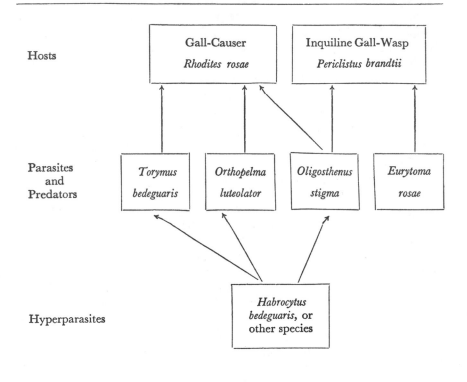

completes the story; for the *Habrocytus* just mentioned, or a closely allied species, seems also to parasitise another Chalcid known as *Oligosthenus stigma*, which in its turn is a parasite of the inquiline *Periclistus* referred to above. This latter insect has another enemy, also a Chalcid, viz. *Eurytoma rosae*. According to K. G. Blair the *Eurytoma* larva is a predator rather than a parasite (see p. 141) since it bites its way from one inquiline cell to another, devouring each occupant as it meets it. Thus, we have enumerated some of the chief actors in the drama that goes on with a single bedeguar gall. There are various other members of this same community about which even less is known than those just mentioned; these we must pass over. The reader may dislike the mention of so many scientific names but reference to the diagram above will help to sort out matters.

Two other kinds of galls are to be found on the wild Rose (Pl. XXIII, p. 202) and are also caused by Gall-wasps of the genus *Diplolepis*. They are much smaller than the bedeguar and, so far as I am aware, both kinds fall to the ground in autumn, the respective Gall-wasps emerging the following spring. These galls are mostly found on the under-side of the leaves and are green at first, becoming reddish later. The smooth pea-galls of *Diplolepis eglanteriae* are often common but escape notice unless specially looked for. Each gall contains a single cell that harbours the Gall-wasp larva but there may be several smaller cells formed by inquilines. The spiny pea-gall, caused by *Diplolepis nervosus*, is easily recognised on account of its sharp-pointed spines, two to four or five in number. This gall is on the whole less often found than the first-named.

Among the few Gall-wasps that attack herbaceous plants a common kind is *Liposthenus latreillei*. It causes galls on the stems and leaves of Ground Ivy (Pl. 33, p. 206, Fig. a), which are present from June onwards. Greenish at first, these galls become tinged with red or purple when mature and are usually rather larger than a pea. Each harbours a single Gall-wasp larva which pupates in the gall, the adult insect emerging the following May.

The other gall-forming Hymenoptera are some of the Saw-flies. They are much larger and more robust-looking insects than the Gall-wasps : they have no constriction or " waist " between the thorax and hind-body and the wings are relatively much broader and more profusely veined. They have received the name of Saw-fly because the ovipositor is finely toothed (though in different ways among the various species), and is used to saw clefts or slits in plant tissues wherein the eggs are deposited.

The most familiar species is *Pontania proxima*, the Bean-gall Saw-fly of Willows. Widely distributed in Britain, it occurs on various species of Willows. The female lays her eggs in May in the leaf-buds and the galls are fully formed in June to July. There is a second brood in August and September. The gall (Pl. 32, p. 191, Fig. b) protrudes equally from both surfaces of the leaf and is at first solid, but the larva eats out a cavity in its centre. Later on it makes a hole on the lower side of the gall but the reason for this opening is uncertain : it has been variously suggested that it is for aerating the gall cavity, for the ejection of the excrement of the larva, or to allow of its exit for pupation. It is formed, however, a long time before the insect is ready to pupate. When fully-fed the larva leaves the gall and forms a golden-yellow cocoon either in the soil or on the bark of the tree. The colour of the galls is somewhat variable : according to Dr. Mary Carleton those formed on *Salix triandra* are dark red above and pale yellowish-green below, whereas on *Salix fragilis* they are pink both above and below, but the colour is more pronounced on the upper side. Anyone who attempts to rear the occupants of these galls will be sure to breed out parasites instead of the rightful occupants in a considerable proportion of the cases. The commonest parasite is the Ichneumon-fly *Angitia vestigialis*. Some of the very early observers mistook this parasite for the true gall-causing insect and figured it as such. Another feature is the numerical predominance of females over males. The male Saw-fly in fact is so rare that it is unlikely that it will be met with.*

A small black Weevil (*Balanobius salicivorus*) is often common on Willows and it lays its eggs in the Bean-galls, especially when the latter are very young. The Saw-fly host seldom seems to survive the invasion but it is difficult to say whether the Weevil larva directly kills the egg or larva of its host or whether the latter perish as the indirect result of its feeding activities. Miss Carleton mentions that in some seasons as many as 40 per cent of the galls in some localities contain the Weevil. On reaching maturity the Weevil larva leaves the gall and turns to a pupa in the earth beneath.

(2) The larvae of Diptera or True Flies cause the formation of many kinds of galls. The surprising thing about them is that these gall-causers are mostly very small fragile creatures too insignificant to attract notice from anyone other than entomological specialists. They mostly belong to the family Cecidomyidae or Gall-midges. As will be seen in Pl. V, p. 46, Fig. a, the antennae in these insects are long and are adorned with characteristic girdles of projecting hairs while their wings are supported by very few veins. The larvae of Gall-midges are minute objects, short or stumpy in build and often yellow or orange in colour. Many members of the family live on or within various parts of plants without inducing any gall-formation. Others live in decaying wood or fungi, while many are predators that devour Mites, Aphids and other equally small creatures.

A wide range of different plants are subject to attacks by Gall-midges and the resulting galls have a great diversity of form. Among herbaceous plants those commonly galled are Compositae of various species, Meadowsweet, Bracken, Nettle, Yellow Bedstraw, Ground Ivy, etc. Of woody plants members of the order Salicaceae (Willows and Poplars) are very subject to attack, besides the Hawthorn, Lime, Yew and others.

Country dwellers must have often noticed numerous reddish or pinkish pustules on the upper surface of the leaves of the Meadowsweet. On some plants there may be from about 30 to nearly 200 of these galls to a leaf (Pl. 33, p. 206, Fig. b). The causative insect is the Gall-midge *Dasyneura ulmariae* whose yellowish-orange larva lives and pupates within the gall cavity. In its later stages the gall projects in a cone-like manner from the lower side of the leaf and is covered with silky hairs. The apex of the cone is easily detached and under natural conditions is pushed aside by the Gall-midge when it emerges. Among other Gall-midges of the genus *Dasyneura*, the species *D. crataegi* forms rosette galls on the ends of the shoots of the common Hawthorn (Pl. XXII, p. 195, Fig. b). The terminal leaves become deformed and are without stalks : their surfaces are covered with small greenish or reddish out-growths and provide food and shelter for the reddish larvae of this Gall-midge. The larvae fall to the ground to pupate and the Midges emerge in the spring. Another kind of rosette gall is caused by the Gall-midge *Rhabdophaga rosaria* on the ends of the shoots of various kinds of Willows. The leaves become crowded and shortened and give shelter to a single pinkish-coloured larva of this species (Pl. XXIII, p. 202, Fig. b). These galls are very persistent and remain on the shoots in a brown dead condition all through the following winter into the next summer.

A very different kind of Fly from the Gall-midge induces gall-formation on the Common Reed (*Phragmites communis*). It belongs to the family Chloropidae (or Oscinidae) and is known as *Lipara lucens*. Close relatives of this insect are the Frit-fly of Oats and the Gout-fly of Barley, both of which are well known to farmers as being serious enemies of their cereal crops. *Lipara lucens* causes the formation of cigar-shaped galls, averaging about 4 to 6 in. long, on the flowering stems of the Reed (Plate XXIV, p. 203). The presence of this gall causes the almost total cessation of growth beyond its apex and the inflorescence does not develop. A central chamber in the axis of the stem contains a single larva of *Lipara*, and the whole is enwrapped in successive layers of leaves which have become crowded together on account of the growth of the internodes being prevented. The galls are fully formed by August when they are yellowish-green in colour. Later they turn brown and remain all the winter with the insects inside them. Emergence of the Flies occurs in June. Each insect does so by issuing from the top of the gall chamber and then making its way along the core of the successive layers of leaves that enclose it until the exterior is reached. New galls begin to develop in that same month and consequently these growths may be found throughout the year. Where the Reeds are cut annually they are much scarcer and are often difficult to obtain.

A special feature of interest associated with these galls, as with so many others, are the parasites and inquilines that live within them in addition to the rightful occupants. The larvae of the *Lipara* are very subject to the attacks of two kinds of parasites. One kind is the metallic bronze Chalcid *Stenomalus liparae*. The other is a member of the Ichneumon family Braconidae (see p. 145) and is the species *Polemochartus liparae*. The larva of the last-named insect lives inside that of the *Lipara* and has the curious effect of accelerating its pupation. The *Lipara* larva normally changes into a pupa in the month of May; but those parasitised by *Polemochartus* undergo the transformation during the preceding autumn, some six months before the normal time, before finally succumbing to the effects of being parasitised.

When *Lipara lucens* and its parasites have emerged from the galls the empty formations are often taken possession of by other insects. In the Fenland, for example, the small black solitary Bee *Prosopis pectoralis* often makes its tier of superimposed cells (Plate XXIV, Fig. a) in the vacant gall-cavity. The cells containing the females occupy the lower half of the gall while those containing males are situated above. The male Bees, it may be added, emerge first. The larva of this Bee has been found by G. C. Varley to be attacked and destroyed by two very different kinds of parasites. One of these is an uncommon member of the Ichneumon-fly group belonging to the genus *Gasteruption*. The other is a highly burnished Ruby-tail Wasp (see p. 282), *Chrysis cyanea*. The *Lipara* galls also often harbour inquilines. Three kinds of small Flies belonging, like the *Lipara* itself, to the family Chloropidae make use of its galls. Also two kinds of Gall-midges do the same thing. Secondary galls on the main gall may be caused by some of these insects, but their presence does not seem to interfere with the growth of the original occupant. Some of these secondary gall-dwellers, in their turn, have their own special parasites. The result is that quite a number of years of very interesting work is still needed before the whole economy of all the occupants of *Lipara* galls can be fully revealed. Further, there are other species of *Lipara* that make distinct but smaller galls on the Common Reed and afford separate problems for investigation.

(3) A number of different kinds of galls owe their inception to the activities of various Aphids. Among the most conspicuous of these are the "purse galls" caused by *Pemphigus bursarius* on the Black Poplar and Lombardy Poplar. The galls develop on the petiole or on the mid-rib of the Poplar leaf (Pl. 32, p. 191, Fig. a), where they are easily accessible on the lower branches of the trees. When fully formed each gall is a hollow receptacle within which the *Pemphigus* lives and feeds. It is about the size of a Hazel-nut and one portion is drawn out into a sort of beak with an opening at its extremity. It is through this hole that the Aphids issue when they are ready to emerge from the gall. When they leave the Poplar they fly away and settle upon the roots of Lettuce, Sowthistle and some other plants but do not induce gall-formation on these secondary hosts. Lettuces affected by this Aphid are recognised by the white mealy substance produced by the insects clustered around the roots.

Another kind of gall caused by Aphids is induced by *Cryptomyzus ribis* (formerly known as *Rhopalosiphum ribis*). It affects White and Red Currants more commonly than Black Currants. In the spring this Aphid is to be found on the undersides of the leaves and especially beneath the red blister-like patches that result from their activities. In the hollows beneath these patches the Aphids live and multiply in great numbers. During the summer winged Aphids appear that leave the Currants and fly to various wild plants of the natural order *Labiatae* (White and Red Dead-nettle, Hedge Woundwort, etc.), where they go on breeding. In autumn returning migrants appear and these leave the plants just named and fly back to the Currants where they pass the winter.

A third kind of Aphid-gall is to be found very commonly on Norway and Sitka Spruce where it is caused by Aphids of the genus *Adelges* (formerly *Chermes*). The young insects make their way in spring to the bases of the growing needles of the Spruce where the soft tissue at these points swells up as the result of the punctures made by their mouth-parts. The swellings increase in size and coalesce so as to form false cones of the appearance shown in Pl. 31, p. 190, Fig. a.   This peculiar gall, when fully grown, may contain 100 or more cavities or chambers, each harbouring a number of growing Aphids.   Towards the end of June openings appear on these galls that enable the insects to crawl out of the chambers on to the needles.   Here, on casting their skins, they appear in the winged state and soon afterwards they fly away to some other kind of conifer, such as the Larch, Pine or Silver Fir, which serves as a secondary host.   No gall like that formed on the Spruce is ever found on these trees.   Several generations are passed through on the secondary host and in July of the second year other winged forms develop which fly back to the Spruce and there give rise to progeny that complete the life-cycle.   This alternation of hosts is a very characteristic feature among Aphids and is further discussed on p. 220.

Space will only allow of the mention of one other gall-causing insect, viz. the Turnip and Cabbage Gall-weevil (*Ceuthorhynchus pleurostigma*).   This creature lays its eggs on or near the roots of plants of the genus *Brassica* (Cabbage, Turnip, etc.), and other Cruciferae. The young larvae feed on the roots in such a way as to induce the formation of rounded galls that may reach the size of small marbles (Pl. 17, p. 78, Fig. c).   If one of these galls be cut open it is seen to enclose a cavity in which the larva lives until fully grown.   It then eats its way out and transforms into a pupa in the soil.   When numerous these galls damage vegetables of the Brassica kind, checking growth when they are attacked at an early stage.   Their rounded form distinguishes them from the more elongated finger-like growths shown by " finger-and-toe " galls caused by a fungus (*Plasmodiophora brassicae*, one of the slime fungi).   This latter organism causes internal decay, a tendency little shown in the Weevil galls even after the larvae have vacated them.

What most readers will probably want to know about galls is how they are actually formed.   To say that they are caused by such and such an insect is only a very partial answer to the question.   The most attention has been given to those galls that are caused by the activities of Gall-wasps.   Many theories have been advanced to account for their formation but the matter is still very far from being explained.   Attempts to produce galls artificially by means of experiments have so far mainly failed.   It seems to be quite clear that the irritation of the tissues produced by the insertion of the insect's ovipositor is not the initial cause. There is also no evidence that if a fluid is injected by the female during egg-laying it plays any part in gall-formation. The mere presence of the Gall-wasp's egg in the plant tissues is not in itself sufficient to cause the gall to grow because ordinarily the latter does not begin to show itself until the larva has hatched : many months may elapse between the time an egg is laid and the hatching of the larva. All that can be said is that the galls are produced as the result of the reactions of the cambium and other actively dividing cells of the plant, in response to a stimulus induced by the presence of the larva. It is probable, but not so far proved, that the larva exudes a secretion that exercises an influence in modifying the otherwise normal growth of the plant.

In the case of galls induced by Saw-flies the causes are very different. The Bean-galls of the Willow referred to on p. 177, for example, develop very quickly after the eggs are laid and may be fully grown even before the larvae have emerged from the eggs. It is believed that the causative agent here is a secretion that is injected at the same time as the egg into the tissue of the Willow leaf. This conclusion is borne out by the fact that if the egg be destroyed by puncturing with a fine needle the gall continues to develop. The insect sometimes saws holes in leaves with its ovipositor and discharges the glandular fluid at the same time, without an egg being laid, and yet galls that are quite normal in appearance result.

It is known that certain substances termed auxins, which in effect are hormones, are of special importance in promoting growth in plants.* The amount of growth that takes place in different parts of a plant is directly dependent on the amount of concentration of the auxin present. The modern view, as expressed by the American authorities F. W. Went and K. V. Thimann in 1937, is that "quantitative relations between different parts of the plant are expressions of the quantitative relation between auxin and its growth effects." Thus in Curly Top, which is the result of a virus disease, the growth of the shoot is much reduced, probably on account of the reduction of the amount of the auxin produced by the infected plant. Very probably the simpler kinds of galls, such as the rosette types shown in Pls. XXII (p. 195), XXIII (p. 202), are in part at any rate due to this same cause. The crinkling or blistering of the leaves of plants by the sucking action of Aphids are in reality incipient kinds of galls. The Aphids insert their mouth-parts into the sieve-tubes and in this way they interfere with auxin production by the phloem. This would have the effect of slowing up and stopping growth of the stem, petiole and leaf-veins. On the other hand the sappy tissue of mesophyll of the leaf goes on growing and is not influenced. This causes bulging of the parts of the leaf affected in some cases and curling in others, owing to unequal growth. The more elaborate galls caused by Gall-wasps, for instance, seem to be due, at least to some extent, to a substance that has been introduced into the plant by the insect and greatly influences growth. This substance seems to act like an auxin. The secretion injected by the Saw-fly that causes the Bean-galls on Willows, for instance, acts in this way. The Dutch investigator M. W. Beyerinck in 1888 called this secretion a " growth enzyme," and it was the first published instance of a substance causing differentiation and growth in plants. While such an explanation may account for some of the simpler examples of gall-formation it is very unlikely that the more elaborate galls can be considered in such simple terms. Some of these galls, for example, are made up of as many as eight separate layers of tissue, that are organised in a very definite pattern, quite different from any found on other parts of the plant.

It is known that diffusible substances which stimulate cell-division and growth are liberated by parts of plants when injured. These substances were called wound-hormones by the botanist Haberlandt. It is probable that the mechanical injury resulting from punctures made by the saw-like ovipositor in some insects or by the feeding activities of gall-inhabiting larvae in others likewise induce the liberation of such substances into the tissues. Injuries, therefore, are probably contributory influences in gall-formation, combined with growth-promoting secretions discharged by the insects concerned. One or both of these causes may, in turn, influence the production of auxin by the affected part of the plants in question. That the more complex galls result from the combined influence of several causes seems, therefore, to be very probable. But we shall never understand the subject of gall-formation properly until we are able to imitate, by experiments, the effects of gall-insects on plants. That is as far as the subject can be discussed here but it expresses in a few words the gist of present-day opinion.

CHAPTER 9

ON WAYS AND MEANS
OF PROTECTION

ANIMALS have enemies of various sorts with which they must contend, and insects form no exception to this cardinal feature of nature. Their most active and inveterate persecutors are birds, other insects, spiders, frogs and toads, and insect-eating mammals. These are all predators intent upon securing an insect meal either for themselves or their hungry offspring. The insects, on their part, react in numerous ways in order to escape detection and ultimate capture by their enemies. Some fight with their mandibles which are sharply pointed for the purpose. Others sting ; and many, which can do neither of these things, just try and make themselves look as repellent as possible by adopting threatening attitudes—a trait that is often associated with a defensive secretion. There are still other insects that depend upon their agility of movement as a means of escape from danger. Some achieve this end by flight, others by speed of foot and quite a number have a capacity for leaping away from the source of disturbance. More sedentary kinds of insects adopt the very opposite procedure—they just play 'possum or in other words when disturbed they draw in their legs and antennae, often letting themselves fall to the ground, and remain stone-still until the danger has passed. By adopting this kind of trickery they simulate the particles of some kind of inanimate matter of no interest or use to their aggressors, or simply escape their attention. These are all more or less instinctive acts on the part of the insects to escape from their enemies. Such methods, however, by no means exhaust the list for there are many other insects that rely upon their own coloration to give them the necessary protection. In this way a great number of different kinds merge into their surroundings so long as they remain quite still. Their colour-resemblance is often combined with characters of shape and attitude which greatly enhance its efficacy. In this way they come to resemble bark, stones, leaves, bits of stick, stems or other items in their surroundings. They have the instinct to rest on or in close relation with whatever object they resemble and in this way manage to cause many of their enemies to overlook their presence.

There are, again, a whole host of different insects that protect themselves by chemical means ; this they do by making the best use they can of the glandular products from their own bodies. Some of those that are endowed in this way are able to eject an acrid repellent liquid quite a respectable distance against their foes. Others, not able to do this, are gifted with an evil odour and often a vile taste which causes their enemies soon to learn to leave them severely alone. As a general rule insects endowed with chemical properties of these kinds advertise their presence as much as possible. This they do by parading in striking uniforms of contrasted colours. Sometimes they find it more effective to advertise themselves by congregating in companies so as to produce a more conspicuous effect. Coloration of this kind is known as warning coloration. It is obviously an advantage for their possessors to flaunt such colours so that their enemies may learn as soon as possible to leave them alone. Black and yellow form one of the standard combinations of a warning significance in nature. Man himself has also found it an efficacious scheme for road signs of a warning character ! But many insects which are extremely palatable to their enemies put up a bluff by closely imitating the colours and patterns of those having inedible properties. They live in the same areas as their models and at the same time of the year. Their resemblance is often so perfect that the uninitiated would fail to discriminate between the mimic and its model.

Finally the reader may be reminded that most insects are much more vulnerable to attack by their enemies at some particular stage in their lives than at others. For many their most helpless condition is when they are in the pupa or chrysalis stage ; various soft-bodied larvae are also exceedingly vulnerable. In instances of this kind the creatures themselves take special measures to ensure their own protection. As a rule they make cases or coverings of various sorts within which they are able to live without attracting undue notice. These devices are usually made so as to resemble parts of the surroundings wherein their owners live or are constructed in concealed situations so as to avoid detection.

With this preamble let us now pass on and explore our subject more fully. Their ways and means of protection form one of the most interesting sides of the natural history of insects. It is a subject nothing like as fully explored as it should be and one in which the amateur, gifted with patience and sufficient leisure, can do useful work and contribute to its advancement. No one who takes walks in the country during spring and summer need go very far before coming across at any rate some of the examples mentioned in this chapter. Others provide additional interest in that they need sharp eyes and a little practice in order to find them.

The advantages of wings as a means of escape from enemies are obvious to anyone who has ever tried to catch a Butterfly or watched a sparrow or other bird chasing a swiftly flying Moth. These organs together with the subject of flight are dealt with in Chapter 3 and no more need be said here. A capacity for swift running aids many insects to escape from their pursuers. It is a special feature in the Silver-fish (*Lepisma*), in Cockroaches, Ground-beetles, among Ants and various other insects. Anyone who, unaided by any special gadget, tries to catch a Cockroach on a kitchen floor will soon become convinced of the value to such creatures of being able to run fast in order to keep clear of enemies. Most of these sprinters of the insect world are either flightless or do not rely upon wings to save them from their pursuers. If their legs be looked at it will be seen that they are of almost equal size and slenderly built. Much indeed can be deduced about an insect's way of living by looking at its legs. As already noted (p. 12), a Crane-fly, for instance, uses its excessively long and slender legs for alighting or for holding on to objects when resting—it is quite unable to run. Other insects use their legs for digging, some for swimming and so on.

The value of leaping as another way of escaping from enemies will be very evident to those who have tried to catch Crickets or Grasshoppers. The leaping powers of such insects, and of Flea-beetles (also of Fleas) reside in powerful muscles that take their origins in the enlarged femora of the hind pair of legs. In a Grasshopper, for instance, the very large levator muscle of the tibia (Text-Fig. 8, p. 36) originates from a large part of the surface of the much elongated and enlarged femur. On contracting, this muscle forcibly straightens the tibia, which has the effect of projecting the insect into the air. It is probable that the depressor muscles of the trochanter act at the same time and perform an accessory function in the process. Among the minute Spring-tails (p. 34) leaping is performed in a different way. The special organ concerned is a two-pronged appendage or furcula which acts as a springing organ and is attached to the 4th segment of the hind-body.

When not in use it is held by a retaining device so as to lie against the underside of the insect with the prongs directed forwards. In leaping the furcula is pulled downwards with its prongs extended so that the organ frees itself from the retaining catch. The action has the effect of causing the insect to jump a distance of several inches. In the " Cheese Skipper," which is the larva or grub of the Cheese-fly (*Piophila casei*), as a preliminary to a jump, the tail extremity of the body is grasped by the mouth-hooks. This causes the whole body to be curved into a loop and put into a state of tension : when the tail is freed the body becomes suddenly straightened and the tension thus released causes the creature to project itself into the air.

The Click-beetles or " Skipjacks " are very common in grassy places in summer (see also p. 58). The acrobatic performances of these long, neat-looking Beetles are very entertaining. If one of them be touched it immediately curls up its legs and lets itself drop to the ground just as if it were shot. It seems generally to land on its back and there it lies for a time as still as in death. Then it gives a stretch and goes off suddenly with a click, thus jerking itself into the air perhaps several inches. If it should come down on its back a second time it tries again and goes on doing so until it alights on its feet, when it runs away. This property of being able to leap when placed on its back is due to the underside of the prothorax being provided with a backwardly directed spine which catches against the edge of a cavity on the mesothorax. So long as the apparatus remains in this position the insect is quiescent. When it moves so as to cause the spine to slip over its catch this instrument becomes driven with force into the cavity just mentioned. The blow thus given seems to cause the wing-cases to strike the surface upon which the Beetle is lying, so giving rise to the leap. This capacity for jumping is much less developed in some species of Click-beetles than in others and may only be just enough to enable the creature to right itself when lying on its back. Click-beetles seem quite unable to turn themselves over with their legs and they can only leap when lying on their backs. These two facts seem to show that the primary function of their leap is to enable them to right themselves. But often this gymnastic capacity has increased so much beyond its original requirement that it also came to be used as a means of escape from, at any rate, some sorts of enemies.

The assumption of a threatening attitude when alarmed is adopted by some insects as a means of protection. Thus the Devil's Coach-horse curves its hind-body over its back and holds its mandibles wide apart, snapping vigorously at any object presented to it (Pl. X, p. 99, Fig. c). Earwigs do very much the same thing under like circumstances. The hind-body is bent over the back and the forceps are held widely open ready to seize any real or imagined enemy. The male Stag-beetle can assume a very threatening attitude with its great mandibles held wide open. These structures, however, can only inflict a feeble sort of bite whereas the much shorter mandibles of the female can give a far more effective nip. In the case of the Devil's Coach-horse the threatening attitude is accompanied by the exudation of a foetid secretion from glands near the anus.

One of the commonest ways of protection lies in the colours and colour-patterns* of many insects. Very often these cause their possessors to resemble with remarkable fidelity the background against which they are seen. The efficacy of this method is often enhanced when colour is combined with features of body-form and resting attitude. The familiar Buff-tip Moth (*Phalera bucephala*) with its violet-grey forewings and oval cream-coloured patch at their tips, when resting reproduces in appearance a broken pale-coloured piece of a dead twig (Pl. 13, p. 66). Here it will be noted that the violet-grey ground colour matches the background on which the insect is resting. The disruptive pattern at the wing-tips, as well as resembling the broken end of a rotten twig, breaks up a continuous colour into what appears to be a discontinuous broken surface. In this way the creature is rendered more difficult to detect on a diversified background than a self-coloured object without any marked pattern. It is, therefore, important to bear in mind that disruptive coloration, that is a pattern of contrasted colours or tones, is often of great importance in serving to blur the outline and disguise the real surface form, which a homogeneous colour is often unable to effect. Another very good example is to be seen in the nymph of a common small Grasshopper (*Chorthippus parallelus*). H. B. Cott mentions that in the New Forest it is an earthen-brown insect whose form is apparently divided down the back by a pale cream stripe just the colour of dried grass. The disruptive coloration thus displayed by this insect as it rests among sun-dried grass and baked earth is truly remarkable since these are the two things which its own colour exactly matches. Other Grasshoppers have a similar pale stripe but are green in colour over the rest of their bodies. When resting upright on growing stems, which the broad pale line down their backs simulates, the green of the rest of their bodies merges into the general tone of their surroundings.

Some of the most perfect examples of protective resemblance are displayed by the familiar twig-like caterpillars of Geometrid Moths (Pl. 34, p. 207). They are so well assimilated to their surroundings that it takes much practice and sharp eyes to discover them. They combine a close resemblance to growing twigs, both in colour and in actual form, with a rigid lifeless resting attitude that accentuates the deception. By remaining stationary during daylight they escape the attention of most of their enemies ; only when night approaches do they move about freely and feed, the disguise then being no longer required.

A variety of insects, when disturbed, fall to the ground where they remain motionless for a longer or shorter period. If, as most often happens, the insect is a Beetle, it draws its antennae and legs close to the body and this, coupled with a more or less rounded contour, may make it look exactly like a seed or a particle of earth. Such insects are usually sombrely coloured, which gives them an excellent chance of escape, especially so long as they remain motionless amid dead leaves, earth, or debris of various sorts. This behaviour is not, as is often believed, an attempt to feign death but is an essential part of a resemblance to stationary inanimate objects. The Click-beetles have already been noted; other examples are met with among Weevils. The dingy-coloured members of such genera as *Ceuthorhynchus* and its allies, which are very abundant among wild and cultivated Crucifers, Nettles and other plants, afford examples. Their somewhat cumbrous name is well chosen, being derived from the Greek words *keutho*, to hide, and *rhynchos*, a beak or snout. When disturbed they draw the beak or rostrum and the limbs beneath the body and present a rather rugged rounded contour which enables them to defy detection among ground debris beneath their food-plants. The *Cionus* Weevils (Pl. 27, p. 150, Fig. b) of Figworts and Mulleins do just the same and are equally difficult to find. A very different sort of Beetle named *Byrrhus pilula*, found near the roots of grass and other vegetation, is a real expert in packing up its limbs. As soon as it is disturbed the head is withdrawn into the thorax, the tarsi fold into the tibiae which in turn pack closely against the femora and its entire legs fit into slots underneath the body. Its Latin name *pilula*, meaning a globule, refers to the insect in this attitude, when it becomes hard to detect amid its surroundings.

There are various kinds of Longicorn Beetles (p. 116), none very

PLATE 31

VARIOUS GALLS (× 1)

a. Pseudocone or gall caused by the Aphid, *Adelges abietis*, on Spruce
S. BEAUFOY

b. Currant-galls on flowers of Oak (above); galls on leaf-stalk of Aspen caused by the Aphid, *Pemphigus bursarius* (below). The small holes in the leaves were caused by Flea-beetles
S. BEAUFOY

PLATE 32

S. BEAUFOY

a. Galls on leaves of Willow caused by the Bean-gall Saw-fly, *Pontania proxima*
b. Galls on leaf-stalks of Poplar caused by the Aphid, *Pemphigus bursarius*

S. BEAUFOY

c. Bedeguar on Wild Rose caused by the Gall-wasp, *Diplolepis rosae*

FAMILIAR GALLS (× ¾)

common but some more plentiful than others, that rest upon the bark of branches of trees, usually of those wherein their own larval life was passed (p. 117). Some of them, including *Leiopus* (Pl. 18, p. 79) and *Pogonocherus*, are found nowhere else and are often uncommonly difficult to find, so well do they blend with their immediate surroundings. Some of our Scale-insects resemble gall-like or other structures on the stems of woody plants. One of these, belonging to the genus *Eulecanium* is shown on Pl. XXI, p. 194. Undoubtedly such insects derive considerable protection from this resemblance coupled with their horny exterior. The present writer has often found the persistent dead shells of these insects remaining attached to the food-plants long after the creatures have died—a fact that seems to suggest that the resemblance just mentioned enables them to be overlooked by tits and other birds. Their family name *Coccidae* is derived from the Greek *kokkos*, a kernal or grain, and was given in allusion to their berry-like appearance. When in the young nymphal stages many Scale-insects, White-flies and Jumping Lice are curiously thin wafer-like green objects closely applied to the leaf-surfaces of their food plants. In these phases they are easily overlooked and probably many escape the notice of insectivorous birds.

One of the most startling examples of protective resemblance among all British insects is to be found among the *Cionus* Weevils previously mentioned. Their larvae devour the green tissue of the leaves of Figwort, skeletonising them since they do not eat the ribs and veins. When fully grown they ascend among the developing seed-capsules where they make neat parchment-like cocoons. These bear a truly startling resemblance in form, size, and colour, to the seed-vessels of the Figwort among which they are found (Pl. 26, p. 143). The advantage to be derived would appear to be due to these cocoons resembling something which insectivorous birds are not interested in and consequently leave alone.

An immense number of different sorts of insects are leaf-green in colour and there is no doubt that many of them derive protection from resemblance to the foliage where they live. The Green Grasshoppers (Pls. 1 and 2, pp. 2, 3) for example are very hard to detect among their leafy surroundings. To look for them in such situations is rather like searching for the proverbial needle in a haystack. Shaking a bush on which they live over an open umbrella is a speedy way of finding them providing they have not already leapt out of range! The numerous Plant-bugs of so many kinds, especially the Capsid-bugs, the many kinds of Aphids or Green-fly, the Green Weevils *Phyllobius* and *Poly-drusus*, all seem to gain some measure of protection owing to their shades of green coloration. We have little or no positive evidence on this point, but if such insects were brown or black they would obviously be much more conspicuous. When we find a high degree of correlation between the particular coloration of an insect and that of its surroundings it is reasonable to assign to it a biological meaning—at least as a tentative explanation until definite evidence is forthcoming.

It is sometimes maintained that we do not know whether those insects that display what is called protective coloration gain any real advantage from the disguise. It is true that while much has been written describing apparently protective resemblance not nearly enough observations or experiments have been undertaken for testing its efficacy. Does such resemblance in actual fact assist an insect in escaping detection by its enemies and in that way prove a real advantage to it in the struggle for existence? Among the Lepidoptera there is considerable evidence of the kind needed and it gives a positive answer to this question. Among other insects the evidence obtained in recent investigations by E. J. Popham[1] will be found to be very much to the point. He was mainly interested in finding out the biological significance of colour-variations in certain of the Lesser Water-boatmen belonging to the genus *Sigara* (p. 228). The first thing that he noticed was that these insects tend to resemble in general colour that of the backgrounds of the ponds where they live. He noticed in the first place that the colour of a nymph or a young adult depends directly upon that of its surroundings during the time when it moulted. A pale-coloured background restrains the formation of the colouring matter in the insect whereas a dark background has not this effect. Secondly the creature prefers to settle on a background with which its colour harmonises ; it becomes restless and tries to fly away when the difference is extreme. Thirdly, selection comes into play. In one experiment Popham introduced three small Rudd into an aquarium. Twelve of the Lesser Water-boatmen were then added, six being of a colour shade that harmonised with the general background in the aquarium and six not so adapted. When an insect was eaten it was replaced by one of the same colour and in this way the population was kept constant, some 200 Lesser Water-boatmen in all being used in these trials. When the results were totted up it was found that the

[1] *Proceedings of the Zoological Society of London*, 1941-43.

three fish destroyed 151 individuals that did not harmonise with the background of the aquarium and only 49 of those that did more or less resemble their surroundings.

Tests done under artificial conditions, however, are very different from the complex situation so often found in nature. Bearing this in mind Popham extended his work into the open country among some small ponds in Lancashire which contained three different kinds of the insects in question. Having fixed upon one pond he made daily sample collections of Water-boatmen for seven successive days. After noting the proportion of those whose coloration harmonised with their general surroundings the living specimens were then returned to the water. Since there were no fish in these ponds and very few other inhabitants it seemed suitable for his experiment. This was the introduction of about 50 Minnows. After it had been effected samples of the insects were taken over the same period as before. The result showed that the proportions of Lesser Water-boatmen that resembled their background were noticeably increased. Various possible explanations were gone into but it seemed that the most likely one was that the Minnows mainly fed on those insects that were the most conspicuous through their colour not harmonising with that of their surroundings. Since the change in these proportions was sudden and coincided with the introduction of the Minnows it would seem that this explanation is probably correct. It should also be mentioned that the Minnows were previously tested in an aquarium and found to feed readily on the three kinds of Water-boatmen in the pond. The results of Popham's trials are summarised below. The numbers in each case are the totals of the samples taken at the end of the two periods of seven days, (a) before the Minnows were introduced and (b) afterwards :—

	Sigara venusta		Callicorixa praeusta		Sigara distincta	
	a	b	a	b	a	b
Adapted	726	859	33	31	29	26
Non-adapted	345	212	31	9	21	1

This example will give some idea of the sort of information that is needed in order to evaluate the efficacy of protective resemblance. Such information is often to be obtained by observation and experiment that can be carried out by persons who have not undergone an elaborate technical training. What is needed is, as J. B. S. Haldane has expressed it, " sufficient intelligence to solve a crossword puzzle." Let any experiments be critically planned and done on as large a scale as possible.   Keep a notebook and record fully everything observed however trivial it may seem, and when an account of the work is finally written up a definite contribution to the advancement of the subject is quite likely to result.

We may now pass on and consider the significance of some of the conspicuous colours and patterns found among our native insects. Coloration of this kind seems to advertise the presence of its possessors to the world at large for they habitually expose themselves freely in nature. Thus, we have the very antithesis of protective resemblance. Instances are provided by very familiar insects and most country-dwellers are acquainted with some of the examples quoted. Even many urban residents have found their Gooseberry and Currant bushes defoliated in parts by the conspicuous larvae of the Magpie Moth (*Abraxas grossulariata*).   These creatures have been the subjects for numerous trials with insectivorous birds, lizards, frogs and also bats— in each case with the same result.   When offered to any of these predators Magpie Moth caterpillars are either rejected at sight, or, if seized, are soon dropped owing to their distasteful properties.   It is easy to experiment with chickens to find how consistently these caterpillars are refused.   Young and inexperienced birds soon learn to recognise them by their conspicuous colour pattern and after a few unpleasant ventures, leave them severely alone.   Colours of this kind are known as warning colours and the insects that have them are either distasteful to their enemies, or emit nauseous secretions or are capable of stinging.

Among Beetles there are many kinds that show warning coloration associated with distastefulness.   The Soldier-beetles (*Cantharis*) and Ladybird Beetles are familiar examples.   The well-known experiments of Lloyd Morgan with young birds showed that both these insects were tasted at first but were avoided afterwards as the result of the experience. Not infrequently a number of individuals of a warningly coloured insect feed in companies, thus greatly enhancing their conspicuousness.   This feature is displayed in various brightly coloured caterpillars of Saw-flies, notably those of *Croesus septentrionalis* and of *Priophorus viminalis*. In the first-named the prevailing colour is green with orange markings and in the *Priophorus* the ground colour is orange studded with black marks.   Both kinds are common on the foliage of various species of Poplar in August and September.   The habit of gregariousness

Plate XXI

A. D. IMMS

a Brown scale, *Eulecanium coryli,* on Hawthorn (× 1)

A. D. IMMS

b Brown scale showing exit-holes made by parasites (× 6)

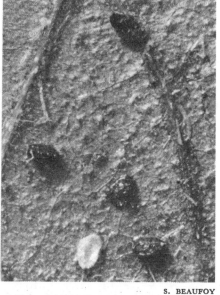

S. BEAUFOY

c Dead Aphids with exit-holes made by *Aphidius* (× 7)

S. BEAUFOY

d Normal (white) and parasitised (black) nymphs of the Greenhouse White-fly on a Tomato leaf (× 8)

STUDIES IN PARASITISATION

Plate XXII

S. BEAUFOY

a Marble Gall of Oak showing the *Andricus* larva within (× 2½)

W. TAMS

b Terminal Rosette Galls on Hawthorn caused by the Gall-midge, *Dasyneura crataegi* (× ½)

F. C. BROWN

c Galls caused by *Biorhiza pallida* on roots of Oak (× 2). Exit holes made by the Gall-wasp are shown

F. C. BROWN

d Currant Galls caused by the Gall-wasp, *Neuroterus quercus baccarum* f. *lenticularis*, on catkins of Oak (× ½)

STUDIES OF GALLS

occurs also in the caterpillars of Lepidoptera and the companies often comprise many more individuals than those of the Saw-flies just mentioned. The black spiny larvae of the Peacock Butterfly (*Vanessa io*) and the yellow and black soft-haired individuals that produce the Buff-tip Moth (*Phalera bucephala*) provide good examples. The caterpillars in both cases keep together until nearly fully grown when, possibly on account of their much larger appetites, they disperse and feed apart.

The " Woolly Bears " of Tiger Moths and other hairy caterpillars are very conspicuous objects, fond of exposing themselves quite openly in the sunshine. Apart from the mere unpleasantness of such a creature in the mouth of a predator such nauseous features as stinging-hairs, eversible glands, etc., are often also present. The caterpillar of the Vapourer Moth (*Orgyia antiqua*) will be familiar to many owing to its armature of defensive brushes or tussocks of bristles along its back, as shown in Plate 35, p. 222, Fig. a.

Caustic or irritating secretions seem to provide many insects with means of defence. The gregarious brightly coloured Saw-fly caterpillars, referred to above, give out a secretion emitting a very unpleasant odour. In the case of the larva of *Croesus septentrionalis* the body is turned forward over the head when alarmed and the ventral secretory organs discharge the products so that the whole company becomes pervaded with their unpleasant odour. This, according to Sir E. B. Poulton, acts as an effective protection. Many Plant-bugs (Heteroptera) and Lace-wings discharge evil-smelling secretions when handled. Carabid Beetles discharge evil-smelling butyric acid from glands around the vent. In the Bombardier Beetle (*Brachinus crepitans*) (Pl. 18, p. 79, Fig. 27) these same glands emit, with a peculiar explosive " crack," a fluid which vaporises into a tiny cloud when it comes in contact with the air. The striking metallic green Beetle (Plate 18, Fig. 18) known as the Spanish Fly (*Lytta vesicatoria*) contains the potent blistering agent, cantharidin. The larva of the Leaf-beetle *Chrysomela populi*, often to be found on dwarf Sallows, has glands which secret the unpleasant-tasting salicylaldehyde, evidently derived from the glucoside salicin present in its food.

The Red Ant (*Formica rufa*) of pine woods is a large Ant that does not sting, nevertheless its poison gland produces quite a large amount of formic acid. As Donisthorpe mentions, it can discharge the acid from the tail end of its body to a distance of 6–12 in. When alarmed or enraged the workers stand on the tips of their feet, with the gaster bent between their legs, so as to eject the venom against any foes that face them. The caterpillars of the Puss-moth (*Cerura vinula*) also can eject a spray containing a high percentage of formic acid against such enemies as Ichneumon-flies in order to discourage their attacks.

In a number of other cases, usually among Beetles, the blood of the insect itself has caustic properties and is discharged in small drops when the creature is seized. This peculiar attribute, which is termed reflex bleeding, is due to the blood oozing from around limb joints or else-where when the insects concerned are attacked or molested. The habit prevails among Ladybirds (*Coccinella*, etc.), in the Bloody-nose Beetle (*Timarcha tenebricosa*), the Oil-beetles (*Meloe*) and others. These three kinds of Beetles, like so many other warningly coloured forms, are sluggish in their movements which, in a way, serves to emphasise their conspicuousness. The two last-named crawl heavily and slowly over the ground, where their blue-black coloration together with their large size render them conspicuous objects (Plates 36 [p. 223] Fig. c, and XI [p. 106] Fig. d). Warning colours in order to be effective must be easily recognised and remembered—bold simple patterns or a single pronounced colour are more likely to be effective in this connection than a delicate blend of markings of different shades.

It needs to be pointed out that protective devices, however efficient they may be, do not confer absolute immunity to their possessors from attack. Such an ideal is probably very rarely if ever attained in nature. For example, the Cuckoo is known to feed upon some of the hairy types of caterpillars that are avoided by almost all other kinds of birds. This same species has even been noted to feed upon such distasteful larvae as those of the Magpie Moth. The fact that one kind of bird, or other enemy, attacks certain kinds of protected insects does not invalidate the utility of the particular protective devices in regard to their efficacy against other and more numerous enemies. By way of analogy the protective steel helmet of the soldier is more or less relevant. This device saves many lives from destruction by shell splinters and spent bullets and its adoption for this purpose is justified notwithstanding the fact that it may be ineffective against high velocity missiles at short range.

Many Hymenoptera adopt very active methods of protection ; they are able to sting their assailants when attacked. The sting, as noted on p. 61, is a modified ovipositor which has changed its function from that of an egg-laying instrument so as to become a weapon of defence.

Among many Ichneumon-flies the ovipositor is used for piercing the skin of other insects. By this means these creatures are able to lodge their eggs right inside the bodies of their victims which ultimately serve as food for their larvae. In Bees, Wasps and many Ants the ovipositor is also a piercing organ but has lost its original function as an egg-laying tool and has become a sting. Solitary Wasps, for instance, sting their prey before storing it as food for their own grubs. The act of stinging consists of piercing or stabbing the prey and at the same time injecting a poison that is produced by associated glands. The result commonly induces rapid paralysis of the motor centres of the prey thereby depriving it of its capacity for movement. In all Bees and social Wasps the sting is not used for this purpose but has become an organ of defence against enemies.

Glands associated with the sting secrete the venom that imparts the painful sensation experienced when a person is stung. In the Hive-bee the venom seems to contain several toxic substances, of which the chief one, called " apitoxin," is a protein of low molecular weight. Histamine is also stated to be present and to cause the cutaneous reaction to stinging, but not very much is known about these constituents. In many Ants venom is also present and in those of the genus *Formica* and its allies the chief constituent is formic acid. The popular belief that this same acid is a constituent of Bee venom is a mistaken one and some other substance must account for the benefits that accrue to rheumatic persons after being repeatedly stung by Bees.

It is remarkable how predominating a black-and-yellow coloration is among Wasps. It does in fact act as a warning that advertises their repellent nature. Most people treat any insect with a similar sort of pattern with respect lest it also might prove to be able to sting. Birds in general avoid Wasps and Bees although they feed on numerous other insects. We have most convincing proof of this in the work of a Dutchman, I. H. N. Kluijver, who carried out series of experiments on the food of nestling Starlings, in a state of nature, over a period of three years. In that time 16,484 insects were found to have been brought to the nestlings by their parents. Among this very mixed diet there were 4,490 Beetles but only two were Ladybirds. There were also 799 Hymenoptera ; these latter insects comprised only a single solitary Wasp, and not one true Wasp or Bee. The findings of other experimenters tell the same story. Thus R. Carrick, in experiments made near Glasgow in 1934, tried out the palatability of various sorts of insects by offering them to wild birds, including the Wren, Willow-warbler and Sedge-warbler. The insects were attached alive to feeding trays placed near to the nests where fledglings of the birds just named were being fed. He mixed up warningly-coloured kinds such as Bumble-bees, Wasps, Cinnabar Moth caterpillars, etc. with neutrally coloured insects (mostly brown or grey Flies and certain caterpillars). What he did next was to watch the behaviour of the birds at a distance through binoculars. Although his experiments were only on a small scale they are of a kind that we need because they were done out in the field where the birds behave in a free manner. In seven tests of this kind 58 neutral insects and 44 warningly coloured kinds were used. It was found that the birds ate 86 per cent of those neutrally coloured and only 9 per cent of the warningly coloured examples. Among the latter the birds refused Bumble-bees and Wasps and only two out of twelve *Andrena* Bees were taken. Rather similar trials, but on a very much larger scale, were done by F. Morton Jones at the edge of a natural woodland on an island in the State of Massachusetts. Other experiments were conducted by him on similar lines in Florida. In both series he found a close relation between types of coloration and acceptability to birds. In so far as Moths were concerned, only 0·74 per cent of those that were cryptically coloured were left on the feeding trays, whereas 86 per cent of those with warning colours remained untouched. Significant as these figures are, one more example of the utility of warning coloration will be cited. In this case we are concerned with the food of Tree-frogs. H. B. Cott has examined the insects and Spiders recovered from 995 frogs in Portuguese East Africa and in the Canary Islands. His results, which are tabulated below, speak for themselves :

	Orthop-tera	Hemip-tera	Coleop-tera	Dip-tera	Hymen-optera	Spiders	Total
No. of prey identified	63	705	273	193	10,300	51	11,585
No. and % of prey with warning colours	0	4	4	5	7	0	20
	0·0	0·58	1·48	2·63	0·68	0·0	0·17

It will become clear to anyone who has read thus far that there is good evidence as to the value of warning colours to those insects that possess them. It has been seen that Wasps, Bumble-bees, Ladybirds and others all display colours of warning significance. There are however, many British insects that are similarly too conspicuous to be overlooked by their enemies. In the absence of definite evidence we can only conclude, by analogy with the examples already mentioned, that these insects are also clothed in warning colours. Three instances only will be quoted, although many more could be given. Perhaps some reader with the necessary leisure and a flair for natural history may be tempted to try experiments with them.

(1) The Common Tiger-moth (*Arctia caja*) shown in Pl. 35, p. 222, Fig. b, is one of our most gaudily patterned insects. It flies, however, by night and hides away by day among herbage, etc. If it has distasteful properties why does it not display its colours openly in order to advertise their warning significance ?

(2) The different kinds of Frog-hoppers or Cuckoo-spit Insects in Britain, with one exception, are so sombrely coloured that they seldom attract notice. The exception is the creature known as *Cercopis vulnerata*, displayed on Pl. 3, p. 10, which occurs locally on Sallows and Alders. It is very strikingly coloured, being black with large blotches of cinnabar-red, and lives openly on its food-plants. Has it distasteful properties which it advertises by its own gaudy livery, whereas all its relations are very dowdy retiring creatures ?

(3) The Cardinal Beetle (*Pyrochroa serraticornis*), shown on Pl. 19, p. 94, Fig. b, is of a deep red colour with jet black legs and antennae. It makes no effort to hide away and crawls slowly exposing itself to view on Nettles and other roadside herbage.

The would-be experimenter should view his subject with an un-biased mind. In the words of Michael Faraday, he " should be a man willing to listen to every suggestion but determined to judge for himself. He should not be biased by appearances ; have no favourite hypothesis ; be of no school ; in doctrine acknowledge no master. He should not be a respecter of persons but of things. Truth should be his primary object. If to these qualities be added industry, he may indeed hope to walk within the veil of the temple of Nature."

The protective resemblance shown by insects to inanimate objects in their surroundings has already been discussed. So far nothing has been said about another and equally striking aspect of animal coloration known as mimicry.* This name refers to a different sort of resemblance—that of one animal to another. The word is often misunderstood and wrongly used for cases of protective resemblance like those that have already been mentioned. Some examples of mimetic resemblance are so marvellous and close as almost to take the breath out of the most hard-boiled naturalist when he first becomes acquainted with them.

Let us consider the theory of mimicry first and then see how far it finds expression among British insects. At the outset it should be remembered that the mimic or imitator presumably benefits because it bears a close resemblance to another creature known as the model. The model itself is protected against attack by enemies owing to un-palatable or other qualities. The mimic lives a life of deception for, although it is palatable itself, it deceives its would-be enemies by its sham warning coloration. It is mistaken for the model and con-sequently its enemies leave it alone because previous experience has taught them that the model is not good to eat. Obviously, in order that the mimic may really benefit by its resemblance, it and its model must inhabit the same locality. Also, the mimic must be less common than the model otherwise it would gain little benefit by resembling a creature that is much less often seen : the model furthermore would tend to be destroyed because of its being mistaken for the mimic. It is significant that whatever resemblance a mimic may bear to its model, this only affects features that are superficial and are *actually seen*—it would be useless for the resemblance to extend to hidden parts. As H. B. Cott remarks, when a white man adopts a theatrical make-up in order to play a negro's part he blackens only those parts visible to his audience. Mimicry works on that same principle, but the super-ficial resemblance of the mimic to its model must be sufficiently close and detailed for the former to be actually mistaken by its enemies for the latter.

The foregoing conditions hold good in well-established examples of mimicry but the subject has aroused much doubt and controversy. The reality of mimicry has been hotly contested and it has even been claimed that the close resemblance of mimic to model is purely accidental and due to other causes than to natural selection. The weight of evidence, however, is very much in favour of the theory and opponents have been very unsuccessful in providing any alternative explanation that would account for the remarkable resemblance of mimic to model on other grounds. Those who gave the first scientific account of mimicry were certain renowned naturalists who made observations out in the field in the tropics. There is no doubt that the most perfect and striking examples of mimicry are displayed in tropical and subtropical lands rather than in the temperate zone. Possibly, the more intense competition and struggle for existence prevailing in tropical nature provided the essential conditions for its evolution.

Let us now look into some of the more striking cases of mimicry between insects that are so distantly related as to be placed in different orders. A good example to begin with is the Wasp-beetle (*Clytus arietis*) whose black and yellow coloration recalls that of its presumed model the common Wasp (*Vespa*). The resemblance is enhanced by the alert jerkiness of movement on the part of the Beetle combined with a quivering motion of its antennae. There is also a more pronounced " waist " than is usual among Beetles. This insect is frequently to be seen on wooden fences and gates—situations often favoured by Wasps for the purpose of gnawing off wood fragments which are used in nest building (Pl. 36, p. 223, Fig. a).

The Reduviid Bug *Nabis lativentris* bears in its nymphal stages a striking resemblance to Ants (Pl. IV, p. 27, Fig. d). This is caused by a sham waist since the sides, where the thorax and hind-body join, are very pale-coloured except for a dark mark in the middle. The dark mark is shaped like the stalk or pedicel that joins the gaster to the thorax in an Ant while the pale patches at the sides look as if they were not part of the insect at all. Its elbowed antennae and slender limbs are further points of resemblance. When looked at in profile there is a definite node or process at the *apparent* constriction of the body just as in Ants, while the shiny abdomen is also Ant-like. The present writer has often noticed this Bug running over pavement in a Cambridge garden. Its rapid movements were very like those of Ants and it always seemed to be near to or in company with Ants that nested among crevices between the paving-stones. The adult Bugs, which are non-mimetic, were chiefly found among low plants growing nearby. Several other of our Bugs and also certain Spiders are noticeably Ant-like in appearance and are commonly found along with Ants.

Some Moths have acquired transparent wings—a condition that is produced by the loose attachment of the scales which rapidly become detached and fall off except along the margins and wing-veins (Pl. 28, p. 159, Fig. 18). In the case of the Broad-bordered and Narrow-bordered

Bee Hawk-moths (*Hemaris fuciformis* and *H. tityus*) the insects emerge from the chrysalis with the transparent areas of their wings scaled, but the scales become detached during the first flight. In this way they have come to resemble Bumble-bees very closely and have diverged from many other members of the Hawk-moth family in being diurnal in habit. A really thrilling experience is to see these remarkable Moths on the wing along with Bumble-bees partaking of nectar from the flowers of Bugle in a wood-clearing during the early summer. The Clearwing Moths likewise have acquired transparent wings. The two largest species, viz. the Hornet Clearwing (*Sesia apiformis*) and the Lunar Hornet Clearwing (*S. bembeciformis*), bear a remarkable resemblance to Wasps, especially the last-named. Their banded Wasp-like coloration, humming sound when flying and diurnal habits are especially noteworthy (see Pl. 28). No other British Moths have departed so much from the outward appearance of the other members of their order.

The attractive but scarce Beetle *Trichius fasciatus* (Pl. 28, Fig. 2), is an ally of the Cockchafer and is chiefly found in Scotland. It bears a very notable likeness to a Bumble-bee when in flight and, like the latter insect, visits wayside flowers in sunshine.

Among Flies there are various kinds shown on Plate 28 that bear a close resemblance to Wasps or Bees, as the case may be. The resemblance it may be added appears to be much more real in the living active creature than in a dead cabinet specimen. The Conopidae deserve special mention : they are a family of Flies that mostly undergo their development as parasites of Wasps or Bees and are consequently closely associated with them. Their resemblance to species of *Crabro*, *Odynerus*, *Nomada* and other solitary Wasps and Bees is clearly shown by their form, size and coloration. Their antennae are also much longer than is usual among the group of Flies to which they belong and heighten their resemblance to the models just named (Figs. 14 and 15).

The largest number of instances, however, are to be found among the Syrphidae or Hover-flies (Plate 28). One of the most prevalent types of coloration in this family is a black-and-yellow banding. A great many species, some large and others small, bear this design. The small kinds, especially those with noticeably slender bodies, may possibly be mimics of Solitary Wasps. Some of the larger kinds bear much the appearance of Social Wasps of the genus *Vespula*, especially the rather rare *Volucella inanis* whose larva lives as a scavenger in the nest of the Hornet. It has been said that this resemblance enables the

Plate XXIII

STUDIES OF GALLS

S. BEAUFOY

b Terminal Rosette Galls on Willow

S. BEAUFOY

a Pea Galls (5) and Spiny Galls (3) on Dog-rose

Plate XXIV

GALLS MADE BY THE FLY, *LIPARA LUCENS*, ON FLOWERING STEMS OF
THE COMMON REED AT WICKEN FEN

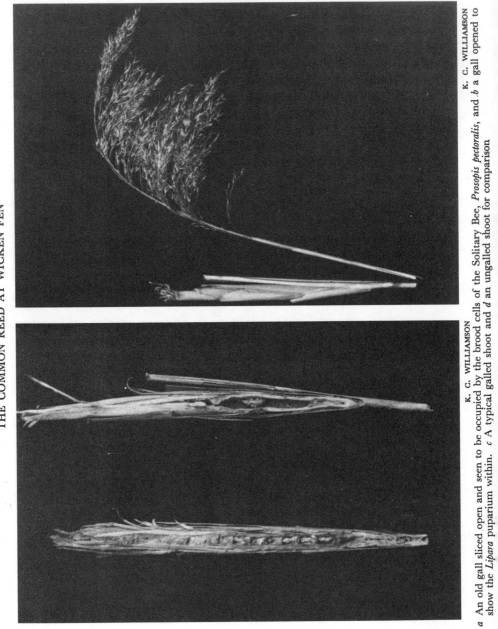

K. C. WILLIAMSON

a An old gall sliced open and seen to be occupied by the brood cells of the Solitary Bee, *Prosopis pectoralis*, and *b* a gall opened to show the *Lipara* puparium within. *c* A typical galled shoot and *d* an ungalled shoot for comparison

insect to be passed over and left unmolested when it enters a Hornet's nest. If this be so, it is strange that a closely related species *Volucella pellucida*, whose larva is likewise a scavenger, but in this case in the nest of the common Wasp (*Vespula vulgaris*), bears no resemblance to a Wasp at all. Indeed, the large *Sericomyia borealis* found about moorlands and woods has a more Wasp-like appearance. Another kind of *Volucella*, *V. bombylans*, is very like a small Bumble-bee and its larva is a scavenger in the Bees' nest where it feeds on wax, pollen and the dead or diseased larvae—it is said never to feed on healthy larvae. Several other kinds of Hover-flies are densely hairy, which gives them the general appearance of small Bumble-bees. Since none is known to have association with Bees' nests, it cannot be claimed that this resemblance is a disguise to enable them to enter such places without being attacked by the rightful occupants. Examples include the handsome *Criorhina floccosa* and other members of its genus, the large *Arctophila fulva* and the Narcissus Fly (*Merodon equestris*).

The abundant Hover-fly known as the Drone-fly (*Eristalis tenax*, (Plates 12 and 23) is almost always mistaken for a Hive-bee by the non-entomological observer. Its deceptive colour and appearance go with its activity in sunshine and it feeds at flowers along with Bees. There seems no doubt that this resemblance was responsible for the Aristotelian belief that Bees could be spontaneously generated by putrefaction.* This ancient and widespread myth held sway until Francesco Redi (1626–98) proved by simple experiments that the claim that insects could arise in this way was baseless. About the same time the Dutchman Jan Jacobz Swammerdam (1637–69) pointed out that there are Flies so like Bees that they might be mistaken for them. It remained for the Baron Osten-Sacken, more than 200 years later, finally to dispose of the ancient fable already mentioned. He showed that the Drone-fly (see p. 237), which often breeds in liquefying carcasses or other putrid organic matter, is so like a Bee as to be the cause of the myth. It is seldom found breeding under such circumstances nowadays because carcasses are not left lying about as they were in ancient times. To return to the resemblance of the Drone-fly to the Hive-bee. The first-named insect seems much too abundant to satisfy the conditions of ordinary mimicry. If this Fly is an edible insect the Hive-bee might often be mistaken for it and suffer heavy mortality in consequence. This complication brings us back, for a brief interval, to the general subject of mimicry.

It will be recalled that typical mimicry involves the resemblance of an edible mimic to a distasteful and more abundant model. This is sometimes called Batesian Mimicry after the traveller and naturalist H. W. Bates who was its first interpreter in the year 1861. Later it became known that another kind of mimicry may prevail wherein two or more specially protected insects may show a common plan of warning colours to their mutual advantage. In order to illustrate how this principle is believed to work let it be imagined that two kinds of insects are present in the same area in about equal numbers ; that both are distasteful to their enemies ; and that they show very different coloration. Let it further be granted that say 500 individuals of each species would have to be destroyed before their enemies learned to avoid them. Now, if instead, the two kinds bore such a close mutual resemblance as to be mistaken for each other, a loss of 500 individuals would still be sufficient for their enemies' preliminary testing of their qualities and consequently each kind would lose only 250 individuals or, in other words, their losses would be halved. This in a few words is the gist of another kind of mimicry which was first explained by Fritz Muller in 1879 and has come to be known as Mullerian Mimicry. It will be clear that under this theory one distasteful species may often be as abundant as another—both kinds will profit by the resemblance.

There is some evidence that the Drone-fly is rarely preyed upon by birds and it is quite possible that it is a distasteful insect. If this be correct then its resemblance to the Hive-bee is most likely to be accounted for on the basis of Mullerian mimicry. The black and yellow Hover-flies, already mentioned, together with very similarly coloured Ichneumon-flies and various sorts of Wasps also very possibly represent an association of mimics of the Mullerian kind. They certainly possess a common likeness and the theory would require that they are all protected in some way—either by stings or nauseous properties. Wasps we know are protected insects and what few experiments have been carried out show that Hover-flies are generally rejected by birds but we know less concerning the Ichneumon-flies. (Here is another promising field for the amateur to investigate.) A third instance of presumed Mullerian mimicry concerns two kinds of Beetles associated with the Red Ant, both kinds being found in and around its nests. One kind is the Ladybird *Coccinella divaricata* which is a member of a family of Beetles well known to have distasteful properties. The other kind is the Beetle named *Clythra quadripunctata* which belongs to a different family and is stated to be avoided by insectivorous animals. The two Beetles seem to be sufficiently alike in their conspicuous black and red liveries for at least some of their enemies to fail to discriminate between them. If this be so then the resemblance is to be regarded as an example of Mullerian mimicry.

In the foregoing example of resemblance between insects belonging to very different groups the primary question is whether mimicry is involved and is accountable for the likeness thus displayed. In so far as British insects are concerned the subject has attracted very little attention— perhaps they seem to pale into insignificance as compared with the amazing displays of mimicry seen in the tropics. Anyway what is needed is more direct evidence by way of both observation and experiment. Circumstantial evidence, however, is often sufficiently definite as to make it probable that the examples quoted in these pages are instances of true mimicry. Here the amateur has an excellent opportunity to conduct observations and critical tests on the coloration and edibility of different insects that may shed light upon a much disputed subject.

The riddle as to how such resemblances have come into being is a difficult problem. One thing is clear and that is that they can *not* be due to community of descent. Perhaps the best statement in a few words is given in the following quotation from the work of A. R. Wallace :—" The number of species of insects is so great, and there is such diversity of form and proportion in every group, that the chances of an accidental approximation in size, form, and colour of one insect to another of a different group is considerable ; and it is these chance approximations that furnish the basis of mimicry, to be continually advanced and perfected by the survival of those varieties only which tend in the right direction."

Before leaving the subject of coloration one other aspect of it should be mentioned. A number of insects show a localised but brilliant coloration displayed in parts of the body which are normally concealed but which flash into conspicuousness when they take to the wing. Such coloration is often called flash coloration. It is displayed frequently among Grasshoppers, both large and small ; in Cicadas, Lantern-flies and certain Moths and Butterflies. In southern Europe, for instance, certain kinds of Grasshoppers have beautiful crimson or blue hind-wings. When such insects are disturbed brilliant flashes of colour appear as the creatures fly away, but the moment they come to rest they seem to vanish altogether. The explanation is that their general colour merges perfectly with their surroundings when they are at rest because the hind-wings are completely hidden when closed. It is claimed that the bright flash attracts the attention of an enemy who becomes mystified when it vanishes and afterwards hunts around for it.   Usually it searches in vain although its prey may remain concealed nearby.

While there are no Grasshoppers that display flash colours in Britain certain Moths show the same phenomenon. The most notable are the Red Underwings and the Yellow Underwings which have red or orange-yellow hind-wings respectively. When disturbed by day these bright colours show up in flight only to disappear the moment the insect closes its wings and comes to rest. The present writer has several times watched sparrows chasing Yellow Underwings which had been disturbed. The Moth pursued an erratic darting flight followed by the bird but when it suddenly settled on the ground and disappeared among the herbage the bird soon gave up the search. In each case observed the Moth got away.

The use of protective coverings is usual among a variety of insects. Thus the various sorts of cases made by Caddis larvae (p. 50) protect their soft bodies when danger threatens. When disturbed in any way they withdraw the head and legs into these shelters and hold fast by their tail-hooks when they become difficult to dislodge. Many cater-pillars and the larvae of some of our Weevils roll the leaves of the food-plant into tubular shelters which allow them to feed in conceal-ment.   A very unusual kind of covering is the froth made by the Frog-hoppers or Cuckoo-Spit Insects (p. 46). The commonest species is *Philaenus leucophthalmus* (Pl. 37, p. 238, Fig. a). A larger kind known as *Aphrophora spumaria* affects a narrower range of plants, especially Sallows and Alders. A more strikingly coloured and less abundant Frog-hopper, *Cercopis vulnerata* (p. 199), occurs locally on the same kinds of bushes. Its nymphs have the unusual habit of living on the roots of grasses, etc., surrounded by froth, about 6 in. below ground.

The production of the spume or froth of Frog-hoppers has caused much speculation. It appears to protect the soft bodies of the nymphs from desiccation while it may also guard them to some extent against predators (Plates 37 and 38). It offers no impediment, however, to the Solitary Wasp *Gorytes mystaceus* which stores its larval cells with the nymphs of *Philaenus* which it drags from their surrounding spume. In *Philaenus*

PLATE 33

MORE STUDIES OF GALLS

S. BEAUFOY

a. Galls on Ground-ivy caused by the Gall-wasp, *Liposthenus latreillei*. The galls are green at first, becoming reddish or mauve later ($\times$ 1)

S. BEAUFOY

b. Galls on Meadow-sweet caused by the Gall-midge, *Dasyneura ulmariae* ($\times$ $\frac{3}{4}$)

PLATE 34

A STUDY IN CONCEALMENT AND DISPLAY

a. Caterpillars of Large Thorn Moth, *Ennomos autumnaria*, on Hawthorn. There are four of these caterpillars in the picture (× 1)

S. BEAUFOY

b. Gooseberry Saw-fly, *Pteronidea ribesii*. The yellow caterpillar above has recently moulted (× 1)

S. BEAUFOY

side-walls of the abdominal segments are extended beneath the body so as to meet below, thus enclosing a cavity into which the breathing pores open. This chamber is closed in front but air can be admitted or expelled by a sort of valve placed behind. The frothing is caused by air discharged through this valve, coming in contact with fluid issuing from the anus so as to blow it into bubbles. On the 7th and 8th abdominal segments are lateral glands whose secretion is believed to mix with the anal discharge so as to enable the spume to maintain its coherence even in wet weather.

Many aquatic insects deposit their eggs in the water where their larval life is passed. Such eggs are frequently laid in masses and coated with a gelatinous product from the body of the female insect. This substance swells in the water into a transparent mucilage which makes them not only hard to find but also so slippery that they would evade the grasp of most enemies. The eggs of many Caddis-flies and Midges are of this description.

The cocoons so characteristic of Moths, Saw-flies and other insects protect the helpless and more or less immobile pupae. In most cases cocoons are hidden away in recesses, beneath leaves, below ground or in other situations and are not easily discovered. In the Puss-moth (*Cerura vinula*) the cocoon bears a remarkably close similarity to the bark of the Willow or other tree upon which it was formed (Pl. XII, p. 107, Fig. f). Many cocoons are sufficiently tough or dense to preclude the entry of most invertebrate enemies, indeed so tough that the contained insect itself often has to be provided with special means (see p. 25) in order to effect its emergence into the outer world when fully developed.

There are still other ways and means of protection that have not been mentioned in these pages. A number of aquatic insects, for instance, rely upon their own swimming powers to dart away from their enemies and lie up among water-plants until the danger has passed. Another means is provided by a particularly hard and resistant integument. With the protection given by such an armature some Weevils and other Beetles are able to withstand very rough treatment and yet escape without injury. Many much-persecuted insects such as Aphids are endowed with an enormous capacity for rapid multiplication which speedily makes good a heavy destruction of individuals. The reader may be reminded that most Moths, besides numerous kinds of Flies, Beetles and other insects hide themselves during the day and are only active at night. This habit secures for them a high degree of freedom from the attacks of day-time enemies, especially birds. Finally the great majority of leaf-feeding insects take up positions on the *under* sides of the leaves, which is perhaps the simplest of all ways of protection from exposure to enemies.

The chief ways and means that insects adopt for protection against their enemies have now been enumerated, and a tabular résumé of the subject is given below :

1. Protection by locomotion, i.e. :—flying ; running ; leaping ; swimming.
2. Protection by adopting threatening attitudes.
3. Protection by coloration.
   a.—Protective or cryptic coloration, imparting a close resemblance to some part of the inanimate surroundings.
   b.—Mimicry or the resemblance of one animal to another. Includes Batesian mimicry or the resemblance by an unprotected mimic to a distasteful (protected) model ; and Mullerian mimicry or the sharing of a conspicuous pattern by several distasteful (protected) species.
   c.—Warning coloration advertising general distastefulness, hairiness, poisonous or irritating secretions, stings, etc.
   d.—Flash coloration.
4. Protection by means of cases, cocoons, leaf-rolls, coverings of froth or mucilage, etc.
5. Protection by other means, i.e. :—high reproduction-rate, nocturnal habits, etc.

THE PHENOMENA
OF REPRODUCTION

REPRODUCTION is a unique property of all living things and separates them from the non-living. Since insects are typically land animals they cannot reproduce themselves as simply and easily as is the case with many aquatic creatures. For example when a Sea-urchin or a Star-fish reproduces, the female liberates her eggs into the water and the male does the same with his sperms. The sperms swim of their own activity through the water and on coming into contact with the eggs they penetrate into them and thus bring about fertilisation. This happy-go-lucky way of doing things is all very well for truly aquatic animals. Those that live on land have to face the ever-present danger of their sperms drying up owing to lack of moisture. This means that external fertilisation is far too precarious to be adopted by terrestrial animals. The only possible way for them is to ensure that the sperms come in contact with the eggs before the latter leave the bodies of the female parents. Insects form no exception; they all practise internal fertilisation.

The actual linking together of the bodies of the male and female constitutes the act of mating* or copulation. The coupling is brought about by the external organ or penis of the male entering the vagina of the female. In cases where the male possesses claspers (see p. 14) he uses them to grasp the female during the process. Among Beetles there are no claspers and the tarsi of the fore-legs in the male are often much broadened and sucker-like. This is specially marked in the Great Water-beetle (*Dytiscus*), and in all cases they are used for holding on to the female. In some of the Oil-beetles the antennae are modified at a certain point so that the male may grip those of the female in the clasp thus formed.

There is plenty of room for observation as regards different mating habits among insects, although a good deal has been written about it already. Most Grasshoppers and Crickets attract their mates with "song," but other insects, excepting the Cicadas, are less romantic. The male Scorpion-fly, for instance, spits out little globules of saliva on to the leaf where a female is sitting. She obligingly turns to this offering and feeds on it: the male then seizes the end of her abdomen and mates with her.

But the Empid-flies are the most accomplished artists in keeping their spouse occupied during mating. Some of the smaller kinds dance or swarm in the air in great numbers over streams or elsewhere. Like the Robber-flies they are carnivorous and, in some of the species, what the male does is to scour the air until he manages to capture some small insect, usually another Fly. This he kills and presents to the first female he meets, who eagerly takes it. Mating then happens immediately and while it goes on the female complacently sucks out the juices of the morsel in question.

The strangest members of the Empididae are little black Flies called *Hilara*. It is their custom for the male, having captured a prey, to bind it up with a few strands of silk, possibly to prevent it struggling, and then bestow it upon a female. Some kinds hunt over the surface of streams and are very cunning in their behaviour. What they do is to pick up a dead insect or other sufficiently light object they may find floating by. They may even use such inedible things as bud scales, buttercup stamens, or petals—daisy florets being specially favoured. Whatever is picked up is enveloped in a silken binding, and probing the bundle seems to keep the female busy while mating takes place. It is not related what happens when (or if) she discovers the fraud.

Hilara produces its silk in a very extraordinary way—not through the mouth like a caterpillar but by means of its fore-legs. The front tarsi have their part nearest to the tibia much enlarged and studded with minute bristles. The silk-forming glands lie in the swollen part of the tarsus, each gland opening into one of the bristles (Pl. 23, p. 126, Fig. 3). Under a high power of the microscope traces of a whitish fluid may be seen issuing from the tip of each bristle. On contact with the air this fluid hardens into a thread of exquisite fineness.

With many Moths the males are attracted to the females by a particular scent produced by the latter from glands situated near the end of the hind-body. Sometimes the product exudes almost like sweat and, in the Vapourer Moth, if it be absorbed on a piece of blotting paper it will attract the male even in the absence of the female herself. Scent-glands, however, are much more common in the male than in the female. They occur not only in Moths and Butterflies but also among Caddis-flies and some other insects. Their odour is often perceptible to human nostrils and in all cases it appears to act as a stimulant or aphrodisiac to excite the female.

The rule with insects, as among most animals, is that the male is the active sex that searches out the partner. There are, however, a few examples in which the female does the searching. The Ghost-moth (*Hepialus humuli*) is a well-known instance. In this case the glistening white of the male presumably helps in betraying his presence as he hovers round on rapidly vibrating wings. In this way he diffuses an odour which gives further aid to the female as she flies among the grass in her search for him. Another instance is found in the Giant Lace-wing, *Osmylus fulvicephalus*. The late C. L. Withycombe noted that the male in this species plays a very passive part in courtship. All he does is to sit about and protrude his scent-glands that are placed near the end of his body. The females do the searching and are obviously attracted by the odour that is diffused and even stroke the glands with their antennae and palpi before mating. The reader will find something more about scents and odours in Chapter 4, including their perception from distances.

The act of mating normally results in fertilisation—that is the merging or fusion of the sperm nuclei with those of the eggs. Whereas the sperms are usually discharged into the vagina of the female, there is often a special pouch or spermatheca present into which they ultimately pass. Here they may be kept alive for some time and are liberated in small numbers as the eggs become ready to be fertilised. In the Hive-bee the sperms may remain alive in her spermatheca for as long as five years after she has once mated. In general, however, fertilisation takes place soon after mating and the female lays all her eggs within a comparatively short time, after which she dies.

While the eggs are in the oviduct of the female each becomes coated with a hard protective shell. Afterwards they pass down into the vagina where fertilisation takes place. It is at this juncture that nature makes a remarkable provision to ensure its happening. Since the egg-shell is impenetrable to the entry of the sperms a definite microscopic area, or micropyle, is provided expressly for the purpose of ensuring their admission. It comprises a pore, or a group of pores, where the egg-shell is not complete and through which sperms can freely pass in order to reach the interior of the egg.

Insect eggs show an amazing diversity of shape and surface pattern :
a better idea of their range of form will be gained from Text-Fig. 32
than from several pages of letterpress. A very frequent type is that of
the House-fly—rather long, cylindrical, and slightly curved, with the
surface either smooth or patterned. Cockroaches, Grasshoppers, Bees
and many Flies lay eggs of this kind. Some of the most beautifully and

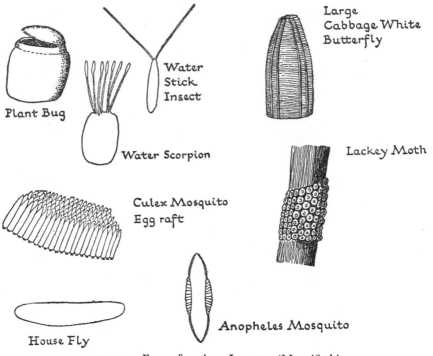

Large
Cabbage White
Butterfly

Water
Stick
Insect

Plant Bug

Water Scorpion

Lackey Moth

Culex Mosquito
Egg raft

Anopheles Mosquito

House Fly

FIG. 32.—Eggs of various Insects. (Magnified.)

elaborately sculptured eggs are found in Butterflies and certain Moths.
The Green Lace-wings lay smooth ovoid eggs attached to leaves at the
extremities of long stalks. These are really most attractive objects, as will
be gathered from Pl. VII, p. 62. In some species the stalks are separate
and apart while in others they adhere so as to form a common stem,
but with the ends bearing the eggs quite separate. Before an egg is
laid the Lace-wing exudes a drop of a sticky fluid on to a leaf. It then
raises the tip of the abdomen so as to draw out the fluid into a fine

thread. This quickly hardens and an egg is laid on the top of the stalk thus formed. Being well placed at a distance from the leaf-surface these eggs are protected from the attention of such marauders as young larvae of the Lace-wings themselves, Ants and other creatures.

Many Plant-bugs lay batches of short cylindrical or urn-shaped eggs provided with neat lids that are pushed open by the young insects when they hatch. The Ox Warble-flies and the Lice attach their eggs to the hairs of the animal upon which their offspring are destined to live (Pl. IV, p. 27, Fig. b). These eggs are so firmly fastened that no ordinary scratching on the part of the host will dislodge them.

The eggs of aquatic insects are a never-failing source of interest to the naturalist. Those of the *Culex* Mosquitoes, for instance, are laid in batches, sometimes of 300 or more. They adhere so as to form a minute raft less than $\frac{1}{4}$ in. long. These rafts are brownish objects that are common on the surface of stagnant water but very easily over-looked. They float so lightly that they become blown about by the least puff of air. They are normally unsinkable and cannot be upset because they right themselves immediately. The individual eggs are arranged upright with the narrow ends in the air and their curious cup-like micropyles resting on the surface film. It has been recently shown by Sir Rickard Christophers that these eggs are individually heavier than water but have properties that make them unwettable. The result is that air enters the chinks and spaces between the eggs and makes the whole raft buoyant. Placed in weak spirit the raft sinks, because this fluid is able to enter the spaces just mentioned and drive out the air. The cup-like micropyles have a special affinity for water and maintain a firm hold on the surface film : this device keeps the raft right side up.

The *Anopheles* Mosquitoes lay their eggs singly : their buoyancy is due to an air-chamber or float on each side of the eggs (Text-Fig. 32).

The Water-scorpion (*Nepa*) and its close relation the Water Stick-insect (*Ranatra*) lay curious eggs with thread-like outgrowths at one end. There are generally 7 of these structures in *Nepa* and 2 in *Ranatra*. The eggs are laid in the stems of water-plants in such a way that only the threads project (Text-Fig. 32). Perhaps these filaments allow of the inward passage of oxygen to the eggs and the outward diffusion of the unwanted carbon dioxide. Eggs have to respire like all living cells and this interchange of gases might prove difficult unless part is freely exposed to the water.

Insects with long ovipositors lay their eggs in hidden situations. The length of these instruments, in fact, is a measure of the depth to which the eggs are deposited. Thus, the Great Green Grasshopper (Pl. 1, p. 2) has a stout blade-like ovipositor with which she lays her eggs well down in the soil. The female Wood-wasp, *Sirex* or *Urocerus*, has a long needle-like instrument which she uses to drill a hole in pine-trees so that her eggs can be lodged deep (Pl. 20, p. 95, Fig. 12).

Our largest Ichneumon, *Rhyssa*, has an even longer tool for egg-laying than *Sirex* has. She needs every bit of it, however, because her ambition is to find the *Sirex* larva and place an egg on its body. Its larva, when it hatches, lives as a parasite on that of the *Sirex*, gradually sucking out its life-blood until it is fully grown (p. 151). *Rhyssa* (Pl. 20, p. 95, Fig. 13) is an elegant bluish-black insect with white markings on its hind-body and the legs are red. A good-sized female measures $1\frac{1}{4}$ in. long and its ovipositor reaches to another $1\frac{1}{2}$ in. In June and July they are to be seen searching for logs infested with Wood-wasp larvae. Having found a trunk to her liking the female explores its surface most thoroughly with the tips of her antennae. She seems to be guided at least partially by her sense of smell in discovering the whereabouts of the *Sirex* larva. When she has picked up the scent she becomes unmistakably excited and after quietening down starts to bore into the solid wood. According to R. N. Chrystal she does this by arching her body upwards and raising the long bristle-like ovipositor with the aid of her hind-legs so that its tip can enter the wood. The parts of this instrument work with incredible rapidity with the result that she can drill a hole $1\frac{1}{4}$ in. deep into solid wood in the space of less than 20 minutes. Often her instinct seems to fail her and she draws a blank —the *Sirex* larva may have moved away but had probably left a deceptive odour trail behind. Anyway, she seems undaunted for she starts another search until she locates the larva she needs and then the boring process is repeated. Her eggs have to pass right down the slender ovipositor which has a central passage for their transit. The eggs become squeezed out of their normal shape in their journey but regain it on reaching the *Sirex* larva.

The present writer once found a dead *Rhyssa* in Wales with her ovipositor buried up to the hilt in the solid wood of a larch tree. Something had happened that prevented her from withdrawing it. In 1944 he found a female *Sirex* in the same predicament, stone-dead and firmly trapped. According to Chrystal this happens when these insects bore in wood that is at all fresh because the wood fibres close up round the ovipositor and hold the insect fast.

In the Saw-flies the ovipositor is like a microscopic fret-saw. With this tool the female literally saws slits, or pockets, to receive her eggs in the stems or leaves of those plants upon which her larvae will feed.

Most insects show instinctive care for the future of their progeny— this is instanced by the meticulous care with which they lay their eggs in places where the offspring (that they will never see) have plenty to eat. There is, however, one elementary axiom about eggs that it is most important to bear in mind. The number that is laid is not a criterion of the relative abundance of a given species. It was Darwin who pointed out many years ago that the Fulmar Petrel lays only a single egg yet it is believed to be one of the most abundant birds in the world. The greatest fecundity prevails among those animals that suffer the heaviest destruction, particularly where, as is usual among insects, the parent has no means for protecting her eggs or young. It will be interesting to look into a few instances that illustrate this general theorem.

A good example is the Sheep-ked (*Melophagus ovinus*) which is a spidery-looking object and almost a complete travesty of what it really is :—viz. a Fly. It has degenerated into a wingless parasite that lives among the wool of sheep and sucks their warm blood. The female Ked only produces a single egg at a time : each grows within her body into a larva which is nourished by a maternal secretion until fully grown. As soon as a larva is born it turns into a pupa among the wool of the host and there develops in the course of a few weeks into a new Ked. It will be noted that the whole life of a Ked is a protected one spent hidden among the wool. It has few enemies other than certain birds that at times perch on the backs of the sheep in order to devour any of these tough morsels that they may find. Since the vicissitudes of free eggs and larvae are done away with, and the adults themselves are adepts at concealment, a numerous progeny is rendered un- necessary. In fact each female is stated to produce only 10 or 12 larvae during her life.

An example of the opposite kind is afforded by the Oil-beetles (*Meloe*). These insects differ from most Beetles in that their wing-covers overlap instead of simply meeting in a line down the back (Pl. XI, p. 106, Fig. d). They are large creatures, sometimes an inch or more long, which crawl about in a sluggish manner in grassy places during sunny days in spring. The female Beetle lays several large batches of minute yellow eggs in the ground. The French observer A. Cros mentions that a single batch laid by the species *Meloe violaceus* contained 3,000 to 4,000 eggs. The fecundity of these insects is, therefore, relatively high. The young larvae are minute yellow objects that are very active and have long legs and projecting bristles at the hind extremity. Their life is a precarious adventure because survival depends upon their coming across *Anthophora* Bees (see p. 266). These larvae wander in swarms over the herbage, generally climbing upwards. In this way some of them manage to reach flowers that are visited by the Bees in question. The *Meloe* larva now has its chance to make good and it tries to hang on to the hairy coat of the bee. If it succeeds it becomes carried to the *Anthophora's* nest where it undergoes a complex metamorphosis. Once there, the first thing it does is to raid one of the cells and feed upon the contained egg. Having thus refreshed itself it appropriates the food-store intended for the Bee larva and completes its growth on this pabulum. The *Meloe* larva seems to be very careless as to the kinds of insects to which it may attach itself. A vast number come to a miserable end through clinging to the wrong kind of Bee or by mistaking a hairy Fly for a Bee. An even larger quota never come in contact with a carrier of any sort. Thus, the hazards of life in *Meloe* are compensated for by the vast numbers of larvae each female Beetle produces. Most insects which experience the ordinary hazards of life each lay several hundred eggs, certainly not more.

In referring to the Sheep-ked it was mentioned that this insect produces living young. Quite a number of other insects do the same thing. What happens is that the eggs, instead of being laid, remain in the body of the female until they hatch out. Insects that reproduce in this way are said to be viviparous (*L. vivus*, alive and *pario*, to produce) to distinguish them from those that are oviparous (*L. ovum*, an egg, and *pario*, to produce), i.e. lay eggs in the ordinary way. The most familiar viviparous insects are the Aphids or Green-fly that abound in summer on many kinds of vegetation. It is only in late autumn that oviparous Aphids are found. Throughout the spring and summer they multiply by the viviparous method. If colonies of these insects be scrutinised newly-born young are almost certainly to be found. They are recognisable on account of being the smallest individuals present. Very often some of the females may be seen in the act of producing offspring.

The Flesh-fly (*Sarcophaga*) also gives rise to living young. If a female be captured and put into a vessel she will often deposit a number of squirming larvae over its interior. Gauze covers placed over meat, unless of exceedingly fine mesh, do not afford protection against this Fly. If she cannot gain personal access to the meat she just sits on the cover and lets her larvae fall through the meshes.

Some insects practise virgin birth or, in other words, the eggs which they lay do not have to be fertilised by sperms. This method of reproduction without mating is called parthenogenesis (*parthenos*, virgin ; *genesis*, origin). It is the usual way of reproduction in Aphids, where it is always associated with the birth of living young. Generation after generation of Aphids reproduce in this way and all the individuals that are born are females. Not even the ghost of a male appears on the scene until the autumn. Then males and normal egg-laying females develop and in due course they mate. The females lay fertilised eggs which remain dormant all the winter and hatch out in early spring into other females. These individuals start practising virgin birth all over again : brood after brood arises in this way until the autumn.

Virgin birth prevails in a great many Hymenoptera. It is well known for instance that in the Hive-bee virgin eggs give rise to the drones or males whereas the queens and workers come from eggs that have to be fertilised in the usual way. This method of sex-control has been carried to a great pitch in other of the Hymenoptera. Among certain of them the male has disappeared altogether as for instance in some of the Saw-flies and Gall-wasps. From among tens of thousands of females of some species that have been reared by entomologists not a single male has ever been known to show his face—the sex has in fact been wiped out.

Some other Hymenoptera have not quite abolished the male. Among certain Ichneumon-flies, for instance, an unwanted male turns up very occasionally from among thousands of members of the opposite sex. The Gall-wasp that makes "Robin's Pincushions" (Pl. 32, p. 191, Fig. c) on the wild Rose rarely produces males—there is generally only about one male to well over 100 females. In another Gall Wasp that makes the oak-apples (Pl. 30, p. 175, Fig. a) so familiar to country dwellers, the spring brood consists of only wingless females whereas the summer brood comprises individuals of both sexes.

It is easy to rear caterpillars of the Gooseberry Saw-fly (*Pteronidea ribesii*)—they are to be found on Gooseberry bushes in most gardens. Individuals of both sexes are readily bred out and if proper precautions are taken so that the females are kept separate from the males they will lay virgin eggs, which produce males in every case. Where mating has been allowed to occur, females only are produced from the fertilised eggs.

Many Moths, kept in captivity, will lay unfertilised eggs that normally do not hatch. Occasionally parthenogenesis occurs and the eggs develop into caterpillars that grow into either male or female Moths. This happens sometimes in the Silkworm Moth, in the Oak-eggar and a few others.

One or two kinds of insects even start to breed before they have grown up. This sort of reproduction is called paedogenesis (Gr. *pais*, gen. *paidos*, child, and *genesis*, origin). Those most addicted to this way of behaving are tiny Gall-midges. Gall-midges, it may be added, are true Flies and are not to be confused with the Gall-wasps already referred to in this Chapter. Why they should be in such a hurry to leave progeny behind them is not known. Anyway, what happens is that the females of certain kinds of these Midges, especially *Miastor*, produce a few very large virgin eggs. Each egg hatches into a transparent larva which gives rise to daughter larvae inside its own body : they arise from precociously developed parthenogenetic eggs. When they are fully developed these larvae gnaw their way out of their unfortunate parent and then start multiplying in exactly the same way on their own account. After several generations have been produced they alter their habits and become more conventional. Each larva turns into a pupa and ordinary male and female Midges arise. After mating eggs are laid and the curious paedogenetic cycle starts afresh.

An even more curious state of affairs prevails among certain of the Chalcid Wasps and their allies. Some of them are so minute that they are able to lay their eggs inside the eggs of other insects, especially of Moths. When the Moth egg hatches the caterpillar that emerges from it comes into the world with the egg of the Chalcid Wasp growing in its interior. It is now that something little short of a miracle happens. The Chalcid egg becomes a sausage-shaped mass of embryonic cells which goes on growing and divides up into a chain of separate embryos that vary in number according to the species of Chalcid concerned. Each embryo grows into a minute larva which in its turn becomes a pupa. All this goes on inside the body of the unhappy caterpillar that is now dead and reduced to skin only. This strange phenomenon, in which an egg may develop and divide into two or more separate embryos, is called polyembryony. In this way a single original egg may give rise to 2, 12, 20, 50 or more Chalcid Wasps according to the species : the maximum number known to originate from the division of a single egg is about one thousand ! Truly we can say with Hamlet :

> There are more things in heaven and earth, Horatio,
> Than are dreamt of in your philosophy.

This achievement of producing a thousand offspring from one single egg is found in the Chalcid *Litomastix* which is by no means a rare insect. It lays its eggs inside those of the common Silver Y Moth (*Plusia gamma*). Another Chalcid (named *Ageniaspis*) uses the eggs of the Small Ermine-moths (*Yponomeuta*) for the same purpose. In this case each egg gives rise to about 30 to 80 offspring—so it is much less prolific than the other Chalcid just mentioned.

But this is not the whole story. If the Chalcid Wasp lays virgin eggs, as she often does, they all develop into males, whereas if mating takes place and the eggs become fertilised, the progeny then consists entirely of females. Sometimes several eggs may be laid within a single host-egg, as happens in the case of the *Litomastix* already mentioned. When such a thing happens, more than 3,000 individual adult *Litomastix* have been counted after they had come out of a single defunct caterpillar. If both virgin and fertilised eggs had been laid in the first place the offspring would be a mixed population of males and females. Otherwise if only the one or the other kind of egg had been laid then all the resulting Chalcids would turn out to be males or females as the case may be.

Up to this point only brief reference has been made to Aphids or Green-fly ; consequently this chapter will close with some further comments on their breeding habits. We have about 450 different kinds of these insects in Britain and among them are many notorious enemies of cultivated plants. Their sucking propensities exhaust the sap when the vegetation becomes heavily infested, the leaves and shoots becoming distorted or shrivelled, if not killed. Most people with gardens are familiar with the sight of innumerable Aphids clustered around the shoots of roses, broad beans or other plants. Their breeding habits, however, display much that is interesting and, as will be shown later, the effective control of Aphids really depends in the long run upon what we know of their reproduction in particular.

In the month of October, when insect life is beginning to decline or becoming dormant, Aphids likewise begin to die off. Before this happens they produce ordinary male and female individuals that mate and lay fertilised eggs. Generally speaking, they are laid on the stems and shoots of woody plants or trees. It is these eggs that carry the Aphids through the winter. Relatively large, black and thick-shelled, they withstand the extremes of weather with impunity and hatch in the following March.

The resulting Aphids are wingless " stem-mothers " which produce living young without participation of the males—in fact there are no males about at this time of the year. As a rule the generation thus produced multiplies on its own account in an exactly similar way but among the progeny are many individuals with wings—these are the migrants.

We now enter another phase of Aphid life. What the migrants do is to fly away and settle down on some other kind of plant, usually of the herbaceous kind, where they begin to give birth to numerous offspring. From now onwards until autumn, generation after genera-tion follows in rapid succession—each generation consisting mainly of either winged or wingless individuals alternating. The winged examples fly away and infest other plants. All the countless individuals produced are females : every one brings forth living young by virgin birth. Never a sign of a male appears on the scene.

A single individual Aphid will give rise to several daughters daily and perhaps to 50 or more during her brief spell of life. The progeny may need only 8 or 10 days before they are grown up and these reproduce in the same way themselves. The warmer the weather the more rapidly multiplication goes on: a cold spell slows it down very appreciably. The progeny of a single Bean Aphid (*Aphis fabae*), for example, may amount to over 1,300 individuals at the end of 14 days under a mean temperature of 71° F. Fewer than 500 will be the net result at the end of 18 days should the mean temperature be only 58° F., so vital is the effect of warmth.

In October males at last appear. They and the winged females usually fly to the same kind of woody plant or tree. The females give rise to wingless daughters by virgin birth and these latter mate with the males. Fertilised eggs are laid and, with this act, provision for overwintering is made and the life-cycle is completed.

The undisturbed progeny of a single " stem-mother," at the end of one season only, would represent a fantastic figure if reproduction were allowed to go without any check. Assuming for the sake of simplicity that 50 young are born to each female Aphid, and that there are 13 generations composed of individuals of this sex, then the total offspring at the end of the season would be $(50)^{12}$. But this figure does not take into account the last generation that produces fertilised eggs. However, enemies of various kinds including other insects and birds, disease, often together with the effects of unfavourable weather, deplete the Aphid ranks. Even then the number of survivors may be almost astronomical.

Anyone with a garden or allotment sooner or later makes the acquaintance of the Bean Aphid (*Aphis fabae*). After overwintering in the egg on the Spindle-tree or perhaps on the Guelder Rose it flies to the Broad Bean. When left to its own devices its progeny smother the growing shoots (Pl. 38, p. 239, Fig. a) and ruin the crop. Besides Broad Beans it has other summer hosts including Dock, Poppies and Sugar-beet. Apple trees suffer heavily from Aphid attacks. The Woolly Aphid or American Blight (*Eriosoma lanigerum*) when abundant, is a sure sign of neglected trees. It generally spends its whole life on the Apple, where groups of individuals attack the branches and are very noticeable on account of their white wool-like coverings of waxy material (Pl. 17, p. 78, Fig. d). Four other kinds of Aphids attack the foliage of the Apple, the most important being the Rosy Aphid (*Dysephis malifoliae*) which causes the leaves to curl up and turn brown. This species lives on the trees until about mid-July when great numbers of winged individuals develop. Most of them fly to other plants, thus leaving the trees comparatively free. To what plants they migrate we do not know but a return migration to Apple trees happens in October and winter eggs are eventually laid on the shoots. The Rosy Aphid has many enemies, including larval and adult Ladybirds, Lace-wing larvae and larvae of Hover-flies. These creatures often check the infestation by July but most of the damage has then been done. The Poplar Gall-aphid (*Pemphigus bursarius*) produces galls on Poplar leaves and their stalks as shown in Pl. 32, p. 191, Fig. a. It also lives on the roots of the Lettuce and Sow-thistle. Mention must also be made of the Rose Aphids (Pl. 29, p. 174, Fig. a) of which there are three different kinds. One kind, *Myzaphis rosarum*, spends its whole life on the Rose, both wild and cultivated, whereas the other two kinds migrate to Cereals and Grasses or to Teasels respectively. This migration often accounts for the sudden clearance of the trees in summer which remain free until they become re-infected late in the season.

There are two periods when the depredations of many Aphids can be best controlled, viz. the winter and the spring. Winter is the time for destroying the hard-shelled eggs on the leafless branches and twigs. The standard way of doing this to use a tar-oil spray, which penetrates the shell. It can only be done in the dormant season because it burns and kills the foliage at other times. The discovery of these sprays in Holland has been a boon to fruit-growers who now rely upon winter treatment as one of the chief ways of protecting their trees.

Spring treatment aims at killing off the early generations of Aphids before they become too numerous and destructive. Once they have multiplied sufficiently to cause the leaves to curl it is too late to apply treatment for so many individuals hide away in the contorted leaves and escape the effects of spraying. Because Aphids feed by piercing the tissues of plants and sucking up the sap they require a different kind of treatment compared with insects like caterpillars, that chew up the foliage. Sprays known as stomach poisons, that cover the foliage with a thin film of poison, are effective against caterpillars but are quite useless against Aphids. These and other sucking insects can only be killed by sprays which, containing either nicotine, paraffin, or derris, kill by coming into contact with the bodies of the insects. Recently insecticides like parathion have been discovered which are absorbed by plants, whose sap becomes poisonous to sucking insects.

It will perhaps be useful to conclude this chapter with a short summary of the ways in which insects multiply. There are four methods as follows :—

a. Ordinary or bisexual reproduction.
b. Parthenogenesis or reproduction by virgin females.
c. Paedogenesis or reproduction by the larvae or immature insects.
d. Polyembryony or multiplication of the developing embryo into two or more daughter embryos. This may happen either with *a* or *b* above.

As a general rule, reproduction in insects is oviparous, or in other words eggs are laid in the usual way. In some insects, and in particular Aphids, the eggs remain in the body of the female until they hatch, and living young are produced in consequence.

PLATE 35

E. J. HUDSON

E. J. HUDSON

a. Caterpillar of Vapourer Moth, *Orgyia antiqua*, densely hairy, hairs in tufts

b. Tiger Moth, *Arctia caja*, presumed warning coloration

S. BEAUFOY

b. Caterpillars of Saw-fly, *Croesus septentrionalis*, warning coloration

(All slightly enlarged)

METHODS OF PROTECTION

PLATE 36

a. Wasp-beetle, *Clytus arietis*   b. Nut-weevil, *Curculio venosus*

c. Bloody Nose Beetle, *Timarcha tenebricosa*, and larva on Goosegrass
[temperature controlled]

(All slightly enlarged)

MORE COLEOPTERA OR BEETLES

Photographs by S. BEAUFOY

AQUATIC INSECT LIFE

MANY kinds of insects have taken to life in the water but in every case they were originally descended from air-dwellers and, in fact, very many of them continue to breathe the atmospheric air. They would drown, like any denizens of the land, if they stayed below the water for a considerable time and are consequently forced to come to the surface for " a breather." There are, however, other kinds of insects that are complete aquatics in that they, like fishes, breathe the oxygen dissolved in the water and no longer have the need to come to the surface to respire the air.

It is perhaps rather remarkable that these numerous aquatic forms do not belong to a single group or order. They are, in fact, a manifestation of the extraordinary plasticity or adaptability of insects in changing from one medium to another. The water-dwellers comprise a very miscellaneous assortment, drawn from numerous families belonging to diverse orders. It follows, therefore, that aquatic insects have not been evolved from a common ancestral stock : the very opposite has occurred since this mode of life has been independently acquired in each of the groups concerned. To take a few instances, many Water-beetles belong to families which often include a large quota of terrestrial species. Again, we have one or two Hymenoptera and a very few Moth caterpillars that have taken to an aquatic life and, in this way, they have deviated from the usual mode of existence common to all the other members of those two orders. On the other hand, the nymphs of Stone-flies together with those of Dragon-flies and of May-flies are all aquatic—there are no exceptions. Among the true Flies or Diptera not only do at least thirteen of the British families include aquatic representatives, but the water-dwelling habit has been acquired independently, in some cases at least several times within a single family.

Aquatic insects* are among the most attractive of all water animals to search for and observe. The interest that they arouse is mainly due to the many fascinating ways in which they have become fitted for their modes of life. The change from a terrestrial to an aquatic existence

has meant many alterations affecting breathing, locomotion and feeding. In these respects some insects are more highly adapted than others
and for this reason it is convenient to sort them out into three groups
as follows (Text-Fig. 33) :—(1) The surface-dwellers, whose adaptations
are relatively slight because they are above-water forms that merely walk

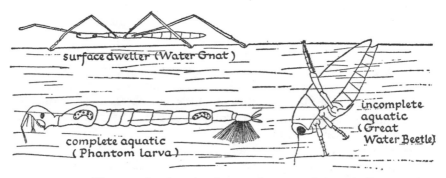

surface dweller (Water Gnat)

incomplete
aquatic
(Great
Water Beetle)

complete aquatic
(Phantom larva)

FIG. 33.—Diagram showing the three main types of Aquatic Insects.

or glide on the surface without being submerged. (2) The incompletely
aquatic forms, which show varying degrees of adaptation towards
overcoming the difficulties associated with their ways of life. Since they
spend most of their lives submerged they are aquatic in respect to most
of their activities but they have to come to the surface in order to take
in air. They are not so completely wedded to the water that they are
unable to leave that medium. They do, in fact, often take to the air
and many are good fliers. (3) The true aquatics, which live wholly
below the water and perish if placed in the air.

1. SURFACE-DWELLERS.—The most familiar of the surface-dwellers
are the Pond-skaters or Water-striders (*Gerris*), which are Hemipterous
insects of the suborder Heteroptera. They form an almost constant
feature in pond life, attracting notice on account of their agility in
darting over the surface of the water. There are ten British species,
which all have long narrow bodies, short fore-legs and elongated
middle- and hind-legs (Pl. XXV, p. 226, Fig. c). The fore-legs are held
above the water surface, being used for seizing and holding other
insects which serve as food : the middle legs are the chief locomotory
organs and the hind pair are used for steering.

The most significant difference between Pond-skaters and ordinary terrestrial insects is their ability to run or even leap on water without becoming wetted. This depends upon two facts. Firstly, the surface of the water is an almost incredibly thin film or membrane owing to the molecules cohering in a peculiar state of aggregation. The film thus formed is in a state of tension and has a rough resemblance to a very fine sheet of stretched india-rubber. Besides being elastic it also has considerable strength since it will support any object whose weight is insufficient to break its continuity. This can be shown by the time-honoured experiment of carefully launching a fine needle on to the surface of water in a vessel. Notwithstanding its being many times heavier than water, the needle will rest on the surface film ; thus proving the strength of the latter. Once the film is broken an object ordinarily becomes wetted and, if heavier than water, it sinks. The second feature is that the Pond-skater has a special covering which prevents it from becoming wetted. This takes the form of a fine velvet-like pile which clothes the legs and body and has the property of preventing the water from coming into actual contact with the insect. If the reader has ever tried to capture a Pond-skater he will know how agile this creature is, but if one be submerged it will be seen to be enveloped in a silvery coat of air which the water is unable to displace, so that when the insect rises to the surface it is quite unwetted. By watching a Pond-skater at close quarters it will be seen that its body does not actually touch the water ; it is, in fact, supported by the legs so as to be just above the surface. When its feet come in contact with the surface film they make tiny pits, which are due to the weight of the insect depressing the film at these points. The claws of the feet, it may be noted, are placed just before the apex of the tarsus which ends in a tuft of hair. This latter is a device which serves to prevent the tip of the legs from pushing through the surface film.

Another kind of surface-dweller is the Water-gnat or Water-measurer (*Hydrometra*)—a fantastically slender creature that makes one wonder how all its internal organs manage to find room in its attenuated body (Pl. XXVI, p. 227, Fig. a). The common *Hydrometra stagnorum* lives near or among vegetation bordering stagnant or slowly moving water. It is incapable of skating or leaping after the manner of *Gerris* and merely moves by a slow crawl over the water-surface, using the same movements as when walking on land ; indeed it is often to be found on nearby damp soil.   Although different in appearance from Pond-skaters *Hydrometra* is closely related to them.

Anyone who has lingered on the banks of pools and gently flowing water can scarcely have failed to have noticed, at some time or other, the Whirligig-beetles (*Gyrinus*) (Pl. 18, p. 79, Fig. 14). They occur on the water surface in large or small companies, whirling about in circles in all directions with movements too rapid for the eye clearly to follow. Early in the season they are about only in small numbers but towards September new individuals have developed and their numbers greatly increase. When alarmed they dive below the water carrying a bubble of air with them at the hind extremity. Whirligig-beetles are good fliers, which enables them to change their abode when desired.

About ¼ in. long, these Beetles are blue-black with a highly burnished upper side which has hydrophobe properties—i.e. the water retreats from such an area, leaving its surface dry. The under-side and the legs, on the other hand, have no such properties and are kept completely wetted and immersed. The middle and hind-legs are very different from the ordinary running kind, being modified so as to become very efficient paddles. The whole of the hind-leg is flattened and oar-like and its effectiveness is much enhanced by the fringe of long stiff hairs. The middle legs are likewise oar-like but to a lesser degree. The fore-legs are very little modified and are used for seizing the food, which consists of other insects, chiefly those dead and floating on the water. The compound eyes are each divided into two separate portions of somewhat different construction. Most authors refer to this feature and many claim that the upper portion serves for vision in air and the other for seeing beneath the water. Whilst this conjecture may be correct more evidence is needed before it can be accepted without question. Also some other explanation has to account for the functions of the divided eyes which are present in some non-aquatic insects (see p. 93).

Whirligig-beetles are well suited to their ways of living ; their stream-lined contour and highly polished surface enables them to offer the minimum resistance to the water during their acrobatics. In their larval stages they live completely submerged and are true aquatic animals. It is for this reason that they are dealt with in Section 3 (p. 245).

2. INCOMPLETELY AQUATIC INSECTS* :—These include a great number of water-insects which, as previously mentioned, have to come

Plate XXV

S. BEAUFOY

a Water-boatman, *Notonecta*, in swimming position, on its back (× 2)

S. BEAUFOY

b Water-boatman, *Notonecta*, resting with its back uppermost

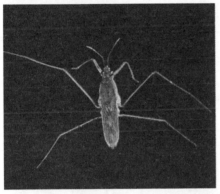

S. BEAUFOY

c Pond Skater, *Gerris*, (× 2) [etherised]

S. BEAUFOY

d Lesser Water-boatman, *Corixa*, in swimming position with back uppermost (× 2)

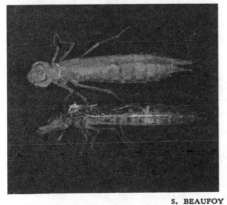

S. BEAUFOY

e Nymph of Emperor Dragon-fly just emerged with the cast skin seen below (× 1)

S. BEAUFOY

f Nymph of Emperor Dragon-fly devouring a small worm; the latter is held by the mask which is bent at an angle beneath the head (× 1)

AQUATIC INSECTS II

Plate XXVI

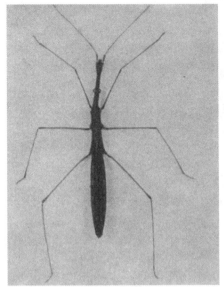

a Water-gnat, *Hydrometra stagnorum* (× 4)
[from a set specimen]

b Cast skin of Emperor Dragon-fly: the white threads are the old linings of the breathing tubes

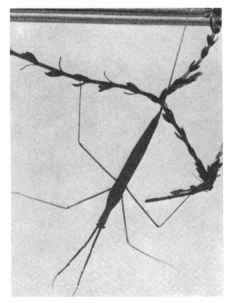

c Water Stick-insect, *Ranatra linearis* (× 1½)

d Water-scorpion, *Nepa cinerea* (× 2)

AQUATIC INSECTS III

to the surface in order to obtain air to breathe. Many are unable to swim and merely crawl about below the water or cling to aquatic plants. This happens in some of the Water-bugs (Hemiptera) of which a good example is the Water-scorpion (*Nepa cinerea*) (Pl. XXVI, p. 227, Fig. d).

Nepa is a flattened, almost leaf-like, dark-coloured insect about ¾ in. long. It is found in shallow stagnant ponds where there is plenty of submerged vegetation. A passable account of the creature was given as long ago as 1634 by the Scottish doctor Thos. Moufet in his *Insectorum Theatrum*, and many naturalists have written about it since. The best way to find *Nepa* is to search the margins of ponds, as it does not wander into the open water. Here it is well camouflaged against a background of dead leaves and water plants. Sometimes it is to be had by scooping up some of the mud in which it may half bury itself. Its movements are not specially adapted to a submerged life since it crawls with the same alternating method of leg movement that insects use on land. At its hind-end *Nepa* carries a long breathing siphon which makes it look as if it were armed with a sting. In fact its name of Water-scorpion is suggested by this feature, along with the peculiarly formed fore-legs which resemble the raptorial limbs of a scorpion and are used for the same purpose. Its breathing siphon is made up of two half-tubes which interlock so as to enclose a central air-passage. Now and again it has to crawl upwards so as to place the tip of the siphon out of the water in order to breathe. The air passes down the siphon to enter a pair of breathing pores at its base. The fore-wings (or hemelytra) are also worth attention. If these dingy-looking organs be raised with a needle they are seen to overlie a pair of very delicate hind-wings that are pinkish with vermilion veins. The upper side of the hind-body is brick-red with black bands. It is hard to understand the meaning of this concealed magnificence. It is certainly not displayed during flight because the creature cannot fly, some of its principal wing-muscles having disappeared !

While looking for *Nepa* search might also be made for its near relative the so-called Water Stick-insect (*Ranatra linearis*) (Pl. XXVI, Fig. c), which is found in similar pools. *Ranatra* chiefly inhabits the south of England, where it is rather local. Ochreous in colour, it has an extremely elongated body, 1½ in. long, with thin legs like those of a Crane-fly. Its siphon is nearly as long as the body and has the appearance of a large bristle. Both *Nepa* and *Ranatra* seek their food beneath the

surface of the water.   It consists of small insects and other creatures
which they seize by means of their fore-legs and suck out the body-
fluids with their piercing mouth-parts.   The fore-limbs are rather
remarkably formed, the tibia and tarsus being capable of being closed
so as to fit into a groove of the femur like the blade of a pocket-knife
into its handle.   Held by this efficient mechanism the prey once seized
has not much chance of escape.

Other Water-bugs commonly met with in ponds or other still
waters include the Water-boatmen or Back-swimmers (*Notonecta*) and
the Lesser Water-boatmen (*Corixa* and *Sigara*).   As with *Nepa* and
Ranatra, the antennae are very small and are stowed away so as not to
incommode their underwater movements.   In other respects they are
very different since they have no breathing siphon.   Also they are
expert swimmers whose hind-legs are specially modified to act as
oars (Text-Fig. 3, p. 12).

Notonecta includes the largest species, 13 to 16 mm. long (Pl. XXV,
p. 226, Figs. a, b).   They are interesting to watch in a small aquarium
or other vessel on account of their active movements which provide a
most attractive display of swimming and diving.   No other creatures
should be confined with them, if it be wished to keep them alive, for
Notonecta has a voracious appetite.   Size is no deterrent for it will feed
on tadpoles and small fish as well as other insects.   As is usual with
Water-bugs, the prey is held by the prehensile fore-limbs while its
body-fluids are being imbibed.

The alternative name of Backswimmer is very appropriate because
Notonecta does actually swim upside-down.   *Corixa* and its allies, on
the other hand, swim in the orthodox way with their backs uppermost.
When occasion demands *Notonecta* comes to the surface to take in air
and protrudes the tip of its hind-end for the purpose.   Having satisfied
its needs it dives by means of vigorous strokes with its oar-like hind-
limbs.   At such times it is seen to carry with it a glistening film of air.
Air fills the space between the body and the wings and also covers the
side of the body which stays uppermost.   This is keeled down the
middle and on either side of the keel there is a neatly designed passage
formed of a double series of interlocking hairs.   The hydrophobe
properties of the hairs forming these two passages enable them to
serve as ducts which convey the air to breathing pores on the thorax.
The air-supply retained in this way, together with that held beneath
the wings, is drawn upon when the insect is submerged.   With its

respiratory needs thus provided for it can stay below for a considerable time. The air, however, renders the Water-boatman very buoyant and the need for its powerful hind-limbs becomes very evident when it swims because it has also to work against its own tendency to float upwards all the time. For this same reason, when it wishes to rest below it has to cling to objects in the water. The hind-legs of *Notonecta* or *Corixa* are well worth examination as examples of mechanical efficiency. As is seen in Text-Fig. 3, they are greatly elongated and flattened so as to offer a broader surface to the water as they work against it. This effect is increased by the closely-set fringes of long hairs along the tibia and tarsus. The tripod method of progression used by land-dwelling insects has been abandoned by all Water-boatmen and their two swimming legs work in unison like the oars of a rower in a boat.

Both *Notonecta* and *Corixa* are strong fliers which is a great advantage when their surroundings become uncomfortable. Ossian Larsen, in Sweden, says that the hard winters of 1927–28 and 1928–29 kept the ponds frozen and killed many Water-bugs. *Notonecta* and *Corixa*, however, escaped by flight before things got too bad. *Nepa*, on the other hand, perished as it cannot fly.

Corixa is quite as interesting a creature as *Notonecta* and is often found in the same waters. It is smaller, with the back more flattened : the upper surface is dark and mottled in contrast with the pale under-surface. Unlike *Notonecta* its middle legs are nearly as long as the hind-legs (Pl. XXV, Fig. d). Also, being a vegetarian, *Corixa* no longer requires its fore-legs to be shaped for seizing the prey as happens in so many Water-bugs. Instead they are used for producing high-pitched sounds in a peculiar way, very possibly attractive to members of the opposite sex. The fore-legs illustrate admirably how a particular organ of an insect may change its function in an almost Gilbertian way. Fore-legs were obviously designed and used, in the first instance, for locomotion ; but among most Water-bugs they have become altered and changed into grasping organs for seizing prey. In *Corixa* and its allies they have further changed so that they are now used for producing " music."

Corixa spends much of its time among weed on the bottom of pools and carries an air-supply in a hollow of its back that is covered by its wings though it is less buoyant than *Notonecta*.

Not only Water-bugs but also some Beetles and other creatures carry a store of air with them in order to enable them to breathe when submerged. A very interesting physical process happens in such cases for as the oxygen contained in this air-supply becomes used in breathing the tension of the remainder will become less than that of the oxygen dissolved in the water. The result will be that oxygen will diffuse in from the water and replace that used up by breathing. By means of an ingenious method of micro-analysis R. Ege, in Denmark, took samples of the air in question and ascertained its composition. In this way he calculated that the supply stored under the wings of *Corixa* lasts from 10 to 30 times longer than if no such diffusion took place.

It will be convenient now to pass to another group of water insects —the Water-beetles—and see what happens to them. The Great Water-beetle (*Dytiscus marginalis*) is an appropriate fellow to look into first. Being 1¼ in. or a little more in length it is easy to find in stagnant ponds—it likes those where there is plenty of weed. It has an oval stream-lined form and is olive-black above with the thorax and wing-covers margined with yellow. The specific name *marginalis* refers to this yellow ornamentation but the name is not a good one as other kinds show the same feature.

Individuals of the two sexes are easy to tell from each other. The male has the wing-covers smooth and the first three segments of the front tarsi much enlarged so as to form a circular pad : the same segments of the middle tarsi are also somewhat broadened. The female has the wing-covers marked with longitudinal furrows and the fore and middle tarsi are unmodified (Pl. XXVII, p. 234, Figs. c and d).

The broadened tarsi in the male are applied to the smooth parts of the upper surface of the female so as to obtain a firm hold while mating. The pad-like front tarsi are provided beneath with cup-like suckers which are moistened with a glutinous secretion. This sticky substance aids adhesion indirectly after the manner of grease in an air-pump and directly by increasing the adhesive force. During mating these suckers hold on to the prothorax of the female and those of the middle legs are applied to the sides of her wing-covers : in this way the male can hold on for many hours continuously.

Dytiscus has two characteristics that are by no means unique but are uncommonly well-developed in this genus, viz. expertness in swim-ming and an insatiable appetite. As in Water-boatmen, the chief swimming organs are the hind-legs. The tibiae and tarsi of this pair of limbs are flattened and margined with a fringe of long bristles. While swimming the tarsus rotates sufficiently so as to present its broad surface to the water when making the stroke and its edge during the return movement. In other words *Dytiscus* feathers its oars like a trained rower. Also, its two hind-legs move simultaneously. As to its appetite it seems to attack all that comes its way, especially other insects and small fishes, which it seizes with its toothed mandibles and the sharply pointed laciniae of its maxillae. The prey is then masticated and consumed.

Dytiscus carries a store of air among the fine hairs covering the back of its abdomen and enclosed by the wing-covers. When it rises to the surface to breathe, little exertion is needed owing to the buoyancy thus acquired. On reaching the surface its hind-end rises above the water so as to expose the last two pairs of breathing pores to the air. At the same time the wing-covers are slightly raised so as to let a fresh supply of air enter beneath them. The remaining breathing pores draw upon the air stored in this way when the insect is submerged.

The eggs are laid in spring, each being deposited singly in an incision made by the ovipositor in the stem of a water-plant. The resulting larva soon grows into one of the most formidable carnivores that roam the under-water pond world (Plate XXVII, Fig. a). When fully grown it is more than 2 in. long and greenish or yellow-brown with very sharp calliper-like jaws that are used for seizing the prey. The larva swims by means of its legs which are fringed with hairs and act as oars ; it is also capable of darting about by wriggling movements of its body. Its food is much the same as that of the Beetle, only it is even more voracious.

The prey is impaled by the mandibles and is not discarded until very little more than its empty skin remains. A very extraordinary thing happens during the interval. The jaws of the larva are each pierced by a fine canal which runs from the pointed tip to the base where it is in communication with the mouth-cavity. Just behind the latter there is a muscular pump which injects digestive fluid from the alimentary system, through the canal in each jaw, into the prey. In this way its tissues become predigested and converted into fluid. The pump then reverses its action and sucks up the ready-prepared meal into the mouth-cavity. This process, which is known as external digestion, is by no means confined to the *Dytiscus* larva but is also practised by various other insects (pp. 129-30). The *Dytiscus* beetle, as already noted, chews up its food in solid form in the usual way and its digestion is internal.

The larva, like the beetle, is lighter than water and, for this reason, can only remain below the surface by holding on to weeds, etc. When it has to ascend in order to take in air it does so by simply allowing itself to float leisurely upwards. Its hind-end is then pushed through the surface-film and the two hair-fringed cerci are spread out horizontally. Owing to their hydrophobe properties the water slides off these appendages and allows the large breathing pores at their base to come in contact with the air. In this position the larva hangs head-downwards from the surface film and takes in air. Its two main breathing-tubes are unusually wide and are consequently able to store sufficient air to serve the needs of the larva when it is below (Plate XXVII).

The fully grown *Dytiscus* larva makes itself a cavity in the damp earth that borders the water and there changes into a pupa. This latter stage only lasts a few weeks and then transformation into the beetle is completed. For a while the Beetle remains in the pupal cell to allow its skin to harden but eventually makes its way out into the water. It is an active flier, which accounts for its sometimes appearing overnight in tubs or other small accumulations of water. The reflection of water in moonlight is stated to give them the whereabouts of pools, into which they drop vertically downwards. This seems to account for their being deceived by the glass roofs of greenhouses, upon which they sometimes let themselves fall with violence ! A long succession of naturalists have written about *Dytiscus* from almost all points of view with the result that the creature has been exceptionally fully investigated. Under the title of *Der Gelbrand* (a name which refers to the yellow margins to its thorax and wing-covers) Professor E. Korschelt in 1923–24 edited two impressive volumes comprising 1,827 pages about this one species of Beetle !

Many members of the family Dytiscidae are abundant in Britain, but space will only allow of mention being made of one other, viz. *Acilius sulcatus* (Pl. 18, p. 79, Figs. 2, 3). This Water-beetle is common in pools and dykes besides being found in the static water-tanks built during the late world war. It is relatively broader and flatter than *Dytiscus*, also much smaller, its length being only a little more than ½ in. As in *Dytiscus* the front tarsi are sucker-like in the male while the female has deeply fluted wing-covers. The larva (Plate XXVII, Fig. b) when fully grown is 1¼ in. long and differs from that of *Dytiscus* in its long neck-like prothorax and its smaller head. The mode of life, both of the larva and the beetle is much the same as in *Dytiscus*.

If the reader be sufficiently interested to search for other Water-beetles he or she may be lucky enough to find the Great Silver Water-beetle (*Hydrophilus piceus*). It is our largest beetle and has a length of 1⅞ in. (Pl. IX, p. 98, Fig. b). The Stag-beetle (*Lucanus cervus*) it is true is a longer insect on account of its huge mandibles, but it has a smaller body. *Hydrophilus* is much less common than formerly and is more or less confined to southern and south-eastern parts of England. It should be looked for in the stagnant waters of weedy ponds, ditches and dykes. It belongs to the family Hydrophilidae, which also includes a number of Beetles that live on land in damp places or among vegetable refuse. A special feature is their very short antennae that end in a club clothed with hydrophobe hairs. These organs provide a good instance of change of function for they no longer serve the usual uses of antennae and have become modified to play an important part in negotiating the surface film when the insect comes up to breathe. On the other hand the maxillary palps are very long and seem to take the place of antennae. When *Hydrophilus* comes to the surface it behaves quite differently from *Dytiscus*. Like the last-named Beetle, it has an air-reservoir between its wing-covers and the upper surface of the hind-body. In addition it carries a large air-film on its underside which gives it a silvery appearance and accounts for the name Great Silver Beetle. The two air-tracts are continuous along the edges of the wing-covers. On rising to the surface it comes up head first (not tail first as *Dytiscus*

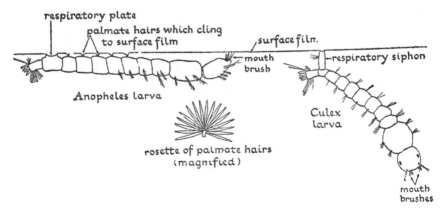

FIG. 34.—Diagram showing *Anopheles* and *Culex* larvae suspended from the surface film of water.

does) and inclined to one side. The antenna of that side is used to break the water-film by means of its unwettable club which is held at such an angle as allows of the passage of air into the cleft between the head and thorax. In this way the outside air comes into contact with that contained in the reservoir on the underside of the body and with the main breathing pores.

The food of *Hydrophilus* is mainly vegetable matter and consequently it does not need the agility of *Dytiscus* which has to catch prey for its living. It is, in fact, a rather poor swimmer with its hind-legs less oar-like than those of *Dytiscus*. They are moved alternately which results in a wavering course through the water.

The larva of *Hydrophilus* is nearly 2¾ in. long when fully grown. It is a fatter and more fleshy creature than that of *Dytiscus* and is also more sluggish in its movements. Unlike the Beetle into which it transforms, it is carnivorous and feeds mainly upon small water-snails ; these, of course, are easy to capture, which probably accounts for its lack of agility. The larva takes in air through a pair of breathing pores at the hind-end of the body and comes to the surface periodically so as to place them in communication with the air.

Among other incompletely aquatic insects are numerous Fly larvae. The most familiar of these are the " wrigglers " or larvae of Mosquitoes.* They are interesting creatures to watch on account of the beautiful ways in which they are fitted to their particular mode of living. There are two chief kinds of Mosquito larvae—viz. the *Anopheles* type and the *Culex* type. In both kinds there is a large head, a swollen thorax, formed of the usual three segments merged together, and a long abdomen (Text-Fig. 34). Only one pair of breathing pores is present, and they are placed on the 8th segment of the abdomen. In *Anopheles* they are located on the surface of the segment itself but in *Culex* and its allies they are carried at the apex of a breathing-tube or siphon. When at rest and during feeding *Anopheles* larvae remain horizontally just beneath the surface-film. The area bearing the breathing pores breaks through the surface and, owing to its hydrophobe properties, water is prevented from entering the respiratory system. This is owing to the area in question being moistened with an oily exudation which does not mix with the water but repels it. The larva is helped to keep its horizontal position by pairs of minute rosettes of palmate hairs on its back which adhere to the surface film of the water as shown in Text-Fig. 34. The larvae of *Culex* and related Mosquitoes

Plate XXVII

S. BEAUFOY

a Larva of Great Water-beetle, *Dytiscus marginalis* (× 1)

S. BEAUFOY

b Larva of an allied Water-beetle, *Acilius sulcatus* (× 1½)

S. BEAUFOY

c Great Water-beetle, male (× 1¼)

S. BEAUFOY

d Great Water-beetle, female (× 1¼)

AQUATIC INSECTS IV

Plate XXVIII

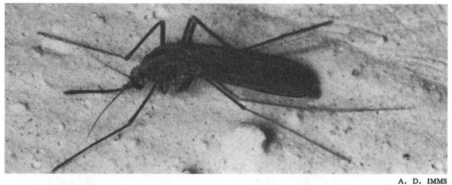

a Culex Mosquito at rest (× 4)

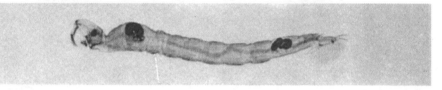

b Phantom larva of *Chaoborus:* the black rounded objects fore and aft are the flotation organs (× 4)

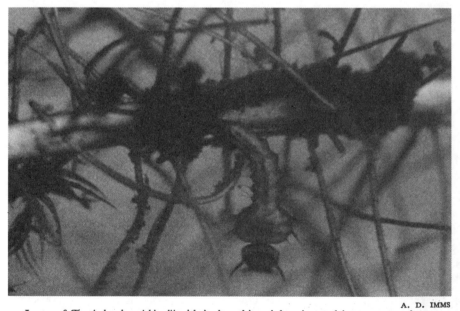

c Larva of *Taeniorhynchus richiardii* with its breathing siphon inserted into a water plant

AQUATIC INSECTS V

rest at an angle with the surface-film and are inclined head downwards. The breathing siphon ends in five tiny flaps which spread out on the surface-film. These flaps have their surface kept " greased " with an oily exudation just as was seen in the case of the area around the breathing pores in the *Anopheles* larva. By this means water is similarly prevented from entering the two breathing-pores which they encircle. If anything alarms the larva it submerges, the flaps immediately close over the breathing pores, and the insect wriggles away as fast as it can. Knowledge of the way in which a Mosquito larva breathes has turned out to be of enormous practical value because it provides the key to a means of controlling these insects. Since the creature must come to the surface sooner or later to breathe advantage is taken of this apparently unimportant fact by coating the water with a fine film of petroleum oil, cresylic acid, or other suitable fluid, which can freely enter the breathing-pores and thus suffocate all the larvae present. The hydrofuge properties of the area around the breathing-pores, so efficient in precluding the entry of water, are of no avail against an oily fluid.

Mosquito larvae are legless, nevertheless they manage to get along with astonishing agility simply by side-to-side wriggling movements of the hind-body, the direction being tail-foremost. Their feeding habits are unusual. On each side, under the front of the head, moustache-like, is a feeding brush. These brushes are vigorously vibrated backwards and inwards, 150 or more times a minute. As the result a current is set up in the water which converges towards the mouth of the larva. As the current flows past and between the mouth-parts, any solid particles held in suspension become filtered out and retained by these appendages and their armature of bristles. These particles form the food of the larva and are collected assiduously, the mouth-brushes being repeatedly combed by bristles on the jaws for any tit-bits that may be adherent to them.

The *Anopheles* larva feeds upon such particles as adhere to the under-side of the surface-film of the water. But to get at them it has to rotate its head through an angle of 180° so that the side bearing the feeding brushes becomes uppermost (Text-Fig. 34). The rotation having taken place the feeding brushes immediately get to work and sweep the under-side of the surface-film rather as a really industrious house-maid brushes a ceiling for cobwebs. The *Culex* larva, hanging head downwards, gets its food from deeper water and does not need a rotary head for this purpose.

surface film

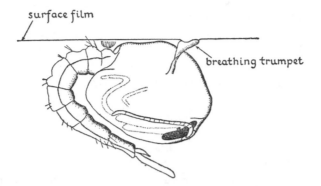

breathing trumpet

FIG. 35.—Pupa of a Mosquito. (Magnified.)

Different kinds of Mosquito larvae inhabit different situations. Those of some species are very particular as to where they live. The larva of *Orthopodomyia pulchripalpis*, for instance, only inhabits water collected in tree-holes and it is useless looking for it anywhere else. The larvae of *Aëdes detritus* and of *Aëdes caspius* breed in salt-marshes. That of *Theobaldia annulata* prefers small collections of water, especially when contaminated with manure or other organic material ; it is often abundant in garden tanks containing manure water. *Culex molestus* seems to prefer dark places and during the Second World War its larvae have been found in accumulations of water in the tunnels of the London tubes and in the basements of bombed houses. *Culex pipiens,*

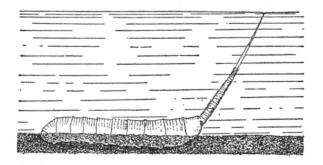

FIG. 36.—Larva, or Rat-tailed Maggot, of the Drone-fly : its breathing siphon is seen suspended from the surface film of the water. (Slightly enlarged.)

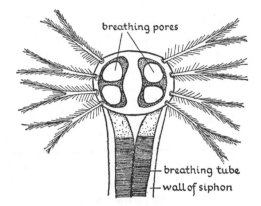

breathing pores

breathing tube

wall of siphon

FIG. 37.—Apex of the breathing siphon of the larva, or Rat-tailed Maggot, of the Drone-fly. (Magnified.)

which is our commonest Mosquito, does not much mind where it breeds for its larvae are abundant in water-butts, puddles, ditches, pools, static water-tanks, etc. Larvae of *Anopheles* like still or slowly-flowing water with surface weeds ; consequently pools, ditches, backwaters of rivers, canals, etc., are the best places to find them.

Mosquito pupae are rather like tadpoles with their tails curved under their bodies. Unlike most pupae they are aquatic like the larvae : also they are very active and swim by flapping their tails up and down. The effectiveness of the tail for this purpose is increased by the two broad plates borne at its extremity. At other times they rest quietly at the top of the water with a pair of " breathing-trumpets " on the thorax piercing the surface-film so as to be in free communication with the outside air (Text-Fig. 35). Less than a week is usually spent in the pupal stage and, when time for the exit of the adult Mosquito arrives, the emergence occupies only about 5 minutes or rather longer.

Some of the most fantastic of all water-insects are the creatures called Rat-tailed Maggots which are the larvae of some of the Hover-flies or Syrphidae (Text-Fig. 36 and Pl. XXIX, p. 258, Fig. a). In order to meet with them it is necessary to search accumulations of very stagnant water rich in mud and decaying leaves or those which seep from manure-heaps, etc. Usually the more contaminated the water the better these curious larvae seem to thrive. They belong to the subfamily Eristalinae, of which the commonest species is the Drone-fly (*Eristalis tenax*). The speciality of such larvae is an enormously elongated telescopic tail which acts as a breathing siphon. A fully grown Drone-fly larva is about 1 in. long and its tail when fully extended reaches almost another 6 in. The two main breathing-tubes of the body traverse the whole length of the tail or siphon and open by means of pores at its apex. Surrounding the latter there is a circlet of eight fringed hairs (Text-Fig. 37). When the apex of the tail is at the top of the water these spread out into an elegant little rosette which lies on the surface-film. Since they are unwettable they prevent water from entering the breathing-pores. The larva rests on the bottom of the water with its tail or siphon at the surface. It spends its time grovelling in the mud and feeding on particles of organic matter that abound in the situations it inhabits. The tail is adjustable like a telescope and can be lengthened or shortened in accordance with the depth of the water (Text-Fig. 36). Where the water is too deep for its tail to reach the surface the larva shifts its position to a place where it is shallower. When fully grown it changes into a pupa which is enclosed within the hardened larval skin (puparium). The outward appearance of the larva is retained but the tail and body have become shortened. The puparium floats with a pair of breathing-trumpets projecting through the surface-film.

Notwithstanding the unsavoury habits of its larva the Drone-fly itself (Pl. 23, p. 126) frequents flowers. Among other Hover-flies which have rat-tailed larvae two species are shown on Plate 28, p. 159, Figs. 21, 10, viz. *Helophilus pendulus* and *Myiatropa florea*. Both kinds are common on garden and roadside flowers all over the country.

A remarkable case of parallel adaptation is that the curious rat-tailed kind of larva is also found in a small group of Crane-flies that form the genus *Ptychoptera* (Pl. 23, p. 126, Fig. 19). If some of the black mud from a small shallow pool be collected in a suitable vessel and allowed to settle, the long lashing tails of the *Ptychoptera* larvae often become evident at the surface. As with the Drone-fly larva the tail is made up of three segments which can be telescoped into one another. The tip of this breathing-tube hangs from the surface-film of the water, being kept in that position by means of a circlet of fine hairs which surround the two breathing-pores. Notwithstanding this likeness the two kinds of insects are only distantly related. The small but distinct head of the *Ptychoptera* larva will serve to distinguish it from the larva of the Drone-fly, whose head is almost non-existent. The pupa is very different from that of the Drone-fly : for one thing, it is not enclosed

PLATE 37

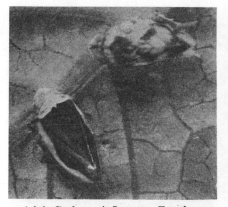

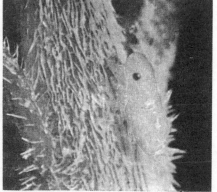

a. Adult Cuckoo-spit Insect or Frog-hopper, *Philaenus eeucophthalmus:* both pale and dark forms are shown

b. Nymph of Cuckoo-spit Insect or Frog-hopper after removal of the enveloping spume

c. Capsid-bug about to insert its mouth-stylets into a plant

(All are somewhat enlarged)

FROG-HOPPERS AND A CAPSID-BUG

Photographs by E. J. HUDSON

PLATE 38

FAMILIAR SUCKING INSECTS × 1)

a. Black-fly or Aphid, *Aphis fabae*, on Broad Bean   S. BEAUFOY

b. Cuckoo-spit or spume of *Philaenus leucophthalmus*, on Thistle   S. BEAUFOY

in a hard shell formed of the old larval skin. Also, it has developed a life-line, over an inch long, to enable it to keep up connection with the outside air : it makes no use of the long breathing-tube of the larva and grows instead a brand new one from the opposite end of the body. It may be pointed out that many aquatic pupae have a pair of breathing-horns or -trumpets on the prothorax—they are well seen for instance in those of Mosquitoes (Text-Fig. 35). In *Ptychoptera* the right breathing-horn has grown out into the enormously elongated tube just mentioned, the left one being very short (Pl. XXIX, p. 258, Fig. b).

A small number of enterprising larvae no longer come to the surface to breathe. Instead, they get their oxygen from water-plants, which they do by piercing the roots with a kind of spine that bears the breathing-pores. This tool is worked into the plant until the breathing-pores reach the intercellular spaces which contain a small amount of oxygen. Among British insects this remarkable way of life is well shown in the larva of a rather local Mosquito—*Taeniorhynchus richiardii* (Map 7). The Mosquito itself is a tawny-brown undistinguished-looking creature that is very prone to attack human beings after dusk. In its larva the usual *Culex* type of breathing-siphon has been modified into a pointed instrument which is used to penetrate the roots of various water-plants (Pl. XXVIII, p. 235, Fig. c). The pupa also gets its air from the same source : this it does by forcing its pointed breathing-trumpets into the plant. It remains attached in this position until the time arrives for the adult Mosquito to emerge, when it then swims to the surface.

The coppery or green Leaf-beetles of the genus *Donacia* (Pl. 27, p. 158) have larvae which similarly tap the roots of plants in order to get their oxygen. The Beetles are found on sedges, rushes and reeds along riversides during summer. In order to see these beautiful objects all that is needed is to drift slowly downstream in a boat and look for them as they bask in the sun. If tufts of the grass *Glyceria maxima* be pulled up by the roots, and the mud carefully washed away, larvae of *Donacia semicuprea* will often be found adhering to them. They hold on only by means of a pair of hook-like tail-spines which bear the breathing-pores. The cocoons containing the pupae are often found along with the larvae (and sometimes also larvae of the Mosquito just described).

3. COMPLETELY AQUATIC INSECTS.—There now remain to be considered those insects that live exclusively in water and die if removed

from it. Like fishes, they obtain the oxygen they need from the supply dissolved in the water. Consequently their breathing organs are not so constituted that they can make use of the oxygen in the atmosphere.

Breathing is usually effected by means of gills. Among insects these organs are simply outgrowths of the integument that are covered with a very thin cuticle and contain a system of fine breathing-tubes connected with those running through the rest of the body. In some cases the gills are very small or absent and breathing then takes place through the skin which is then very thin.

Completely aquatic insects have a specific gravity greater than that of the water and, since they have no need to come to the surface to take in air, they can economise their energies for use in other ways. For the most part they do not use their legs for swimming. They usually propel themselves by body-movements of various types which in certain cases are aided by the vibratory motion of the gills.

Among insects that breathe by means of gills are nymphs of three kinds, viz. those of May-flies, of Dragon-flies and of Stone-flies. To these must be added several kinds of larvae. It is noteworthy that adult insects have very rarely adopted the completely aquatic mode of life.

It will be convenient to begin with the nymphs of May-flies. There are many kinds to be found and all are most attractive objects to watch in a small glass vessel or aquarium. It is necessary to keep them in some of the original water from where they were found and, when not being watched, the vessel should be placed in the dark with a cover to exclude dust. If a ditch or pond of clear water is at hand nymphs of the small May-fly *Cloëon dipterum* are often to be found at almost any time of the year (Pl. III, p. 26, Fig. c). Its specific name of *dipterum* refers to the adult insect which is two-winged owing to the loss of the hind-wings. Almost all our May-flies have the hind-wings much reduced in size and a few others (like *Cloëon*) have lost them altogether. These latter species fly quite as easily as the others and the loss of the hind-wings seems in no way to be a handicap.

The nymphs of *Cloëon* are best caught by fishing out some water-weed, among which they hide, and then separating it apart in a flat vessel. It will be noticed that a series of rapidly vibrating gills project from each side along the hind-body. The latter ends in three tail-like filaments rather like those of the Silver-fish (p. 34). The gills are oval flat plates and each pair, excepting the last or 7th pair, is double.

The first six pairs are kept in constant vibration and, in this way, currents are set up in the water immediately around the insect. The 7th pair of gills are stationary.

The working of the gills of May-fly nymphs has been studied by Prof. L. Eastham of Sheffield University. In many cases the gills of the two sides of the body work in pairs like a series of oars, but they do so in a special rhythmic manner. The first pair of gills begins the movement and the other pairs then follow on and take up the stroke in rapid succession. In this way a current is set up which brings a fresh supply of water into direct contact with the gills for breathing purposes. In the nymph of *Cloëon* the current flows backwards until it reaches the last or stationary pair of gills. These act as buffers which strongly deflect the water flow to each side so that it will not be immediately used again. The speed with which the gills vibrate depends largely upon the amount of oxygen that is dissolved in the water. If the water is highly charged with oxygen the gill-movements are slow and leisurely. On the other hand when the nymphs are transferred to water that has been deprived of its oxygen by having been previously boiled and allowed to cool down to the original temperature, the gill-movements are enormously speeded up. The insect accelerates its gill movements in its efforts to bring much needed oxygen to its gills so as to counteract the danger of suffocation. These movements may become so rapid as to produce the appearance of a halo along each side of the body. It is well known that our own rate of breathing, and that of other mammals, becomes likewise accelerated in conditions of low oxygen supply.

Among other abundant May-fly nymphs those of *Ephemera* are burrowers. Consequently the place to look for these is the bottom of sandy or muddy lakes and slow streams or rivers. Their bodies are cylindrical with the fore-legs short and stout. These appendages, together with the long projecting mandibles, are used in excavating the burrows. The gills are double with long fringes to their margins and are held on the back so as to be out of the way in the tunnel-like burrows. They fit over one another from before backwards like the tiles of a roof and their movements give them the appearance of a continuous undulating membrane. The three tail-filaments are long and fringed with fine hairs. These nymphs are very unhappy if placed in a glass vessel in a strong light and not provided with mud. They exhaust themselves speedily in their efforts to burrow on the hard surface of the vessel. In natural surroundings the burrows are open at both ends and the current set up by the movements of the gills can be demonstrated by introducing a little powdered carmine or lamp-black into the water, in front of the entrance to a burrow. The current is then seen to be in the form of a straight flow over the gills along the middle of the back and out at the hinder end of the tunnel.

If the reader has access to a swiftly running stream with a stony bed the nymphs of *Ecdyonurus* are likely to be found. They are very different from those of *Cloëon* and *Ephemera*, being exceedingly broad and flattened. The place to look for them is beneath the stones, where they lie with their heads usually directed upstream. Their whole form and make-up provide an excellent example of how the shape and structure of animals becomes adapted during evolution to suit their conditions of life. The *Ecdyonurus* nymph clings to the stones by means of the strong claws on its widely spread legs. Its whole body and limbs are so flattened as to look as if they had been trodden upon. This flattened smooth surface presents the smallest possible obstacle to the fast-flowing water and so reduces the danger of becoming dislodged and carried away downstream. Also it enables the creature to work itself into the crevices between the stones to take up its usual position beneath them. The eyes are no longer at the sides of the head but on top near the middle. The gills consist of an oval plate together with a bunch of filaments which lies at its base. The first pair is very small and the seventh pair has no filaments at its base. The function of the gill-plates is to set up a current in the water by means of their rhythmic movement. This ensures that an adequate supply of oxygenated water is carried to the filaments which are the true breathing organs. The water-flow passes from the sides of the body upwards, between the gill-plates, to the middle line of the back ; from there it passes backwards to join the downstream flow of the river.

Among the real tyrants of the underwater world the nymphs of Dragon-flies share first place only with the Great Water-beetle (*Dytiscus*). Few other insects can compete with them for voracity. The nature of their food depends a good deal upon their size and age. The older nymphs are stated to be very much addicted to devouring those of May-flies as well as smaller examples of their own kind. Mosquito larvae also figure among their fare, while the large *Aeshna*[1] nymphs are not above negotiating a tadpole or an occasional small fish.

---

[1] Formerly spelt *Aeschna*.

Dragon-fly nymphs are mostly brownish or dull green and, in a general way, their colour merges into that of their immediate surroundings. Thus protected from their enemies they rely upon the same concealment as an aid in capturing their prey. Remaining as still as inanimate objects, they wait until unsuspecting victims come into their close vicinity. Then the mask (p. 41) shoots forward with great rapidity on its long arm that had remained folded beneath the head. The prey is impaled on the grasping hooks and spines of the mask. This is then retracted so as to bring the victim within reach of the jaws, which speedily chew it up.

For the most part Dragon-fly nymphs wander in a leisurely fashion on the beds of ponds and streams or among the submerged water-plants. They are not expert swimmers and would fare badly if they depended for their living on their agility. When necessary the large sturdy nymphs of the Anisoptera (p. 41) use an accelerated mode of locomotion and advance by a series of apparently jet-propelled spurts. The source of the motive power may not be obvious at first but sooner or later it will be noted that a little cloud of mud or sand is stirred up in a rhythmic manner around the hind-end of the body. The cloud is caused by a jet of water that is squirted forcibly through the rectum of the insect. This chamber pulsates in a regular manner involving alternating expansion and contraction which has the result of taking in and then forcibly expelling water through the anal opening. The propulsory action of the rectum is not its only function because it is also the main breathing organ of the nymph, besides conveying excretory matter to the exterior. Its inside wall is drawn out into an elaborate series of gills, each supplied with fine breathing-tubes. They are similar in function to the gills of May-fly nymphs but instead of being external they are internal in position. When the rectum draws in water it brings fresh oxygen to the gills within and when it expels the water it acts as an organ of propulsion—the latter action being the more vigorous of the two.

The more slenderly built nymphs of the Zygoptera (p. 41) propel themselves by side-to-side wriggling movements of the abdomen aided by the three tail-lamellae. These latter function in the same way as a single oar when worked from the stern of a boat. The lamellae also function as gills, there being no rectal gills. The fact that they are often broken off or missing without causing the insect any obvious discomfort has given rise to the misconception that they are of little value for breathing purposes. There is no doubt that the skin plays an important part in breathing but that the gills extend the actual surface that is available for respiratory purposes. Loss of the gills, therefore, may embarrass the insect only slightly for the time being as new ones are grown to take their places, though it would be serious in conditions of low oxygen-supply.

The nymphs of Stone-flies might be mistaken for those of May-flies. They are, however, easily distinguished by the possession of two tail-filaments instead of the usual three that prevail among May-flies. Also, the gills of Stone-fly nymphs are like fine tubes or threads which are usually grouped into bunches on the underside of the thorax or at the hind extremity of the body (Pl. III, p. 26). They are not found along the sides of the abdomen as in the nymphs of May-flies.

Stone-fly nymphs are inhabitants of clear unpolluted waters with a stony bed. Consequently the best places to find them are in streams, rivers and along lake-shores. They are not often found where there is silt and are especially partial to flowing, well-oxygenated water. Hilly and mountainous country yields many more kinds of these insects than flat districts. Some of the larger species spend two years as nymphs but more generally the whole life-cycle lasts about a year. Many of these nymphs feed upon algae and other vegetable material but the larger sorts also prey upon other aquatic insects.

Most Stone-fly nymphs are more or less flattened (Pl. III, Fig. d) and live beneath stones. Our largest forms belong to the genus *Perla* and are often found in company with nymphs of the May-fly *Ecdyonurus*. The eggs of Stone-flies are deposited in groups or masses, on or in the water, where they sink and often become separated. The young nymphs are at first without any gills and have to breathe through the skin. In some kinds this way of breathing persists and no gills are developed—a peculiarity which obtains in the nymphs of our green Stone-flies belonging to the genera *Chloroperla* and *Isoperla*.

Many ponds and slowly-moving streams or rivers are inhabited by the larva of the Alder-fly (*Sialis lutaria*) which belongs to the order Neuroptera. It needs to be searched for among silt or mud and the specific name of the insect, *lutaria*, means muddy. If the creature (Pl. III, Fig. b) be looked at through a pocket lens, when in a shallow dish of water, its broad head is seen to carry a pair of projecting pointed mandibles that betray its carnivorous habit. The body tapers backwards and ends in a slender hair-fringed tail. The thorax carries three pairs of strong legs and the hind-body has seven pairs of slender jointed gills that are similarly fringed with hairs. The insect is brown in colour with pale gills and, when fully grown, measures about an inch to the extremity of the tail. It swims by undulating movements of the body. About May the adult larva leaves the water and seeks a suitable place in the earth to make a cell or chamber wherein it changes into a pupa. When the Alder-fly is ready to emerge the pupa works its way upward until it reaches the surface of the ground. Here the final moult into the adult insect takes place.

Another member of the order Neuroptera which has an aquatic gill-bearing larva is the Sponge-fly (*Sisyra*). In order to find this larva the reader needs first to learn to be able to find a freshwater sponge. There are two kinds of these strange animals found in Britain. One, the River Sponge (*Ephydatia fluviatilis*), encrusts plant stems, pieces of wood or the undersides of stones in rivers and canals. The other, known as the Pond Sponge (*Spongilla lacustris*), is only found in still water. The *Sisyra* larva is to be looked for in the cavities of both kinds of sponges. Here it lives and feeds as a parasite, probing the sponge tissues with its long needle-like sucking jaws. Like the *Sialis* larva it bears seven pairs of gills, but they lie underneath the body and are not seen from above. When the time comes to pupate the larva deserts the water and spins a cocoon on a bridge, tree-trunk or other situation not far from the water side.

The larva of the Whirligig Beetle (*Gyrinus*) is likewise a gill-bearing completely aquatic creature. It might be mistaken for that of the Alder-fly except that the body does not taper to any noticeable degree : also, it bears ten pairs of long slender gills and there is no median tail. It is found in much the same situations as the Alder-fly larva.

Most people who are familiar with the countryside have come across Caddis cases which are the portable habitations made by the larvae worms of Caddis-flies (order Trichoptera). These larvae are found in most types of fresh water excepting those which are foul. On the bottom of still waters the cases of several species of *Limnephilus* are often common ; other species only inhabit streams. The genus *Rhyacophila* and its allies need to be looked for in torrents and fast-flowing rivers, while large pools and lakes have their own quota of Caddis larvae. The cases are made in many different ways which vary a good deal according to the species and sometimes according to the materials that are available for their construction : only a very few are shown on

Pl. XXX, p. 259. As a rule larvae that inhabit swift streams attach heavy particles of stone to their cases, to serve as ballast whereas those living in still waters tend to use lighter materials possibly so as not to hamper them in moving about. A typical Caddis larva has three swellings on the first segment of its hind-body (Text-Fig. 12, p. 51). These appear to help in maintaining the insect in a median position in its case so as to allow of a free flow of water all around it. This flow can be demonstrated when Caddis larvae are confined in vessels of water. All that is necessary is to drop some finely powdered lamp-black or other suitable material into the water just in front of the entrance to a Caddis case. It will be seen that some of the particles are being wafted into the case and reappear in the water at the hind-end. This is due to the breathing current that is set up by movements of the insect inside to ensure a steady flow of water over the gills.

A Caddis larva is difficult to remove from its case by force, in fact it can almost be pulled asunder before it will let go. This firm hold is effected by the action of a pair of limbs at the hind-end of the body, which bear large grappling hooks that grip the lining at the end of the case. The best way to remove a larva is to slit open the case as carefully as possible so as not to injure the occupant. If a fresh supply of building materials be made available the Caddis larva will set about making a new abode and often complete it within an hour. Sometimes it will oblige by using such things as small coloured beads, bits of glass, broken fragments of shell, etc. Some Caddis larvae will use pieces of mica to build their cases with if nothing else is available : in a habitation of this kind that is nearly transparent something of the movements of the creature within can be seen.

In ponds and lakes during early summer a small Caddis larva belonging to the species *Triaenodes bicolor* is often common. For its size it makes an unusually long case which is formed of vegetable fragments arranged in a spiral manner. It is able to swim freely, propelling itself, case and all, through the water by means of its third pair of legs. These are exceptionally long and fringed with hairs.

There are other kinds of Caddis larvae that make no cases at all. These free larvae, as they may be termed, mostly inhabit swiftly flowing streams and hold on against the current by means of the pair of grappling hooks at the hind-end of the body. They lack the three swellings on the first segment of the hind-body of case-builders and they may or may not bear gills. Those without gills are sometimes mistaken for larvae of some kind of Water-beetle, but the apparent absence of antennae will easily distinguish them. Among the commonest of the free larvae are the green and brown members of the genus *Rhyacophila* which are found underneath stones. Those of *Hydropsyche* inhabit similar places but they make silken retreats beneath the stones ; each of these is expanded into a funnel-like opening which faces upstream. Small insects and plant material carried down by the current become caught in these snares and are used as food. The free larvae only make protective coverings when about to turn into pupae. Such shelters are usually made of small pebbles bound together by silken material and enclose a cocoon which is the immediate covering for the pupae.

It will probably come as a surprise to many people to find that the caterpillars of certain Moths figure among aquatic insects. These belong to the family Pyraustidae, of which there are five species in Britain which display this habit. The Moths have delicately patterned wings which evidently suggested the popular name of China-marks for some of them. They are mostly common insects wherever the food-plants of their caterpillars are abundant. Their life-histories will repay much closer study than has been given to them hitherto and consequently a small but attractive field for investigation is open to enterprising observers. The caterpillars have the usual three pairs of thoracic legs and five pairs of claspers on the abdomen. They do not feed openly and exposed but make for themselves cases of bitten-off pieces of their particular food-plant. One kind—*Nymphula stratiotata*—has a series of thread-like gills on most of the body-segments and leads a completely aquatic life. Pale yellowish or greenish with a translucent appearance it lives among the leaves of the Water-soldier (*Stratiotes*) or other water-plants which it binds together with silk to form a case around itself. In this habitation it lives and feeds from about mid-summer until the next spring when it forms a submerged cocoon. The Moth is on the wing from about June to September. The Small China-mark (*Cataclysta lemnata*) is perhaps the commonest of the five species. It has a darkly coloured caterpillar that lives in a floating case made up of leaves of the Duckweed (*Lemna*). The Beautiful China-mark (*Nymphula stagnata*) is also abundant, and its caterpillar spins together leaves of the Bur-reed (*Sparganium*). This same food-plant is also utilised by the caterpillar of the Brown China-mark (*Nymphula nymphaeata*), which makes a floating case of its leaves or of those of

Potamogeton or other water-plants. The fifth species, *Acentropus niveus*, seems to be less common and more local than the others. It is a very remarkable creature since it has two kinds of female. One kind, which is fully-winged, leads an ordinary life ; the other kind lives submerged, has much reduced wings and swims by means of its legs.

A number of Fly larvae live entirely in water without ever coming to the surface for oxygen. They utilise the skin for breathing for they either have no gills or those organs are of little importance. It will, however, only be possible to refer to a few of these larvae. The kinds chosen are the larva of the Gnat *Chaoborus* (often known as *Corethra*) because of its amazing transparency and equally remarkable organs for flotation ; and that of the Midge *Chironomus* on account of its red blood, due to haemoglobin as in ourselves and other vertebrates.

Chaoborus belongs to the Culicidae or Mosquito family but differs from typical members of that group because its mouth-parts are not formed for piercing and sucking. Its larva, which when full-grown is about $\frac{1}{2}$ in. long, is to be found in still clear water in pools, ditches and dykes. Its popular name of Phantom Larva is well chosen on account of the creature's transparency. It is in fact so nearly invisible when poised motionless in the water that the eye has difficulty at first in seeing it at all. Only its black eyes and dark pigmented flotation organs give the clue to its presence. It will be obvious that a transparent animal that keeps still for quite long periods is not easy for its enemies to find. These two properties—transparency and immobility—also serve the *Chaoborus* larva to very good purpose in another way. It feeds upon small crustaceans, water-insects, etc., and when one of these unsuspecting creatures comes within reach it suddenly seizes the morsel more quickly than the eye can follow and devours it. This it achieves by means of the antennae which are modified into pre-hensile organs armed with sharp curved spines for impaling the prey. When alarmed the *Chaoborus* larva swims by jerky side-to-side movements of the body. An elaborate tail fin, made up of a comb of feathered bristles, plays an important part in propelling the insect through the water (Text-Fig. 33, p.224, and Plate XXVIII, p. 235, Fig. b).

Normally the *Chaoborus* larva remains poised in the water without the exercise of any muscular effort. Its ability to do so is due to the possession of a pair of dark bean-shaped sacs near each end of the body. These bodies are hydrostatic organs, filled with some gas, possibly air, whose size can be altered, shrinking or expanding as occasion may require. In this way the buoyancy of the larva can be adjusted to the density and pressure of the water. A change in the latter results in a corresponding change in the hydrostatic organs just mentioned which causes the larva to rise or fall accordingly. The actual mechanism which alters the size of these organs has been much discussed but is still not properly understood.

The pupa of *Chaoborus* floats more or less upright in the water, supported by the pair of prothoracic horns, which contain the gas formerly in the hydrostatic organs of the larva.

If some of the muddy deposit from the bottoms of sluggish streams, water-butts, stagnant pools and the like be scooped up with a large spoon or ladle most likely the larva of *Chironomus* will be brought along with it, sometimes in company with the rat-tailed larva of *Ptycho-ptera* mentioned on p. 238. It is easily recognised by its blood-red colour which has led to its popular name of Blood-worm. This larva is about one inch long when fully grown and lives in a vertical tube-like burrow made up of debris held together by its viscous saliva. Both fore and aft it carries a pair of false feet armed with hooklets. Also, at the hind-end there are two pairs of long tubes filled with blood; these latter organs are usually termed blood-gills but their real function is uncertain.

This blood-red wriggling larva of *Chironomus* is a real biological curiosity. While it is true that a very few other insects contain this same red colouring matter it is only found in certain organs of the body. The spectroscope and other tests show that the red colour is due to haemoglobin which is dissolved in the blood. Owing to the transparency of the cuticle the whole animal appears red. The haemoglobin acts as an oxygen-carrier just as it does in our own bodies. In the *Chironomus* larva it only gives up its oxygen to the tissues under conditions where the amount of oxygen present is very small. This is just what happens in the mud where the larva lives. Unlike most insects the blood here plays a significant part in respiration and the usual breathing-tubes are correspondingly reduced.

In the same mud along with the *Chironomus* larva, water-snails of the genus *Planorbis* are often present and sometimes also the small red worm *Tubifex*. Both these creatures contain haemoglobin in their blood, which similarly enables them to live in surroundings very poor in oxygen.

The female *Chironomus* lays her eggs in masses on the surface of the water. They are coated with a gelatinous substance which swells rapidly into a transparent mucilage. Many hundreds of eggs are bound together in this way into a mass, rope, or cylinder that floats on the water and is attached to some foreign object. Their transparency makes these masses hard to see and they are so slippery that they would evade the grasp of most enemies. This habit of coating the eggs with a mucilage prevails also among Caddis-flies and various other aquatic animals, including pond snails and certain fishes. To these instances must be added the familiar frog-spawn.

A great many species of Midges belong to the family Chironomidae and it is remarkable that while the Flies show an almost monotonous similarity of build their larvae often display notable differences. It is only certain of the larvae, and particularly those of the genus *Chironomus*, that are blood-red and are burrowers. Others are green, yellowish, blue-green or colourless. These often live near the surface of the water and feed upon weeds. Some form mines in the leaves of aquatic plants and one or two kinds even live in the sea. These latter are small green larvae which inhabit the salt water of the rock-pools along the sea-shore. They are mostly found among the bright green algae that are common in such pools and are easiest to obtain by collecting some of this weed and spreading it out in a shallow dish of sea water.

Here we must bring this chapter to a close. The reader will understand that no effort has been made to include every sort of aquatic insect found in these islands. Kinds in plenty will be met with that find no mention, but this is inevitable within a limited space. The object of this chapter has been to give some account of the remarkable and often unique devices that enable water-insects to live in their own particular ways. Consequently special notice has been taken of their means of locomotion : how they manage to capture their food : and the contrivances by which they can breathe. No one lives very far from where at least some of these creatures are to be found. For the town-dweller it may be only a water-butt ; others may have recourse to ponds or streams. In any case it is this accessibility that is one of the advantages that fresh-water insects have to offer to the naturalist.

CHAPTER 12

GREGARIOUSNESS AND SOCIAL LIFE

MOST insects, like the majority of other animals, lead solitary lives. Each individual usually lives for itself and by itself. It is true that association with members of the opposite sex occurs for mating but this contact is but of short duration. The partners afterwards have no further concern for one another and the female shows no interest in or solicitude for the welfare of her offspring. There are, however, quite a number of other insects that are by no means solitary in their habits. Some of these are merely gregarious while others are more or less social in their ways of life.

GREGARIOUS INSECTS.—A tendency to form aggregations is quite common among insects ; in some cases it is merely a temporary phase while in others it is a more established way of life. May-flies and Midges congregate at times and form temporary swarms in connection with mating. Thus, swarms of the Midge *Chironomus* perform aerial dances of an evening. The whole crowd often rises and falls in unison while occasionally a pair of mating flies leaves the rest and passes to the ground. Generally the number of females in these swarms is small, the males greatly predominating.

The swarming of May-flies, referred to on p. 40, is a performance familiar to country-dwellers. As with Midges it is a nuptial flight and is the embodiment of graceful aerial motion. It is to be witnessed most often on calm warm days near the waterside. Cold, windy weather seems to stop the performance altogether. In most cases these swarms are made up only of male individuals which perform their aerial evolutions while awaiting the females. The latter enter the swarm singly or a very few at a time and usually soon become mated. When this happens the paired couple flies away without disturbing the collective dances of the rest of the crowd. The ceremonial is probably connected with the necessity for May-flies to mate while on the wing. Concerning this process J. G. Needham says that the male flies beneath the female and reaches upwards with his long fore-legs so as to get hold of her. He then turns the hind end of his abdomen forward so as to seize the extremity of the female by means of his claspers. In this way the openings of their genital organs are brought into contact and fertilisation is effected.

The males of the smaller Crane-flies and of the Winter Gnats, which are allied to them, also show the habit of congregating in dancing swarms in the late afternoon. They aggregate in smaller numbers than May-flies or Midges but the significance of this behaviour appears to be the same. The common Winter Gnat (*Trichocera hiemalis*) is often seen in mid-winter dancing in companies whenever sunshine lures it into activity.

There are other insects that congregate in numbers when about to hibernate. The Two-spot Ladybird (*Adalia bipunctata*) is an example. It often hibernates in numbers of perhaps fifty or more under bark or in some other suitable place. The same individual tree may be used for this purpose for several years in succession.

The Cluster-fly (*Pollenia rudis*) is another example (Pl. 23, p. 126, Fig. 2). It is related to the Blow-fly and has received its name from its habit of clustering together, often in large numbers, for hibernation. Favourite retreats for this purpose are disused rooms or the roofs of churches or lofts ; it also uses thatch or hides behind boards, curtains, etc., that are likely to remain undisturbed. This insect is larger than the House-fly and when resting, its wings, instead of diverging at their tips, completely overlap like the closed blades of a pair of scissors. It is clothed with fine shiny golden hairs without any noticeable pattern. This Fly is of especial interest to the biologist on account of its extraordinary life-history which is mentioned on p. 152. Sometimes another Fly, known as *Musca autumnalis*, occurs in large numbers under similar conditions of hibernation and often in company with the Cluster-fly. It breeds in cattle droppings and is consequently found in country districts. Being very like the House-fly (*Musca domestica*) in appearance it is often mistaken for it but the House-fly does not congregate and overwinter in this way.

There are other kinds of Flies, of very small size (one-sixth of an inch in length, or less) that sometimes appear in thousands on the window panes and ceilings of houses from August to about October. Such swarms are often found in the same house for several years in succession. The record seems to be held by the small greyish-brown Fly *Limnophora humilis* which is known to have congregated annually for 16 years in the same house. All the individuals were impregnated females, as dissections of a representative sample showed the presence of active spermatozoa in every case. The tiny black and yellow Fly *Thaumatomyia notata* behaves in a similar way and is known to congregate on the same part of the ceiling in the same room of a house for several successive years. The swarms in this case were composed of individuals of both sexes, as also happens with those of the Cluster-fly.

The causes that promote individuals of the same species to congregate are not easy to discover. In some cases there seems to be little doubt that a fall in temperature is largely responsible. Thus, when the temperature falls below 50° F. it has been found that the Cluster-fly alters its habits and seeks dark places and, at the same time, becomes extremely sensitive to contact with external objects.   These two peculiarities cause it to hide away in dark corners and numerous individuals cluster together so as to be in close contact with one another. A rise in temperature alters this behaviour and the Flies disperse and seek the window panes where they become a mild source of annoyance. A sudden warm sunny day in winter, or the lighting of a fire in the room where they are living, has this effect.

When flies aggregate in the same room and at the same period in successive years, often in thousands of individuals, it is a complete mystery what attracts them or guides them to so small an area.   In the absence of evidence one can only speculate. It seems not unlikely that individuals of previous years may leave an odour trail where they have rested which induces newcomers to use the actual area themselves for the same purpose.   Insects are well known to be highly sensitive to odours—far outside the limits of human perception.

Some insects only become gregarious when they migrate to other areas.   Locusts and certain Butterflies are well known to indulge in great migratory flights over long distances.   There are, for instance, many records of large flocks of Butterflies seen crossing the English Channel or arriving on the south or east coasts.   Such flights are commonly composed of the Large or Small Cabbage White Butterflies. Locust swarms fortunately do not reach our islands—only stray individuals have been noted from time to time.   The Dragon-fly *Libellula quadrimaculata* is well known to form migratory swarms.   On several occasions swarms of this insect have been observed in the Dover area and others off the Essex coast.   On other occasions immense numbers of individuals have been recorded off Heligoland and in

INSECTS ON FLOWERS OF COW PARSNIP (ETHERISED)

3
SOLDIER-BEETLE
Rhagonycha fulva

4
Malachius viridis

6
Oedemera lurida

5
Malachius bipustulatus

9
CAPSID-BUG
Leptopterna dolabrata

1
DRONE-FLY
Eristalis tenax

7
CAPSID-BUG
Leptopterna dolabrata

8
CAPSID-BUG
Leptopterna dolabrata

2
HOVER-FLY
Volucella inflata

11
SOLDIER-BEETLE
Rhagonycha fulva

10
LONGICORN
Leptura livida

1 and 2 DIPTERA; 3-6, 10 and 11 COLEOPTERA or BEETLES; 7, 8
and 9 HEMIPTERA or PLANT-BUGS.

PLATE 39

S. BEAUFOY

PLATE 40

PLATE 40

255

BUMBLE BEES (× 1)

1 *Bombus terrestris* QUEEN	7 *Bombus lapidarius* MALE	13 *Bombus agrorum* QUEEN
2 *Bombus terrestris* WORKER	8 *Bombus pratorum* QUEEN	14 *Bombus agrorum* MALE
3 *Bombus lucorum* QUEEN	9 *Bombus pratorum* WORKER	15 *Psithyrus vestalis* QUEEN
4 *Bombus lucorum* WORKER	10 *Bombus hortorum* WORKER	16 *Psithyrus vestalis* MALE
5 *Bombus lucorum* MALE	11 *Bombus hortorum* MALE	17 *Psithyrus rupestris* MALE
6 *Bombus lapidarius* QUEEN	12 *Bombus hortorum* QUEEN	18 *Psithyrus rupestris* QUEEN

Denmark and Southern Sweden. In the foregoing examples it would seem that a great number of individuals respond to some common stimulus at the same time. Very little is known about what urges them to swarm or to take a definite course in their flight. The whole problem of migration of insects, like that of birds, is of great interest, but before much progress can be made in understanding the subject many more facts are needed. Anyone who is willing to join in this work or has observations to record, should write to the Keeper of Entomology, British Museum (Natural History), London, S.W.7, who will put him or her in touch with a committee specially interested in insect migration.

So far reference has only been made to insects that become gregarious during some particular phase or restricted period of their lives. Other kinds show the gregarious instinct in a more pronounced way by living in large companies during a continuous period of their lives. This trait is invariably associated with the habit of the female insects to deposit their eggs or offspring together in large batches in situations where the progeny will have a sufficiency or, in many cases, an abundance of food.

The reader is most likely familiar with the large colonies of Aphids that so often infest both wild and cultivated plants (Pl. 29, p. 174). These insects frequently go on multiplying until they literally smother parts of their food-plants. Sooner or later winged individuals appear that fly away to other plants where they found new colonies.

There are caterpillars that live in communal webs. Those of the Small Ermine Moths (*Yponomeuta*) usually form their webs on the common Spindle-tree (*Euonymus*). Often webs made by the progeny of different females merge and envelop quite long stretches of hedgerow. Such webs are shelters wherein a whole brood of larvae indulge in communal feeding. Caterpillars of the Small Eggar Moth (*Eriogaster lanestris*) form webs on Blackthorn and Hawthorn (Pl. XXX, p. 259). Such a web may contain several hundred individuals and its size is increased as the caterpillars spread themselves further for food. They do not wander very far from it and always retire into the shelter when not feeding. In their fully-grown state they become much less gregarious and form their cocoons solitarily. The caterpillars of the common Lackey Moth (*Malacosoma neustria*) also make communal webs on fruit trees, etc.

Large populations of insects are found infesting grain, flour, and other stored products. Patches of dung are often crammed with Fly maggots and the same applies to decaying carcasses, etc. Quite a number of studies of insect populations have been made in recent years and especially with the cosmopolitan Flour-beetle *Tribolium confusum*. To the ordinary observer these dense populations may seem hopelessly overcrowded. They do not degenerate into slums, however, because natural tendencies exert a check on any undue increase in relation to the amount of food that is available.

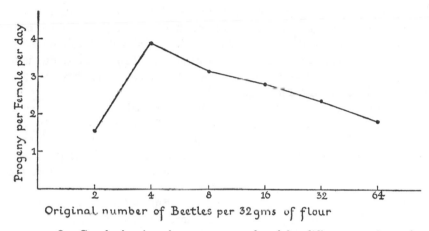

FIG. 38.—Graph showing the progeny produced by different numbers of Flour Beetles each day over a period of 11 days.

Populations of the Flour-beetle have been rather fully studied by various investigators, notably by R. N. Chapman. It seems that both overcrowding and undercrowding are definitely disadvantageous. If for instance we take a number of similar vessels each containing 32 grammes of a standard kind of flour and conduct a test with 1, 2, 4, 8 or more pairs of Beetles (male and female) we get a result like that shown in Text-Fig. 38. In this graph the number of eggs and larvae produced by each pair of Beetles each day over a period of 11 days is indicated. It will be noticed that the number is greatest when two pairs of Beetles are present. Then with increasing numbers of pairs of Beetles there is a progressive reduction in the rate of multiplication although it is still higher than when only a single pair of Beetles is present. Analysis of the results shows that two very different tendencies are at work in such populations. In the first place the Beetles roam at

will through their floury microcosm eating not only flour but also eggs
on their way. This habit has the effect of reducing the rate of increase
of the population and the larger the number of pairs of Beetles present
the greater the destruction becomes. In the second place there is the
opposite tendency for increasing numbers of Beetles to stimulate
repeated matings and thereby produce more eggs. The final outcome
of the two tendencies is to regulate the increase of the population within
the limits mentioned.

We have seen in the foregoing pages of this chapter that under
natural conditions various sorts of insects become gregarious for longer
or shorter periods in their lives. The advantages of the habit may not
always be apparent but it is more than likely that such behaviour is in
the interest of the species concerned. We have seen that there is
evidence of this in the Flour-beetle *Tribolium*.

Gregariousness and social life are not necessarily closely connected.
Some writers, however, see in gregariousness* the beginnings of social
life in mammals but among insects there seems to be no evidence
that the one has led to the other. All that can be said is that both
gregarious and social insects have this much in common—that the
individuals have learned to tolerate the close presence in a limited
space of other members of their species. But, with the exception of
gregarious web-making caterpillars, there is no evidence even of
rudimentary co-operation resulting in benefit to the community, which
is one of the important attributes of social life.

THE BEGINNINGS OF SOCIAL LIFE.—There are few chapters in insect
life of more absorbing interest than the habits of those kinds that live
in societies. Anyone who ponders at all over this remarkable development, which finds its nearest parallel in human society, naturally
speculates as to how such a complicated pattern of habits originated.
Social insects are indeed

> Creatures that by a rule in Nature teach
> The act of order to a peopled Kingdom.
> *(Henry V*, Act 1, Sc. 2.)

Before going further it is desirable to say what is meant by a social
insect.* It may be defined as one in which parent and offspring live
in mutual co-operation in a common shelter or nest. This mode of
living is made possible because the life of the female parent has become
sufficiently lengthened to allow of association with her offspring. It

Plate XXIX

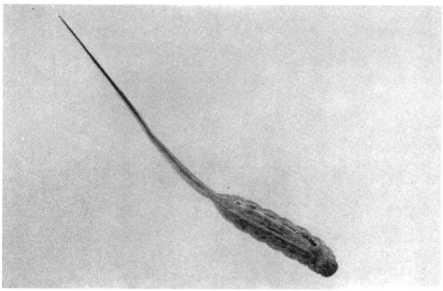

a Rat-tailed maggot or larva of the Drone-fly, *Eristalis tenax* (× 1½)

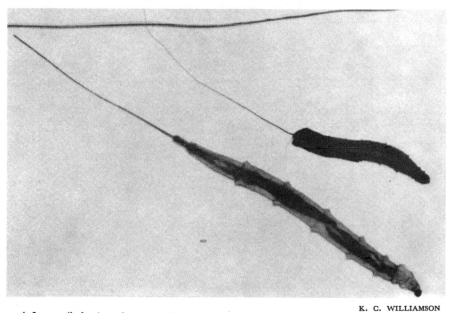

b Larva (below) and pupa (above) of the Crane-fly, *Ptychoptera contamanita* (× 2)

AQUATIC INSECTS VI

CATERPILLARS AND CADDIS-WORMS

A. D. IMMS   S. BEAUFOY

a Communal web spun by caterpillars of Small Eggar Moth,   *b* Caddis-cases of various types: in three of them the head of
Eriogaster lanestris (× ¼)   the occupant is visible (× 2)

will be clear, therefore, that the basis of insect society as of human society is the family.

In Britain we have some 70 kinds of social insects, all members of the one order Hymenoptera. From among the 6,000-odd British species of this order it is only certain kinds of Bees and Wasps, together with all the Ants, that have attained a social organisation. The only other order of social insects is the Isoptera or Termites but since none of these inhabit Britain only incidental reference will be made to them.

Various insects have made shots at developing a social mode of living but most of them have only reached an early stage in the process and no further. These beginnings or attempts at developing a co-operative life are very interesting and several examples are to be found among our native insects. We have seen that web-making caterpillars have made but a groping beginning without getting on to the real track of social development. A much better effort is made by the Shield-bug, *Elasmucha griseus*, whose female lays her eggs in a batch of 30 or more on the underside of a Birch leaf. Here she remains over them on guard, almost concealing them by means of her body (Pl. 11, p. 42, Fig. a). If they are interfered with in any way she becomes greatly agitated. When the eggs hatch she still maintains the same position of guard over the young nymphs. As the latter grow older they make excursions away for feeding but the parent manages for a short while to gather them beneath her again. Finally they disperse and shift for themselves. The present writer once kept one of these Bugs in captivity and the parent ultimately died while still shielding the young nymphs.

The Common Earwig (*Forficula auricularia*) has evolved a stage further. Not only does the female parent show a sort of brood-care instinct for the eggs and young but she has even contrived to make a communal shelter in the form of a cavity excavated beneath the soil, wherein the community lives during its young stages. It is interesting to note that the early naturalist Carl Degeer (1720-78), a compatriot of Linnaeus, gave an excellent account of the maternal instincts of the Earwig in his *Mémoires pour servir à l'histoire des Insectes* (vol. III, 1773, p. 548). In this same work Degeer also recorded the maternal behaviour of the Shield-bug previously noted.

A further step in the evolution of social life is shown by some of the small inconspicuous Bees that belong to the genus *Halictus*. We have some 35 species of this genus in Britain. Each makes a burrow or shaft that goes deep down in the soil and from off this main gallery a group of about 15 or more brood-cells is constructed. Some few kinds of *Halictus* might be regarded as semi-social in habit because the female Bee is long-lived and having stored her brood-cells with pollen closes them down. She then guards them, sometimes even until the young Bees emerge.

The next stage in social development entails the co-operation of the female parent and her offspring for the common good. This step in fact has been attained in *Halictus malachurus*, a Bee that is mostly found in southern England. Fertilised females of this species appear in early spring and, along with many other Bees, they help to pollinate fruit-blossoms. They soon begin to make brood-cells which they provision and in which they then deposit their eggs. The brood that emerges consists entirely of females. These are smaller than the mother, with a differently sculptured cuticle, and were once thought to belong to a different species. These individuals are infertile and are known as workers. They take over the construction and provisioning of further brood-cells from the parent female, or queen as she may be termed, who then devotes herself to egg-laying. By August there are about a dozen of these workers in an individual colony. At this time young fertile females or queens, that resemble the original parent, begin to appear, and with them a certain number of males or drones. The latter mate with the newly-emerged females but take no notice of the workers. The original queen dies at the end of the season and the males and workers meet a similar end. The young fertilised females hibernate in the parental burrow and are the next season's queens. In the spring they get restive and fight for the possession of the burrow. Usually only one remains and the losers have to seek accommodation elsewhere which generally means that they have to dig new burrows of their own. Thus we see in this small *Halictus* Bee a social organisation on a miniature scale. There is even a division of labour in the colony, the queens ultimately devoting themselves to egg-laying and the workers to enlarging the nest and tending the brood.

BEES, SOLITARY AND SOCIAL.—There are some 240 different kinds of Bees found in Britain. The great majority of them are solitary insects and it may come as a surprise to the reader to learn that only 27 species among them are social in habit. The lives of all Bees, whether solitary or social, are closely linked with those of flowering plants. Bees are dependent upon them for obtaining nectar and pollen and, in return, ensure that the flowers are pollinated. The value of Bees as pollinators far exceeds that of all the honey obtained from the hives. Without Bees the fruit crop would be greatly reduced and their aid in effective pollination makes these insects essential for clover-seed production, apart from their value in connection with other plants such as fruit-trees. It is generally known that flowers are mainly pollinated by Bees and other insects and it is not the place here to describe the various beautiful devices that flowers display in order to ensure that this happens. The various floral shapes, colours and alluring scents mainly invite visits from Bees and other insects and direct them to the nectar. The nectar is of course the primary attraction and, in order to obtain this much desired product, the insect becomes inadvertently dusted with pollen from off the stamens. In its efforts to reach the nectary of another flower some of this pollen becomes attached to the stigma and so cross-pollination is effected. Bees begin visiting fruit and other blossoms early in the year and the solitary kinds are among the greatest benefactors in this respect.

All Bees have mouth-parts that are adapted for lapping or licking fluids. The more primitive solitary Bees visit flowers with exposed nectaries, hence their value in pollinating the Plum and Pear. Their maxillae and labium are short as in Wasps. In the more highly developed Bees these organs are much lengthened which enables them to reach the deeply-seated nectar of long tubular flowers. The labium in such Bees is drawn out into a sort of tongue, by means of which the Bee imbibes the nectar. After traversing a deep channel in the tongue the nectar enters the pharynx and then passes into the crop. In the latter chamber it becomes mixed with a ferment or enzyme and is finally regurgitated into the cells of the nest or hive where it is kept as food. Nectar is a watery solution of cane-sugar, and the enzyme just mentioned changes this sugar into two others, namely laevulose and dextrose. When this process is complete the product is honey. Dextrose and laevulose, it may be added, have the advantage of not requiring hydrolysis before they can be absorbed as food.

Pollen very readily adheres to the furry coat of Bees, which is ideal for the purpose. Branched or feathery hairs, mixed among the ordinary pile, help to hold the pollen until the Bee combs it off by means of its legs. Most Bees collect the pollen into tiny masses, moisten them with honey and transfer them to special " pollen-baskets " for conveyance to the nest. The commonest position for the pollen-basket is on the hind-legs.   In Bumble-bees and the Hive-bee, for example, the tibia and first tarsal segment of the hind-legs are specially broadened and flattened.   The actual pollen-basket is formed by the hind tibiae whose smooth shining outer surface is bordered by long hairs for keeping the pollen mass in place.   The inner side of the corresponding broadened tarsal segment is spiny, forming a comb.   Pollen adhering to a very similar comb on the middle legs is scraped on to the comb on the hind tarsi.   Thus impaled, the mass is transferred to the pollen-basket of the leg of the other side.   The mass is scraped off over the lower edge of the tibia and on reaching the pollen-basket is pressed into position.   In the Leaf-cutting Bees and some other solitary Bees the pollen-basket is placed underneath the abdomen where it is constituted by flanges of long hairs.

Before going on to deal with the economy of social Bees it is necessary to say something regarding the solitary kinds because they form the predominating element in any Bee fauna.   Solitary Bees make their nests in the ground, in cavities in stems or other parts of plants, in ready-made crevices in walls, holes in timber, etc.   Most of the materials used are derived from plants and no solitary Bee produces wax.   The nest itself consists of a small number of cells, usually arranged in a linear series.   As soon as a cell is finished it is provisioned with " bee-bread," which is pollen soaked with honey :   an egg is laid within and the chamber is then closed down.   Except in a few cases, the parent never sees her offspring and usually dies before they appear.

Among our numerous solitary Bees the most primitive belong to the genus *Prosopis*—small, black, hairless, shiny insects that do not look like Bees at all (Pl. 21, p. 110, Figs. 1, 2).   Their structure is so little advanced and their habits so rudimentary that Maeterlinck in his *La Vie des Abeilles* claimed that they stand in relation to the Hive-bee in more or less the same position as cave-man does in regard to people who live in large cities.   *Prosopis* cannot collect pollen in the orthodox Bee fashion, firstly because it is nearly naked and secondly because its legs are not adapted for the purpose.   All it can do is to gorge its crop with pollen along with nectar and regurgitate the combined product when it reaches the nest.   These small Bees are often found on fruit blossoms and on bramble flowers.   Their nests are formed in hollow bramble stems, in the ground, or elsewhere, there being much variation in this respect.

The immense genus *Andrena* is represented in Britain by about

60 different species (Pl. 20, p. 95).   Most of them have very much the appearance of the Hive-bee, but some are smaller and others larger. Their tongues, however, are short and they consequently visit flowers with readily accessible nectaries.   These Bees are very abundant in spring when they visit the Sallow catkins and fruit blossoms : later on they resort to the flowers of Dandelion, Blackberry, Ragwort, Scabious, etc.   Some Andrenas, like the Halicti to be mentioned later, select a particularly favourable area of ground and form their burrows in close proximity to one another.   In this way dense colonies arise.   R. C. L. Perkins mentions one comprising numerous burrows of *Andrena humilis* which persisted for *at least* some 40 years in one small patch of ground in Gloucestershire.   It was observed at intervals from 1876 until 1914, when it was still present.   The very common *Andrena albicans* is partial to the flower-heads of Dandelion, and other Andrenas show general or even exclusive preference for certain other flowers.   Some of these Bees are very distinct and are easily identified.   Thus, *Andrena carbonaria*, an early Bee found on Dandelion and Sallow blooms in spring, is easily recognised by its predominating coal-black colour.   Another black *Andrena* is *A. cineraria* but it is a blue-black with conspicuous ashy-grey hair on the thorax (Fig. 24).   *Andrena fulva* (Figs. 22, 23) is one of the most familiar sorts ; the female is densely clothed with orange-coloured pile while the male is a rather ordinary-looking brown Bee.   Like most *Andrena* it burrows in sandy or other light ground : the resultant tiny pyramids of fine soil so common in spring on lawns and paths often

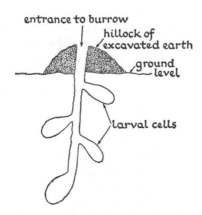

FIG. 39.—Section through the nest of an *Andrena* Bee.

attract notice (Text-Fig. 39). The first heaps are made of the soil pushed up by the Bees that have emerged from last year's burrows, but very soon these are to be seen sinking new shafts on their own account. The entrance-hole leads into a burrow six or more inches deep, from which brood-cells lead off, one below the other. These most attractive Bees cause no harm to lawns and should not be interfered with. Their excavations do not offend the eye of the fastidious for very long as they are soon closed down and become no longer apparent.

Most of the species of *Andrena* are liable to be very much interfered with by other and very different Bees known as *Nomada* (Pl. 21, p. 110, Fig. 13) of which we have some 27 species. Most of them are very like small Wasps in appearance with black-and-yellow or brown-and-yellow banded abdomens. The antennae and legs are generally brownish-yellow and the whole body is bare or very sparsely hairy. These Bees lay their eggs in the cells made by *Andrena* (and other solitary Bees) and the larvae on emerging consume the provisions intended for the rightful occupants of the cells, who perish in consequence. The smooth shiny bodies of the *Nomada* Bees and the absence of any pollen-baskets indicate the lack of any need for collecting pollen for their offspring. Bees like *Nomada* that live at the expense of others are often referred to as parasites ; but some authorities consider that the term inquilines (Lat. *inquilinus*, a tenant) better indicates their relations with their hosts. It will be noted that *Nomada* lives as a dweller, or uninvited guest, in the nest of *Andrena* : the latter Bee apparently does not suspect its injurious activities and tolerates its presence. Many entomologists, therefore, use the term inquiline rather than parasite for this type of relationship wherein the host itself is not the direct subject of attack.

Mention has been made previously of the sub-social propensities shown by some of the species of *Halictus*. The Halicti are smaller than the Andrenas and comprise some of the smallest of all our Bees. None of them is very hairy and many are dark-brown insects of not very distinguished appearance ; others, however, have a very definite metallic sheen. They are short-tongued Bees which make their nests in companies in banks, pathways, etc. Sometimes the individual nests are very numerous and such aggregations might be called villages. In most cases, however, these are not true communities since there is no sign of co-operation for the common advantage. Each Bee in fact works for itself only and is an isolated unit amid the multitude. In some of the species, however, a number of females work together in excavating a common burrow leading to their respective brood-cells.

A number of other small solitary Bees are comprised in the genus *Sphecodes*. They are, however, not at all like the popular conception of a Bee, since they are shiny black and red insects, the red being confined to the hind-body. In some kinds almost the whole abdomen is red, while in others it is limited to a band across that region. They have only slight traces of a pollen-collecting apparatus, which is probably a survival from the period when these Bees were industrious, and provisioned their own nests. There is definite evidence that they lay their eggs in the already provisioned nests of various kinds of *Halictus* and *Andrena*. Like *Nomada* their offspring live at the expense of those of their hosts, in whose nests they are, therefore, parasites or inquilines. A very common species, *Sphecodes monilicornis*, is shown in Pl. 21, p. 110, Fig. 8.

The Leaf-cutting Bees (*Megachile*) are familiar to many people on account of their habit of cutting out extraordinarily neat smooth-edged pieces from the leaves and petals of roses and other plants. There are nine species of these attractive Bees found in Britain. They resemble the Hive-bee in general appearance but are rather more robust, with broader heads. Their nests are mostly made in the ground or in dead wood, hollow stems, or other situations. The brood-cells are constructed entirely of layers of excised pieces of leaves or flower-petals and are shaped like thimbles. The cutting process is carried out with a precision that suggests the work of a machine. The female Bee holds on to a leaf with her legs while she speedily cuts out a piece of the required shape by means of her mandibles. The wall of each cell is formed of oval pieces ; the lid which closes the receptacle is composed of smaller rounded pieces (Pl. XV, p. 122, Fig. c). These Bees are often seen speeding away with their burdens looking very like flying leaves. At least three of the species utilise Rose leaves but those of Lilac, Laburnum, Willow and other plants are also resorted to by various members of the genus. The species most likely to be found is *Megachile centuncularis* (Pl. 20, p. 95, Fig. 25) which is very partial to gardens where there are rose-bushes available, the cells of its nest being made from the leaves. It generally tunnels in a decaying post or other piece of worn-out woodwork : the burrow may extend about a foot in depth and the cells are placed end to end from the bottom upwards. Several of the burrows may be made adjoining one another by the same Bee.

The genus *Osmia* includes eleven British species, some of which are very like the Hive-bee in appearance ; several are larger insects while others are much smaller with a metallic sheen. They are easily distinguished from the Hive-bee because their pollen-baskets are beneath the abdomen instead of being on the hind-legs. These Bees show great diversity of nesting habits, even within an individual species. For the most part they are very prone to use ready-made holes or cavities rather than excavate on their own account. As a group they are called " Mason-bees " because they form their cells of agglutinated particles of earth, sand, minute pebbles or raspings of wood glued together with a secretion presumably from the salivary glands. The commonest species, *Osmia rufa* (Pl. 20, Figs. 8, 9), is reddish-brown and nests in key-holes, crevices in walls, nail-holes in wood and other refuges. Several kinds use empty snail-shells and *O. leucomelana* bores into dead stems of bramble. Another kind, *O. inermis*, is known to nest in hollows beneath stones.

In addition to *Sphecodes* and *Nomada* quite a number of other solitary Bees live as parasites. They have no apparatus for collecting pollen for the reason that they collect no pollen ; also, they never make nests and never provision any cells. They provide for their progeny by taking a mean advantage of the labours of the more industrious and orthodox members of the Bee fraternity. Having entered the burrow of an unsuspecting Bee they seek out the cells and lay an egg on the stored food contained in each. The provisions are consumed by the larva of the intruding bee which often also preys upon the rightful larval occupant of the cell. In many cases the host Bee seems quite oblivious of the baneful significance of the parasitic species and shows no resentment to its presence. In other species the intruding Bee is stated to avoid contact with the host Bee but it must be admitted that there is not very much known about these relationships in different species and careful observations are greatly to be desired.

Among other parasitic Bees the large and handsome *Melecta* is very different from the small *Sphecodes*. The name *Melecta* is a misnomer since it implies a honey collector which this Bee is not. There are only two British species : both of them rear their brood at the expense of the genus *Anthophora*. *Melecta luctuosa* is about ½ in. long and is an intensely black bee with its head and thorax toned with ashy grey hair while the hind-body is ornamented with side tufts of silvery

Plate XXXI

NESTS OF VESPIDAE

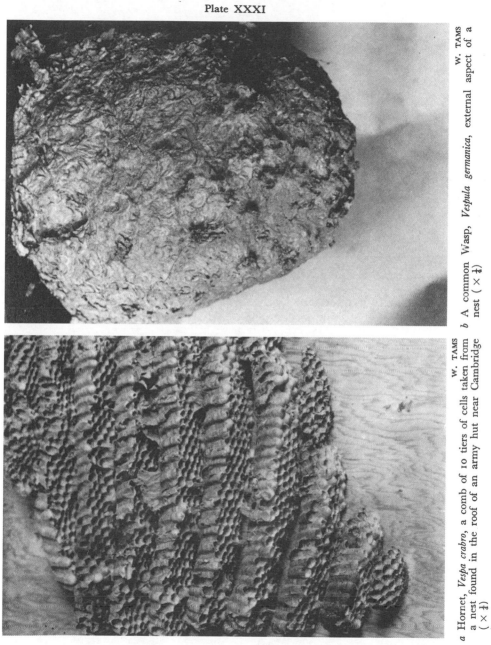

a Hornet, *Vespa crabro*, a comb of 10 tiers of cells taken from a nest found in the roof of an army hut near Cambridge (× ¼)

W. TAMS

b A common Wasp, *Vespula germanica*, external aspect of a nest (× ¼)

W. TAMS

Plate XXXII

W. TAMS

a External view

W. TAMS

b Opened to show cells within

NEST OF CARDER BEE, *BOMBUS AGRORUM* ($\times \frac{1}{2}$)

pubescence. The Anthophoras which it parasitises include the largest of all our solitary Bees. They are long-tongued Bees that mostly nest in banks in the ground or in old walls, etc. Our two largest kinds, viz. *Anthophora retusa* and *A. acervorum* (*pilipes*), are very like small Bumble-bees and appear along with them in early spring. Their females are black with orange hairs on the hind-legs (a feature which separates them from a black Bumble-bee), whereas the males are to a large extent clothed with fulvous or brown hair. *A. pilipes* receives its name from the fringe of very long hair borne on the tarsi of its middle pair of legs (Plate 20, Fig. 10).

Mention has been already made of the Bee *Anthidium manicatum*—the " Carder-bee " of Gilbert White. It belongs to the same group as *Osmia* and *Megachile*. The members of all three genera are long-tongued Bees and have their pollen baskets on the under surface of the abdomen where they take the form of long hairs for holding the collected pollen in position. We have only this one species of *Anthidium* (Pl. 20, Fig. 14) in Britain : it presents the unusual feature of the male being larger than the female. This insect is not so much an excavator as an upholsterer. The female evidently does not believe in making her own tunnels and consequently looks round, like the Osmias, for some ready-made borings of the right sort. Having found one suitable for her requirements she seeks out plants with downy leaves or stems such as Mullein. She rapidly shaves off the cottony hairs by means of her mandibles until she accumulates a ball almost as large as herself. Flying away with this cargo held between her legs she lines the selected burrow with the soft material. The cells are formed of a secretion which hardens to form a kind of membrane, which prevents the honey from the food-mass percolating into their downy outer covering.

Having briefly discussed some of our most characteristic solitary Bees we will now pass to the social kinds which have unquestionably been derived from them in the course of evolution. The social Bees include the Bumble-bees *Bombus* and *Psithyrus* and the Hive-bee (*Apis mellifera*). The *Halictus malachurus* mentioned on p. 260 must also be included with them.

The Bumble-bees are friendly creatures known to everybody as they fly from flower to flower intent upon collecting pollen and nectar. The names " bumble " and " humble " are both used for these insects and refer to the characteristic buzz or hum which they make while in flight. In Britain we have 19 species of true Bumble-bees belonging to the genus *Bombus* and 6 species of parasitic Bumble-bees of the genus *Psithyrus*. Each kind of true Bumble-bee has three kinds of individuals, viz. :—the queens or fertilised females ; the workers or small females ; and males or drones. The queens are larger than either the workers or drones and are most often seen in spring when they are founding their colonies. The antennae have 12 segments and a sting is present. The hind-legs are broadened and flattened with a " basket " of hairs for holding the collected pollen. The workers are similar in all these characters to the queens the only difference being their smaller size. The males have longer antennae than the queens and workers, with 13 instead of 12 segments. They have no sting ; the hind-legs are more slender and are not used for carrying pollen. Their coloration resembles that of the queens and workers but they often have extra yellow bands that are wanting in the former individuals.

Our six commonest Bumble-bees (Pl. 40, p. 255) are *Bombus terrestris*, black with two deep yellow bands and a tawny or tawny-white hind extremity ; *B. lucorum*, which is very similar but the yellow bands are slightly paler and the hind extremity pure white ; *B. hortorum*, which might easily be confused with *lucorum* but has three yellow bands instead of two ; *B. lapidarius*, black with a deep orange-red extremity ; *B. pratorum*, very much smaller than *B. lucorum*, but like it in coloration excepting the hind extremity which is pale orange ; and *B. agrorum*, also a small Bee, but tawny yellow or pale brown all over with some black hairs on the abdomen.

Bumble-bees begin to appear in March or April. The individuals seen at that time are the queens which have just come out of hibernation and are getting busy looking for suitable sites for their nests. Generally the nests are located in ready-made holes that have been vacated by field-mice, voles or other small animals. Bumble-bees use fine grass, moss, dry leaves, etc., which they form into hollow ball-like nests. Access to a nest is by means of a subterranean tunnel which varies a good deal in length. *Bombus agrorum*, and several other Bees, however, make surface nests (Pl. XXXII, p. 267) generally hidden among grass or other vegetation. They are known as Carder-bees from their habit of using materials nearby and plaiting them together with their legs and mandibles. Having prepared her nest the Bumble-bee places in it a mass of pollen moistened with honey. Upon this paste she builds a circular wall of wax and deposits a batch of eggs in the cell thus formed. She then seals it over with wax and proceeds to build a waxen honey-pot nearer to the entrance to the nest. This may hold nearly a thimbleful of honey ! The queen sits over her eggs to incubate them, only leaving the nest to obtain food. During bad weather she draws upon the reserve contained in the honey-pot nearby. The eggs hatch out in four days into white crescentic legless grubs. When they have devoured the original mass of food provided for them the queen adds more of the same kind. She also cuts a hole in the roof of the cell and discharges a honey-pollen mixture through her mouth for their benefit. As the larvae grow more wax is added to the cell, which gradually expands in size. When fully grown each larva spins a cocoon and changes therein into a pupa. About three weeks after the first eggs were laid, the adults begin to emerge : these are all workers. Meanwhile the queen has provisioned more cells and deposited more eggs. The workers relieve her of much of the duties of feeding and tending the brood. The queen still flies abroad to gather food but ultimately, when enough workers have developed, she remains in the nest and devotes herself to egg-laying, her other nest functions being delegated to the workers. These latter take over the protection of the nest, the making of new cells and honey-pots and the general provisioning of the community. Up till this time the queen has laid only fertilised eggs which develop into worker-bees but towards the end of the season she lays both fertilised and unfertilised eggs. The larvae from the fertilised eggs, laid at this time, are fed more abundantly than those destined to become worker-bees : they grow larger, make larger cocoons for pupation and develop into queens. The unfertilised eggs develop into males. If the workers lay any eggs, as they often do, these eggs are also unfertilised and give rise to males.

After mating, the young queens disperse and ultimately burrow into banks or beneath trees where they overwinter in a state of torpor until roused by the warmth of spring. All the other members of the colony perish on the advent of cold weather. A large colony of Bumblebees may number about 400 individuals, but the populations of *Bombus pratorum* and *B. agrorum* are much smaller. The interior of a nest (Pl. XXXII) presents an irregular appearance, the new cells being built on top of the old ones, which are not used a second time. Bumblebees will often withstand much provocation before they sting and in some cases, especially with *B. pratorum* and *B. agrorum*, a nest may be taken without receiving a single sting. The amount of honey yielded by a single nest is too small to make its collection a practicable proposition although it is not difficult to keep a colony in captivity. The honey, however, is very pleasant to the taste, as country schoolboys often know. Since the tongue of a Bumble-bee is much longer than that of the Hive-bee the insect can extract nectar from long tubular flowers such as Red Clover, Foxglove, Nasturtium and many others. A habit of biting a hole near the bases of some flowers, to establish a short cut to the nectaries, robs the flowers without the benefit of pollination.

The legend of the " trumpeter " Bumble-bee seems to date from the year 1700 when a Dutchman, J. Goedart, published a treatise on insect life. Among the naïve beliefs expressed in this work is his claim that an individual Bumble-bee rouses the occupants of the nest early in the morning by sounding a reveille by means of " his " rapidly vibrating wings—thus playing the part of a bugler in the army. His observation that a Bee mounts the comb and produces a humming note in this way, at the time stated, has often been confirmed and the charming story of its *raison d'être* has received credence, on and off, for over 200 years. Perhaps the last observer of the performance to believe in Goedart's legend, was the German M. Bachmann, who published his findings in 1915. But his fellow-countryman, H. von Buttel-Reepen, had earlier provided a more probable explanation of the " trumpeter's " activity. Just as individual Hive-bee workers ventilate the hive so the " trumpeter " ventilates the Bumble-bee colony. Her rapidly vibrating wings set up an air-current which reduces the temperature and expels excess of moisture from the nest.*

In addition to the true Bumble-bees, forming the genus *Bombus*, we have in Britain six kinds of Parasitic Bumble-bees of the genus *Psithyrus* (Pl. 40, p. 255). These Bees have no labours of their own to perform and comprise only males and females (or queens), the worker caste having disappeared. They impose themselves upon the hard-working Bumble-bees, devouring their stored food, laying their eggs in the ready-made cells, and leaving their offspring to be fed by the workers of the host species. The parasitic Bees behave, therefore, very like the Cuckoo in that they lay their eggs in the nests of species other than their own. F. W. L. Sladen, who has specially observed the habits of *Psithyrus*, tells us that the queen does not always gain entry into a Bumble-bee colony without a struggle, especially if the workers be numerous. In any event the *Bombus* queen is ultimately stung to death

*On a cold morning wing vibration—like shivering—may warm the bee's wing muscles to the temperature needed for flight. *G.C.V., B.M.H.*

so that her worker daughters will then only rear *Psithyrus* offspring instead of her own. The *Psithyrus* queen is well adapted for this nefarious task for she has a harder, more shiny and less densely hairy skin and a more powerful sting than her *Bombus* rival. When flying from flower to flower the two kinds of Bees are hard to distinguish by the eye, being very alike in size and general appearance. *Bombus*, however, makes an unmistakable humming sound when on the wing whereas the note emitted by *Psithyrus* is very faint and soft.

Each kind of *Psithyrus* breeds only in nests of its particular host species. Our common *Psithyrus rupestris*, for instance, only parasitises nests of *Bombus lapidarius*, and *P. vestalis* has *Bombus terrestris* as its host. Certain kinds of *Psithyrus* bear a close colour-resemblance to their respective hosts and some authorities believe that this is because each kind of parasitic Bee arose originally from its particular host species. In support of this view is the fact that late-appearing queens of some kinds of *Bombus* do not always take the trouble to start nests of their own and, instead, enter nests of other members of their species and may even kill the rightful queens. Sladen mentions that this habit may extend to attacking closely related species. Thus, *B. terrestris* may enter a nest of *B. lucorum*, kill the queen and use the workers for rearing her own *terrestris* brood, thus behaving in the same way as a *Psithyrus*. If this habit became permanent an important stage in the evolution of *Psithyrus* would have been reached, and it is claimed that its further development has in fact led to the evolution of the parasitic Bumble-bees as we know them to-day.

The Hive-bee (*Apis mellifera*) and its economy is dealt with at length in books on Bee-keeping, or the reader may turn to the writings of Maurice Maeterlinck and of Eugène Evrard. It will not be necessary, therefore, to recount the story of its life and habits in any detail. During more than 40 centuries man has kept colonies of this insect for his own advantage. Being a singularly adaptable creature the Hive-bee has become dispersed all over the world. The fact that it can use the most diverse kinds of flowers as sources of food and can keep its nest warm enough to resist a good deal of cold have proved great assets in this respect. Yet it is rarely found nesting in its primitive, natural state. It needs a cavity for the purpose and consequently seeks a hollow tree, a hole in a roof or other structure or a cave. The man-made hive fulfils its requirements to a singularly complete extent. The original land of origin of the Hive-bee is probably the Orient, and in particular the Indo-Malayan region, which is the only part of the world where species of the genus *Apis* occur wild. In support of this belief it is interesting to note that the native Bee of India, *Apis indica*, is almost indistinguishable from our Hive-bee and hybridises with it. It is thus likely that the Hive-bee is merely a race of the oriental Bee just mentioned. The fact that the colonies of the Hive-bee are perennial and give off swarms as a means of founding new societies also suggest a tropical origin for it. Neither habit features in the lives of the social Bees or Wasps of temperate lands, in all of which the colonies are annual affairs and swarming does not occur.

The Hive-bee colony represents the highest attainment of social development among Bees. Differentiation into the three forms of drone, queen and worker (Pl. 20, p. 95, Figs. 19-21) is more pronounced than among Bumble-bees. The drone, for instance, is larger and stouter than the worker and is easily distinguished by his broader head and larger eyes. The queen has a longer hind-body which reaches beyond the closed wings. Since she performs none of the functions of comb-building or feeding and tending the brood she secretes no wax or " royal jelly " (to be mentioned later), nor do her hind-legs form pollen-baskets ; also her tongue and sting are slightly shorter than in the workers and her brain is smaller. She has become in fact a highly developed egg-laying machine, and plays no other active part in the economy of the hive. The workers alone secrete the wax for comb-building. This is produced by the younger individuals only from glands situated on the under-side of the segments of the hind-body. This substance is moulded to form pendant combs of hexagonal cells (Pl. XIII, p. 114, Fig. a) placed back to back. The drone-cells are larger than those in which workers develop while the cells for queen-rearing are more or less sac-like and hang downwards. Other cells are devoted to the storing of pollen and honey for use during bad weather and also for feeding during winter.

The queen lays a single egg in each cell. An egg takes about three days to hatch. The young larvae are all nourished at first upon so-called " royal jelly," a secretion produced by the pharyngeal glands of the workers. Larvae destined to grow into queen bees are fed exclusively on this substance, which is very rich in protein ; in the case of drone and worker larvae it is replaced from the 4th day onwards by a diet of pollen and honey which contains a higher proportion of carbo-hydrate. Experiments by transferring eggs or very young larvae from worker-cells into queen-cells, and the reverse, show clearly the decisive importance of these differences in diet in determining the two types of individuals. In this way an egg from a worker-cell can be made to develop into a queen or, conversely, one from a queen-cell made to produce a worker.

The difference between drones and females (queens and workers) is determined by heredity, according to whether an egg is unfertilised and contains only a single set of chromosomes, or is fertilised and contains the usual two sets. There is evidence that the queen herself controls the sex of the egg she lays by opening, or by keeping closed, the sphincter muscle of the duct of her sperm-containing sac and, by this means, regulating fertilisation (or its absence). Presumably the stimulus is provided by the sight, or by the feel, of the brood-cells, worker or queen as against drone. But to some extent the regulation is seasonal, drone-producing eggs being laid chiefly in spring.

The population of a strong hive may number 50,000 to 80,000, the vast majority being workers. When the population increases sufficiently a swarm is emitted, but the underlying causes of swarming and the best means of its prevention are still very debatable topics among bee-keepers. A first swarm consists of the reigning fertilised queen and a large number of workers. The original colony becomes dominated by a new queen which had been previously guarded from attacks by the original queen by the workers. Being a virgin, she leaves the colony at an early opportunity on her marriage flight, followed by an eager crowd of pursuing males. Mating takes place in mid-air and the now fertilised queen then returns to the hive. If the colony gives off an after swarm in the same season the workers are accompanied by one or more virgin queens.

Here it will be necessary to close the subject of Bees and to leave consideration of Wasps and Ants to the next chapter. A fitting introduction to the relationships between Wasps and Bees is provided by those primitive solitary Bees known as *Prosopis* which have been previously referred to. *Prosopis*, it will be recalled, has a simple tongue like that of a Wasp : its body is almost hairless and it has neither pollen-collecting-apparatus nor any trace of a pollen-basket. It shares all these negative characters with wasps and the question arises as to how Bees of this kind are to be distinguished from solitary digging Wasps. The real difference lies in difference of habit, not in structure or colour or appearance. Whereas all Bees explore the vegetable world for their means of sustenance, Wasps are essentially carnivorous and feed their brood upon various insects and small related animals. Bees are in fact Wasps that have forsaken an animal diet and come to rely upon the products of the vegetable kingdom. The name " Blumen-wespen " or Flower-wasps, used by some German entomologists, well expresses this fact.

SOCIAL LIFE
(continued)

IN THE preceding chapter a brief account was given of the economy of social and solitary Bees and how they are adapted to exploit the nectar and pollen yielded by flowers. We now extend our subject to the Wasps (social and solitary) and the Ants, all of whom are social in habit.

SOCIAL AND SOLITARY WASPS.—Although there are in Britain more than 290 different kinds of Wasps, only a very small proportion are true Wasps or Vespidae. All the rest are known as Fossorial or Digger Wasps. True Wasps are easily recognised because their wings are folded into longitudinal creases when closed over the body. In all other Wasps these organs are closed flat and without being folded in the way just mentioned. The only Wasps familiar to everybody belong to the genera *Vespa* and *Vespula* (Pl. 25, p. 142). These are the creatures endowed with painful stings that enter houses and also help themselves to fruit in our gardens and orchards. There are seven species; and they are our only social Wasps. Those most usually seen are the Common Wasp (*Vespula vulgaris*) and the equally abundant German Wasp (*Vespula germanica*). Both these kinds make their nests underground. The reddish-tinged *Vespula rufa* has similar nesting habits but rarely enters houses. Two other species, viz. the Tree-Wasp (*Vespula sylvestris*) and the Norwegian Wasp (*Vespula norvegica*) nest in trees or bushes. The Cuckoo-wasp (*Vespula austriaca*) is rather rare and lives at the expense of *Vespula rufa* in whose nests it lays its eggs. It bears just the same relation to this host as *Psithyrus* does to Bumble-bees. The seventh kind is that super-wasp known as the Hornet (*Vespa crabro*), which nests chiefly in hollow trees (Pls. 25 [p. 142] Fig. a and XXXI [p. 266] Fig. a). It is easily known by its much larger size with brown instead of black markings combined with a deeper yellow coloration. The Hornet is chiefly found in Southern England and is much commoner in some parts than in others. It is frequent for instance in the New Forest, parts of East Anglia, the Wye Valley and in Devonshire. Near London it is known from the district around Richmond Park.

The social system of *Vespula* and *Vespa* is much more like that of a Bumble-bee than of the Hive-bee. The colonies are annual affairs only and never give off swarms. Also there is very little difference between the queens and workers other than that of size—the colour-difference being very slight. The large Wasps that attract notice on sunny days in early spring are young fertilised queens that have survived hibernation. On being aroused from their long winter's sleep their first business is to find a suitable site for nest-building. In the case of our two commonest Wasps, previously mentioned, the nest is formed inside a deserted mouse-hole or other cavity some distance below the soil surface. The next operation is to gather the material for nest-building. Unlike social Bees, Wasps do not produce wax for this purpose. Instead, they use weather-worn but sound wood from posts and trees, particles of which are rasped off by means of the mandibles and worked up with the aid of saliva into what is called " wasp-paper." Layers of this material are applied to the roof of the subterranean cavity and from the disc thus formed a pendent stalk is soon made. The lower end of the stalk becomes widened out and to it is attached a horizontal comb or layer of cells. The cells are hexagonal and face downwards, being widely open below but closed above. An umbrella-like covering is suspended from the roof of the cavity so as to protect the comb as it is formed. The eggs are laid one in each cell, and are glued down so as not to fall out. Those first laid all produce workers. Very soon these individuals take over the duties of brood-care and nest-building, leaving the parent queen to devote herself entirely to egg-production. When a nest is fully formed it is roughly spherical in outward shape and is covered with several layers of wasp-paper (Plate XXXI). New cells are added to the outer sides of those already made and when one layer of comb has reached a suitable size new tiers or combs are added below and are firmly attached by stalk-like pillars to the combs immediately above. This goes on until seven, eight, or more combs have been formed. The distance between the edges of the combs and the nest-covering is just sufficient to allow of the free movement of the occupants. Towards the end of summer larger cells are formed and these " royal cells " are used for rearing the females or queens that will found the next year's colonies. Males are also produced about the same time. The fertilised eggs, as with Bees, give rise to queens and workers dependent upon the amount of food given to the larvae. The workers are females which have aborted reproductive organs and are incapable of being fecundated. Male Wasps are always produced from unfertilised eggs laid by the queen and, under certain conditions, by the workers. Just as with Bees, male Wasps have no sting and are distinguished from the workers by their somewhat longer antennae.

Wasps feed their larvae on other insects, portions of which they masticate previously for the purpose : both fresh and decaying meat and fish are also sometimes resorted to. The Wasps themselves mostly like substances rich in sugars and consequently resort to such energy-producing foods as ripe fruits, nectar and honey-dew. Their short tongues prevent them from reaching deeply-seated nectaries and for this reason the range of flowers visited by Wasps is limited. They are, however, very constant visitors to the flowers of the Figwort and in autumn to Ivy bloom. When a worker enters the nest after a foraging expedition the hungry eyeless larvae raise their heads at her approach. In return for the food which they bring, the worker Wasps eagerly imbibe the saliva that flows from the mouths of the brood. There are times when this larval product is exploited without any reciprocal exchange of nutriment. The saliva has apparently lost its digestive function and is mainly a sugary fluid. The inert larva itself needs protein for its growth rather than carbohydrate. The saliva on the other hand provides the worker Wasps with an ideal food for an active insect that is no longer growing. Thus an interchange of nutriment takes place. This explains much of the behaviour that has been attributed to a maternal brood-care instinct on the part of the workers. It is curious that among Bees there is no evidence of any such mutual exchange of food-stuffs. Possibly this is because the nectar of flowers satisfies all their needs for carbohydrates without the Bees exploiting their larvae also. Or, if the necessity does arise there is usually enough honey stored in the comb to satisfy their requirements.

When the Wasp larvae are ready to transform into pupae each spins a cocoon and closes the mouth of the cell with a floor of tough silk. About four to six weeks after the eggs are laid the fully-formed Wasps bite their way out of the cells and emerge. After the males and virgin queens have mated the colony begins to disintegrate. The daughter-queens, which will be the foundresses of the colonies of the next year, hibernate in concealed situations, whereas all the other occupants of the nest gradually perish as autumn advances.

Passing now to the remainder of the Wasps, the first thing to be noted about them is that they are all solitary insects. There is no community, and each female operates on her own account without any workers to assist her. Solitary Wasps are smaller and more slender than the familiar social Wasps just discussed and are not often noticed unless specially looked for. Nevertheless their habits and instincts are very remarkable and have attracted the attention of some of the most famous observers of insect life. The Frenchman J. H. Fabre (1823–1915) has contributed in his *Souvenirs Entomologiques* some of the most graphic word-pictures of the behaviour of these insects.

In the discussion of the ways and doings, not only of Solitary Wasps but of all Hymenoptera, the reader needs to bear in mind that the female insects alone are being referred to. The activities of the males, apart from mating, are of very little biological significance. They enjoy, in fact, " that indolent but agreeable condition of doing nothing."

Solitary Wasps, unlike the social kinds, feed their larvae upon whole insects which are not premasticated or dismembered. The prey, however, is stung first. This paralyses it and renders it incapable of activity ; in some cases death results but the injected venom also has antiseptic properties which keep the victim fresh for many days or even weeks. Solitary Wasps are very particular as to the prey they capture and most kinds have the instinct to attack certain creatures only and no others. Thus, *Ammophila* stores her cells exclusively with non-hairy caterpillars ; *Pompilus* is a spider-hunter ; *Mellinus*, *Crabro* and *Oxybelus* mostly capture Flies of various sorts ; *Cerceris* usually selects Weevils ; *Philanthus* captures Bees ; *Gorytes* drags Frog-hopper nymphs from their " cuckoo-spit " while *Pemphredon* stores Aphids.

Among the true Wasps of solitary habit the genera *Eumenes* and *Ancistrocerus* are found in Britain (Pl. 20, p. 95). They can be separated from the social Wasps by the claws of their feet being either toothed or forked. Our only species of *Eumenes*, *E. coarctata*, has the abdomen joined to the thorax by a tapering stalk, whereas in *Ancistrocerus* a mere constriction separates the two regions of the body. *Eumenes* is found on sandy heaths and commons: it is a potter Wasp which makes exquisite vase-like cells of moulded earth attached to the twigs of Heather and other woody plants. Each of the cells is provisioned with several very small caterpillars and over these a single egg is suspended, like a ceiling droplight, by a delicate thread from the top of the receptacle. The young *Eumenes* larva eats its first caterpillar while attached to its egg-shell and still hanging from its suspensory filament. By this means it appears the larva is protected from being crushed by movements of its victims until it is strong enough to descend among them. *Ancistrocerus* and allied genera comprise nineteen British species, some being common and widespread. They suspend their eggs and provision their cells much as does *Eumenes,* but in some cases small Beetle-larvae are used instead of caterpillars. Their cells, however, do not show the same refined workmanship and are mostly constructed in the ground or in walls or posts, while certain kinds burrow in bramble stems.

Our other Solitary Wasps are a very mixed assemblage and are often referred to as Fossorial or Digger Wasps. For the most part they are burrowers and excavators, working with their mandibles, which act as grapplers, and with their tarsi, which are highly efficient rakes. Among the best known of them are *Ammophila* and its allies, which belong to the Sphegidae. Their habits are exceptionally interesting and it is not surprising they have received attention from many naturalists. Our four British species are very much alike in coloration with the hind-body narrowed to form a slender stalk, which in *Ammophila subulosa* is very long (Plate 20, Fig. 18). They are well named Sand Wasps because they frequent commons and other sandy areas— mostly in southern England. The female Wasp makes a vertical or sloping shaft in the ground ending in a bulb-shaped cell. She spends much time selecting its site and does not live in the burrow while she makes it. Some kinds close the entrance hole temporarily with a small fragment of stone during the process of formation. The Wasp then often flies into the air over the burrow, apparently taking an orientation flight in order to learn its position in regard to neighbouring objects. In this way she is enabled to find it again after being away on an expedition to seek her prey.

Ammophila sabulosa uses a single caterpillar to provision each burrow she makes. *A. hirsuta* only preys upon night-feeding caterpillars that hide away by day in the soil at the base of their food-plant. By an undiscovered instinct, possibly smell, this Sand-wasp is able to locate its prey while hidden from view. Having found a caterpillar of the right sort she stings it until it becomes immobile. Fabre claimed that the victims are stung in very definite places so that the sting enters the main nerve-centres that govern bodily movements and induce paralysis. He claimed that the number of stings *Ammophila* and other

Solitary Wasps administer to their prey is largely dependent upon the number of motor nerve-centres.   Later observers have doubted this attractive explanation and rather discredit Fabre's claim : they find that the number and position of the stings that are administered to a prey are more variable than Fabre thought.   The stinging usually goes on only so long as the victim struggles and is often supplemented by the Wasp biting the creature vigorously in the neck and even imbibing the exuding blood.   Also, it is not necessary for the sting to pierce the nerve-ganglia to induce paralysis, as the venom soon circulates in the blood.   We have to conclude, therefore, that *Ammophila* and other Solitary Wasps are not the skilled surgeons gifted with an intuitive knowledge of their victims' anatomy as was implied by Fabre.   Nevertheless, anyone who has witnessed the process will agree that they are clever operators that soon overcome their prey.

Having stung the caterpillar into immobility, the Sand-wasp either flies with its victim or drags it to the nest.   Here she drops her burden ; after inspection of the burrow she hauls it down into the cell and deposits an egg on its surface.   She then selects sand grains or a stone for closing the burrow, taking much care in the process.   In the allied Sand-wasp *Sphex* a number of experienced observers have witnessed the insect seize a minute stone and use it as a rammer when closing the burrow.   This astonishing habit affords a unique example of an insect actually selecting and using a tool to serve its needs.   So far this performance has not been witnessed among our British species of *Ammophila*.

In another family of Solitary Wasps, the *Pompilidae* (Pl. 20, Figs. 3, 4), we have a group of spider-hunters.   There are 39 British species, all of which store their cells with spiders.   They are mostly found where the soil is light and sandy ; commons and sand-dunes support the largest numbers of different kinds.   Most of our Pompilidae measure about $\frac{1}{2}$ in. or a little more across the outstretched wings and are black or black with a red-brown band across the hind-body.   Attention is often drawn to them on account of their extremely active movements as they run on the ground with their wings and antennae quivering all the time.   Some of the tropical kinds are among the largest of all Wasps and are able to overcome the great Mygalid spiders with which they provision their nests.

The life of a typical *Pompilus* is briefly as follows.   In early summer, after mating, the female starts looking for her spider prey and does so before she has made any nest for its reception. When a suitable spider is recognised she either drives it from its web or routs it from its burrow. A chase then usually ensues until she can get a hold on its back and, having succeeded, she curls her abdomen round so as to sting the hapless victim underneath. A curious thing is that the spider makes very little effort to defend itself. W. S. Bristowe mentions that the spiders seem to have an instinctive fear of Pompilids and show signs of panic when confronted by these adversaries. As a rule the larger Pompilids effect complete paralysis of their victims, the venom evidently being very potent. Having captured and stung a spider the *Pompilus* either hides it or deposits it near-by while she proceeds to make a burrow. When the nest is ready the immobile spider is seized and dragged backwards to the entrance. The Wasp then enters, turns round and, reaching out, hauls the victim within. After packing the spider in the cell at the bottom of the burrow she lays an egg on its underside and then closes the entrance to the nest. Having sealed up one burrow the whole performance is repeated each time an egg is to be laid until the full quota is deposited.

The family Philanthidae includes members of a more orthodox wasp-like appearance, with black and yellow banded bodies. One of our commonest kinds is *Cerceris arenaria* (Pl. 20, Fig. 2) which, like some other species, stores its nests with Weevils. Some nests contain Weevils all of one species only, while in others they are a mixed lot but much about the same size. Among their prey are the Nut Weevils *Curculio* (Pl. 36, Fig. b). The *Cerceris* manages to pierce the hard shell of Weevils · by stinging them in the membrane between the legs or between the thorax and abdomen. How the *Cerceris* larva negotiates this crusty diet does not seem to be recorded.

Some of the most abundant of all our Solitary Wasps are members of the family Crabronidae (Pl. 20, p. 95, Fig. 7) which provision their nests with Flies of various sorts. Their burrows are often very numerous in old stumps of dry wood. Leading off from each is a linear series of brood-cells. Other kinds tunnel into the pith of Bramble, Elder, etc. ; still others burrow into the ground, light or rather heavy soils being preferred according to the species. To find these insects one often need not go outside the garden, where they may have their burrows in the ground or in old woodwork, etc. While certain kinds seem to restrict their prey to members of a single family of Flies others are much less fastidious. *Acanthocrabro vagabundus* preys upon Crane-flies and

Clytochrysus cavifrons selects Hover-flies, yet *Metacrabro quadricinctus* captures Blow-flies and Flesh-flies as well as Horse-flies and Hover-flies. Some of these victims, it may be added, are large strong creatures much more bulky than the Wasp itself.

The metallic Ruby-tail Wasps (Chrysididae) always attract notice whenever they are seen. Usually they are to be met with diligently exploring sheltered walls and fences during hot sunshine. On such occasions they are searching for the burrows of other insects in whose nests they lay their eggs. Their hard cuticle is like a magnificent coat of mail studded with elaborate patterns and coloured brilliantly blue-green, green or copper according to the species. One of our most characteristic kinds is shown in Pl. 21, p. 110, Fig. 9. These beautiful Wasps have indeed sordid habits, since their larvae devour those of other Solitary Wasps and Bees, particularly of the genera *Ancistrocenus* and *Osmia*.

Before closing this digression on Solitary Wasps we must ask whether any of them betray a trend towards social habits. The answer is that here and there we can detect traits which seem to point in this direction, more especially in regard to the feeding of the offspring. The usual method consists in the rapid accumulation of enough food to provide for the larvae until they reach maturity and then in closing down each cell, even before the eggs have hatched. The French entomologist, E. Roubaud, has aptly designated this procedure " mass provisioning." In some few species, however, the eggs hatch before the cells are fully provisioned and the parent Wasp then continues feeding her offspring—a method which Roubaud calls " progressive provisioning." This process involves the lengthening of the life of the parent, who at the same time gains some acquaintance with her brood. It is in fact the beginning of a habit that finds its full expression among social insects.

It will be recalled that such Wasps as *Ammophila* and *Pompilus* construct their cells singly and isolated, each with its own entrance-burrow. Others, like the Crabronidae, tend to form their cells collectively : each Wasp makes its cells in a group connected with a single entrance burrow. Thus we have a sort of rudimentary comb and the beginnings of the true nest-formation which features in all communities of social insects.

An even more rudimentary social tendency is shown also among some of the Crabronidae, in that they have learned to tolerate the close proximity of other members of their kind. A number of females may nest in the ground so closely together that they have developed mutualism to the extent of using a common entrance tunnel.

Thus we see among Solitary Wasps, as among Solitary Bees, tendencies that are rudimentary beginnings of communal life.

ANTS.—Ants must be given first place among social insects. They are indeed the highest-developed and the most successful exponents of this way of living. All Ants are social in habit and their colonies endure from one year to another. There are more different kinds of Ants than of all the other social insects together and they are found throughout the world from the poles to the equator. Their longevity is remarkable, which in itself gives stability to their colonies ; worker Ants are known to live up to seven and queens for more than fifteen years. Their feeding habits are more catholic than those of Bees and Wasps. Some kinds of Ants, for instance, are carnivorous and feed upon insects or other small animals, dead or alive ; other kinds feed upon seeds, while fungi, nectar and honey-dew form the diet of certain species. Ants are essentially creatures of the ground, their nests in most cases being subterranean. They owe much of their superiority to their terrestrial habits. Aerial insects make long flights without meeting obstacles or gaining experience whereas, on the earth, not a movement can be made that is not a contact with something and, in this way, experience becomes rapidly accumulated. Ants construct no combs, their food and their young in various stages of growth being lodged within intercommunicating chambers. Nest-building, therefore, has become a less dominant occupation than with the social Wasps and Bees and this, in itself, allows freedom to develop other phases of life. Their subterranean habit has led to Ants largely dispensing with wings which, after all, would be of very little use under the circumstances. They seem to make up for this by being some of the most agile and tireless runners in the whole insect world.

If there be any doubt whether a particular insect is an Ant or not, note the following rules. Look at the hind-body : in all Ants it consists of a slender stalk or waist joining it to the thorax and continued backwards into a globular gaster (Text-Fig. 40). The stalk bears a hump or tubercle (sometimes two) on its upper surface, which is not found in other insects with stalked hind-bodies. Also, the antennae of Ants are sharply bent or elbowed. Only male and fertile female Ants bear

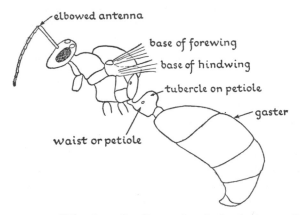

FIG. 40.—Side view of a Queen Ant (only the bases of the wings and legs are shown). (Magnified.)

wings and these only for the nuptial flight. The fertile females are generally very much larger than the males.

On a suitable day, most often in July or August, the male and female Ants leave the nest on their nuptial flight. The air is sometimes literally filled with these winged reproductive agents ; swallows and other birds soon detect such swarms, chasing and devouring their members in immense numbers. Whatever causes this exodus affects the colonies of the same kind of Ant often over a large area at the same time. H. Donisthorpe mentions that on August 8th, 1915, swarms of the Garden Ant (*Lasius niger*) and a closely related kind were noted over the greater part of England from the Isle of Wight to Leicester and even into Northumberland. Some atmospheric influence probably extended over an extensive area simultaneously, moisture and warmth being perhaps two of the factors concerned. The workers become very much agitated near the swarming period and prevent the winged individuals from leaving the nest before the right time. Mating occurs in the air during the flight and intercrossing of individuals from different colonies often happens. After the function is over the fertilised queen descends to earth once again and the first thing she does is to divest herself of her wings. This she effects by working them backwards and forwards, by rubbing them against stems etc. and by pulling them with her legs and jaws until they break away. Once the queen becomes wingless her instincts alter and she now shuns daylight and hurries to escape below ground. In some Ants artificial removal of the wings before mating will evoke these same instincts in a virgin queen. During her marriage-flight the queen receives enough sperms from the male to last her lifetime. On coming to earth she usually does one of three things. Either she may return to her original nest or enter another one, or she may found a new nest of her own. The latter course of action is the usual one and she excavates a cavity in the soil or uses a ready made one. This she closes up and remains there in seclusion until her eggs are ready to be laid. During this period, which may run into several months, she has to draw upon reserves in her own body to keep herself alive. The degenerating muscles of her cast-off wings yield a store of food-materials for this purpose. When her eggs hatch she feeds the larvae with her own saliva until they turn into pupae. The individuals that emerge are all workers and their first act is to break their way through the soil so as to establish connection with the world at large. Just as in social Bees and social Wasps, the queen then devotes the rest of her life to egg-laying, leaving her worker daughters to carry on with all other nest functions. The queen, as already mentioned, is long-lived and during her life within the nest she is fed with liquid food regurgitated from the mouths of successions of workers.

Worker Ants, as is the case with worker Bees and Wasps, are females with rudimentary sexual organs. Numerically they form the greater part of every Ant colony. They are wingless, with large heads and much reduced eyes. In some species the workers (and the queens) are able to sting but the effects on man are very slight. Ants keep their eggs, larvae and pupae in separate chambers of the nest. They move them from place to place whenever conditions become unfavourable. Great attention is paid to the larvae ; the workers not only feed them but continually clean and lick them. This contact between the workers and the brood involves the same process of mutual feeding as we have seen prevails among the social wasps. The workers bring various kinds of food to the larvae and the latter respond by exuding drops of salivary or other secretion which is eagerly imbibed by the attendant ants. The larvae are legless blind maggots, as in Bees and Wasps ; many kinds spin cocoons before transforming into pupae.

The Small Black Ant or Garden Ant (*Lasius niger*), already referred to, is one of our commonest species. It seems to occur almost everywhere—not only in gardens but in woods and fields, in towns and even in houses. It nests usually in the earth, where it often forms low mounds, or beneath stones, but can adapt itself to a variety of circumstances and may even use old stumps or live under pavements, in or out of doors. Beneath pavements the entrance holes are in the chinks between the paving stones. This Ant frequently nests below hard paths in gardens, where long tracks worn by the feet of constantly passing workers are very noticeable. These tracks lead out from the entrance-holes of the nests to the foraging grounds. The food comprises various kinds of small insects, as well as honey-dew ; at times, seeds are collected and stored in reserve. The Garden Ant is exceedingly fond of the honey-dew discharged by Aphids and Scale-insects. Its relations with these " ant-cows " are rather like those of a stock-keeper and his cattle. Some kinds of these insects are harboured by the Ants within chambers in the nest where they are tended for the sake of the honey-dew they yield. Such Aphids themselves mostly feed on the roots of plants that penetrate into these abodes. This Ant is also a pastoral farmer that collects and deposits Aphids on nearby vegetation so that it can " milk " these obliging creatures under convenient circumstances. Often the Ant stimulates the Aphids to yield their honey-dew by stroking them with its antennae. Sometimes slight earthen sheds are constructed over low plants in order to retain and protect the Aphids present.

The Common Yellow Ant (*Lasius flavus*, Pl. 21, p. 110, Figs. 7, 12) is a near relative of the Garden Ant. It prefers to nest in fields and other grassy places and is seldom to be found in gardens. Sometimes the nests occur in hundreds. Each is in the form of an elongated mound with its long axis pointing eastwards. A Swiss observer, C. Linder, has shown that this Ant keeps extending its nest in an easterly direction in such a way that only the extreme end of it is inhabited. In the Alps it is stated that the orientation of these nests serves as a compass to the shepherds should they lose their way in fog or darkness. For the Ant the advantage appears to be that the nest is kept warmer and drier than if it faced in any other direction.

This species of Ant is even more addicted to keeping flocks and herds of Aphids than the foregoing kind. During the winter groups of small dark-shelled eggs are also often found in its subterranean galleries. As Lord Avebury was the first to show, these are hibernating eggs of certain Aphids that are collected by the Yellow Ant in autumn and stored under protection until the following spring. When the young insects emerge they are carried out of the nest by the Ants and deposited on the appropriate food-plant. It is really very extraordinary that such care is taken of these eggs, for they are useless to the Ants until they hatch. Yet the Ants protect them all the winter with an amazing foresight which Lord Avebury regarded as being unexampled elsewhere in the animal kingdom. Another notable thing about this Yellow Ant is that although it keeps Aphids like domestic cattle in its nests the eggs just mentioned give rise to a species that is never found living under such conditions.

We may next take note of the Wood Ant (*Formica rufa*). It is our largest species of Ant and is found in woodlands, especially where pine-trees prevail (Pl. 21, Figs. 5, 6). Its large mound nests attract immediate attention. Each is the habitation of a vast community of perhaps 100,000 or more individuals. The nest consists of an underground labyrinth of intercommunicating chambers surmounted by a conical heap made up of pine-needles, small sticks, straws and the like, often reaching to a height of three feet or more with a circumference of sometimes 30 feet and over. This hillock itself is penetrated by galleries connected with those below ground and has entrances at different places on its surface. These gateways are closed with twigs by the workers at night and are guarded by sentinel ants. If left undisturbed these nests may remain tenanted for twenty, forty or more years. Charles Darwin, in a letter to the Swiss myrmecologist A. Forel, mentions the case of an old man of eighty who had noticed one very large nest in the same spot ever since he was a boy. Tracks, or streets as we may call them, extend from a nest out to foraging grounds, especially to trees abounding with Aphids. These trackways vary very much in length, ranging from a few yards up to 80 or more. Their course is usually remarkably straight and direct. According to Donisthorpe the Ants sometimes cut down the vegetation in order to keep their tracks clear. This Ant is so numerous and strong that very few other insects venture on the trees which it uses (literally) as Aphid farms. The population of each nest has its own territory for exploitation, and is served by its own trackways that do not communicate with those of neighbouring nests. These great Ant strongholds have few enemies excepting Woodpeckers and Man. The cocoons of this species in particular are collected and sold under the name of Ants' eggs by dealers in bird-food. W. M. Wheeler mentions that this practice proved so destructive to *rufa* nests near Aachen that the

Germans passed a law in 1880 forbidding anyone interfering with the nests, under the penalty of a fine or imprisonment !

The Wood Ants feed extensively on various kinds of insects and the workers are often to be seen dragging such booty along the trackways to the nest. In this way woods and forests are cleared of an immense quota of insect pests. Donisthorpe, from a consideration of how many insects the Ants of one large colony were seen to bring home per minute in favourable weather, considered that they would collect nearly one hundred thousand daily. This Ant is well endowed with means of protection. Besides having sharp mandibles, it secretes a large amount of formic acid which it discharges forcibly from glands in the hind end of the body to a distance of six to about twelve inches. Other insects soon become immobilised by this form of chemical warfare. Anyone who interferes with the nests is liable to experience unpleasant sensations on the skin of the hands from these discharges. The colonies of the Wood Ant contain numerous queens instead of a single individual. This feature seems to be linked up with the loss of ability of the queen to form independent colonies. After mating, numbers of queens return to the shelter of their original homes or to other *rufa* nests in the vicinity. Individuals that have strayed outside the nest area may enter the nests of the related species, *Formica fusca*. This intrusion is not always successful and the *fusca* workers may drive such queens away or kill them. Should a queen Wood Ant manage to establish herself in a *fusca* nest the colony becomes a mixture of the two species of Ant but with a *rufa* queen. The usual way for the Wood Ant to form new colonies is for a few queens to emigrate along with a number of workers and found a branch nest somewhere outside the confines of the original community.

The nests of most Ants and especially those of the Wood Ant give shelter to a varied assortment of other creatures, chiefly insects, that are known as myrmecophiles (Gr. *myrmex*, gen. *myrmekos*, an Ant, and *philos*, loving). There are more than 300 different kinds of these Ant-nest inhabitants in Britain alone.* Some of them are true guests, being in fact hospitably received, fed and tended by the Ants. These guests are mostly certain peculiar kinds of Staphylinid Beetles (p. 57) ; and in order to ingratiate themselves they produce secretions that are eagerly licked up by the Ants. One of the best known of these Beetles is *Lomechusa* which lives in nests of the Robber Ant. Although its larva eats the brood of its host with impunity, the Ants tend the Beetle in all its stages with every care, apparently because they are so fond of the secretion it produces.

A much more numerous fraternity of myrmecophiles are the indifferently tolerated lodgers. They receive no attention from the Ants and are chiefly scavengers feeding on refuse within the nests. Quite a variety of Beetles come under this category, together with larvae of the Hover-fly *Microdon* and those of a rather rare Beetle, *Potosia cuprea.*★ The female *Microdon* lays her eggs in the nests of the three kinds of ants already considered besides those of some others. The larvae are slug-like and for many years they were in fact described as slugs. When, however, they were found to transform within a hard-shelled puparium their true nature was revealed. The Flies on emerging leave the nest and seek their mates in the open. Another group of myrmecophiles are hostile lodgers ; these comprise various Staphylinid Beetles of agile and carnivorous habits. They force themselves into the nests where they prey upon the larvae and pupae. The Ants try to eject them but they are well protected by discharging an offensive liquid from their hind-end which they thrust into the faces of the Ants. Finally there are parasites that live and feed at the expense of Ants and their brood. These are mostly larvae of Ichneumon-flies, Chalcids and of certain True Flies. Some others are Mites and Nematode worms.

Returning to the Ants themselves, the blood-red Robber Ant (*Formica sanguinea*) is of special interest since it is our only slave-making species. Nearly as large as the Wood Ant, it is of a brighter red with a greyish black gaster. It nests below ground and has no mound or hillock to betray it. It avoids the haunts of man and should be looked for on commons and heaths or open spaces in woods (Map 8). The workers attack the nests of other Ants, more especially those of *Formica fusca*. Their object is to seize and carry off the worker pupae to their own colony. When the alien Ants emerge they live as slaves, working in the abodes of their captors. An attack by the Robber Ant is quite an organised procedure. Advance guards are sent out in order to explore the situation and find the weak places. When needed, reinforcements are called up. They fight with great courage, biting and ejecting formic acid with vigour. When resistance is stiff they tend to attack their quarry in the rear instead of meeting them in a frontal advance. It should be mentioned that the Robber Ant is not wholly dependent upon slave labour for its welfare, since it can and does form slaveless colonies on its own account. There is, however, another kind of Ant known as *Anergates* which is an obligatory slave-maker. It has no workers of its own and its queens live in nests of a very different Ant—*Tetramorium caespitum*—whose workers assassinate their own queen and tend the *Anergates* brood. *Anergates* is only known from the New Forest where it seems to be very rare. It is a very small Ant, the queen being only 2–5 mm. long.

Myrmica is another genus of British Ants which includes some abundant species. They and their allies form the subfamily Myrmecinae whose members have two nodes or swellings on the waist—a feature which makes them easily recognisable under a pocket lens. These Ants are able to sting whereas *Formica* and *Lasius* have lost that capacity. *Myrmica* includes the Red Ants which dwell in medium-sized colonies under stones, in banks, or beneath small mounds which they build of earth. Several kinds have curious relations with the caterpillars of the Large Blue Butterfly (*Lycaena arion*). These larvae feed on the flowers of the wild Thyme until their third and last moult. What happened to them afterwards, before they became Butterflies, remained a mystery for many years. Ultimately it became known that *Myrmica scabrinodis* was implicated in the matter. The caterpillars of *L. arion*, and other of the " Blues," are much sought after by certain Ants because they exude a fluid that is extremely attractive to them. The Ants stroke the caterpillars with their antennae and lick up the palatable product as it issues from a gland near the hind-end. In the case of the Large Blue the caterpillars eventually leave the wild Thyme and roam abroad until they make contact with the right sort of Ants. They seem to anticipate what is shortly to happen for they hunch themselves so that the fore-body becomes swollen. When this occurs the *Myrmica* seizes the caterpillar with its mandibles, just behind the swelling, and carries it off to its nest. Here it does not seem to cause the least commotion although it actually takes to feeding on the Ants' own offspring. Finally the caterpillar changes to a chrysalis within the nest and the resulting Butterfly has to make its way through the galleries in order to reach the outer world.

The caterpillars of the Large Blue, like certain Aphids (p. 286), are myrmecophiles of a rather different kind to those mentioned on p. 288. They are sought out by the Ants whereas the other, or true myrmecophiles, seek and enter the Ants' nests of their own accord, the Ants themselves being passive agents in the matter.

Sometimes Ants are troublesome in houses where they are attracted to the contents of larders and store-cupboards. Numbers can be destroyed by placing old pieces of sponge soaked in sugar and water in their haunts, and by periodically collecting these lures in a vessel of boiling water. A surer way is to watch the files of Ants coming and going, following them to their nest which may be a surprisingly long way off, often in the garden : when the nest is located a kettleful of hot water will usually rid the householder of the trouble.

A really serious invader is Pharaoh's Ant (*Monomorium pharaonis*)— a tiny yellow insect about $\frac{1}{12}$ in. long with a dark tip to its gaster. It may invade houses, factories, stores, etc., in numbers that almost defy our comprehension. Usually this Ant nests in the foundations, or at the backs of ovens or in other situations that render it uncommonly difficult to eradicate. It is found nearly all over the world and has become a permanent (and undesirable) resident in Britain for many years. The Argentine Ant (*Iridomyrmex humilis*) is another troublesome alien species that is rapidly becoming cosmopolitan.

EPILOGUE.*—What appeals so forcibly to the imagination is not the structure of social insects but their extraordinary instincts which compel them to live in communities. Interest is still further aroused because of the undeniable resemblances of their communal life to our own.

The immensely populous communities of Ants afford the nearest approach to civilisation in the insect world and betray many similarities to human society. It will be evident that in communal life, whether it be human or insectan, a regular and abundant food-supply is a prime consideration. The more primitive societies are hunters that largely live on flesh. The highly organised and densely populated communities such as those of the Hive-bee, of the more advanced of the Ants, and of all Termites, have come to rely more and more upon the surer and more easily procurable supplies afforded by plants. The collecting and apportioning of food among adults and young, economy in its use, and competition in obtaining supplies find many parallels in human society. Thus we find that social insects have established food-stores ; they tend and " milk " domesticated animals ; some Ants and Termites even cultivate crops of fungi. Ants send out marauding expeditions in order to discover new sources of wealth ; they establish slavery ; and their activities may involve them in wars with their own and other kinds. Also we have noticed that the shelter and security afforded by their nests, just as with human habitations and buildings, have been exploited by numerous alien invaders that are more or less tolerated by their hosts.

The higher kinds of social insects, like human communities, are faced with the problem of overpopulation. The indulgence of unbridled reproductive instincts would result in chaos and disorganisation unless means were found for alleviating such a state of affairs. This problem was solved by social insects ages ago—even before our simian ancestors began to show any real semblance of human form ! Their methods are, firstly swarming, which is in fact emigration, and secondly, inhibition of reproduction. The latter accomplishment has been effected by confining procreation to a single female (queen) or to a small number of such individuals. The female is biologically the social sex *par excellence* and insect societies are matriarchal institutions. The male is a mere fecundating agent who is excluded from participation in communal life and only tolerated for a short time and in small numbers. The Termites have solved the problem of the male in a different way. The particular individual or " king," which fertilises the queen, is forced to live a monogamous life with her in a dark cell deep in the earth, the monotony of existence only being broken by periodic mating so as to enable his spouse to produce up to 30,000 eggs a day. Thus, with a single monogamous male, all the rest of the males are sterile workers and soldiers as numerous as their non-productive sisters.* The males are therefore forced to work with their sterile sisters instead of hanging around until they are forcibly ejected. The Termites have, indeed, actually succeeded in socialising their males—Wheeler claims that they are the only animals that have succeeded in doing so !

By concentrating the propagation of the species in a single or a few individuals of enhanced fecundity, the rest of the social insect community has become available for other services. They are sterile individuals that show a remarkable division of labour which finds analogies among nurses, farmers, builders, soldiers and the like in the human community. As with man, social insects have achieved remarkable control over the inanimate world. It is true that they have not acquired the use of tools but instead they are marvellously endowed with a capacity for using their natural equipment of heads, jaws, legs, stomachs, stings, together with sundry glandular products, to good purpose. Their achievements in nest-building—whether we visualise the elaborate and beautiful nests of our common Wasps with their suspended tiers of storied cells and surrounding insulating envelopes, or the underground chambered labyrinths that accommodate Ants—exemplify the control that social insects have achieved over the use of materials.

It is a very remarkable fact that the social way of life should have arisen independently in two orders of insects so wide asunder as the Isoptera or Termites, which are in reality socialised Cockroaches, and the Hymenoptera. The Ants, Bees and Wasps of the last-named order are probably the most highly evolved of all invertebrate animals. They are just about as different in structure from Termites as Marsupials are from Man. Insects are indeed strange animals and one of their most remarkable achievements is that they should have evolved a social life at all. The author would commend anyone in need of change of outlook and a new interest to read everything he or she can get hold of on the social life of insects. It is surprising how inexhaustible are its problems and how many lines of thought they will stimulate.

DOCUMENTARY APPENDIX

An asterisk in the text indicates that a reference will be found, under the appropriate Chapter and page, in the Documentary Appendix.

A dagger in the text indicates that the group has been fully covered in a Royal Entomological Society Handbook.

INTRODUCTION.

p. 3.—A considerable number of different insects inhabit the sea-shore below high-water mark and undergo daily submersion by the tides. Very few, however, actually live in the sea and the only known kind that is submarine in all its stages, including the adult, is a species of Midge found by P. A. Buxton in Samoa. The greenish larvae of several kinds of Midges live submerged in rock-pools and in deeper water around our British coasts but their adults are aerial. What barriers have prevented insects from invading the sea is uncertain but perhaps the combination of currents, tides, waves and the salinity of the water are collectively responsible. See Buxton, *Proceedings of the Zoological Society of London* 1926, 807-14.

CHAPTER I

p. 16—In the remote ancestors of insects there was undoubtedly a single nerve-ganglion to each segment, but many of them tend to fuse together to form larger and more complex centres. Thus the brain is made up of at least six originally separate ganglia and the ventral head-ganglion is composed of three fused ganglia. The segmental arrangement of the nerve-ganglia is most often retained in the thorax where there are three such centres and in the abdomen where there may be as many as eight separate ganglia.

p. 21—See Wigglesworth, *The Physiology of Insect Metamorphosis*, 1954.

p. 25—It is only among the most primitive wingless insects, viz. the Spring-tails and the two orders of Bristle-tails, that moulting goes on throughout life. In all other insects moulting ceases when the final or adult stage is reached. The only exception is the subimago of May-flies which is, in reality, an immature adult and undergoes a final moult before it becomes a functional adult.

CHAPTER 2.

p. 30.—For a general discussion of the problem of species, subspecies and biological races see J. S. Huxley's excellent book *Evolution: the Modern Synthesis*, 1942, and A. J. Cain, *Animal Species and their Evolution*, 1954.

p. 32.—More detailed information on insect structure and classification is given in *Outlines of Entomology* by A. D. Imms, 2nd ed. 1944. For an advanced work see the same author's *General Textbook of Entomology*, 9th ed. 1964. For an acquaintance with insect physiology the following books should be consulted:—*The Life of Insects* by V. B. Wigglesworth, 1964, and the more advanced *Principles of Insect Physiology*, 1953, by the same writer. As a guide for collecting, rearing, mounting and preserving insects *Instructions for Collectors* by J. Smart, 1954 (British Museum: Natural History; is recommended. See also R. L. E. Ford, *Practical Entomology* (1963), and H. Oldroyd, *Collecting, Preserving and Studying Insects*, 1958.

p. 33.—The number of species (given in brackets) in the different orders of insects is based for the most part on *A Check List of British Insects* by G. S. Kloet and W. D. Hincks, 1945, not the second edition 1964—.

p. 34.—When searching for examples of the Silver-fish in order to photograph them for this book Mr. S. Beaufoy came across an allied but more local insect of very similar appearance known as the "Fire-brat" (*Thermobia domestica*). This creature is portrayed on Plate I, p. 18, and can be recognised by its much longer antennae and tail-feelers. It derives its name from its habit of living near bakers' ovens and other equally warm situations.

p. 35.—See *Grasshoppers, Crickets and Cockroaches of the British Isles* by D. R. Ragge, 1968. *British Grasshoppers and their Allies* by M. Burr, 1936. *British Orthoptera* by W. J. Lucas, 1920, can also be recommended but is somewhat out of date.

p. 39.—See *A Revised Key to the British Species of Ephemeroptera* by D. E. Kimmins, 1954: Publication 15 of the British Freshwater Biological Association (Ambleside; For the nymphs see Ferry House Publication No. 20 by T. T. Macan (1961).

p. 40.—According to C. E. Hicke the word Odonata refers to the sharply toothed maxillae of these insects.

p. 42.—See *Dragonflies*, 1960 by P. S. Corbet, C. Longfield and N. W. Moore. The older work *British Dragonflies* by W. J. Lucas is useful for its excellent coloured plates.

pp. 47-9.—See *British Neuroptera* by F. J. Killington, 2 vols, 1936-37, and *Mecoptera, Megaloptera and Neuroptera* by F. C. Fraser (1959).

p. 52.—Useful books are *Butterflies*, 1946; *Moths*, 1955, both by E. B. Ford; *Butterflies and Moths of the British Isles* by R. South, 3 vols, 1906, 1939; *Revised Handbook of the British Lepidoptera* by R. Meyrick, 1938.

p. 55.—See *Coleoptera of British Isles* by W. W. Fowler, 5 vols. and supplementary volume, 1887-1913, and *British Coleoptera* by N. H. Joy, 2 vols, 1932.

p. 60.—Among books on Hymenoptera are *The Hymenoptera Aculeata of the British Isles* by E. Saunders, 1896; *British Ants* by H. Donisthorpe, 2nd ed. 1927; *Ants, Bees and Wasps* by Sir John Lubbock, new ed. 1929; *The Bumble Bee* by F. W. L. Sladen, 1912; *The World of Bees* by G. Nixon, 1954; and other works mentioned under social insects.

p. 61.—See *Flies of the British Isles*, by C. N. Colyer and C. O. Hammond, 1951; *British Blood-sucking Flies* by F. W. Edwards, H. Oldroyd and J. Smart, 1939; *The British Mosquitoes* by J. F. Marshall, 1938; *The Natural History of Flies* by H. Oldroyd, 1964.

p. 64.—See *Fleas, Flukes and Cuckoos: a study of Bird Parasites* by M. Rothschild and T. Clay, 1952.

CHAPTER 3.

p. 68.—Detailed accounts of insect flight mechanisms are given by J. W. S. Pringle in his book *Insect Flight* (1957) and on pp. 283-333 of Rockstein: *The Physiology of Insecta*, Vol. 2 (1965). The subject is also discussed in *Principles of Insect Physiology* (6th Edition, 1965), by V. B. Wigglesworh.

CHAPTER 4.

p. 89.—For a general account of the olfactory sense see *The Physiology of Insect Senses* by V. G. Dethier, 1963.

p. 89.—Interesting personal observations on assembling in the Oak Eggar Moth are given by F. R. E. Wright in the *Entomologists' Monthly Magazine*, 1929, *65*: 265-66.

p. 98.—See "Types of Learning in Insects and other Arthropods" by W. H. Thorpe in *The British Journal of Psychology*, 1943, *43* and 1944, *44*.

p. 100.—For a more detailed account of the "light-compass" reaction see *Animal Navigation* by J. D. Carthy, 1956. An interesting book on insect behaviour is *The Psychic Life of Insects* by E. Bouvier, 1922.

CHAPTER 5.

p. 105.—Under certain conditions the Blow-fly, and almost certainly the House-fly also, is able to draw back its labella so as to expose a series of fine denticles which are then used for rasping purposes. When feeding in this way the creature is able to rasp off particles from a lump of sugar for example, and to take in larger food fragments than can be absorbed during the more usual feeding position.

p. 108.—In the old but still useful monograph by H. T. Stainton entitled *The Natural History of the Tineina* 1855-73 (13 vols.) the mines made by the larvae of these small Moths are beautifully illustrated in the numerous hand-coloured plates. The text of this work is unique in that it is written in English, French, German and Latin, arranged in parallel columns. For further information see *Biology of Leaf-Minors* by E. N. Hering, 1951.

p. 113.—For a general account of wood-borers and bark-borers see *The Insects of British Woodlands* by R. N. Chrystal, 1937.

p. 117.—See also *The Woodworm Problem* by N. E. Hicken, 1963.

p. 122.—Readers interested in the Wireworm problem should consult *Wireworms and Food Production*, 1944 (Bulletin 128, Ministry of Agriculture and Fisheries).

p. 123.—A close ally of the Rose-chafer is *Potosia cuprea*, which is much scarcer and confined to northern Britain where its larva is found in Ants' nests. The *lapis myrmecias* or ant-stone is supposed, according to a continental legend, to grow in Ants' nests and combine the nature of an Ant with that of a stone and to be effective in alleviating certain human ailments. The belief seems to have originated by finding that the earthy cocoons of this Beetle in Ants' nests give rise to a veritable living jewel of an emerald or golden green.

CHAPTER 6.

p. 124.—This fly is now thought to be the same as one whose larva feeds on wheat, cabbage and also decaying vegetable matter, which is known as *Egle radicum*. *Cf. Genera Insectorum, 205*, p. 111.

p. 133.—For works on blood-sucking Flies see under Chapter 2, p. 61.

p. 138.— See *Man's Mastery of Malaria* by P. F. Russell, 1955.

p. 141.—For a general account of insect parasites see *Recent Advances in Entomology* by A. D. Imms, 2nd ed. 1937, Chapters 12 and 13.

p. 147.—A general account of the natural control of the Large Cabbage White Butterfly is given by J. E. Moss in *Journal of Animal Ecology* 1933, *2*: 201-231. O. W. Richards has investigated the same problem in the Small Cabbage White Butterfly and his account is published in that same journal, 1940, *9*: 243-88.

p. 149.—Papers by G. Salt on *Trichogramma* are to be found in *Proceedings of the Royal Society, B.* 1934, *114*: 450-76; 1935, *117*: 413-35; 1937, *122*: 57-75.

CHAPTER 7.

p. 158.—See *Biological Control of Insect Pests and Weeds* by P. de Bach and E. I. Schlinger (1964). For a popular account see H. Nicols' *Biological Control of Insects* in the Pelican Books, 1943.

CHAPTER 8.

p. 170.—For identifying galls the following books will be found helpful: *British Galls* by E. W. Swanton, 1912; also E. T. Connold's *British Vegetable Galls*, 1901, and *British Oak Galls*, 1908. See also *Ecology of Plant Galls* by M. S. Mani (1964). See also R. R. Askew, Ent. Mon. Mag., *95*, 1959, p. 191.

p. 172.—See R. R. Askew's paper *On the Biology of the Inhabitants of Oak Galls of Cynipidae (Hymenoptera) in Britain* in Trans. Soc. Brit. Ent., *14* (XI) pp. 237-268 (1961).

p. 175.—For a short account of the inhabitants of the Bedeguar Gall see K. G. Blair's articles in the *Entomologists' Monthly Magazine* 1943, *70*: 231-33, and *Proceedings of the Royal Entomological Society* 1945, *20*: 26-30.

p. 178.—An interesting illustrated account of the Bean-gall Saw-fly of willows is given by M. Carleton in the *Journal of the Linnean Society, Zoology*, 1939, *11*: 575-624.

p. 183.—For a modern account of growth-promoting substances in plants, *Plant Growth Substances*, by L. J. Audus, 1953, should be consulted.

CHAPTER 9.

p. 189.—See H. B. Cott's finely illustrated book *Adaptive Coloration in Animals*, 1940.

p. 200.—See *Mimicry* by G. D. H. Carpenter and E. B. Ford, 1933.

p. 203.—Virgil in the *Georgics* gives instructions for obtaining Bees. A dead ox is procured and laid out. It is then beaten vigorously, so that it will presumably decompose rapidly, and afterwards left until Bees develop in the carcass. Virgil's recipe is based upon a direct observation which he wrongly interpreted, his "bees" of course being Drone-flies.

CHAPTER 10.

p. 209.—An interesting account of the mating habits of insects is given by O. W. Richards under the title "Sexual Selection and Allied Problems in the Insects" in *Biological Reviews* 1927, *2*: 298-364.

CHAPTER 11.

p. 223.—*The Natural History of Aquatic Insects* by L. C. Miall, 1934; *Animal Life in Fresh Water* by H. Mellanby, 1938; *An Angler's Entomology*, by J. R. Harris, 1952. Also the publications of the Freshwater Biological Association, Ferry House, Ambleside, Westmorland.

p. 226.—Among incompletely aquatic insects, the Water-bugs live in water during all their stages from the eggs to the adults. The latter, however, in many cases readily take to the wing when occasion demands. Among Beetles it is seldom that any kind spends its whole life in water. The great majority leave the water and bury themselves in nearby moist soil when about to turn to pupae. Among completely aquatic insects the adults are almost always aerial. There are extremely few exceptions to this rule and one is mentioned in the note to p. 3.

p. 234.—For a full account of the larvae and pupae of British Mosquitoes see *The British Mosquitoes* by J. F. Marshall, 1938.

CHAPTER 12.

p. 256.—See *Insect Migration* by C. B. Williams, 1958.

p. 258.—For interesting accounts of gregariousness and its relations to social life see W. C. Allee's two books *Animal Aggregations*, 1931, and *The Social Life of Animals*, 1939.

p. 258.—For a more detailed treatment of social insects see *Social Life among the Insects* by W. M. Wheeler, 1922, also the same author's larger work *The Social Insects*, 1928, the small introductory book *Social Behaviour in Insects* by A. D. Imms, 2nd ed. 1938, *The Social Insects*, by O. W. Richards, 1953, *The World of Bees*, by G. Nixon, 1954, and *The World of the Honeybee*, by C. G. Butler, 1954.

CHAPTER 13.

p. 288.—See *The Guests of British Ants* by H. Donisthorpe, 1927.

p. 289.—See note to p. 123.

p. 291.—For comparison between the social lives of Ants and human beings see the suggestive book *Ants and Men* by C. P. Haskins, 1945.

p. 292.—The fact that the sterile individuals in Termites consist of both males and females is a fundamental difference separating them from all other social insects. In the latter it will be recollected that the sterile individuals are all females.

A very comprehensive guide to existing literature is the *Bibliography of Key Works for the Identification of the British Fauna and Flora*, published by The Systematics

Association, British Museum (Nat. Hist.). Illustrated Keys are given in the series of *Handbooks for the Identification of British Insects* in course of publication by the Royal Entomological Society of London.

MAPS SHOWING
THE DISTRIBUTION OF CERTAIN INSECTS
IN THE BRITISH ISLES

The following maps are intended to give a general idea of the distribution of certain of our native insects. In each case distribution by counties or vice-counties is indicated rather than by means of individual localities. The maps only give, therefore, the approximate ranges of the different species dealt with in this way. Much work still remains to be done in collecting and observing our native insects —including the few kinds whose range is indicated on the accompanying maps. Outside the Butterflies and many Moths the distribution of all other native insects is still very imperfectly known. Here the amateur can give valuable help.

The names in brackets, following the titles of the maps, are those of the authorities from whose works the data have been taken in drawing up the maps.

1. Emperor Dragon-fly, *Anax imperator* (C. LONGFIELD AND OTHERS)

2. Mole-cricket, *Gryllotalpa gryllotalpa* (W. J. LUCAS AND OTHERS)

3. Giant Lace-wing, *Osmylus fulvicephalus* (F. J. KILLINGTON)

4. Field-cricket, *Gryllus campestris* (W. J. LUCAS AND OTHERS)

5. Great Green Grasshopper, *Tettigonia viridissima* (W. J. LUCAS; M. BURR)

6. Carabid Beetle, *Calosoma inquisitor* (J. H. COOK)

7. Mosquito, *Taeniorhynchus richiardii* (J. F. MARSHALL)

8. Robber Ant, *Formica sanguinea* (H. DONISTHORPE)

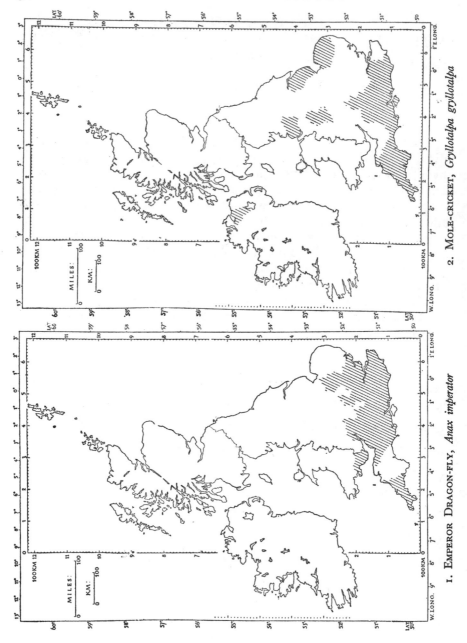

2. MOLE-CRICKET, *Gryllotalpa gryllotalpa*

1. EMPEROR DRAGON-FLY, *Anax imperator*

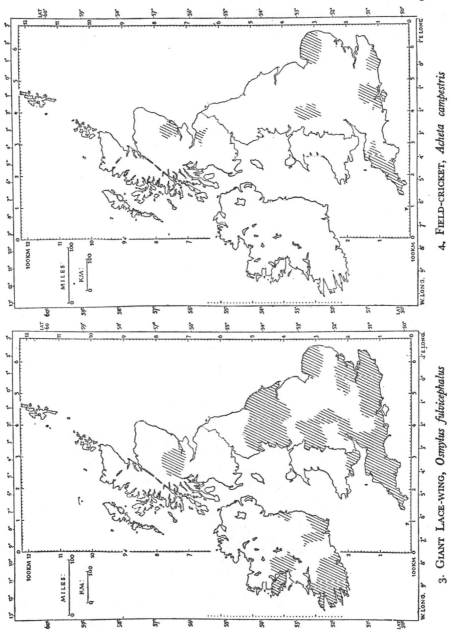

4. FIELD-CRICKET, *Acheta campestris*

3. GIANT LACE-WING, *Osmylus fulvicephalus*

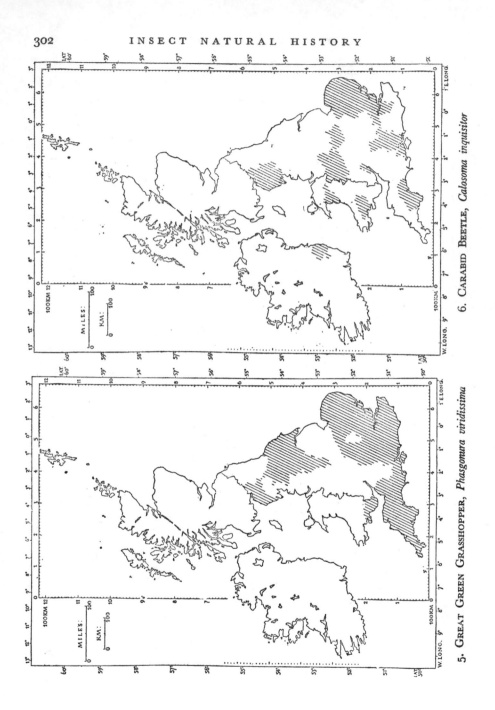

5. GREAT GREEN GRASSHOPPER, *Phasgonura viridissima*

6. CARABID BEETLE, *Calosoma inquisitor*

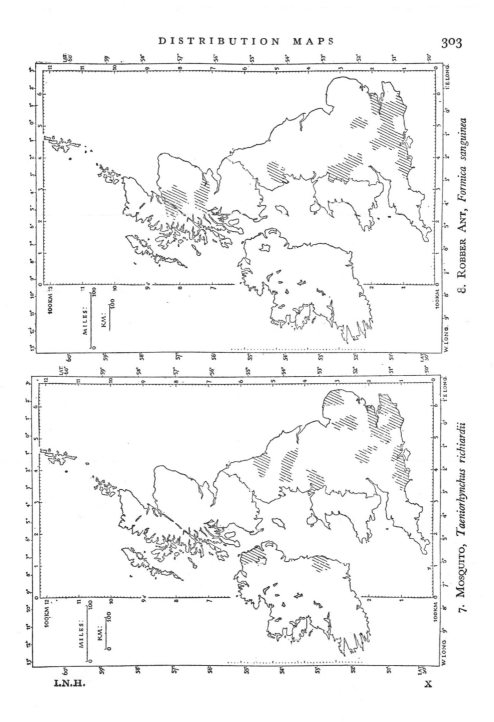

8. ROBBER ANT, *Formica sanguinea*

7. MOSQUITO, *Taeniorhynchus richiardii*

L.N.H.

X

INDEX

Insects are indexed under their English names, with a cross-reference from their generic names, except where the latter are the only names available. Arabic numerals in heavy type indicate Colour Plates; roman numerals refer to Black-and-White Plates. Letters, or superior figures, after Plate numbers indicate individual figures on each Plate.